Canada and the United States: Differences that Count

Canada and the United States: Differences that Count

edited by David Thomas

broadview press

Canadian Cataloguing in Publication Data
Thomas, David.
Canada and the United States : differences that count
Includes bibliographical references and index.
ISBN 1-55111-018-0
1. Canada - economic conditions - 1991 -   .
2. United States - economic conditions - 1981 -   .
3. Federal government - Canada. 4. Federal government - United States. 5.
Canada - Constitutional law. 6. United States - Constitutional law.

F1008.C3 1993   971.064'7   C93-095601-X

Broadview Press
Post Office Box 1243, Peterborough, Ontario, Canada, K9J 7H5

in the United States of America
Post Office Box 670, Lewiston, NY 14092

in the United Kingdon
c/o Drake Marketing, Saint Fagan's Road, Fairwater, Cardiff, CF53AE

Broadview Press gratefully acknowledges the support of the Canada Council,
the Ontario Arts Council, and the Ontario Publishing Centre.

George Hoberg's article "Comparing Canadian Performance in Environmental
Policy" from Canadian *Environmental Policy: Ecosystems, Politics, and Process*,
Robert Boardman ed. (Toronto: Oxford University Press, 1992) pp. 246-262 is
reprinted by permission of the author.

Cover: One effect of the differences in Canadian and American policies can be
clearly seen in this satelite image of the Milk River crossing the Alberta-Montana
border; American policies encourage grain growing in this sort of terrain; the
Canadian landscape is dominated by rangeland.

ERS-1 Image acquired by CCRS on August 13, 1991; © ESA 1993; courtesy CCRS
and Radarsat International Inc.

PRINTED IN CANADA

10 9 8 7 6 5 4 3 2 1

Contents

Part Three: Rules, Rights, and Roles

Part Four: Cultural Reflections

Preface

There are so many people whom I wish to thank that it is difficult to know where to start, so a merely chronological sequence seems best. I want therefore to first of all acknowledge my debt of gratitude to Don LePan, the President of Broadview Press, for supporting the idea of the book from the outset. His advice throughout the project has been invaluable.

I next want to thank all the contributors. Facing the deadlines they already had, they had every right to turn down my request for their respective chapters. But they did not, because they liked the idea of the book and what it is trying to accomplish: my admiration for their work is unbounded and it has been my privilege to work with them. And I do want to single out one name, for I owe Dr. Roger Gibbins a special debt of gratitude for his ongoing support. He exemplifies the best that our universities have to offer.

My colleagues in the Department of Economics and Political Science at Mount Royal College must also be thanked, for as the book got fully underway it is possible that on occasion I became preoccupied with it, and was even boring on the subject. They have put up with this with good humour and helpful advice.

Finally I want to acknowledge the contribution made by my wife, Maureen, who served as my "mythical average reader." She was able to offer helpful and detailed comments on many of the chapters at the crucial first draft stage, and she could do so from a non-specialist's standpoint that was most useful.

We are living in what might euphemistically be called yeasty times. I hope that *Differences that Count* enhances, in some small manner, the quality of the debate about what distinguishes Canada from the United States, and illustrates clearly the ways in which our ongoing differences really do matter.

David Thomas
Calgary, 1993

Introduction

Canadians and Americans alike are often subject to the "availability error." This is to say we judge things not after careful, logical, empirical analysis but rather by what first comes to our mind, and what does so is what is "available." Usually this is something recent, particularly if it is dramatic, concrete, readily understandable, emotional, and seems symbolic. So, if a Canadian's last trip to the United States resulted in a successful shopping spree, good food at reasonable prices, friendly "have a nice day" service, and inexpensive, decent accommodation, then news and information about the United States will be filtered through a positive frame of reference. The *whole* American system is likely to be seen in a better light and other conclusions will follow: taxes must be lower, competition is a great thing, there's more liberty and opportunity.

On the other hand, if a Canadian has just read about yet more murders and mayhem, or goes to the United States and drives through a ghetto, or becomes ill and sees the bills (let alone pays them), then the United States becomes a Darwinian/Reaganite universe in which the rich get richer, the cities crumble, the social fabric rots, the melting pot is a myth if you're black, and special interests hold sway. Similarly, positive and negative views of Canada may be held by American visitors depending upon what information and immediate experiences are available to them; they too will judge by what comes immediately and readily to mind. Canada can thus appear clean, well run, friendly, and safe — or boring, overpriced, anti-American, and inefficient.

We also want to cling to what we think we already know, and we try to make new information fit our preconceptions. It has been argued that throughout the nineteenth century:

> Canadian views...were not really derived from actual use of observation, they were arrived at...by a psychological necessity to believe that the principles of the Canadian system were better than those of the United States.[1]

In the words of a recent book on the subject of rational and irrational thought, versions of the availability error, which include the unexamined primacy of certain assumptions, "permeate all reasoning."[2] None of us is immune from such a subjective rush to judgement; neither the leaders nor the led. Making sensible, well grounded, comparative judgements is extremely difficult.

Differences that Count attempts to put certain things into a more balanced perspective. The authors each analyze a particular area where Canadian and American differences are assumed, at least initially, to be important. Each chapter offers a frame of reference that has depth and substance, providing a kind of intellectual foothold, or vantage point, from which to assess the route we have followed and where we are going.[3]

The nineteen areas were chosen because they seemed to be relevant, important, illustrative of differences from which we might learn, and in dire need of illumination. This is not to say that information on these topics is not, in many cases, already available; there is hardly anything on which a good book has not been written. However, people just do not have the time, the resources, or the desire to track down lengthy specialized works, and the op-ed sections of our newspapers cannot, in a mere page, do justice to the complexities of things.

Yet people do want and need more information. Disillusionment with politicians notwithstanding, there is a very high level of interest in economic, political and social questions. Over ninety million people watched the Clinton-Bush debates. In Quebec, in October 1992, over two million people (of a population of less than seven million) saw Robert Bourassa debate Jacques Parizeau about whether to vote "yes" or "no" in the referendum on the Charlottetown Accord. People sense that there is a dearth of usable information even as we drown in newsprint and will soon have more TV channels than days of the year.

Differences that Count is designed to offer readable, useful, and interesting analysis on a broad range of significant topics. What does it deal with; what has been left out; who are the intended readers; who are the authors; and does the book have any particular axes to grind?

There is, first of all, a cluster of "economic" issues, all with serious social and political overtones: health care, taxation and deficits, unionization, banking systems, and environmental policies. Each of these areas is a veritable minefield of conflicting information, opinion, and diagnosis. Does Canada face a worse deficit and debt situation; how do our banking and financial institutions differ and could Canada face a savings and loan type collapse; what is happening to organized labour; how do the tax regimes compare; are American environmental laws tougher; will, and should, the United States adopt a more Canadian-style health care system? These are the kinds of policy issues discussed.

There are five chapters on our respective political, institutional, and constitutional arrangements. Although both countries share a political heritage that is similar, it may well be that, in the words of a recent essay, "Canada and the United States are more distinctive politically than they are in any other way."[4] Our societies look similar; our institutions do not. Chapters on provincial and state power, presidents and prime ministers, the two Senates, electoral systems and representation, and constitutional change, explore our differences at a time when political institutions and arrangements are in the spotlight.

These are followed by chapters that have a predominantly legal focus — on the two judicial systems, the Charter of Rights and the Bill of Rights, native rights, and gender equality. (The latter illustrates how difficult compartmentalization is; gender questions are also institutional, cultural, and economic, as well as legal.) In both countries "rights" are a matter of considerable controversy, the workings of the legal systems are a source of fascination and frustration, and important differences are easily overlooked or misunderstood.

Finally there is a discussion of more obviously cultural and sociological questions: the images of the melting pot and the mosaic in theory and practice; political reporting styles and their consequences; the cultural leadership and sponsorship undertaken by the state in Canada; the foreign policy traditions of our two countries; and the socializing power of post-secondary education.

This is intended to be a book in which one can browse, picking first those chapters that are of special interest, and moving on to others as time and events dictate. The chapters will not date easily, for although they mention current events and personalities, they are illustrative of larger, far more permanent, themes.

There is certainly no dearth of topics to include in a book on Canadian-US differences and comparisons; the more I thought about it and discussed it with others, the longer the list grew. The final choice was made with difficulty. If I were able to start all over again I would, for example, include a chapter on the funding of local government. Two other omissions may seem curious. The first of these is a discussion of the linked topics of guns, violence, poverty, race, and crime. For unavoidable reasons this was a chapter that did not come to fruition. Luckily, it is probably the area where we are already most aware of the enormous differences that exist, for it is difficult to open a newspaper without being reminded of the American murder rate, the weapons problem in general, the plight of those living in inner city ghettos and the incarceration rates of young black men. In 1990 the United States had over 10,500 deaths involving handguns; Canada had a mere 68. The number of gun-related deaths in the United States during the past five years is put at over 60,000. There are an estimated 200,000,000 weapons in circulation; there are 286,000 gun dealers and the number of applicants for licences to sell guns (in 1991) was an astonishing 34,000, of whom only 37 were refused a permit. The National Rifle Association has successfully prevented the adoption of computerized record-keeping (of gun sales and ownership) by law enforcement agencies, and its lobbying power is legendary. Overall, there were approximately 22,500 reported murders in the United States in 1991; in Canada there were 762.[5]

Likewise, Canadians and Americans are, for the most part, already aware that Canada does not face a similar race problem. Not that racism or race-related violence are absent from Canadian cities or from Canadian history. The fact is, however, that in Canada there is nothing comparable to the horrific gun- and drug-related violence that stalks black and other neighborhoods in American cities. America has a "killing culture" linked to crime and drugs and it is extracting an extraordinarily high price. And Canada does not have 2,600 inmates on death row.

The second topic that might stand out as absent is Quebec. This was a deliberate omission for there is nothing comparable on the American scene. If a single state contained one-quarter of the population who spoke a different language, were of a different faith and had been the first Europeans to arrive, American history would probably be rather different. Yet Quebec's presence can be felt throughout the book, particularly in those chapters that discuss federalism and Canada's constitutional problems; the ways in which Quebec has shaped Canada markedly are bound to emerge continually, regardless of whether or not a separate chapter is devoted to them.

Certain larger themes are also avoided. This is because the question of such things as national values and political culture in general are dealt with extensively elsewhere, in books meant for the general public. I think particularly of Seymour Martin Lipset's *Continental Divide: the Values and Institutions of the United States and Canada*.[6] Lipset and others proceed from the assumption that it is precisely because the two North American democracies are so similar that scholars can isolate and identify the factors responsible for our differences. This is a view borne out in *Differences that Count*.

Through depressions and wars, booms and busts, the two federations have had to make ever-changing adjustments to international circumstances. One might assume that, for functional reasons alone, convergence is inevitable. But, on the other hand (there is always an "on the other hand" in the social sciences) specific differences can add up, and their cumulative effects will shape the lives of citizens in very important ways. This is a point also made in a new book with a very similar title to the one chosen (entirely independently) for this volume. In *Small Differences that Matter: Labor Markets and Income Maintenance in Canada and the United States*[7] (edited by David Card and Richard Freeman) the contributors explore "the principal differences in income inequality, poverty rates, unemployment, and other labor market outcomes between Canada and the United States." Inter-country differences did indeed widen during the 1980s; the poverty rate in Canada actually fell while in the United States it rose, particularly for single-parent families. Canada's unemployment insurance programs are more generous (50 weeks in Canada, 26 in the United States), more workers are eligible and a higher percentage of those who qualify actually apply for assistance. And there is a broader range of benefits, including maternity and sickness leave. The same is true for other income support systems; comparable American programs are "more narrowly targeted and less generous." Canada pays a price for this: in taxation, in government deficits, and in some labour market effects. The major empirical finding of Card and Freeman's volume is that Canadian labor market and income support policies have worked to stand against "the rising trend of (income) inequality that swept the United States." Three chapters in *Differences That Count* (those on health care, taxation, and unionization) cast further light on these important matters.

The most common line of argument in books that have tackled our macro-level national values and their effects on institutions, beliefs, and behavior has been that Americans are more individualistic, anti-statist, self-absorbed, moralistic, egalitarian, religious, ideological, and imperialistic — to mention but a few of a long list of value-laden attributes. Canada is seen as more British, elitist, deferential, bureaucratic, state-oriented, collectivist, orderly, and conservative; as lacking heroes and founding myths, and as being preoccupied with unity in a bi-national political setting.[8]

One could spend days debating such judgements for they are fascinating and frequently paradoxical. The problem is that if we do so, we are often none the wiser about the details that are needed in order to make sensible comparative evaluations in a less sweeping way. We need to assess our differences at the so-called "mid-range" level where operational comparisons are easier and more precise, and may cast light on broader generalizations. It must be remembered also that our citizens often know little of their own systems. Canadian task forces and commissions from the Pepin-Robarts report of 1979 to the *Citizens' Forum on Canada's Future* of 1991 have lamented this lack of knowledge: "We are dying of our ignorance and of our stubborn refusal to learn."[9] Americans similarly suffer from a lack of ability to see themselves as others see them: to understand that American ways of doing things are not necessarily the only ways, and that much can be learned from the successes of others.

A problem for Canadians is that a great deal of the Canada-US information they receive and consume is filtered through the lens of the American media, including arguments about whether or not things (like medicare) work effectively north of the 49th parallel. And, for Americans, Canada remains virtually invisible. Although there are more than two dozen centres for Canadian Studies in the United States, there are probably as many scholars studying Albania or Taiwan as there are studying Canada. Additionally, North Americans are often parochial when making comparisons. Canada compares itself to the United States and the United States compares itself internally. "If the Canadian-American border has little or, in most cases, no impact on the world view of Americans, it has a major, even constricting impact on the world view of Canadians."[10] There should be a far more wide-ranging comparison and a greater awareness of what other countries are doing in everything from currency rates to social policy.

Differences that Count is written for an audience that wants to know more and is intended to be useful both in an academic context and to the general public. The chapters were written to be accessible. Not all are easy, but they have been written with a view to minimizing footnotes and academic jargon and with an emphasis on a clear theme for each. (Footnotes if necessary but not necessarily footnotes; where they are used they are often informative and not merely citations. Lists of recommended readings have likewise been kept short.) We hope that this dual focus has worked and that the book is suitable both as a starting point for academic study and as a contribution to public debate.

The authors deserve a special vote of thanks. None of them needed to write for the book, for all were already fully committed to their own projects. (These are individuals from whom the taxpayers get their money's worth!) What made them take up the challenge and the extra work was, I suspect, a belief similar to mine; namely, that they had important things to discuss and that there was too little contact between the world of academe and the public at large. As the British historian David Cannadine has argued forcefully in another context, scholars must:

give more attention to our audience than the cult of professionalism has tended to allow...we should seek for general interpretations...we should deliberately set out to regain our position
as public teachers who deserve both public attention and public
funding.[11]

In their willingess to contribute to *Differences that Count* the authors
have demonstrated their commitment to enhancing public debate.
(Only one chapter, "Comparing Canadian Performance in Environmental Policy" by Dr. George Hoberg, was not written especially for
this volume: it captures exactly what I had in mind for this topic.)
With one exception the contributors live in Canada. Several are
American citizens, however, and many were educated or have taught
in the United States; all are well aware of the difficulties of comparison and are experts in their area. They were not chosen because they
occupy any particular place on the political spectrum and not all
work in universites: David Perry is Senior Research Associate for the
Canadian Tax Foundation, Jamie Portman is the national fine arts
correspondent for Southam Press Inc., Dr. Philip Bartholomew is Director of the Bank Research Division at the Office of the Comptroller
of the Currency in Washington, D.C., and Mr. Justice R.P. Kerans is
a senior member of the Alberta Court of Appeal.

This is not a book that sets out to praise or to blame. It does not
specifically focus, as do a spate of recent works, on NAFTA, the Free
Trade Agreement, or the legacy of Brian Mulroney, although what
it says often has a bearing on these questions. It does not contain,
as far as I can see, any conspiracy theories. This is not to suggest
that there are no grounds for concern over the effects of economic
integration, particularly at a time when the American economy itself
is in such disarray. Integration may, in Canada's case, as was predicted, exacerbate regional fragmentation, further homogenize cultures and political systems, and erode the regulatory and redistribu-
tive powers of the federal government.[12]

However, the chapters in *Differences that Count* reveal, I think, a
more complex picture, and show how seemingly modest differences
can have substantially different consequences. Some chapters do have,
in places, a prescriptive tone. The move from analysis to suggestion
is an easy one, and scholarly work is often the more interesting for
it.

Finally, I should probably make my own biases clear. I think of
myself as a moderate Canadian nationalist, but a nationalist nonetheless: proud of being the citizen of a "middle" power,[13] grateful
for Canada's mix of ideological debate, and appreciative of its history
as well as its geography. At the same time, who could fail to be

fascinated by the on-going experiment that is the United States? Canadians live in the shadow of a great nation and are perhaps always destined to remain ambivalent towards it — as are many Americans, some of whom are savage critics of precisely those things that concern Canadians.[14]

At a time when there is gloom and doom on both sides of the border, *Differences that Count* puts nineteen topics into the spotlight to see what can be learned. In many respects it is quite clear that the ways things are done in Canada are not better or worse, they are simply different. What other evaluative conclusions readers wish to draw, I leave up to them.

NOTES

1. S.F. Wise and Robert Craig Brown, *Canada Views the United States* (Macmillan: Toronto, 1967), 122. For American views on Canada see Reginald C. Stuart, *United States Expansionism and British North America, 1775-1871* (Chapel Hill: University of North Carolina Press, 1988).

2. See Stuart Sutherland, *Irrationality: The Enemy Within* (London: Constable and Company, 1992), 16.

3. I am indebted to Charles F. Doran for this notion of an "intellectual foothold." See his still important work *Forgotten Partnership: U.S.-Canada Relations Today* (Markham: Fitzhenry and Whiteside, 1984), 4.

4. See Roger Gibbins, "The Impact of the American Constitution on Contemporary Canadian Politics" in Marian C. McKenna (ed.), *The Canadian and American Constitutions in Comparative Perspective* (Calgary: University of Calgary Press, 1993), 133.

5. These figures are all taken from readily available sources, namely newspapers and magazines, in particular *The Globe and Mail* and *The New Yorker*.

6. Seymour Martin Lipset, *Continental Divide: the Values and Institutions of the United States and Canada* (New York: Routledge, Chapman and Hall Inc., 1990).

7.   David Card and Richard B. Freeman (eds.), *Small Differences that Matter: Labour Markets and Income Maintenance in Canada and the United States* (Chicago: University of Chicago Press, 1993).

8.   For a full discussion of these ideas see Lipset, *op. cit.*, especially chapters 1-3. Also note his earlier work, *Revolution and Counter-Revolution* (New York: Basic Books, 1968). See also Doran, *op. cit.*, chapter 3; Norman Hillmer, *Partners Nevertheless* (Toronto: Copp Clark Pittman Ltd., 1989) Section 4; Everett C. Hughes, "A Sociologist's View" in John Sloan Dickey (ed.) *The United States and Canada* (New Jersey: Prentice Hall Inc., 1964), 8-29. For a completely updated version of Dickey (ed.), *op. cit.*, see Charles F. Doran and John H. Sigler (eds.) *Canada and the United States: Enduring Friendship, Persistent Stress*. For a less scholarly but "affectionate look" at our differences, see Andrew H. Malcom, *The Canadians* (Markham: Fitzhenry and Whiteside, 1985). It is interesting to note how many titles reflect ambivalence (or trepidation). Some recent scholarship has attributed some of Canada's key values (Toryism and socialism for example) to anti-Americanism and defensiveness.

9.   *Citizens' Forum on Canada's Future.* (Ottawa: Supply and Services Canada, 1991), Chairman's introduction, 9.

10.   See Roger Gibbins, *Canada as a Borderlands Society* (Borderlands Monograph Series #2), 12. Gibbins notes that the border extends much more deeply into Canada. This means that Canadian defence of the border "does not take place along the border as such but extends backwards into the national community".

11.   David Cannadine, "British History: Past, Present — and Future?" *Past and Present*, No. 116, Aug. 1987, 169-191.

12.   For an excellent pre-Free Trade discussion of these issues see Charles Pentland, "North American Integration and the Canadian Political System," in Denis Stairs and Gilbert R. Winham (eds.), *The Politics of Canada's Economic Relationship with the United States* (Toronto: University of Toronto Press, 1985). This is volume 29 of the Royal Commission on the Economic Union and Development Prospects for Canada series.

13. There is an enormous literature on Canada as a "middle power," some of it arguing that Canada is not, in fact, such an entity or that the term is not particularly useful. For a comprehensive review of the foreign policy literature, including works on free trade, see Maureen Appel Molot, "Where Do We, Should We, or Can We Sit? A Review of Canadian Foreign Policy Literature," *International Journal of Canadian Studies*, 1-2, Spring-Fall, 1990, 77-96.

14. The American novelist John Irving had this to say recently: "Compared to Canadians, Americans are isolated by their extreme selfishness, their personal avarice, their complete suspension of a social conscience, not to mention their terror of the so-called welfare state; we simply don't accept our domestic obligation to care for those who can't take care of themselves." *Saturday Night*, Feb. 1993, 41. Not even the most ardent Canadian nationalist could be more viscerally anti-American.

Part One: The Price We Pay:
Taxing, Spending & Regulating

ROBERT G. EVANS

Less is More:
Contrasting Styles in Health Care

Our system of universal public insurance for health care is by a considerable margin Canada's most successful and popular public program. We think of it, not just as an administrative mechanism for paying bills, but as an important symbol of community, a concrete representation of mutual support and concern. It expresses a fundamental equality of Canadians in the face of disease and death, and a commitment that the rest of us will help as far as we can.

Perhaps as important for our national identity, the Canadian approach to health insurance also clearly distinguishes us from the United States. The fact that we have developed such a different system suggests that, despite outward appearances, we really are a separate people, with different political and cultural values. Even better, our system *works*, and compared to most other systems works well, while the American alternative does not.

Yet the American alternative is always there, the ever-present "Other" with which we compare virtually everything we do. So large, so self-absorbed, Americans implicitly assume that their own arrangements in any field are the best, the "natural" forms (possibly even ordained by God) towards which the rest of the world should be guided and assisted. We absorb that subliminal message through many channels, even when we know on a conscious level that it is false.

The comparison of health care systems is particularly instructive, precisely because our very similar societies, with quite similar health care delivery systems, have adopted such different modes of funding — a sort of vast social experiment. The large differences in system performance can thus be attributed with some confidence to the effects of funding. These differences are observed both at the aggregate level — coverage, costs, equity — and in the provision of care for individual patients with similar problems.

Most of the comparisons, on objective measures, favour us. Americans like to point with pride to their mastery of the commanding heights of medical technology; and the best in America is very good indeed. The less thoughtful pour scorn on "rationing" and waiting lists for care in Canada and Europe. But the worst in America is very bad indeed, and would not be tolerated anywhere else in the developed world. Alain Enthoven, one of the leading American students of health care, has put the point rather brutally: "...it would be, quite frankly, ridiculous...to suggest that we have achieved a satisfactory system that our European friends would be wise to emulate."

But it is too easy to be self-congratulatory, and to miss the fact that in health care as in hockey, the Americans are not the team to beat. (Russian health care, however, is not so hot either.) Most European countries also have universal, comprehensive health care systems. Like our own, all the European systems are facing serious problems and studying or implementing significant reforms. But their problems, like ours, are much less severe than those of the United States; and as in Canada, most European observers have concluded that their systems are fundamentally sound. We may learn more from the experience of relatively successful systems than from comparing ourselves with the least successful.

There may still be much to learn from the more successful components of the highly diversified American "system"; Canadians have long admired the efficiency and effectiveness of some of the American staff-model Health Maintenance Organizations such as Kaiser, or special clinics like Mayo. But "cherry-picking" can be misleading; if the success stories have not been generalized in the United States, they may not generalize here either.

The most insidious danger, however, is that in devoting close and exclusive attention to the United States, we become drawn into their internal debate and begin to see *ourselves* in that very distorted mirror. The intense struggle over health care reform which has developed south of the border over the last five years has included a massive reaction by the beneficiaries of the *status quo* — principally the private insurance industry and members of the American Medical Association — to defend the indefensible by discrediting any plausible alternatives. Since advocates of reform have long pointed to Canada as a working model of a much superior system, the reaction has included deliberate and extensive "disinformation campaigns" to misrepresent the characteristics and experience of the Canadian system through selective reporting, distortions, and outright lies.

Since our news media are so closely interlocked, we become unintended targets of these efforts. Indeed the campaign may reach into Canada, to locate and highlight specific failures which can then be recycled for American audiences as if they were systemic features. So we have allegations of Canadians "dying in the streets" or pouring south of the border because adequate care is not available under "socialized medicine."

The claims may be fabricated; that is irrelevant so long as they play in Peoria. But they may also raise anxiety in Toronto, particularly when they appear to match the periodic claims from domestic sources of "underfunding," the "orchestrated outrage" which is an inescapable part of fee, wage, and budgetary negotiations in a publicly funded system. Outside the United States, Canadian health care is the most generously supported in the world, not only in absolute amount but as a share of national income. But the average Canadian who tunes in to the American "debate" does not know this.

Simplistic distortions are easy. But it is not at all easy to describe, without misleading, a field of activity which now accounts for roughly one-tenth of the energy, effort, and skill of an entire society, and then to compare it with another. From the user's perspective, it may be helpful to compare the two systems under the heads of: (1) Complexity; (2) Choice; and (3) Costs and Consequences. But the reader is warned that all generalizations are false.

COMPLEXITY:

Health care systems are probably the most complex organizations in any modern society. Users need not be aware of this, any more than they need to understand the science and technology behind the diagnostic and therapeutic interventions offered to them. National systems differ considerably both in the inherent complexity of their organization and financing, and in the extent to which individual users are required to cope with this. The Canadian system is from the user's point of view one of the simplest in the world; the American is unquestionably the most complex.

All Canadian residents are fully covered for all "medically necessary" hospital and physicians' services, through a program administered and financed by the government of their province of residence. All costs are met from general tax revenue; out-of-pocket charges in the form of either copayments or provider extra-billing are not permitted. Entitlement follows from residence; some provinces levy "premiums" but these are in fact taxes and coverage is not conditional

Table 1: Insurance Coverage in the United States

Type of Program	Percent of Population Covered	Percent of Expenditure Covered
Private Insurance:	61.7%	31.5%
Medicare:	12.9%	16.8%
Medicaid:	8.3%	15.2%
No Coverage:	14.1% (about 37 million people)	
Out of Pocket	—	18.6%
Other:	3.0%	17.9%**

* "Primary" source of coverage.

**Other public programs, plus non-personal expenditures (public health, research, construttion).

upon payment. Private insurance is permitted only for peripheral services not covered by the public plans.

The individual seeking medical care normally contacts a general or family practitioner who is in private fee-for-service practice. The fees are uniform for all practitioners, determined by periodic nego-tiation between provincial governments and medical associations, and paid directly by the public plan without patient involvement. Roughly half of all medical practitioners are generalists. Specialist care, diag-nostic services, and hospital care are available upon referral by the primary practitioner. Specialists, who are also in fee practice, con-centrate on referral work; the American "primary care specialist" is largely unknown.[1] The hospital is a not-for-profit institution with a Board of Trustees, funded through a global operating budget nego-tiated annually with the provincial government. Diagnostic services may be provided either in a hospital or by private practitioners.

It is not, however, possible to generalize in the same way about the American patient. Her insurance coverage will depend upon her age, employment status (past and present), income, place of resi-dence, and increasingly on the nature of her illness and on the fi-nancial health of her employer. Her possible sources of care will be a very diverse set of organizations, while her access to and use of care for a particular problem will be highly variable depending on the specific form of her coverage. And her out-of-pocket costs will vary from none to ruinous.

The major forms of primary health insurance coverage in the United States are (1) a large and diverse collection of private plans for employees and their dependents; (2) Medicare (federal) for those over sixty-five; (3) Medicaid (state-administered, with federal contributions and regulation) for (some of) the low income population; and (4) none. Their shares of population covered and of total health spending are shown in Table 1, above (1992 estimates).

While 61.7% of Americans rely primarily on private coverage, this pays only 31.5% of all health care costs. Private insurers prefer to insure healthy people: the employed, non-elderly, non-poor are, on average, healthier than the remainder. Moreover, few private plans provide comprehensive coverage; most insured patients also have to pay significant amounts out-of-pocket.[2]

In addition to limiting their liabilities by providing incomplete coverage, and only for the better risks, private insurers also receive an indirect subsidy from the income tax system. Employer-paid premiums are deductible from income by the employer but not taxed as income in the hands of the employee. Without this public subsidy, valued at $40 billion in 1992 or nearly 20% of premium revenue, it is not clear how much private coverage could be maintained. Roughly half of all expenditure in this nominally "private" system thus comes directly or indirectly from public sources.

Nor do the public programs provide comprehensive coverage. The federal Medicare system, for example, requires patients to pay a large deductible (in 1993, the first $670 of hospital expenses in any one year, and the first $100 of physician bills), plus a copayment of 20% of all subsequent allowable expenses, plus any amount which a provider may choose to extra-bill above the allowable rates. These amounts can be substantial; consequently there is a large market in "Medigap" insurance, privately sold, to cover them. Alternatively, some employment contracts include continuation of coverage for retirees, to pay the charges which Medicare does not. Thus patient copayments, which according to economic theory and political rhetoric are intended to "control costs" by deterring use, serve instead to provide a market for private insurers and to shift costs from taxpayers back to the covered population.

Such cost shifting, under the rhetorical cover of "cost control," makes up a large part of American health care policy, public and private. Highly competitive efforts to transfer responsibility for costs, and for the people who generate them, onto someone else, account for much of the complexity and cost of that system. As the federal government struggles to control its budget, it reduces Medicare benefits and increases the copayments, thereby increasing not only patients' out-of-pocket payments, but also employer liabilities for retirees and private Medigap premiums. This compounds the problems of employers, who are themselves struggling with escalating health benefit costs that now exceed the total value of corporate after-tax profits. Increasingly employers are finding themselves unable to meet these costs; in extreme cases they may be driven into bankruptcy.

Indeed, a number of large firms may already be technically bankrupt in the sense that if they carried on their books an actuarial estimate of the present value of their contractual obligations to pay for future health care, it would exceed the shareholders' equity. (This is a source of some concern to those who set accounting standards.) American firms are thus trying to negotiate or impose lower rates of benefits — more exclusions and copayments — so as to shift costs yet again, back to employees. But the American courts also permit them unilaterally to rewrite their contracts with past employees. The retiree's supplementary coverage vanishes.

The same can happen to those now employed, particularly with small firms. If an employee develops a very expensive medical problem, this will lead to either very large premium increases for everyone else in the small employee pool, or large losses for the employer. Another option, however, is to rewrite the group coverage so as to exclude that problem — or that employee. This too, the courts have permitted. If you become very (expensively) ill, your coverage may vanish just when you need it most — and your job may go with it. The root of the problem is that small employee groups are simply not large enough to pool the financial risks of modern medical care. And the "restructuring" of the North American economy is greatly increasing the proportion of jobs in small firms.

Thus, in addition to those known to have no insurance coverage, there is another very large group who have grossly inadequate coverage to deal with any serious medical problem. Some of them can be identified if one reads the fine print, the limits and exclusions, in their contracts. But others emerge only after the fact; the contract is rewritten to exclude them after the event has occurred. Private coverage is simply unpredictable.

A further form of unpredictability is introduced because private insurers typically deal with the patient, not the provider. If there is any dispute over the bill, the patient has to struggle with the insurer, and is liable for the provider's bill whether or not the insurer pays. In some cases it appears that the insurer simply refuses to pay a legitimate claim, counting upon the difficulty of the struggle to deter the claimant. In any case, the costs of complying with the insurer's requirements in order to be reimbursed represent another major "cost" of private health care which is never recorded in the formal accounts, though most Americans are only too well aware of it.

The insurer has no incentive to reduce these costs; quite the contrary. From that point of view, increased complexity is desirable as a way of reducing claims. The same problem emerges in a different form in the Medicaid program. While nominally a federal-state program for "the poor," Medicaid allows the states to set their own eligibility criteria. In some states these include income tests that are *half* the income level used by the federal government to define poverty. And bureaucratic barriers to enrolment are an obvious way of limiting program costs.

The incentives for the insurer, public or private, are obvious; the extraordinary complexity of the American system is not accidental. Why is Canada different? Two important reasons, neither particularly mysterious. First, provincial payers deal with providers, not with patients. Providers have much more influence, individually and particularly collectively, to negotiate with payers. Onerous payment rules, slow or non-payment, and bureaucratic hassle, will find their way onto the annual negotiating table — and into the press — along with the level of fees paid.

But second, and perhaps most important, the Canadian programs are administered by governments which are responsible to the whole population. When most of the population has private coverage, why should the average voter/taxpayer be concerned if poor people have difficulty getting coverage or care? Taxes may be lower, after all. And private insurers are not politically accountable, at least not directly. Any problems an individual faces in dealing with them are personal, not political. But in Canada such problems *are* political; everyone is potentially involved. The "political marketplace" in Marmor's terms, is much better balanced.

CHOICE (AND COMPULSION):

The choices available — or not available — to people in different health care systems follow from their patterns of funding. At a very general level, the Canadian and American systems appear as reversed mirror images of each other in the choices they provide for patients. Canadians can choose any colour of health insurance they like, so long as they like black. There is one system of coverage in each province, a public monopoly; no competitors are allowed. We do *not* have "socialized medicine," but we *do* have socialized insurance. Americans can, in principle, choose from among a rich menu of options for range or depth of coverage. The market offers whatever you want — if you can pay for it. If you cannot, then as in any other market, your choices are more limited. They may be zero.

But with her universal, uniform public coverage the Canadian has free, or at least financially unimpeded, access to any primary care provider in the system, subject to the corresponding freedom of that provider to accept or refuse new patients. Access to specialists and hospitals is similarly unrestricted, on referral from the primary provider. Of course physicians have admitting privileges only at specific hospitals; thus in choosing the physician, the patient will also have chosen the hospital.

The American, on the other hand, will in general have much more restricted access to particular providers, and these restrictions are increasing with the spread of "managed care" systems. The variety of such systems is immense, but the general principle is that the third party payer — employer, insurance company, government — approves certain providers on the basis of their relative costliness, and then requires patients to use those providers, or else forfeit some or all of their coverage. The "preferred" providers may simply offer price/fee discounts to that particular payer in return for the business, or may have relatively conservative practice styles which result in lower per capita utilization.

It was not always thus. Twenty-five years ago, when Canada completed its universal public systems for hospital and medical care, most Americans had public or private coverage permitting them the "free choice of doctor" that Canadians have always had. This was a fundamental principle for medical associations; they fought bitter battles to suppress "closed panel prepaid group practice" plans whereby a group of physicians would offer to provide all necessary services in return for a capitation payment, a fixed payment per person per time period. Enrolees in such plans were free to use other providers as well — at their own expense.

But this principle was lost long ago under the pressure of relentless cost escalation. By the mid-1980s, the majority of Americans with employer-based coverage were in some form of "managed care" plan placing restrictions on their choice of provider. And most American observers believe that this trend will continue, not only to include more of the population, but also to tighten the restrictions on choice. As the pressure for health care reform has built up in the United States, the advocates of "managed care" have become increasingly influential; and their fundamental idea is that patients must be steered, and steered firmly, to the most cost-effective providers. Of course, one can always purchase whatever care one wishes, from whomever one chooses — if one can pay for it. But few can, even in the United States.

Restrictions on choice are not confined to the privately insured. Most obviously, those with no insurance have a difficult time finding *any* provider. Defenders of the American system point out, quite correctly, that the uninsured do in fact receive some care, sometimes quite a lot. Public hospitals in particular are under obligation to care for them, and do. But such care can be very difficult to find, and provided under very demeaning conditions. Moreover the increasing competitiveness of the American system is making it more and more difficult for institutions that provide "uncompensated care" to offset its cost by overcharging self-payers or those with private insurance.

Evidence is accumulating that the uninsured receive significantly less care for specific conditions (such as heart disease, and pre- and post-natal care) than the rest of the population, and that their health outcomes — including survival — are worse as a result. Coverage does matter.

Those who qualify for Medicaid are better off, but only partly. In order to control costs, Medicaid programs pay significantly lower fees than Medicare or private insurers. So, many providers refuse to accept Medicaid patients. Again, the choice of provider is limited by the mode of reimbursement.

This is not, of course, the end of the story. The Canadian may have "free choice of doctor", as the American used to have, but what about the *doctor's* choices? Those who allege that the Canadian system is "underfunded" emphasize the effects of global cost controls on the availability of care — rationing, waiting lists, and all that. They point out that universal access to care which is comprehensive in principle but unavailable in practice should not be a cause for self-congratulation. The rate of cardiac by-pass graft surgery in Canada, for example, is only half that in the United States, and the availability of high tech diagnostic imaging facilities is much less.

While the point is valid in principle, its application to the most well-funded system in the world (outside the United States) is simply part of the "disinformation" campaign referred to earlier. Defenders of the Canadian system reply along two lines: (1) the real issue is not the volume of particular procedures, which are in fact in excess in the United States, but the outcomes achieved; and (2) the very real problems of the Canadian system, as in those of most of Europe, are problems of management of the present resources, not overall inadequacy. Shortages and "crises" exist, but are highly localized in both place and time. Problems in cardiac surgery in Vancouver and Toronto in 1990, which were sorted out relatively rapidly, are still being referred to in the United States as if they were universal and permanent features of Canadian health care.

That said, however, it is also true that in all modern health care systems payers are increasingly intruding upon the professional autonomy of physicians and limiting their freedom to perform or recommend any interventions which they see fit. The objectives are both cost control and improved effectiveness of care; there is some disagreement as to the relative weights of each. This intrusion is occurring in both Canada and the United States, although in quite different ways.

The Canadian provinces restrict the availability of various forms of capacity — the number of hospital beds, or operating suites, or particular pieces of diagnostic equipment. The practitioner is free to recommend whatever she wishes, but if the total of such recommendations exceeds the available capacity, priorities must be set. The result can be overt waiting lists for certain services, or explicit rationing, sometimes with intense publicity.[3]

But the rhetoric of "rationing" is misleading in both countries. The reality of medical practice is that indications for intervention, "needs," are rarely black-and-white. Much of the clinician's work consists of judging among varying shades of grey — should a particular service be offered in this case, how often, and in conjunction with what others? Each clinician develops her own implicit criteria, and these "thresholds of intervention" vary widely among clinicians.[4]

The Canadian adjusts her criteria for intervention in response to the availability of facilities and services. For some procedures, thresholds are higher in Canada.[5] But the American makes the same adjustments, in response to the patient's ability to pay. Both systems "ration" — as do all others — but in Canada the priorities are set by (far from perfect) professional judgements of relative need. In the United States they depend upon the financial resources — insurance, public program entitlement, own funds, provider "charity" — on which the patient can draw.

In the absence of capacity restrictions, the American with sufficient resources has immediate access to any services offered. For him, the system is still open ended. The result is that clinical thresholds for intervention have been declining, and utilization and costs correspondingly increasing. This has obvious implications for insurers (and behind them for those who pay the premiums) — "exploding" costs. Thus payers have in recent years moved from utilization review to pre-intervention approval. Before admitting a patient to hospital, or initiating some expensive line of diagnosis or treatment, the practitioner must get permission from the insurer *of that patient*. She must describe the case and the reasoning behind the proposed intervention; if these do not match the protocols used by the insurer, approval for payment is denied. This usually means that the service is denied.

In both systems, professional autonomy is under attack, and practitioners are correspondingly angry and frustrated. The difference is that in Canada the constraints are collective and global; the care of the individual patient is rarely scrutinized. The professional community must work out among themselves how to deal with the discrepancy between the capacity they would like, and that which is available.

This focuses collective frustration and anger on "the government," who is so irresponsible and short-sighted as to fail to meet professional demands. "The system is underfunded!"

The American practitioner must defend to the payer her decisions and intentions with respect to an individual patient; the intrusion is thus much more personal and direct. But the corresponding frustration and anger is more difficult to focus. The constraints which are in Canada a political problem for the profession, are in the United States a personal problem for each physician. American physicians are no less angry; indeed recent surveys show a *greater* level of professional dissatisfaction in the United States. This is very clearly linked to the growth of "managed care." Physicians do not like to be managed, especially by outsiders.

But it is going to get worse, in both systems. "Managed care," in yet unspecified forms, is the leading contender in American debates over health care reform. To the north, every commission or review body which has examined the Canadian system has concluded that it is undermanaged, not underfunded. All have made recommendations for greater external accountability, and a shift of emphasis from traditional "doctors and hospitals" to home and community care, with a redeployment, not an addition, of resources. It is far too soon to say whether these efforts at reform will be successful, in either country. But they will in any case involve still further encroachment on professional autonomy, at least in its traditional form of "Give me the tools I (say I) need, and leave me alone."

COSTS AND CONSEQUENCES:

The pressure for "reform" of health care is virtually universal throughout the developed world. Much of the reform rhetoric focuses on "exploding costs" and our "inability to pay" for the increasing cost of health care. But much of this rhetoric is profoundly misleading, and it is important to be careful in identifying just what the problems really are. "Solutions" based on ignorance (or in some cases deliberate attempts to mislead) can be both dumb and disastrous.

First, health care costs in Canada are *not* "exploding" or "spiralling" or doing any other mathematically interesting thing. In real terms (that is, after adjusting for inflation) and per capita, they have been rising at about the same annual average rate for the last twenty years. And that rate, it should be noted, is considerably *slower* than during the previous twenty, prior to the completion of universal coverage for hospital and medical care. What *has* happened is that since 1980 the *general* rate of economic growth has fallen sharply away from its trend over the previous two decades. If economic growth in Canada (real Gross Domestic Product per capita) had maintained its 1960-80 growth through to 1991, we would still be spending about 7.5%, not 10%, of our GDP on health care. Health care did not explode; the rest of the economy shrank.

The real problem, then, is to adapt a health care system which has been habituated over decades to steady expansion, so as to fit it within the new, low-growth environment. The ballooning of health care costs as a share of GDP during the 1980s, and the corresponding deficits in provincial budgets, reflect the fact that this has not yet been achieved. Hence the pressure for reform.

The American problem is rather different. They failed to achieve universal coverage in the 1960s, so failed to put limits on the growth of their spending even during the "fat" years. In Canada, health care spending fluctuated around 7% of GDP during the 1970s, reaching 7.5% in 1980; in the United States it rose from 7.4% in 1970 to 9.2% in 1980. The economic decline of the 1980s has not moderated this growth; by 1991 the American ratio was 13.2%. The United States Congressional Budget Office projects over 18% by the year 2000.

In essence we (like most of the Europeans) learned in the 1970s to limit the growth of our health care system to match our then rates of general growth; the Americans did not and have not. But we (again like the Europeans) are now struggling to impose even tighter restraints, without damaging the effectiveness and political acceptability of our systems. The Americans have yet to find even a partial solution to the cost problem, and to make matters worse they must now address not only the issue of the uninsured — embarrassing but politically acceptable so long as most of them do not vote — but the instability of coverage for many more. The problems everyone else solved in the 1960s and 1970s are still on the American agenda as they, like we, face the management issues of the 1990s.

Behind the rhetoric of cost explosions and underfunding, however, is the more fundamental and more difficult question — what do we get for our money? Implicit in the objective of cost control, shared throughout the developed world by those who pay for health care, is the assumption that, at the margin, either more spending does not buy more health, or if it does, the amount it buys is not worth the cost. Exactly the reverse assumption is made, again usually implicitly, by those who claim that the system is underfunded, or those in the United States who argue that Canadians are dying in the streets because penny-pinching governments have "rationed" access to needed care.

Canadian health care is more egalitarian: American is more intensive and expensive. What can one say about the relative contribution of each to the health of the population that supports, undergoes, and pays for it? The traditional answer has been, "Not much, at least not directly." But that is changing quite fast.

One line of attack on this question is to ask, "Do Americans actually receive, on average, more health care than Canadians?" Or do they simply pay more for what they get? It turns out that when one examines the differences in cost between the two countries, they factor quite neatly into three categories: (1) administrative expenses; (2) provider incomes; and (3) servicing intensity. Only the third of these has any direct connection with the amount of services received.

An estimate of the administrative costs of the American system, including both the overhead costs of insurers and the administrative costs incurred by providers in dealing with insurers, concluded that the *excess* costs in 1987 were between $69 and $83 billion, compared with those required to administer a Canadian-style system. This excess administrative cost accounted for between 10% and 15% of total health care expenditure in that year. Thus roughly half of the additional spending in the United States is simply paper-pushing, and not health care at all.

Others have questioned the size of these estimates, but every analyst agrees that American overhead costs are very large. One has only to look at the size of the billing departments of comparable hospitals on the two sides of the border, or the ratio of benefit payments by private insurers to their premium collections. Americans are paying dearly for complexity, not care. Interestingly, the Hall Commission predicted precisely this result in 1964, when they recommended a universal public system for Canada.

Secondly, international studies of physicians' incomes find Americans to be at the top, earning over five times the average compensation of American employees. In Canada, physicians earn somewhat under four times as much as the average worker. And American fees have risen much faster than inflation over the last twenty years while Canadian fees have been more or less constant in real terms. A recent study by Fuchs shows fee levels in the United States (adjusted for exchange rates) to be about twice as high as in Canada — 50% higher for office visits, and three to four times as high for diagnostic and surgical procedures. But American physicians' incomes are not twice as high, because the average Canadian doctor bills for a larger number of visits and procedures. Expenditures on physicians' services are much higher in the United States, but Canadians actually receive more services because American doctors are paid more for doing less work.[6]

Thus much of the difference in costs between Canada and the United States goes to pay for administrative overheads and higher prices. One might argue that one or both of these factors correlate in some way with the "quality" of health care, and thus contribute to health outcomes — and some apologists for the American *status quo* have done so. But there is neither empirical evidence nor any *a priori* theoretical basis for such a claim.

Detailed cost comparisons thus suggest (but do not prove) that Canadians may receive much the same level of health care services as do Americans. What they emphasize is that there is no necessary connection between overall spending levels and levels of servicing. Moreover Mackenbach has recently shown that in Europe there is no detectable connection between national levels of health spending, and health outcomes — as measured by avoidable mortality. Thus there is simply no basis for the assumption *a priori* that, in terms of health outcomes, "You get what you pay for."

Statistics Canada has recently published a number of aggregate measures of the health status of Canadians and Americans, suggesting that the former are, on average, healthier. If we are "dying in the streets" for lack of adequate medical care, our vital statistics have failed to include the body count. (The stories of large numbers of Canadians flocking across the border for care are equally illusory; the snowbirds flock to Florida and Arizona, but for different reasons.) But the range of other factors which influence these rates makes it impossible to say that Canadians are healthier *because* of their health care system. The crucial question remains: "What, if anything, can one say about the patterns of care in the two countries, and about its relative contribution to the health of their populations?"

Evidence on this question has been very thin, but has recently begun to accumulate quite rapidly. It is quite clear that it is *patterns* rather than overall *levels* of care which differ. Canadians spend significantly more time in acute care hospitals, even after adjusting for the much larger proportion of Canadian hospital beds taken up by *de facto* long-term patients, but undergo fewer and less sophisticated procedures, on average, than do American inpatients. Canadian hospitals do have the latest technology — sometimes ahead of the Americans — but significantly less of it, so rates of utilization are lower (although typically each facility or machine is more intensively used north of the border). Canadians make more visits to general practitioners, fewer to specialists, again resulting in a less procedural, less technically oriented style of care.

From an American perspective, all of this looks very inefficient — people sitting around in beds for a long time with nothing, or at least less, going on. Don't just let them lie there, *do* something — preferably something dramatic, complicated, and expensive — and then get them out and get on with the next case. Some of the subtler

American critics of Canada have shifted their allegations from "Cheap and nasty!" which for the second most expensive system in the world is silly, to "Costly but inefficient!" And those supported by the private insurance industry add, "Inefficient because of *insufficient* spending upon administration."

Such criticisms have some validity. Students of Canadian health care have been pointing out for thirty years that hospitals in particular are inappropriately used and overused. The capitated payment systems in the United States have shown that North Americans can be perfectly adequately cared for with about *half* as much time in hospital beds as is typical in Canada. Provincial governments all across Canada are now struggling, against intense political resistance, to close hospitals and rationalize the use of inpatient care.

One must be very careful, however, to distinguish two very different forms of critique. A large community of students and providers of health care, on *both* sides of the border, are concerned about the extent of inappropriate and costly servicing — whether it be excessive use of hospitals in Canada, for example, or excessive diagnostic and surgical interventions in the United States — judged against the standard of whether one can show a health benefit for the patient. Re-designing the processes of health care delivery, payment, and regulation so as to encourage the provision of effective care, and to discourage ineffective, is a world-wide problem. No country can claim, to this point, to have found *the* answer. On this score the Canadian system is open to plenty of criticism — and has received it.

The internal political struggles over health care reform in the United States, however, have generated quite a different kind of critique. The Canadian system is declared inefficient *because* its patterns of care differ from those in the United States. The American way — shorter hospital stays with more high tech interventions, less time in the offices of more highly specialized and procedurally oriented specialists, all overseen by an extraordinarily complex and expensive administrative bureaucracy — is taken as the standard against which to judge the shortcomings of Canada, and by implication everyone else. But the crucial bit that is missing is the demonstration that such "American" patterns of care actually lead to better outcomes. What Americans do is right, not because it has been shown to work better, but because Americans do it. And Canadians, sadly, have always been very vulnerable to this form of argument.

Cardiac by-pass surgery is perhaps the most frequently cited example of the "inadequacies" of Canadian health care. Americans are about twice as likely, on average, to undergo this "lifesaving" procedure; its use has been expanding rapidly in both countries but the ratio has held fairly steady. There are "waiting lists" in Canada, and from time to time someone on a list dies. Clearly Canadians are dying unnecessarily because their system is either underfunded, or inefficient, or has the wrong priorities. This sort of story makes wonderful propaganda in the United States. The reality is, of course, rather different.

In the first place, there is only a limited range of conditions for which by-pass surgery offers increased life expectancy. People with these problems are not kept waiting in Canada. Waiting lists are *not* "first come, first served"; they are managed by clinicians on the basis of need. Second, as such procedures are being offered to older and sicker people, the composition of the "waiting list" is changing. Very elderly people with heart disease do not have long life expectancies, and in most cases their life expectancy is not increased by the procedure. Dying *while* on a list is not the same as dying *because* one is on a list, rather than being operated on immediately. People, particularly elderly and ill people, die on operating tables too, or shortly thereafter. In fact some people who are too old and ill to undergo the procedure are nevertheless placed on "waiting lists" as a humane way to preserve hope. And finally, as noted above, the American system also "rations" care according to insurance coverage or personal resources. Under- or uninsured persons get less care, but never show up on a waiting list.

Which is better? Unless one starts from the assumption that whatever is American is right, the answer is not clear. American analysts have concluded that their own rates of by-pass grafting are too high, and include a good deal of inappropriate, ineffective, and perhaps harmful interventions. Enthoven, quoted earlier, has conjectured that more people die during inappropriate by-pass surgery in California than die on waiting lists in Canada.

Propaganda campaigns are no substitute for the hard work of studying what patterns of care *and their outcomes* are, on the two sides of the border. Such studies show no evidence of a systematic, much less a major, advantage for the "American style."

WHERE NEXT?

While the Canadian health care system has rather conclusively demonstrated its superiority to American arrangements *in their present form*, the implications for the future are not as obvious as might appear. It does not necessarily follow that Americans should implement a Canadian-style system at the earliest possible date, while we sit back and congratulate ourselves.

As a number of thoughtful American commentators (as distinguished from the professionally mendacious) have pointed out, the United States *is* different in a number of important respects, not least in its form of government. An attempt to graft Canadian institutions onto American traditions might come out very differently — and much worse — in both structure and functioning.

Moreover, most Canadian analysts have concluded that present arrangements are not sustainable into the future — "business as usual" is not a viable option. The reports of conflict and "crisis" in the daily news do not represent accidental or temporary events; we too must change. Nor are we unusual; the same pressures for reform are felt throughout the developed world.

The general objectives of reform are clear; they are both technical/administrative, and political/ethical. We need to know more about the effectiveness of services, what works and what does not, and we need to know *much* more about how to translate this knowledge into actual practice. This is probably the most immediate task. As citizens we want to receive and pay for effective services, efficiently provided. But this requires evaluation, accountability, management, and change — major threats to established values and ways of doing things.

But we also have to work through the political/ethical choices implicit in the phrase, "medically necessary" care.[7] We want all such services to be provided free, but we have never decided what they are. Is *any* medical benefit, however small, worth paying for? And where are the boundaries? Quality of life is an important dimension of the outcome of care. Yet a commitment to provide any service that would improve someone's quality of life would be infinite.

Nor is the issue one of "public" versus "private" funding. "Privatization" in Canada, in the sense of moving back to more payment by users and private insurance (with, advocates say very quietly, public subsidies through the tax system) would lead to *higher* overall costs (particularly administrative costs and fees), lower efficiency, and greater inequity of both access and cost bearing. It is a way of keeping the historic cost expansion going, by shifting the burden from governments, who have had some success at cost control, to users and employers, who have not. Such proposals are simply disguised calls for "More money!" rather than more management and accountability, and will solve nothing.

Yet such "quack" remedies remain popular, for good reason. A shift from tax to private funding lowers the share of costs carried by the healthy and wealthy — the two are highly correlated — while giving them better access. A small contribution buys your way to the front of the line. And it increases the incomes of those who can charge for access to services supported from public funds, while opening up new markets for sellers of overhead services — all costs without benefits. Yet, as the Americans are finding, such costs are deeply entrenched politically.

The institutional changes being proposed to reform health care are very diverse, and system-specific. But certain general principles have emerged, in North America and internationally:

(1) More management, not more money;

(2) Money follows the patient; and

(3) Separation of purchaser and provider.

Interestingly, all have roots in American "managed care" ideas and initiatives.

Perceived health "needs" always expand beyond available resources. Adding more is no solution; we must make better use of the huge amounts already committed. Resources should be allocated to providers on the basis of the size, composition, and estimated needs of the populations they serve, not just their level of activity or historical budgets.[8] And those who pay for services (governments, insurers, employers, depending upon the country) must play a larger role in making decisions over what services shall be provided, by whom — becoming "purchasers" rather than simply complaining about the bills.

"Managed care," in various guises, is what everyone is trying to establish. In Canada provincial governments are ultimately responsible for this function, but its effective performance will require co-operation from both the professions and the population at regional level. In the United States a diversity of agencies are trying to play the role of purchaser. So long as both purchaser and patient can choose each other, however, the over riding incentive is for purchasers to enrol healthy people and exclude the "bad risks" who are in most need.

Every country is wrestling with the same problems; none can yet claim to have found the answer. Canada and the United States at least have a clear picture of the high costs of failure. In Canada, this means the political defeat of reform, continued cost escalation and/or political conflict, followed by governments progressively abandoning their central role — as the federal government is already doing — under increasing fiscal pressure. A little "privatization" is followed by more, and we slide back to an American-style system, down the road we were on prior to the introduction of the public plans. Thus the penalty for failure may be the same on both sides of the border — the present American system!

NOTES

1. In the United States, by contrast, patients freely "self-refer" to specialists (some self-designated) and the general practitioner has almost disappeared. The absence of a generalist "gatekeeper" may add significantly to inappropriate care and costs.

2. In 1986, average out-of-pocket expenditures for health care were $1135 per household in the United States, and $446 (US) in Canada. For hospitals and physicians American households paid $346, Canadians paid $33. The gap increases rapidly with age: American households with heads over 75 paid $1834 for health care, or 17.1% of total personal consumption. Canadians paid $301, or 3.2%. Hospitals and doctors took $648 from this group in the U.S., and $42 in Canada.

3. Allegations of "shortage" are an important part of the political negotiating process, whereby providers of health care bargain for more resources. Aggregate "waiting list" data in particular are virtually meaningless, at least as a measure of the adequacy of overall system resources. But the publicity surrounding this negotiating process is seized upon and amplified in the American disinformation campaign.

4. They also vary greatly from one community to another, without any corresponding differences in outcomes or "quality of care." A classic study by Wennberg has demonstrated very large differences in such thresholds — and in resulting costs — between Boston (Harvard) and New Haven (Yale).

5. For others, Canadian thresholds are lower — cardiac pacemakers, for example — and in fact both total hospital use and total numbers of surgical procedures are *higher* (per capita) in Canada. These differences receive no attention outside the research community, because they assist no political interest in either country.

6. This observation undercuts an "explanation" commonly offered for high costs in the United States — malpractice litigation. The claim that malpractice *premiums* explain the difference is easily dismissed as specious; these represent on average less than 5% of American physicians' gross receipts. Spectacular premiums for some individuals create a com-

pletely false impression. The secondary claim is that *fear* of suit leads to unnecessarily intensive and costly defensive medicine. But this would be reflected in *higher* levels of use in the United States, not lower. What the malpractice story demonstrates is the popularity of glib excuses.

7. In the United States, the same question is framed as the design and implementation of a "basic benefit package", to be universally provided. The state of Oregon has received a great deal of attention, with its plan to set priorities based on scientific evidence of efficacy, and community judgements of appropriateness. Procedures with little or no demonstrable benefit should not be paid for, nor should those that may be of value to the individual but which the community does not regard as a public responsibility. But in Oregon the community at large is setting priorities only for the Medicaid program — the poorest citizens —not for themselves. Moreover the cut-off point on the priority list will be determined by the budget for that program, rather than the budget being determined by the cost of an independently defined "basic benefit" package.

8. In such "capitated" systems payers allocate a certain sum for the care of residents of region R, or enrolees of plan P, from which the providers caring for those residents or enrolees are paid. In Canada, this might take the form of regional budgets allocated by provincial governments; in the United States, Health Maintenance Organizations charge a fixed annual contribution per enrolee, in return for providing all "needed" care.

FURTHER READING:

The United States:

R.J. Blendon and J.N. Edwards, eds., *System in Crisis: The Case for Health Care Reform*, New York: Faulkner and Gray, 1991.

Organization for Economic Co-operation and Development, *U.S. Health Care at the Cross-Roads* (Health Policy Studies #1), Paris: the OECD, 1992.

United States Congress, *Congressional Budget Office Projections of National Health Expenditures* (A CBO Study), Washington, DC October, 1992.

Canada:

A.O.J. Crichton, D.H.-S. Hsu and S. Tsang, *Canada's health care system: Its funding and organization,* Ottawa: Canadian Hospital Association, 1990.

Both:

A. Bennett and O. Adams (eds.), *Looking North for Health: What We Can Learn from Canada's Health-Care System* San Francisco: Jossey-Bass, 1993.

C. Nair, R. Karim, and C. Nyers, "Health Care and Health Status: A Canada-United States Statistical Comparison," Health Reports, 4:2 October, 1992, Ottawa: Statistics Canada (cat. no. 82-003), pp. 175-183.

Journal of Health Politics, Policy and Law, 17:4 Winter, 1992.

Yale Law & Policy Review, 10:2 (1992).

DAVID PERRY

What Price Canadian?
Taxation and Debt Compared

Is there a price to be paid for staying in Canada? There are certainly convincing reasons for staying, or even moving north of the border, just as there are equally convincing arguments for moving south. Most of these involve political or philosophical considerations, not simple questions of dollars and cents. There are a number of economic advantages that pull people south, including the size of the population and the advantages that a large and varied market can offer to those in search of wealth or fame. The same differences in size can offer advantages, on the other hand, to those whose specialties match Canadian economic strengths, or those who prefer a smaller pond. Canadians' expectations of their government are different from those of Americans, and this creates variations in taxation and fiscal policy that can be compelling factors. It is these variations that this chapter examines.

PITFALLS AND A WARNING

The old adage about lies, damn lies, and statistics, was never more apt than when comparing government activities and fiscal policy between Canada and the US. It is possible to use perfectly valid figures produced by each government to prove either side in most arguments. Three reasons make such international comparisons areas where angels fear to tread.

The first relates to the different forms of government and distributions of responsibilities. A comparison of the federal or central governments in each country will be misleading unless you adjust, for example, for the fact that unemployment insurance is a federal responsibility in Canada and a state responsibility in the US.

The second minefield hidden in public finance statistics arises from the different accounting systems used in each country, and even the variation between provinces or states within each country. In one government, a particular function may be carried out by a department and related revenues lumped with all other tax and non-tax revenues. In this case, the related spending and revenue is included in budgetary figures and the difference between them is revealed in the budget surplus or deficit. In another, the same function may be performed by an independent commission or agency, collecting related revenue itself, and using budgetary funds only to the extent that it requires subsidy from the sponsoring government. As a result, the surplus or deficit may be comparable to the all-public-sector system, but budgetary revenues and spending miss most of this activity.

The third trap awaiting the unwary stems from the different responsibilities assumed by the public sector (government as broadly defined) in each country. The most obvious example is medical care, discussed elsewhere in this volume, which is provided primarily by government in Canada and by the private sector in the US. The public finance data will, however, miss all private sector fees, charges and spending, thus distorting the true picture.

In this chapter, I have adjusted for only the first two pitfalls. I have confined most of the comparisons to consolidated data; that is, figures combining results from the federal, provincial or state, and local governments, along with special agencies. Similarly, tax comparisons will include all levels and social security systems to ensure that adjustments are made to make the situations truly comparable. To ensure that the differences in accounting systems have been minimized, I relied primarily on data from the Organization for Economic Co-operation and Development (OECD) and the International Monetary Fund (IMF) for Canadian-US comparisons. The latest years available are thus 1989 or 1990.

There are other instances where the two countries do things differently. The social security system in the US provides a major part of individuals' savings for retirement — the system is designed to provide about one-half of the pension for an individual earning the average industrial wage. In Canada, the comparable Canada or Quebec pension plans (CPP or QPP) provide about one-quarter of the pension for someone retiring after earning the average industrial wage. Thus, a quick comparison would indicate that our system is less generous and less expensive. The CPP and QPP, however, are designed to augment the basic, universal pensions available under the federal old age security program, bringing Canadian pension levels up to about one-half of the average-earnings pension.

Table 1: Total Government Outlays Canada and the US 1971 to 1991

	As Percentage GDP		As Percent G-7 Average	
	Canada	US	Canada	US
1971	36.1	31.6	110.4	96.6
1972	36.6	31.3	111.2	95.1
1973	35.4	30.6	108.3	93.6
1974	36.8	32.2	106.7	93.3
1975	40.1	34.7	106.4	92.0
1976	39.1	33.4	106.3	90.8
1977	40.1	32.2	110.5	88.7
1978	40.3	31.6	110.4	86.6
1979	39.0	31.7	105.4	85.7
1980	40.5	33.7	105.5	87.8
1981	41.5	34.1	106.7	87.7
1982	46.6	36.5	115.3	90.3
1983	47.2	36.9	116.5	91.1
1984	46.8	35.8	118.8	90.9
1985	47.1	36.7	118.6	92.4
1986	46.4	37.1	116.3	93.0
1987	45.2	36.8	113.6	92.5
1988	44.3	36.1	113.3	92.3
1989	44.6	36.1	115.2	93.3
1990	46.9	37.2	111.1	88.2
1991(a)	49.4	38.1		

(a) Estimated by author.
Source: OECD Outlook, 52, December 1992, p. 215.

Furthermore, the Canadian tax system provides more generous tax concessions for retirement savings, using public resources — tax expenditures — as a supplement. When comparing spending on social security — specifically assistance to seniors — between the two countries it is necessary to examine direct spending (the old age security pension and US welfare spending on seniors), off-budget items (benefits paid from the CPP and QPP funds or the US social security fund), as well as the tax expenditures in each country for retirement savings (and additional tax concessions provided for seniors).

To avoid the problems of exchange rates and the difference in size, most comparisons of aggregate public sector income, spending,

Table 2: Consolidated Government Spending Canada and the US

Canada, fiscal year ending March 31, 1990

	Amount in $millions	Percentage distribution	as a % GDP
Total spending	294,661	100.0	44.1
Health	39,095	13.3	5.9
Education	34,195	11.6	5.1
Soc Sec & Welfare	72,184	24.5	10.8
Interest payments	51,237	17.4	7.7
Debt	522,815	na	78.3

US, fiscal year ending September 30, 1990

	Amount in $billions	Percentage distribution	as a % GDP
Total spending	2,032	100.0	36.8
Health	262	12.9	4.7
Education	293	14.4	5.3
Soc Sec & Welfare	403	19.9	7.3
Interest payments	248	12.2	4.5
Debt	3,137	na	56.8

na not applicable
Source: IMF Government Finance Statistics Yearbook, 1992

deficits, or debt in this chapter will look at their relative importance, that is, expressed as a percentage of gross domestic product (GDP).

A BROAD REVIEW OF PUBLIC SECTOR SPENDING AND INCOME

Spending

Total government outlays in each county are summarized in Table 1, which indicates that spending by all levels of government in Canada, including hospitals,[1] was equivalent to 46.9% of GDP in 1990. On a comparable basis, public sector spending in the US was equal to only 37.2% of GDP. The table indicates that the trends over recent years have been similar. In both countries, the relatively high levels of the early 1980s have been exceeded in 1990 and subsequent years, as the recession increased spending (on income support programs) while reducing the denominator — GDP — in relative terms. If the data available from individual country sources are used to project these OECD numbers, Canada's spending rose to about 49.4% in 1991 and the US to 38.1%. The most appropriate standard by which to measure Canadian and US performance is the Group of 7 nations (G-7) — the US, Germany, France, the United Kingdom, Japan, Italy, and Canada.

Canadian spending reached a high, relative to the G-7 average, in the mid-1980s — 118.8% of the average in 1984 — and has declined in recent years to 111.1% in 1990, about the level recorded in 1972. The US ratio, 88.2% of the G-7 average in 1990, is down from 95.1% of the average in 1972.

Based on consolidated expenditures,[2] government spending on social security and welfare was relatively larger in Canada, as shown in Table 2. Government spending on health care was also relatively more important in Canada, taking up 13.3% of total public sector spending and representing 5.9 percent of GDP. In the US, the comparable numbers for government spending on health care were 12.9% and 4.7%. Government spending on education was relatively more important south of the border, as was spending on defence. Interest payments on the public debt were significantly higher north of the border because public sector debt and interest rates were higher in Canada.

The Income Side

Current receipts of the Canadian and US public sectors are summarized in Table 3. These figures include not only tax but also revenue from fees and fines, the sales of goods and services, interest income earned on investments, and certain levies imposed on non-renewable resources (such as sales of oil and natural gas exploration and development rights). This time, the patterns in the two countries are distinctly different. In the US, the level of current receipts has varied surprisingly little; it was around 30 percent of GDP over the 18 years shown. Canadian public sector revenues stayed around 35% of GDP until 1981, when they began a climb that had sent them to 41.6% by 1990. Later figures indicate that the climb has continued in 1991 and 1992. Much of the increase can be explained by the growing

Table 3: Total Government Current Receipts Canada and the US 1971 to 1991

	As Percentage GDP		As Percent G-7 Average	
	Canada	US	Canada	US
1971	34.7	28.2	113.4	92.2
1972	35.2	29.3	113.5	94.5
1973	34.9	29.6	110.8	94.0
1974	37.2	30.4	113.8	93.0
1975	36.1	28.8	112.1	89.4
1976	35.8	29.5	109.8	90.5
1977	36.1	29.7	109.7	90.3
1978	35.7	29.9	108.8	91.2
1979	35.5	30.5	104.7	90.0
1980	36.2	30.8	104.6	89.0
1981	38.5	31.6	110.0	90.3
1982	39.1	31.1	111.7	88.9
1983	38.7	30.7	111.5	88.5
1984	38.7	30.7	112.2	89.0
1985	38.7	31.3	111.2	89.9
1986	39.5	31.4	112.2	89.2
1987	40.0	32.0	110.8	88.6
1988	40.2	31.5	112.3	88.0
1989	40.1	31.8	111.1	88.1
1990	41.6	31.6	104.0	79.0
1991(a)	42.6	31.8		

(a) Estimated by author.
Source: OECD Outlook, 52, December 1992, p. 215.

concern, at the federal level, with the increasing size of the deficit. Since 1984, the federal government has introduced a number of tax increases which contained the deficit, even in times of recession, but which, helped by provincial tax increases aimed at containing deficits and ensuring continued levels of public services, raised the ratio of public sector revenue to GDP. The Canadian pattern has been closer to that of all OECD nations, and of the G-7, than to that of the US.

More Detail On Taxation

There is a surprising degree of diversity between the Canadian and US tax systems. The relative importance of the main forms of taxation are shown in Table 4. In Canada, all taxes were equivalent to 37.1% in 1990. This includes not only federal and provincial taxes on personal income and corporate profits, but also levies for unemployment insurance and the Canada and Quebec pension plans, provincial and local property taxes, some of the provincial levies on natural resource industries, and provincial revenues from the sale of alcoholic beverages, which the economist considers to be taxes. In the US, taxes as broadly defined were equivalent to 29.9 percent of GDP in 1990.

Of more significance in this table is the change in the relationship between the tax levels in the two countries over the past decade. In the US the ratio changed very little over 20 years, but in Canada, the 1970 and 1980 ratios — 31.3% and 31.6% — were significantly lower than in 1990. The Canadian ratio jumped to 33.7% in 1981 and remained at approximately that level until 1987. By then, the full effects of federal deficit reduction measures had begun to take effect, and they were reinforced by a series of provincial tax increases, combined with a similar trend in local property taxes, pushing the tax ratio well above the US level. Projections indicate that the 1991 ratio for Canada increased to 39.4 and even higher for 1992 and 1993. The 1990-92 recession lowered GDP and thus raised the ratio, but this cannot be blamed for all of the change; deliberate tax increases designed to restore balance in fiscal policy have been the major factor. By expressing the Canadian and US ratios as percentages of the average ratio for all OECD countries, it is obvious that the Canadian tax system evolved much as that for the community as a whole until 1987, when it began to climb closer to the OECD average. The US system, on the other hand, fell below the average before stabilizing over the past seven years.

Not only is there a major difference in the level of total taxes, there are also differences in the utilization of each of the major taxes, as shown in Table 4. In Canada, the personal income tax rose from 10.1 percent of GDP in 1970 to 15.2% in 1990. In the US, personal income taxes remained at about 10% throughout the period. Corporate income taxes, on the other hand, declined in both countries from about 3.5% in 1970 to 2.5% or less by 1990. Canada has always used sales or consumption taxes more aggressively than the US, although there has been little change in collections of such taxes over the two decades shown in the table, despite a succession of rate increases and extensions to the bases. In the US, on the other hand,

Table 4: Taxes as a Percentage of GDP, Selected Calendar Years, 1970 to 1990

	Taxes on Personal income	Taxes on Corporate income	Taxes on Goods & services	Taxes for social security	Total Taxes
Canada					
1970	10.1	3.5	9.9	3.0	31.3
1975	10.6	4.4	10.4	3.3	32.4
1980	10.8	3.7	10.3	3.3	31.6
1985	11.6	2.7	10.5	4.5	33.1
1986	12.4	2.7	10.0	4.7	33.7
1987	13.4	2.8	10.1	4.7	34.7
1988	12.8	2.9	10.1	4.7	34.5
1989	13.6	3.0	10.4	4.7	35.4
1990	15.2	2.5	10.2	5.3	37.1
United States					
1970	10.3	3.7	5.6	5.6	29.2
1975	9.5	3.1	5.4	7.1	29.0
1980	10.9	3.0	4.9	7.7	29.5
1985	10.4	2.1	5.2	8.6	29.2
1986	10.2	2.0	5.1	8.6	28.9
1987	10.9	2.4	5.0	8.7	30.2
1988	10.2	2.5	5.0	8.7	29.4
1989	10.6	2.5	4.8	8.6	29.6
1990	10.7	2.2	4.9	8.8	29.9

Source: OECD, Revenue Statistics of Member Countries, 1965 to 1991

such taxes have declined slightly but perceptibly over the same period. In Canada, special levies for social security programs — the Canada and Quebec pension plans, the federal unemployment insurance program and provincial workers' compensation programs — while increasing from 3.0 percent of GDP in 1970 to 5.3 percent in 1990, have not kept pace with similar US levies.

Real property taxes, the main tax source for local governments on both sides of the border, are high relative to other OECD countries, but have declined slightly over the period from 4.1 percent of GDP in Canada and 4.0% in the US in 1970 to 3.3% and 3.2% respectively

Table 5: Percentage Distribution of Tax Revenues by Level of Government, OECD Member Countries, 1990

	Supra-national	central	state/prov.	local	Social Security
Australia	-	79.6	16.8	3.5	-
Austria	-	50.3	10.7	11.2	27.8
Belgium	1.3	60.8	-	3.7	34.2
Canada	-	41.9	35.1	8.9	14.2
Denmark	0.6	65.6	-	30.7	3.1
Finland	-	60.8	-	27.3	11.8
France	0.6	46.2	-	9.0	44.2
Germany	0.9	32.9	21.1	8.3	36.8
Greece	1.0	69.8	-	1.2	28.1
Iceland	10.9	71.4	-	17.7	-
Ireland	1.4	82.7	-	2.5	13.4
Italy	0.5	63.7	-	2.9	32.9
Japan	-	46.2	-	24.6	29.2
Luxembourg	0.5	61.1	-	11.2	27.2
Netherlands	1.4	59.0	-	2.2	37.3
New Zealand	-	94.6	-	5.4	-
Norway	-	54.8	-	20.7	24.4
Portugal	-	67.8	-	4.6	27.6
Spain	0.5	51.9	-	12.5	35.1
Sweden	-	52.5	-	28.8	18.7
Switzerland	-	29.6	21.6	16.0	32.8
Turkey	-	71.6	-	8.8	19.7
United Kingdom	1.0	75.7	-	5.7	17.5
United States	-	39.0	18.8	12.6	29.5
Average: federal states	0.9	45.6	20.7	10.1	23.5
Average: unitary states(a)	1.8	63.8	-	12.4	22.6

(a) Turkey is excluded
-nil.
Source: Same as Table 4.

in 1990. This long-term view, however, masks the fact that over the past three years both countries have shown a gradual rise in this ratio.

The distribution of tax revenues between the three levels of government — federal, provincial/state, and local — is different. As shown in Table 5, Canada has the most decentralized tax system of all federal countries in the OECD. In 1990, 44.0% of all tax revenues went to the ten Canadian provinces and about 8,000 local governments. This figure includes personal and corporate income taxes imposed by the provinces but collected on their behalf by the federal government. In the US, the 50 states and about 83,000 local governments collected only 31.4% of all taxes levied in the country.

Social security taxes (mainly CPP, QPP, and unemployment insurance levies) accounted for 14.2% of all taxes in Canada, while the comparable figure for the US, where the federally run social security system represents the largest proportion, is 29.5%. Thus, while taxes under Ottawa's control represented 56.1% of all taxes, its influence was smaller than Washington's, which was responsible for about 68.5% of all taxes when the federal element of social security levies was taken into account.

HOW MUCH DO WE PAY IN TAXES?

While the comparisons of aggregate tax collections give a clear picture of the relative burden placed on the economy as a whole by the public sector, they seldom relate directly to the amounts of tax actually paid by representative taxpayers. These kinds of analyses must be based on a clear understanding of how the tax systems in each country actually work.

To begin with, the US federal government dominates the income tax system to a degree not seen in Canada for forty years.[3] While most, but not all, states levy some form of personal income tax, their structures are far from uniform and their rates well below those imposed by Canadian provinces. The US federal tax income tax system treats such state income taxes as deductions from taxable income. In Canada, on the other hand, the provincial personal income taxes are an integral part of the system and no deduction is thus allowed for provincial taxes. In nine provinces and the two territories, the federal government administers and collects the provincial income taxes. Quebec has its own personal income tax system, which it collects.[4]

There is a high degree of uniformity between the federal and provincial personal tax systems in Canada, even when the provinces

Table 6: Combined Federal and Provincial/State Personal Income Tax, Highest and Lowest Top Marginal Rates, 1993

		Percent
Canada		
	Quebec	52.9%
	Ontario	52.3%
	Saskatchewan	51.9%
	Alberta	46.1%
United States		
	North Dakota	46.8%
	New York(a)	46.4%
	California	46.2%
	Nevada	39.6%
	Florida	39.6%

(a) includes city income tax

have chosen to collect their own taxes. Under the tax collection agreements, the federal government allows additional provincial taxes on high-income taxpayers or reductions for low-income groups. No provincial variation is permitted in the determination of taxable income or the basic rate schedule.[5] In the US, on the other hand, the states levy and collect their own taxes and so are free to decide what incomes are to be taxed, the rate schedules, and special relief for particular situations. Table 6 compares the rates of combined personal income tax in selected provinces and states in 1993.

The federal government also collects some provincial corporate income taxes in Canada, but three provinces — Quebec, Ontario and Alberta — levy and collect their own taxes. The federal allowance for provincial taxes is more explicit than in the personal income tax system. The statutory federal rates are reduced by 10% of taxable profits to make room for the provincial taxes. All provinces are free to set their own rates, but only the three independent provinces are not bound to express their rates as a percentage of the federal base. In practice, these provinces have kept their tax bases close to the federal definition of taxable profits. The states are free to develop corporate profits taxes as they wish, with the predictable result of a high degree of variation.

The US federal government does not impose a general sales tax, relying only on customs duties and special sales taxes — what are often referred to as sin taxes — on such products as motor vehicle fuel, alcoholic beverages, and tobacco. Ottawa has similar special taxes but also imposes a value-added tax (VAT) — the Goods and Services Tax — on most goods and services. The provinces levy sin taxes and, except for Alberta and the territories, general retail sales taxes, on a narrower range of goods and very few services.[6] In the US, many of the states and a number of local governments impose retail sales taxes and sin taxes, and represent the main tax collectors in this area.

In both countries, the local levels rely primarily on taxes levied annually on real estate for the bulk of their tax revenue. In the US, this level also extensively uses personal property taxes (on such items as automobiles), but local governments in Canada seldom rely on this form of tax.

TRANSLATING THE THEORETICAL INTO THE PRACTICAL

One of the biggest differences between tax burdens north and south of the border, and the one often overlooked when comparing income taxes alone, arises because of the variations in social security systems. The CPP and QPP impose taxes of 2.5% of earned income up to an annual maximum of $752.50 at an income of $34,300. The US counterpart, social security, imposes a tax, in 1993, of 7.65% on income up to $57,600, producing a maximum tax, at that income, of $4,406.40. In each country, employers pay a matching amount for each employee, and the self-employed are assessed double the employee contribution.

Personal income tax burdens are even more difficult to compare because the two systems do not tax precisely the same thing. In Canada, for example, capital gains (profits) on the sale of a home are not taxable, but in the US such gains are eventually taxed. In the US, on the other hand, mortgage interest is deductible from income for tax purposes, while it is not deductible in Canada. Offsetting this is the deduction allowed under the Canadian system for contributions to a registered retirement savings plan (RRSP), which is much more generous than the roughly analogous deduction for contributions to an individual retirement account. Since both are in addition to the tax relief available for contributions to company pension plans, cross-border tax comparisons will be influenced by the extent to which the examples are able to take advantage of the tax relief for RRSPs. Capital gains are taxed at full rates in the US, giving an effective top rate of up to 46.8 percent. In Canada, such income is taxed at

Table 7: Comparisons of Canadian and US personal income taxes, 1993 Federal, Social Security, and Provincial/State For Saskatchewan and North Dakota: Selected Income Levels

A) Single person, no dependants

Annual Earnings	Saskatchewan As % of income	Saskatchewan Amount	North Dakota As % of income	North Dakota Amount
$10,000	11.1	$1,114	13.9	$1,386
$20,000	23.1	$4,622	20.2	$4,046
$30,000	27.1	$8,137	23.8	$7,140
$40,000	31.8	$12,719	28.2	$11,281
$50,000	34.5	$17,263	31.0	$15,518
$60,000	36.4	$21,856	32.8	$19,677
$70,000	38.6	$27,001	33.8	$23,659
$80,000	40.2	$32,196	34.6	$27,683
$90,000	41.5	$37,390	35.3	$31,756
$100,000	42.6	$42,585	35.8	$35,829

B) Married couple, two children, assuming one earner provides 100 per cent of family income

Annual Earnings	Saskatchewan As % of income	Saskatchewan Amount	North Dakota As % of income	North Dakota Amount
$10,000(a)	(26.8)	($2,681)	7.7	$765
$20,000(a)	(1.4)	($272)	11.0	$2,190
$30,000	14.8	$4,451	15.1	$4,537
$40,000	24.8	$9,937	18.2	$7,276
$50,000	29.8	$14,912	20.4	$10,175
$60,000	33.3	$20,006	23.2	$13,902
$70,000	36.3	$25,441	25.0	$17,519
$80,000	38.3	$30,636	26.5	$21,229
$90,000	39.8	$35,830	27.7	$24,943
$100,000	41.0	$41,025	28.7	$28,740

(a) Refundable child tax benefits and refundable GST credit exceed income and social security taxes in Saskatchewan.

75 percent of the regular rates, producing an effective top rate of up to 39.7 percent.

The final consideration in comparing the personal income tax burden between the two countries rests on differences in the progressivity of each system. Canadians at lower incomes tend to pay less tax than their US counterparts, while those at higher levels pay more, as shown in Table 7. The Canadian system, with its special refundable tax credit system for children and for the GST, produces significantly lower burdens for those taxpayers with children than those without. The US system has a system of exemptions for dependent children that provides less assistance for low-income families and more for high-income families.

As indicated earlier in Table 4, taxes on goods and services are significantly higher north of the border, largely because Ottawa levies a general sales tax and Washington does not. Unfortunately, sales taxes are seldom consistent across provincial or state borders, so it is difficult to compare the two countries without making some assumptions about housing and spending patterns, especially spending on alcoholic beverages, tobacco, insurance premiums, and a host of other relatively minor but heavily taxed goods or services.

In summary, comparisons of the tax burden on individuals or families are highly dependent upon the examples chosen. Income and spending patterns are of crucial importance. Unfortunately, many of these taxes are state or provincial taxes and local taxes, so the picture is complicated by deciding where to locate the examples. Comparisons of high-tax provinces with low-tax states exaggerate the differences in favour of the US; the reverse situation minimizes the differences. The best comparison is a highly individualized one, as often performed for businesses about to transfer personnel between countries or even between cities. In that case, the family size and make-up is set to be appropriate, not to typical residents, but to the type of person about to be transferred. The comparisons take into account not only taxes, but also housing and other living costs. Implicitly, benefits received from the public sector, such as free medical care in Canada, and a more generous social security retirement pension in the US, are also taken into account.

BUSINESS TAXES

If you despair of making sweeping generalizations about the family tax burden on each side of the border, remember that even more difficulties lie below the surface of comparisons of the tax burden on businesses. Nominal federal corporate income tax rates are shown

Table 8: Canadian and US Top Corporate Income Tax Rates Including Federal and Provincial/State Taxes: 1993 Tax Year

	Percentage of taxable profits
Canada Federal rate	28.8
Combined federal and provincial	
Ontario	44.3
Saskatchewan	45.8
British Columbia	45.3
Alberta	44.3
Quebec	45.1
Prince Edward Island	43.8
US Federal rate	34.0
Combined federal and state	
New York(a)	46.4
Pennsylvania	42.1
Connecticut	41.6
North Dakota	40.9
California	40.1
Nevada	34.0
(a) includes New York City tax	

in Table 8, and indicate a surprising degree of uniformity. Would that it held in practice! Table 9 shows the relative position of Quebec corporations in relation to those in Ontario, and three of the states most in competition with Quebec for new or expanded business. It illustrates the importance of the examples being considered. A more recent study from the Government and Competitiveness Initiative of the universities of Ottawa and Queen's states that corporate tax levels vary little across the border, a fact that is confirmed by Table 4.

Business also pays special taxes on payrolls and capital employed, as well as general levies such as property tax, gasoline taxes, and some retail sales taxes. The burden of such taxes will vary widely depending on the extent to which such taxed goods are used in the specific business.

Taxes buy different services for businesses, just as they do for individuals. Many large businesses provide medical care insurance

Table 9: Effective Burden on Business of Taxes on Profits, Capital, Payrolls, Purchases and Property Using Simulation Techniques (a)

Provincial or state taxes as a percentage of those payable in Quebec in 1989

	Ontario	Massachusetts	Michigan	New York
Average for all small businesses	108	109	109	124
Specific industries				
Women's clothing	121	112	117	123
Aircraft and parts	99	98	93	115
Pharmaceuticals	106	109	108	131
Communications equipment				
Average for all large businesses	100	98	104	115
Specific industries				
Women's clothing	118	111	118	120
Aircraft and parts	101	102	107	114
Pharmaceuticals	116	113	107	123
Communications equipment	97	98	109	115

(a) Present value of taxes payable over ten-year period to reflect difference of deductions for asset depreciation

Source: Province of Quebec, Budget Speech and Additional Information, 1989, Appendix F.

for their employees. In Canada, much of this is provided by the public plans, through taxes, and employers need only provide coverage for services not covered by those plans. In the US, however, employers must buy even basic medical and hospital care insurance from private insurance companies.

BEYOND TAX COMPARISONS

Deficits

While much can be made of the differences in taxation, only the aggregate numbers are really useful — specific tax comparisons are too dependent on the assumptions used at the beginning of the exercise. It is clear from those aggregate numbers that Canada has a higher level of taxation than the US, and this is confirmed by the studies regularly done by relocation firms. Canadians have a higher expectation of the public sector and the higher level of services have a higher cost.

There are not only present costs, but future ones as well. The international concern over government deficits and rising public debt loads has had a strong impact on public debate in Canada and the US. The responses have been different, and the long-term consequences of these responses will influence the traditional Canadian-US comparisons for years to come.

If both countries had balanced budgets, these spending and tax comparisons would be stable. But with both running substantial deficits, the prospects for maintaining present levels of tax and spending are not good. What is unknowable, however, is the extent to which each country will reduce spending, and perhaps cut services, in order to hold the line on tax levels.

The combined deficit of all levels of government in Canada was, in 1991, equivalent to 6.1% of gross domestic product (GDP), as shown in Table 10. The federal government showed a deficit equivalent to 0.3% of GDP on its own operations, but transfers to lower levels of government pushed the overall federal deficit to 4.4% of GDP. The combined provincial, local, and hospital deficit was 1.9% of GDP, and the Canada and Quebec pension plans showed a surplus of 0.2%. In the US, the federal government showed a deficit equivalent to 3.0% of GDP in 1991, before taking into account its transfers to state and local governments, which pushed Washington's deficit up to 5.7%. Thanks in large part to those transfers, the state and local governments registered a surplus of 0.4%. As a result of the surplus in federal social security transactions — 0.9% of GDP in 1991 — the public sector showed a combined deficit equivalent to 4.3% of GDP.

Most states are precluded, by law, from budgeting for deficits, but in the national accounts analysis, they can and do show deficits. Using this analysis, capital expenditures are taken into national account spending as the work is completed. In their own accounts, however,

Table 10: Public Sector Deficits in Canada and the US National Accounts Basis, 1991 Calendar Year As a Percentage of GDP

	Canada	US
Federal	-4.4	-5.7
Provincial/state and local(a)	-1.9	0.4
Social Security federal only	0.2	0.9
Total public sector	-6.1	-4.3

Note: Figures based on national data as determined by each country. Figures may not be strictly comparable.
(a) includes hospital sector in Canada
Source: Budget of the United States Government for Fiscal Year 1993, US GPO, Washington, 1992. Statistics Canada, National Income and Expenditure Accounts, Annual, 1980-1991, Catalogue 13-201.

state governments will keep such expenditures separate and finance them from borrowing, taking interest and principal repayments into current expenditures over the life of the asset. With tax revenues meeting such annual payments, they show a balance each year on current account. The Canadian provinces are under no similar formal restrictions on their fiscal policy.

Local governments in both countries are also required to balance their budgets, and so treat most capital spending as the states do.

OECD projections of the overall public sector balance for the next few years indicate that Canadian governments have better control over their fiscal situation than their US counterparts. After peaking in 1991, Canada's overall deficit will decline steadily to 3.2% of GDP by 1994, almost half the 1991 figure. The comparable US deficit was expected to rise to 4.7% in 1992, and then fall back in 1993 and 1994 to the 1991 figure of 3.4% of GDP.[7]

There are a number of ways to look at deficits, including separating out the cyclical and structural components. According to the OECD, Canadian governments have been able to reduce the structural element[8] of their deficits from 4.3% of GDP in 1989 to 2.7% in 1992, while the US saw its structural deficit increase from 2.3% to 3.8% over the same period. Overall our deficit increased, because the recession hit earlier and harder in Canada, increasing the cyclical element of the deficit by reducing revenues and increasing spending on unemployment benefits and social assistance. The corrective measures introduced at the federal and provincial levels, increasing taxes and reducing spending in areas unrelated to unemployment insurance or social welfare, reduced the structural element of the deficit. In the US there was not as much effort to reduce the deficit until 1993.

In the long run, this could change the tax comparisons. As both countries recover from the 1990-92 recession, Canada should come much closer to a balanced budget than the US, allowing either lower tax rates, higher spending, or a more stable debt position.

Debt

Debt levels are more difficult to compare, simply because there is no single commonly accepted definition of debt. Deficits represent the amount by which income flows within a year fall short of spending. Debt should theoretically represent the borrowing undertaken to finance deficits incurred in past years, less, of course, amounts that have been applied from surpluses to reduce those borrowings.

The problem arises because not all deficits are financed by borrowing and not all borrowing is to finance the deficit. Governments may use the current surplus in social security funds or employee pension plans to cover deficits and worry later about finding the money to pay future retirees. Does this "borrowing" represent debt, or a contingent or actuarial liability, neither of which are considered debt?

Governments borrow to re-lend to other levels of government, the private sector, and other national governments. They borrow to finance their own business enterprises — Crown corporations in Canada. These borrowing may or may not show up in debt figures; on a net basis, the amount borrowed should be offset by the liabilities of other governments, the private sector, and equity in, or notes received from, the enterprise. The practice is not uniform. Some lending may in fact be to national governments or enterprises that are virtually insolvent, or where the terms provide for ultimate forgiveness. In these cases, the assets that offset the debt may be worthless. While most analysts concentrate on net debt, they frequently use different definitions.

Table 11: General Government Net Debt, Canada and US, Selected Calendar Years, 1974 to 1994

| | As a percentage of GDP | | | As Percent OECD Average | |
	Canada	US	OECD Average	Canada	US
1974	4.9	21.7	14.2	34.5	152.8
1979	12.1	19.1	22.7	53.3	84.1
1989	40.3	30.4	39.8	101.3	76.4
1992	53.9	37.9	43.6	123.6	86.9
1994 (est.)	55.6	41.9	47.7	116.6	87.8

Source: OECD Economic Outlook, 52, December, 1992, page 20.

The Fraser Institute compared Canadian and US federal government gross debt, showing that as of December 1992 our debt represented 73% of GDP, while US federal debt at September 31 1992 equalled 67% of GDP.[9] Moody's, the US bond rating agency, recently calculated that federal debt in Canada, after adjusting for assets and lending to other levels of government in Canada, represented only 50.3% of GDP, compared with 47.9% for the US.[10] These two sets of figures differ significantly from those shown in the OECD economic outlook, which calculated net debt of all levels of government, excluding borrowing for government enterprises. As shown in Table 11, Canadian net debt represented 53.9 percent of GDP in 1992, while the comparable US debt amounted to 37.9 percent of GDP.

The level of debt in each country is regularly judged by the domestic and international investors who buy government bonds and treasury bills. So far, they have shown no reluctance to buy and hold Canadian or US debt, although the slightly higher interest rates charged Canadian borrowers reflects, in part at least, our higher debt load. The money markets have been watching Canadian governments very carefully in the last two years, looking for signs that the federal and provincial governments are making serious efforts to reduce deficits and lower the rate of growth in debt.

These governments have their own reasons to lower the rate of growth in their debt. The interest costs associated with high debt loads severely restrict the room that such governments have in setting fiscal and economic policy. During the recession of 1990-92, for example, Canadian governments were unable to lower taxes or increase spending — the classic policies to stimulate economic activity — simply because interest costs made up such a large portion of their spending, and had pushed most into deficits before the recession began. As noted earlier, Canada seems to have a better handle on deficit reduction, and thus on debt growth, than the US in recent years.

SUMMARY

From this chapter it is clear that there is a price to be paid for staying in Canada, but because the art of public finance is still inexact, it is impossible to determine exactly what it is. As indicated here, and in later chapters, it is the price of choosing a different role for government. Each individual must decide which services should be provided collectively and which privately, and on the basis of those decisions choose his or her country. At the same time, however, both countries are continuously re-examining their governments, to re-arrange, for example, the delivery of health services in Canada and to change the financing of such services in the US. Comparisons between the two countries will always be changing, as the individual's perspective and the functions of government change.

Government spending has increased faster in Canada in recent years, and we have attacked the deficit more vigorously. Not surprisingly, then, our levels of taxation have increased more rapidly than those in the US. In addition, the two tax systems are quite different in their emphasis, as we rely more on sales taxes and relatively less on social security taxes on wages, salaries, and payrolls. Because of this, comparisons of tax burdens on specific individuals or businesses will produce quite different results, depending on the underlying assumptions. Within these wide variations, the fact remains that most individuals will pay more tax in Canada than had they lived in the US. Most businesses will see little difference in the overall tax burden.

The deficit of the Canadian public sector is well above the US level at present, but the differences should shrink because our governments have had more success at reducing deficits, albeit at the expense of higher taxes. Our public debt burden is well above that in the US, but remains within the acceptable limits imposed by our creditors.

In the final analysis, however, the differences in the cost of government — taxes imposed now or likely to be imposed in the future — represent a small part of the cost, or benefits, of being Canadian. The philosophies of the two countries and the economic opportunities available will determine where people wish to live. Most will not ask the price until they have opted for the philosophy and chosen their own opportunities. By then, the price is of little concern.

NOTES

1. In Canada, most of the income of hospitals comes from provincial governments, under the various health care schemes. In the Canadian national accounts the entire hospital sector is therefore considered as an integral part of the public sector, and one of its five components, along with the federal, provincial, and local governments, and the Canada and Quebec pension plans. The unemployment insurance system is integrated with the income and spending of the federal government.

2. Consolidated figures must eliminate grants from the expenditure of the paying government and the revenue of the recipient government in order to eliminate double counting.

3. While both countries introduced emergency measures at the beginning of the war to ensure that each federal government had sufficient resources, the provinces re-entered most tax fields over the next two decades. The states did not proceed as far as the provinces.

4. The federal government provides additional tax room to Quebec to compensate that province for opting out of some conditional grant programs.

5. Recent discussions between the federal and provincial governments have explored a different approach — imposing provincial tax on the federally defined taxable income. This would allow the provinces the added flexibility of setting their own levels of basic tax relief and progressive rate schedule. This would reduce the complexity of the present provincial systems where surtaxes, flat taxes, and low-income tax relief, incorporated after the determination of a basic tax level, cloud the true nature of the provincial tax systems.

6. The province of Quebec has modified its retail sales tax into a modified VAT, with a coverage close to that of the GST. It has an arrangement under which it also collects the GST on behalf of Ottawa from Quebec businesses. Constitutional limitations prevent it from adopting a true VAT.

7. These projections are contained in the *OECD Outlook*, December, 1992, page 7.

8. Structural surpluses or deficits are calculated by the OECD as the outcome if the national economy had been growing at its long-term rate of growth. Cyclical surpluses or deficits are those that can be attributed solely to the fact that the economy diverged from the long-term rate of growth. See the *OECD Economic Outlook, 52,* December 1992, pages 20–40.

9. The Fraser Institute, *Fraser Forum,* Vancouver, B.C., May 1993, page 25.

10. *The Globe and Mail,* June 10, 1993, page B1. "Canada given 'low risk' rating."

FURTHER READING & REFERENCES:

The annual budget statements of the Canadian and US Governments.

OECD Economic Outlook, published regularly in December and July by the Organization for Economic Co-operation and Development, Paris.

Revenue Statistics of OECD Member Countries, published annually by the OECD, Paris.

Joel B. Shoven and John Whalley (eds.). *Canadian-US Tax Comparisons,* Chicago: University of Chicago Press for the National Bureau of Economic Research, 1992.

Robert D. Brown. *The Comparative Impact of Direct Federal and State/Provincial Taxes on People Transfers in the Canada/US Context: Tax Equalization,* Toronto: Price Waterhouse, 1992.

JOHN RICHARDS

A Tangled Tale: Unions in Canada and the United States

By the mid-1980s Canadian union density (the ratio of unionized workers to all paid workers) was more than twice that in the United States. Here is one of the more dramatic and interesting differences between the two countries: dramatic because of the magnitude; interesting because, in attempting to explain it, we are obliged to address variations on classic questions about the two countries. Are Canadians in general more "collectivist" and hence more pro-union than the "individualist" Americans? Does the proportionately larger Canadian public sector have much to do with the union density gap? Since trends in the United States often portend the Canadian future, is the prospect for Canadian unionists as grim as the present reality for their American comrades?[1]

The obvious point of departure in any comparison of Canadian and American labour relations is the 1935 Wagner Act, a key piece of Roosevelt's New Deal legislation intended to regulate the violent labour conflicts that had erupted in many cities during the Great Depression. The Act proclaimed the right of workers "to bargain collectively through representatives of their own choosing." It codified mechanisms to grant a legal monopoly over collective bargaining to a particular union for a particular group of workers. It introduced the concept of "unfair labour practices" that limit employers' efforts to prevent or evade collective bargaining. It replaced the courts operating on the basis of the common law with a powerful tribunal (the National Labor Relations Board) as the arbiter of industrial disputes. In sum, the Act gave a secure legislative basis to collective bargaining, and placed the United States well ahead of Canada in devising a satisfactory set of rules to govern the conflicts entailed in dividing corporate revenues between those who provide finance and those who provide their labour.

Passage of the Act enabled American union density to increase dramatically. (Refer to Table 1.) Not surprisingly, Canadian unionists lobbied intensely for a Canadian equivalent and, during the 1940s, Ottawa and the provincial governments each adopted variants of the Wagner Act. Canadian union density rose in the 1940s, and in both countries density was approximately one third during the 1950s. Beginning in the mid-1960s, Canadian and American experience began to diverge. American union density began a slow decline that has yet to halt; it is now back to levels prevailing in the early 1930s. Canadian union density, by contrast, experienced a modest increase from the mid-1960s to early 1980s. Since its peak in 1984 it has experienced a small decline. The rebound in 1991 and 1992 is not related to an increased rate of growth in Canadian union membership; indeed the rate of growth has actually declined relative to the 1980s. However, the rise in unemployment during the recent recession disproportionately affected non-union workers; hence union density rose. The same process took place during the recession in the early 1980s.[2]

What explains this post-1960s divergence in union density between the two countries? There are basically four lines of argument.

The first — attractive to left-of-centre Canadian nationalists — is that Canadians and Americans have fundamentally different attitudes toward collective behaviour such as joining a union. Canadian workers are allegedly more inclined to choose "collective" institutions like unions.

A second line of argument is that structural differences in characteristics that determine unionization are the fundamental explanation. Some industrial sectors (e.g. forestry) are highly unionized; others (e.g. banking) much less so. Younger workers tend to be less unionized than older workers. The idea here is that no fundamental difference exists in the demand for, or supply of, union jobs between, say, British Columbia and Saskatchewan, or Ontario and Ohio. Differences in union density obviously exist among these four jurisdictions, but that is primarily the reflection of different union-determining characteristics among workers in each.

A third line of argument can be summarized as "lagged convergence". Rather than attempt to explain the present union density gap, writers in this tradition undertake the opposite: an analysis of factors that will tend to bring about — in an ill-defined long run — convergence, at least in the private sector. Country-specific factors may favour unions in one country or the other — for periods extending beyond a decade — but in the long run the choice by workers to certify or decertify a union, and by employers to accept or resist certification, is a kind of institutional market in which more efficient institutions drive out the less efficient. Since the benefits offered by unions in the two countries are similar, we should expect in the long run that similar proportions of workers in both countries will opt for a unionized work environment.

The final argument explains the Canada-US union density gap primarily in terms of the relative success of Canadian organized labour in realizing its legislative goals. Unions may arise spontaneously in craft industries but in mass-based industry, and in the public sector, their success depends on favourable legislation that lowers the cost of certification, raises the cost of decertification, and increases the effectiveness of collective action to raise the union/non-union wage differential. According to this explanation, Canada's parliamentary form of government and disciplined political parties, when combined with narrow parliamentary majorities, have accorded significant influence to organized labour in determining labour law and salary awards in the public sector. This process has sometimes taken the form of NDP (and Parti Québécois) electoral victories. It also has been evident in NDP influence on minority governments of other parties, or in pre-emptive initiatives of non-NDP parties. By contrast, the collapse of the New Deal coalition in the 1960s has resulted in fragmentation of American interest groups and the inability of unions to secure equivalent legislative support.

I shall take up each argument in turn.

1. DIVERGENT POLITICAL CULTURES

Among the most persistent in pursuing this line of argument is the prominent American sociologist, Seymour Martin Lipset (1986).[3] He argues that Canadians are carriers of a more "collectivist" political culture — whether it be the commitment to "la langue et la foi" among the clerical elite of eighteenth-century New France; to "peace, order and good government" among nineteenth-century colonial leaders whose forefathers had rejected the liberal faith of American revolutionaries; or the class-based union solidarity among twentieth-century British working-class immigrants. By contrast, Americans are allegedly individualists who basically want to preserve the freedom of contract in labour markets, and who resort to "collectivist" legislation such as the Wagner Act only at times of acute political crisis. Thus, divergence in union density is a gradual adaptation to underlying differences in national cultures.

There is obviously something to this line of argument: British immigrants have contributed more than their share of Canadian union leaders, and Canada has no real parallel to "right to work" legislation enacted by many American states. (Such legislation bans provisions in collective bargaining agreements whereby workers are obliged to join a union as a condition of employment.[4]) Admittedly there is something to this argument — but if one seeks to go beyond casual observation, one cannot!

Serious attempts to measure public attitudes toward unions conclude that, in general, they are remarkably similar on both sides of the border. For many years pollsters have posed identically worded questions to Canadians and Americans about confidence in leaders of major institutions. On both sides of the border, union leaders are among the least popular, enjoying "a great deal of confidence" among only 10 to 12% of the population. Conversely, when asked whether, in general, they approve or disapprove of unions, a majority in both countries approve. Contrary to predictions of the political culture theorists, this majority (expressed as a share of the population sample) has been larger among Americans than Canadians. Furthermore, while the majority has declined since the end of World War II in both countries, it has declined at a slightly faster rate in Canada than in the United States. A third set of questions explores attitudes about union political influence. More Canadians than Americans think unions exercise too much political power. This result is hardly surprising since Canadian union density is more than twice that of the United States, and Canadian unions undoubtedly do exercise more political influence than their southern comrades. It is worth noting that over 70% of Canadians disapprove of unions contributing to the NDP, that union workers disapprove by the same margin as non-union, and, by a ratio of two-to-one, even NDP supporters disapprove. A final dimension of comparison shows similar majorities of union members satisfied with their unions' performance in both countries, and similar majorities of non-union workers wanting to remain that way in both countries.[5]

2. STRUCTURAL DIFFERENCES

Unlike the first line of argument, which is almost entirely without empirical support, structural differences between Canada and the United States do explain a little of the union density gap — but not much.

In the most rigorous attempt to date to measure structural differences, Craig Riddell analyzed two large sample surveys (approximately 4000 per sample in each country) conducted simultaneously in 1984, one in each country. The probability of a Canadian worker in the sample being either a union member or covered by a collective bargaining agreement was 45%; the analogous probability for a U.S.

worker was 19%. Riddell concluded that, if the average Canadian worker had the characteristics of the average American worker (in terms of age, gender, part- vs. full-time status, public vs. private sector employment, industry and occupation), her probability of being unionized would be four percentage points lower. In other words, structural differences explain roughly 15% (4 points out of a total gap of 26 points) of the difference.

The only structural difference that matters is the relatively larger public sector employment in Canada — and it does not explain much. With the Canadian public sector reduced to the same relative size as in the United States (and no other change in characteristics), the probability of a Canadian worker being subject to a collective agreement would be 2 percentage points lower (i.e. 43 percent instead of 45 percent).[6]

3. LAGGED CONVERGENCE

The point of departure for this line of argument is to separate public from private sector unions. Once this is done — and it requires detailed data to do accurately — it becomes evident that divergence is most dramatic in the public sector. In the private sector, Canadian union density has been declining since the early 1980s — if not well before.

One recent study estimated that Canadian private sector union density peaked at 34% in 1958 and by 1990 had declined to a level of 18%.[7] This study doubtless exaggerates the decline but "lagged convergence" is occurring in the private sector. Two public sector trends have offset this process in the aggregate data. First, in both countries, public sector union density rose significantly in the last quarter century. According to the 1984 surveys analyzed by Riddell, 74% of Canadian public sector workers (defined broadly to include not only civil servants but those in crown corporations and quasi-government sectors like education) were union members, as were 34% in the United States. The respective private sector densities in the survey were 29% and 15%. A second trend is the growth in the public sector share of employment, more pronounced in Canada than in the United States but a trend present in both countries.

The ultimate "boss" facing public sector unions is politicians, who are constrained in their ability to negotiate improvements in wages and work conditions by the willingness of citizens to pay taxes. Hence, public sector unions engage in active political lobbying over the size of government budgets. Private sector unions face a "boss" subject to quite different constraints. Firms in particular markets may enjoy a measure of monopoly power, and unions may negotiate a share of the ensuing above-normal earnings. But the ability of competitors to sell more cheaply acts as the ultimate constraint on private sector negotiations, and hence private sector unions have a stake in the productivity implications of collective agreements. The combination of rising public sector union density and a larger public sector have shifted the relative weight within organized labour in favour of public sector unions, and this has probably made organized labour less sensitive, in general, to their impact on economic productivity.

Union leaders and their intellectual allies typically view collective bargaining as an egalitarian institution redistributing corporate revenues from a few wealthy shareholders to many unionized workers. Relative to non-union firms in the same industry, unions do in fact equalize the distribution of wages and do lower corporate profitability. Furthermore, union defenders assume that unions have either no effect on overall productivity of the economy — or that they actually enhance it by acting as an efficient "collective voice" of workers within corporate hierarchies.[8]

The actual effect of unions on both equality and efficiency is, however, far more complex than the above paragraph implies.

Once established in an industry, unions frequently become a powerful interest group on behalf of "inside" workers intent on preserving advantages against potentially more productive "outside" workers. Unions may, for example, effectively restrict employer ability to hire recent immigrants or younger workers. Growing "insider" power within private unionized firms and governments probably lies behind the disturbing decline over the 1980s in incomes of young Canadian workers (aged 16 to 24) relative to older workers (aged 25 to 64). We are left with the "insider" power thesis by a process of elimination. Because it affected all workers, regardless of education level or industrial sector, the trend cannot be explained by changes in education levels or in industrial structure. Nor are changes in relative age-cohort size an explanation. By the 1980s, children of the "baby bust" generation were entering the labour market and young workers constituted a smaller share of the labour force than in either the 1960s or 1970s.[9]

As mentioned earlier, decisions by workers to certify or decertify a union are a kind of institutional market in which, over time, more efficient institutions drive out the less efficient. Take the example of construction unions. In both Canada and the United States, unions have disappeared from many subsectors of this industry. In part this has been a successful employer strategy to gain access to cheaper unskilled labour; in part, this has been an efficient response to the inefficient constraints on adoption of new techniques imposed by craft unions. In many sectors, successful firms — partly to avoid un-ionization — seek to devise personnel policies that respond better than does collective bargaining to worker demands.[10]

These writers disagree as to whether unions are inevitably doomed to decline due to their inherent inefficiencies, or whether some al-ternate union strategies can reverse the trend. In either case, the inefficiencies of collective bargaining, as practised under Wagner Act rules, are sufficiently important that both employers and employees increasingly prefer a non-union environment. At the risk of some oversimplification, the inefficiencies can be summarized as follows:

Collective bargaining is usually an efficient institution for negotiating the division of current corporate revenue between wages and profits; it is a cumbersome institution for workers to bargain a fair share of the potential gains from productivity-enhancing investments.

In the modern firm, workers' skills have become increasingly im-portant relative to technology embodied in physical plant and equip-ment. In economic jargon this evolution is reflected in use of the term "human capital" to describe skills and training acquired by em-ployees. Workers, as owners of human capital, and shareholders, as owners of physical capital, are in conflict over distribution of current corporate revenue, but they also have a shared interest in maximizing the long-run returns to their combined investment.

Collective bargaining and debt financing are analogous contractual instruments. One fixes a wage rate for labour; the other an interest rate for lenders of finance. Neither provides any share in the gener-alized right to manage the firm. Typically, investors whose financial stake in a firm is large are not content to buy bonds; they buy equity which gives them a share in the right to manage the firm's assets as unforseen events arise. If labour law encouraged it, an analogous process would probably emerge on the labour side wherever workers have a significant investment in industry-specific skills. Workers would continue to engage in collective bargaining but they would also participate more actively in negotiating the adoption of produc-tivity-enhancing investments.

Such investments usually entail the scrapping not only of obsolete equipment but the layoff of workers with obsolete skills, who become unambiguous losers unless explicitly compensated. In the absence of institutions to bargain over the distribution of benefits from new investment, current collective bargaining inevitably generates a good deal of "Luddism" by unions resisting new investment and "union bashing" by management intent on implementing change. After many years of industrial conflict, a majority of both workers and managers in an industry may come to see collective bargaining as a suboptimal strategy, and a non-union environment as offering advantages to both.

It is important to realize this is a critique of collective bargaining as practised in Canada and the United States, not of unions in general. Labour law in continental Europe and Scandinavia places far greater stress than does the Wagner Act tradition on institutions whereby workers and managers permanently negotiate policy affecting long-run employment in the firm.

Decentralized collective bargaining with overlapping contracts imparts inertia to wage-price inflationary spirals. The higher the union density the greater the inertia, and the higher must be the unemployment rate to stabilize inflation.

When, for whatever initial reason, market forces permit one set of unions to realize high wage increases, that provides a powerful precedent to other unions. In sectors where firms possess some measure of monopoly power, they pass on higher wage costs via price increases and inflation develops momentum. When, for example, in the resource boom at the beginning of the 1980s, union A negotiated a large x percent wage increase for 1981-83, it required high unemployment to persuade members in union B to settle for less than x percent in their contract for 1982-84. And it required much idle capacity to persuade corporate managers to lower price increases.

High inflation is associated with lower economic productivity. For example, it increases the uncertainty of financial outcomes and, with hindsight, a higher proportion of investments are seen to be mistakes. In the last two decades, Canadians wasted large sums in high-cost offshore and Arctic oil investments justified, at the time, by inflationary oil price expectations. Similarly, inflationary expectations in real estate induced inefficient overinvestment in the sector. Due to the inefficiencies arising from inflation, a majority of citizens acquiesce — albeit reluctantly — to government policies designed to generate enough unemployment to stabilize prices. Canada and the United States have experienced similar inflation rates over the last decade. Given our greater union density, this equality could probably not have been achieved without Canada simultaneously tolerating an unemployment rate that on average has exceeded the American rate by over 2 percentage points.[11]

Adversarial collective bargaining restricts the potential of tripartite arrangements to improve the efficiency of government labour market programs.

Some portion of this extra 2% of unemployed is a cost paid to control inflation in a context of higher union density; some other portion is a cost of inefficient government labour market policies. Canada devotes a share of GDP equivalent to that of most other OECD countries on programs intended to help people find jobs. Relative to many other countries, however, our priorities are excessively skewed toward provision of "passive" income support (via an overly generous unemployment insurance scheme) and away from "active" job training and mobility.

The most successful example of active labour market programs is that of Sweden. Central to the working out of detailed apprenticeship and retraining programs in Sweden has been tripartite administration of these programs by representatives of government, labour, and business. They are a domain of the Swedish welfare state that the new (elected in 1992) Swedish Conservative government has praised and intends to preserve.[12]

One reason for Canada's failure to develop adequate apprentice programs between school and work, or adequate retraining for workers with obsolete skills, is our heritage of adversarial collective bargaining. It would require an ideological earthquake before representatives of Canadian labour and business could, for example, efficiently collaborate on unemployment insurance programs in a manner analogous to the Swedes.[13]

Collective bargaining under Wagner Act rules tends to restrict the efficient participation of workers in administration at the level of the work site.

Workers' demands have become more complex over the decades: working mothers want flexible schedules; workers expect better occupational health and safety. Simultaneously, managers want access to workers' practical knowledge on how to make a better "widget," and want to cut down abuse of sick-leave by transferring its administration to the union. Joint labour-management health and safety committees and "quality circles" are two examples of reforms attempting to realize benefits from collaborative work site management. Wanting to preserve the Wagner Act tradition of adversarial collective bargaining, union leaders have mistrusted collaborative work management as an employer device to erode employee commitment to the union. And indeed, employers have used such innovations as an anti-union tactic. The net result is the failure to realize the potential of such reforms.

An apt summary of the efficiency impact of unions is that of Richard Freeman, an American economist who has generally written sympathetically about the labour movement:

> Perhaps the most sensible conclusion to draw from the evidence is that the economy functions best when there are both union and nonunion sectors. Competition reduces the "monopoly wage" costs of unionism and encourages the positive aspects of unionism. Competition keeps nonunion firms from taking advantage of their workers and forces them to adopt union-initiated work practices and modes of pay favoured by employees to maintain their nonunion status.... An economy is likely to operate efficiently when there is a sufficient number of union and of nonunion firms to offer alternative work environments to workers, innovation in workplace rules and conditions, and competition in the marketplace.[14]

4. COMPARATIVE POLITICS

"Lagged convergence" may explain a good deal about trends in the two countries; it doesn't explain why the union density gap is currently so large. The basic explanation is probably that, over the last three decades, Canadian legislation has been generally more "pro-union" than in the United States, particularly in the public sector.[15]

A straightforward example of more favourable Canadian labour law is given by the certification rules for new union locals. In Canada, a union in the federal jurisdiction and in most provinces can certify a new local by simply "signing up" a majority of workers in the proposed unit. In the United States, a new local can become certified only after a government-conducted election demonstrates by secret vote that a majority of workers want a union. Union leaders prefer the Canadian system because it limits the employer's ability to state the anti-union case and because, being quick, the certification process gives employers no time to retaliate against union activists. Anti-union employers prefer certification via elections for more-or-less the same reasons that union leaders oppose it. Some polling evidence suggests that a majority of Canadians actually prefer American certification procedures, but only a few provinces have ever legislated accordingly.[16]

Several effects have combined to make the weight of public sector unions more pronounced among organized labour in Canada than in the United States. First, private sector union density has declined in both countries, while it has risen in the public sector. Coincidentally, convergent trends have apparently generated an approximate two-to-one Canada/US density ratio in both the public and private sectors. Second, the Canadian public sector has grown over the last three decades faster than in the United States. Canadian public sector unions have used their political influence to obtain legislated powers — including the right to strike — far more generous than those enjoyed by American public sector workers. Since the rise in public sector union density is itself a function of favourable legislation, it is circular to explain the more favourable Canadian labour law as a function of a growing public sector union sector. What really underlies the relative success of Canadian public sector unions?

In an important article studying the timing of major changes in labour law, Peter Bruce has provided much of the answer.[17] His conclusion is that major pro-labour changes occurred when a pro-labour party held office, or when intense electoral competition gave organized labour heightened influence. Periods of intense competition have occurred when the governing party enjoyed only a minority of elected members and depended on NDP support, or polls indicated that a labour-backed political party could win a current election. For example, Ontario under an unpopular Liberal government introduced the first Canadian approximation to the Wagner Act in 1942. At the time, the Co-operative Commonwealth Federation (the NDP's predecessor) posed a major electoral threat. (Incidentally, the Conservatives and not the CCF defeated the Liberals in the subsequent provincial election.) The first Canadian jurisdiction to extend full collective bargaining rights to public sector workers was the CCF government of Saskatchewan in 1945. These rights were extended to federal employees twenty years later — at a time when a minority Liberal government depended on the support of the small contingent of NDP MPs.

In the United States, the role of the national government is relatively more important in determining labour law, and in Washington New Deal Democrats sympathetic to organized labour have been continuously a minority for the last four decades. Furthermore, the American Congressional system displays much weaker party discipline. Political parties are less able to sustain complex programmatic compromises in which pro-union Democrats could effectively barter their votes on other policies in exchange for pro-labour votes from other Congressmen.

But even in the public sector, "lagged convergence" may be under way. Just as the choice by workers to certify or decertify a union is a kind of institutional market, general elections serve as a (very imperfect) market in which voters choose the desired size of the public sector. The evidence is admittedly shaky, but voters in major OECD countries — Japan and the United States as notable exceptions — have converged in the extent of their desired public spending. Public spending has stabilized in these countries in the range of 40 to 50% of domestic GDP. Canada is currently at the upper end of this range. The Americans have just elected a president committed to universal health insurance and whose overall policy priorities are similar to those of social democrats in western Europe. If Clinton Democrats succeed, they may well raise American public sector spending above 40%.

On the other hand, Canadians are becoming increasingly convinced that their public sector should shrink somewhat relative to GDP. That is the logical implication of the public demand for an end to public sector deficits with no increase in tax levels. In this context, the compensation advantage of public over comparable private sector workers has become a highly visible political issue. Measuring the size of this compensation advantage is subject to controversy — recall, for example, the acrimonious "social contract" negotiations between the Ontario NDP government and provincial public sector unions during 1993 — but the advantage undeniably exists. Reasonable estimates place it in the range of 5-10 percent.[18] The advantage accrues primarily to workers at the low end of the wage scale, and in the form of better deferred benefits such as pensions. These measures of the compensation advantage do not take into account the benefit — a significant benefit during the recent recession — of greater job security enjoyed by public over private sector workers.

Given these political constraints — to balance budgets and not raise tax rates — the public sector pay advantage has become a politically irresistible target for ministers of finance across the country. Complete elimination of the advantage would realize the majority of spending cuts required, under reasonable assumptions about performance of the economy, to balance budgets without raising tax rates by fiscal year 1997-98.[19]

CONCLUSION

What should we make of this tangled tale?

In general, the first line of argument is building ideological castles from statistical sand. Theories that claim to have found distinct national patterns in individual attitudes toward unions have no empirical basis. Recall that the ranking in union density between the two countries has not in the long run been stable. If the present higher Canadian density is due to a greater Canadian "collectivism," then presumably we must interpret the data from the 1930s and 1940s to mean that Americans were, at the time, more "collectivist" than Canadians. And how do we explain the reversal in national attitudes in the 1950s and 1960s? Should we interpret the decline in Canadian union density over the last decade as the beginning of yet another reversal? Structural differences fare somewhat better as an explanation, but do not take us very far.

"Lagged convergence" explains a lot — particularly in the private sector — but the subtle differences between cabinet government in a parliamentary system and Congressional politics clearly matter.

The final point I make is a plea against parochialism. Any comparative discussion of American and Canadian unions must by definition ignore most of the industrial world. Many of the efficiency arguments against North American unions are criticisms of an industrial relations environment which places inordinate emphasis on adversarial collective bargaining and very little on collaborative institutions.

Table 1: Union Density*, United States and Canada

Year	United States	Canada
1935	13.5	14.5
1940	22.5	16.3
1945	30.4	24.2
1951	31.7	28.4
1955	31.8	33.7
1960	28.6	32.3
1965	30.1	29.7
1970	29.6	33.6
1975	28.9	35.6
1980	23.2	38.5
1981	22.6	36.7
1982	21.9	37.0
1983	20.7	37.9
1984	18.8	38.8
1985	18.0	38.1
1986	17.5	37.7
1987	17.5	37.0
1988	17.0	36.5
1989	16.4	36.2
1990	16.1	36.2
1991	—.	36.3
1992	—.	37.4

* Percentage of paid nonagricultural workers belonging to a union
Sources: U.S. data: cited in Industrial Relations Centre. *The Current Industrial Relations Scene in Canada.* Kingston, Ontario: Queen's University, annual.
Canadian data: Labour Canada. *Directory of Labour Organizations in Canada, 1992-93.* Ottawa: Supply and Services, 1992.

NOTES

1. Several colleagues have been generous in instructing me on the subtleties surrounding unions in the two countries, and in critiquing an earlier draft of this article. Bob Rogow, Steve Havlovic, Steve Blumenfeld, and Craig Riddell each deserve credit in correcting errors and improving the presentation. David Thomas also supplied helpful editorial improvements.

2. Union membership figures are drawn from Labour Canada, *Directory of Labour Organizations in Canada, 1992-93* (Ottawa: Supply and Services, 1992).

3. Seymour Martin Lipset has honoured Canadians by maintaining an intellectual interest in us ever since he devoted his doctoral thesis to an exploration of why North America's most rural jurisdiction, Saskatchewan, had in the 1940s elected the continent's most explicitly socialist government. His explanation — which I think basically correct — was that the Saskatchewan Co-operative Commonwealth Federation (predecessor to the NDP) had replaced the rhetoric of European socialists with that of agrarian populism, a political culture that flourished until the mid-twentieth century on both sides of the national border. In other words, a shared economic environment of homesteaders growing cash crops for export produced similar political movements on both sides of the 49th parallel. Lipset has never reconciled this early work with his later emphasis on cultural differences between the two countries. See S. Lipset, *Agrarian Socialism* (San Francisco: Berkeley University Press, 1950); and S. Lipset, "Labor Unions in the Public Mind," S. Lipset ed. *Unions in Transition: Entering the Second Century* (San Francisco: ICS Press, 1986).

4. For a discussion of American "right to work" legislation see S. Slichter et al., *The Impact of Collective Bargaining on Management* (Washington, DC: The Brookings Institution, 1960).

5. For details of the survey results quoted in this paragraph and for a more elaborate discussion of comparative attitudes see the following articles: P. Bruce, "Political Parties and Labor Legislation in Canada and the U.S.," *Industrial Relations*, XXVIII:2:115-141 (1989); J. Richards, "Playing Two Games at

Once," J. Richards et al. eds. *Social Democracy without Illusions* (Toronto: McClelland & Stewart, 1991); C. Riddell, "Unionization in Canada and the United States: A Tale of Two Countries," Working Paper Series QPIR 1993-1 (Kingston, Ontario: School of Industrial Relations, Queen's University, 1993).

6. See Riddell, *op. cit.*

7. See L. Troy, "Convergence in International Unionism Et Cetera: The Case of Canada and the US," Working Paper Series QPIR 1991-3, (Kingston, Ontario: School of Industrial Relations, Queen's University, 1991).

8. That unions act as a "collective voice" for workers, thereby improving industrial productivity of union relative to non-union firms, is an idea developed by Richard Freeman and his colleagues. See, for example, R. Freeman, "Effects of Unions on the Economy," S. Lipset ed. *Unions in Transition: Entering the Second Century* (San Francisco: ICS Press, 1986).

9. For a discussion of trends in "young" vs. "old" workers see G. Betcherman & R. Morissette, "Recent Youth Labour Market Experiences in Canada," paper presented at a workshop of the Canadian Employment Research Forum, Vancouver (June 1993).

10. A local example is the large credit union, Vancouver City Savings Credit Union. The majority of its directors have for many years been "left wing" and sympathetic to unions, but the personnel policies have been sufficiently attractive that the staff has preferred to remain non-unionized. A writer who has emphasized this interpretation of declining union density is Thomas Kochan. See, for example, T. Kochan, *The Transformation of American Industrial Relations* (New York: Basic Books, 1986).

11. Summary data in this paragraph are drawn from D. Card & R. Freeman, "Introduction," D. Card & R. Freeman (eds.), *Small Differences that Matter: Labor Markets and Income Maintenance in Canada and the United States.* Chicago: NBER and University of Chicago Press (forthcoming).

12. For a recent discussion of trends in Swedish labour market policies see P. Trehörning, *Measures to Combat Unemployment in Sweden: Labor Market Policy in the mid-1990s* (Stockholm: The Swedish Institute, 1993).

13. A recent comparative survey of the potential of tripartite arrangements is that of Roy Adams. See R. Adams, *Labour, Management, Government Relations and Socioeconomic Performance: Lessons from the Experience of Germany, Japan, Sweden and the United States* (Ottawa: Canadian Labour Market and Productivity Centre, 1992).

14. Freeman, "Effects of Unions on the Economy," *op. cit.*, p. 200.

15. Riddell conducts an intriguing analysis of the results from union-sponsored surveys on desire for unionization in the two countries. The difference in probability of being unionized in Canada relative to the United States can be decomposed into two terms: the first is the effect of different proportions of American and Canadian workers who want union status; the second is the different proportion of workers desirous of a union who actually are unionized. The first term measures differences in the demand for unionization and is less than one-half the value of the second which measures differences in the supply of union jobs to those wanting them. The much larger value for the second term suggests the explanation for the density gap lies primarily on the "supply" side, a central component of which is government labour laws. See Riddell, *op. cit.*

16. During the 1980s British Columbia's Social Credit government changed provincial certification procedures to require elections. Upon its election in 1991, the NDP government restored former rules, allowing certification by "signing up" a majority of the proposed bargaining unit.

17. P. Bruce, op. cit.

18. See Riddell, *op. cit.*, Table 11, and Quebec, *Quebec's Public Finances: Living Within our Means* (Québec: Ministère des Finances, 1993).

19. This conclusion is based on a forecast by the author: J. Richards, "The Design of Intergovernmental Transfers in a Federal State," paper presented at the Fourth Annual Canada-Germany Symposium, Centre for Trade Policy and Law, University of Ottawa-Carleton University (September 1993). The base for projections IS aggregate revenues and expenditures contained in 1993-94 federal and provincial budgets, which predict a combined federal-provincial public accounts deficit of $51.7 billion for the fiscal year. The forecast assumes an average 3% annual rate of real GDP growth and a decline in average real interest rates on debt. If the aggregate tax/GDP ratio remains unchanged relative to 1993-94, Ottawa and the provinces will realize an additional $29.0 billion (all figures in 1993 dollars) revenue, and annual interest payments on debt will fall by $6.6 billion. Cutting the aggregate federal-provincial payroll by 10% would generate more than half the $16.1 billion required expenditure cuts.

FURTHER READING:

Trade unions are both a means for working people to voice their collective concerns, and a means to improve their economic well-being. All of the following references analyze unions in their second role — which is not to deny the importance of the first. (Incidentally, detailed references for each of the following texts can be found in the endnotes to this article.) In *Unions in Transition*, a book he edited, Seymour Martin Lipset states his divergent political culture thesis. The book contains a number of other good essays, including Richard Freeman's "Effects of Unions on the Economy," in which he argues that unions pursue both a "collective voice" and "monopoly" goals. Leo Troy argues for "lagged convergence" in "Unionization in Canada and the United States." Thomas Kochan makes somewhat similar arguments about declining worker demand for unionization in *The Transformation of American Industrial Relations*. Craig Riddell has undertaken an important empirical study of Canada-U.S. differences in union density in "Unionization in Canada and the United States" (soon to be republished in *Small Differences that Matter*, a book edited by David Card and Richard Freeman). Peter Bruce's article, "Political Parties and Labor Legislation in Canada and the U.S." summarizes well the case that legislative differences matter. Finally, Roy Adams's *Labour, Management, Government Relations and Socioeconomic Performance* is a good statement of the case for continental European corporatist labour law, as supplement to the Wagner Act tradition.

HELMUT H. BINHAMMER & PHILIP F.
BARTHOLOMEW*

Is Your Money Safe?
Depository Institutions in Canada
and The United States

The large number of bank and nearbank failures in both our countries since the early 1970s might well make us apprehensive about
entrusting our funds to depository institutions.[1] As we shall show,
however, government safety nets have substantially reduced the risk
of depositors losing funds despite the high incidence of failures.
These safety nets — principally the national systems of deposit insurance operated in both countries — have contributed to the stability
of both countries' financial systems. Recent experience with American thrift failures, however, shows that operation of these safety nets
can be incredibly expensive to taxpayers.

In this essay we begin by recounting the failure experience of
depository institutions in Canada and the United States and by providing an overview of the financial and banking structures in the
two countries. This is followed by an analysis of our governments'
different approaches in the use of safety nets and regulatory structures to protect depositors. It will be shown that these have created
adverse incentives resulting in costs to the users of financial services
and in some cases the taxpayer. These costs and the sharing of them
have become a public policy issue in both countries.

---

*   The views expressed are those of the authors and do not necessarily reflect
       those of the Congressional Budget Office.

FAILURES OF DEPOSITORY INSTITUTIONS

From 1985 through 1992 some 1300 banks failed in the United States. These failures are estimated to have cost the Federal Deposit Insurance Corporation (FDIC) more than $31 billion. In the third quarter of 1992, the FDIC reported that 909 of the nation's 11,590 banks still remained on the problem bank list. These problem banks — many of which we expect to fail — hold almost $500 billion in assets.

In contrast to the American experience, no bank was liquidated in Canada after the Home Bank closure in 1923 until the official liquidation in 1985 of the Northland Bank and the Canadian Commercial Bank, two relatively new small banks in Alberta. Three other small troubled banks survived ultimate liquidation during the 1980s by being merged with other banks. Although these failures did not constitute a crisis, they prompted government enquiries and subsequently some restructuring of bank regulators.

During the 1980s, hundreds of American thrifts failed. The United States Congressional Budget Office estimates the total cost of these thrift failures to be about $180 billion. These failures swamped the thrifts' deposit insurance fund and most of the cost will be paid by taxpayers.

These American savings and loan associations and savings banks — whose deposits were insured by the Federal Savings and Loan Insurance Corporation (FSLIC) — were the largest provider of mortgage finance. From 1980 through 1988, 489 failed thrifts were resolved at great cost to the FSLIC and another 333 were merged by arrangement with the primary federal thrift regulator — the Federal Home Loan Bank Board (Bank Board).[2] By 1989, it was apparent that the FSLIC's resources were depleted and it could no longer resolve failed thrifts without an infusion of taxpayer funds. Major legislation in 1989 abolished the FSLIC and the Bank Board, replacing them with the Savings Association Insurance Fund (SAIF), administered by the FDIC, and the Office of Thrift Supervision (OTS). The Resolution Trust Corporation (RTC) was established in 1989 as a temporary agency to resolve the hundreds of failed thrifts that FSLIC could not deal with. Funded almost exclusively with taxpayer funds, the RTC resolved 653 failed thrifts through the end of 1992. The RTC still has more thrifts to deal with before the SAIF takes over its responsibilities permanently in October 1993, but the RTC effectively ran out of its appropriated funds in March 1992. Of the 1,855 thrifts operating at year-end 1992, more than 200 were identified by the OTS as problem institutions.

Canada has experienced failures of nearbanks which are similar to American thrifts. Both in terms of the number of trust and mortgage loan companies that have failed and the consequent resolution costs, the Canadian failures have not assumed the crisis proportions of the American thrifts. In the 1980s, the Canada Deposit Insurance Corporation (CDIC) was called upon to resolve 19 institutions, most of which were relatively small. However, since then another nine have been resolved, including two of the country's largest institutions.[3] Unlike the United States, where the taxpayer has to bear most of the cost of the thrift problem, in Canada it is expected that higher deposit insurance premiums will, over time, repay federal government loans to the insurer.

FINANCIAL AND BANKING STRUCTURE

Historically, the Canadian financial system and, after the depression of the 1930s, its American counterpart, were highly structured and highly regulated. This resulted in enforced specialization and limited competition. This was considered a necessary condition to satisfy the regulatory goal of "safety and soundness."

The Canadian financial system was separated into five principal groups: chartered banks, trust and loan companies, the co-operative credit movement, life insurance companies and securities dealers. Each group was characterized by its core business activities and to a lesser extent by the jurisdiction under which it operated — federal or provincial or a combination of the two. After the 1950s the lines of separation became increasingly blurred, especially between the depository institutions as they penetrated each others' primary area of business. For example, the chartered banks added personal residential mortgage lending to their traditional core functions of commercial lending. The trust and loan companies, which specialized in mortgage lending, added personal and to a lesser extent commercial lending. While the chartered banks initially offered transactions (chequable) deposit accounts and the trust and loan companies savings deposits accounts, each now offers both types of deposits as do the credit unions and the *caisses populaires*, their Quebec counterparts. Trust companies are a uniquely Canadian institution, in that they remain the only institution permitted to offer discretionary fiduciary (trust) services.

In Canada, federal legislative reform in 1992 provided a new financial framework to allow the banks and nearbanks to respond to market forces and competition made difficult under the traditional policy of separateness. Under the new legislation all federally incorporated or chartered financial institutions are now able to offer most kinds of financial services, either directly through financial institution subsidiaries or as an agent through a networking relationship. As explained later, these structural changes to enhance competition and to ensure the more efficient provision of financial services have been accompanied by changes in prudential regulations and supervision to assure safety and soundness in the system.

After the financial crisis of the 1930s, American financial institutions also were locked into narrow roles. As in Canada, this resulted in four major types of institutions: commercial banks, thrifts, insurance companies, and investment banks. This market segmentation was imposed to limit competition and to achieve social goals of credit allocation. Many policy-makers were convinced that competition among depositories led to their taking on undue levels of risk which contributed to their failure. Massive numbers of failures had disrupted the financial system by creating a loss of confidence in the safety of individuals' savings that had been entrusted to the banks and nearbanks. Financial panics associated with these failures also created regional, sectoral, and national credit crunches which were felt to have deleterious effects on the national economy.

One of the more significant changes legislated in the 1930s was the separation of commercial from investment banking and the separation of banking from insurance. The depository industry was also segmented into commercial banks, thrifts (including both savings banks and savings and loans), and credit unions. Each type of depository was regulated in such a way that each served a different market. Commercial banks served businesses; thrifts and credit unions served consumers, but thrifts especially provided housing finance.

The concept of separateness has also become increasingly blurred in the American financial system as institutions have penetrated each other's turf. Although reform has been proposed, comprehensive restructuring of the American regulatory structure has not been achieved.

BANKING STRUCTURE

While the overall structures of our financial systems have developed along broadly similar lines, this has not been the case with our banking systems. Canadian banks have always been chartered and regulated by the federal government. Early on, as a result of mergers and amalgamation, the structure of the Canadian banking system evolved into a few large banks with nation-wide branch networks. There are now eight domestic banks with some 7,600 branches. In addition, there are some 58 foreign bank subsidiaries. Only one of these subsidiaries has an extensive branch network; most have less than five branches. In order to promote more competition in banking the federal government first allowed, in 1980, foreign banks direct entry to Canadian banking through the establishment of wholly owned bank subsidiaries.

Nation-wide branching is generally considered to have enhanced the soundness of the Canadian banking system. It has provided the banks a stable base of retail deposits and it has allowed them to reduce their overall credit risks by geographic diversification of their lending. In the 1980s new banks were formed in western Canada with a regional orientation. Without appropriate diversification of their lending, these institutions found themselves in trouble when the economy in western Canada suffered a downturn. Adding to their distress was a lack of a retail deposit base and their dependence for funds on brokered deposits which took flight at the first appearance of trouble. These banks subsequently failed.

In the United States, all depository institutions can be chartered either by the states or the federal government. Until the 1980s, commercial banks were severely limited in operating branch networks; some states prohibited the operation of branches altogether while others permitted state-wide branching. National banks are prohibited from multi-state banking or branching and they must abide by state rules for intrastate (within a state) branching. This feature of American banking contributed to the large numbers of individual institutions. Bank holding companies control about 70% of the banks and 93% of the assets in the banking system. Bank holding companies, subject to federal regulation, are structured allowing the parent company to own either a number of bank subsidiaries or one bank and many non-bank subsidiaries. The non-bank subsidiaries, however, are not permitted to engage in activities such as insurance underwriting that are considered not to be "closely related to banking."

Under the Douglas amendment to the Bank Holding Company Act, states have the authority to restrict out-of-state holding companies from acquiring bank subsidiaries within their state lines. In the 1980s, many states joined in regional pacts which permitted state chartered banks to operate within the regions. This has contributed to the consolidation of numbers of banks. By 1991 all but four states permitted some form of interstate banking and 27 states permitted out-of-state bank holding companies to operate within their jurisdictions.

Prohibitions to bank branching in the United States have left a large proportion of American banks with a regional orientation. As a result many of the American banks do not enjoy the same benefits that are attributed a branch banking system. To some extent this has been compensated for with active federal funds and interbank markets and the establishment of loan production offices throughout the country.[4] More recently the banks also have diversified their credit risks with the development of a market for loan sales and the sale of securitized assets in national markets.[5]

REGULATION AND PRUDENTIAL SUPERVISION

The two major regulatory goals are to ensure "safety and soundness" on the one hand and to "enhance competition and efficiency" on the other. Until recently it was generally held that by insulating and protecting financial institutions from one another with the heavy hand of regulators the goal of safety and soundness could be achieved. Hence legislation sets out, among other things, requirements for the chartering of institutions; parameters for the activities in which they can engage; the type and proportionate amount of investments, capital and liquidity requirements; and standards of sound business and financial practices. Regulatory agencies in turn are responsible for regulatory oversight and prudential supervision. However, the regulatory process has involved different political jurisdictions in both our countries and a multiplicity of regulators in each jurisdiction, so the process has not always achieved its intended objectives.

SAFETY NETS

Banks and other depository institutions are unique in that they play a central role in our payments systems and in the transmission of monetary policy. The traditional function of banks has been to make illiquid and risky loans to the public and in turn provide the public with liquid and riskless deposit liabilities which serve as a medium of exchange.[6] The public holds these deposits as a safe haven of purchasing power to be called upon via cash withdrawal, cheque, or plastic.

The public can repay its loans over time while the banks are an immediate provider of cash (coin and central bank notes). This can cause problems because at any one time the amount of cash held by a bank in its tills, vaults and automatic teller machines, is only a fraction of its deposit liabilities. This is called a fractional reserve banking system. If depositors become aware that their bank is operated unsoundly and the safety of their deposits may be at risk, they have the incentive to run to it and withdraw their money or transfer it to another bank where it is considered to be safe. An unsound bank unable to meet its depositors' immediate cash demand has no alternative but to close its doors — temporarily if not permanently. A further problem arises if a run on one bank makes the public suspicious about other banks regardless of how soundly they are operated. Under these circumstances runs on other banks can spread like a disease — a phenomenon referred to as contagion. When this happens, the liquidity and stability of the entire financial system is threatened. The Canadian branch banking structure probably is less susceptible to destructive system-wide runs than the American unit banking system.

To prevent contagious runs, in both our countries, two safety nets have been put in place. The oldest of these is the central bank's lender-of-last-resort facility. The other is federal government deposit insurance.

The lender-of-last-resort facility of central banks, as originally designed, was meant to be a liquidity facility for banks with temporary cash needs. It was recognized that, with fractional banking, demands on the banks for cash cannot be predicted with certainty under the best of circumstances. It was not intended that central banks, who are the ultimate source of cash, should come to the aid of banks whose cash shortages are the result of imprudent behaviour. Rather, the central bank is intended to assist sound banks with temporary liquidity problems.[7]

In the United States, the central bank is the Federal Reserve System which is comprised of twelve Federal Reserve Banks governed by the Board of Governors. Loans are made to banks through the Federal Reserve Banks' so-called discount window, and have taken three forms: seasonal loans, typically to small agricultural banks; short-term adjustment loans, when a temporary cash deficiency cannot be met in the national funds markets; and extended credit, when a bank no longer has normal access to the funds market and needs time to find alternative sources. Traditionally, the Federal Reserve Banks used their discretionary power to avoid continuous borrowing by their member banks and to lend only to sound institutions who could back such loans with appropriate collateral. However, in the 1980s the Reserve Banks made advances of extended credit to maintain the liquidity of banks whose solvency was questionable. In 1991, the Federal Deposit Insurance Corporation Improvements Act (FDI CIA) established guidelines and limits on the use of the Federal Reserve's discount window. For example, advances to undercapitalized institutions were limited to no more than 60 days in any 120-day period.

In Canada, the Bank of Canada has typically only made short-term loans to the chartered banks and now also some nearbanks that are solvent and require temporary cash assistance. These loans are collateralized and made at the Bank Rate which is a penalty rate in that it is higher than the rates for similar borrowing in the money market. In the 1980s, however, the Bank of Canada also made extraordinary large loans for extended periods of time to institutions that subsequently failed. In both countries, the practice by the central banks of extending other than temporary last-resort loans, in some cases to insolvent institutions, has probably resulted in these institutions managing their cash less prudently than they would otherwise.

Federal government deposit insurance was introduced in the United States in response to the financial crisis of the 1930s when the public lack of confidence in its banking system contributed to thousands of bank failures. This lack of confidence was exacerbated by the Federal Reserve System's delay in providing last-resort lending to meet the cash needs of banks experiencing runs. This delay has been attributed to the Federal Reserve's mistaken desire to discipline banks rather than to address their liquidity problems. Federal deposit insurance was introduced to protect small and unsophisticated depositors and to prevent bank runs by restoring public confidence in the safety of their deposits.

Today, deposits held at American commercial banks and thrifts are insured up to $100,000 per deposit by the FDIC. The FDIC operates two separate funds: the Bank Insurance Fund which guarantees deposits at banks; and the Savings Association Fund which guarantees deposits at thrifts. In 1970 with the establishment of the National Credit Union Share Insurance Fund, federal deposit insurance was extended to the credit unions.

Government deposit insurance was not established in Canada until 1967. While it has similar goals, even though bank runs have not been a chronic problem, it has allowed the nearbanks whose deposits are also insured to compete more readily with the banks for deposit funds.

The Canadian deposit insurance system is somewhat less comprehensive than its American counterpart. Deposits are insured only up to $60,000. The federal government's Canada Deposit Insurance Corporation (CDIC) protects deposits at all chartered banks and those at trust and mortgage loan companies with the exception of deposits accepted in the Province of Quebec by provincially incorporated institutions. The Province of Quebec has its own deposit insurance plan administered by the Quebec Deposit Insurance Board (QDIB). By agreement between the CDIC and the QDIB, deposits made in Quebec with provincially incorporated institutions are insured by the

QDIB. The CDIC backstops the QDIB in that it can make loans to it. Deposits made with federally incorporated institutions are insured by the CDIC regardless of the province in which the deposit was made.

Under normal conditions the federal government deposit insurers in Canada and the United States are expected to meet current insurance claims from insurance reserve funds accumulated with annual premiums paid by member institutions. However, in the event of extraordinary loss, the respective governments have been called upon to make up deficiencies with loans to the insurers. This amounts to an unconditional government guarantee and provides deposit assurance rather than deposit insurance.

In the 1980s and more recently, deposit insurance reserve funds experienced large shortfalls which have had to be financed by the government. It is expected that the Canadian government will recover its loans to the CDIC from higher insurance premiums. The banks have complained because most of the losses have been due to failures of trust and loan companies; because of their proportionate size, the banks provide the bulk of CDIC's premium revenue, and therefore they are left less competitive. Insofar as higher premiums pay for insurance underwriting losses, the Canadian government's deposit insurance system can be said to be self-financing. This is not the case in the United States.

Given the massive amount of financing approved by Congress to bail out American deposit insurers, most of the costs will have to be born by taxpayers. Full recovery of the taxpayer's contribution through higher deposit insurance premiums would leave depository institutions uncompetitive with other financial institutions and probably result in further failures. Some would argue that having the taxpayer pick up the tab can be justified in that all citizens benefit from the confidence instilled in the payment system by government deposit insurance.

There is no question that government deposit insurance has met its goals of protecting small and unsophisticated depositors and preventing contagious bank runs. However, it has also had a major drawback in that it has created a "moral hazard problem" — that is, financial institutions have an incentive to undertake riskier investments with depositor's funds when these are insured. Moral hazard problems are not uncommon in the insurance industry because insurance coverage can alter the behaviour of the insured and thereby increase the probability that the event underwritten by insurance will happen. For example, with fire insurance on our homes we probably take less care to prevent fires and with theft insurance less care to lock doors. Deductible provisions are a common feature of householder policies to guard against the moral hazard problem. Similarly, with deposit insurance, depositors have little incentive to monitor the risk-taking activities of depository institutions. As a result, these institutions are able to obtain deposits to fund risky investments without paying higher rates of interest that would reflect these higher risks. Nor are these higher risks reflected in higher insurance premiums, since deposit insurers have set insurance premiums at a uniform percentage of the amount of insured deposits. With all institutions paying the same premium rate this also results in less risky institutions subsidizing the additional risk that the more aggressive institutions take on. Deposit insurance gives institutions, especially those already in trouble, the incentive to assume more risk because their shareholders benefit from favourable outcomes while the cost of unfavourable outcomes is borne by the insurer, and ultimately taxpayers. Where insurance losses are recovered through higher premiums, future customers of depository institutions are victimized.

The methods used by deposit insurers to resolve failed institutions increased the moral hazard problems during the 1980s. In Canada, the CDIC preferred not to immediately close an institution that had been determined to be insolvent. Rather, it arranged with other institutions, through agency and operating agreements, to administer the insolvent institution during a winding-down process. During this process, the CDIC advanced funds or guaranteed funds that the agent used to meet depositors' claims. In so doing, the CDIC in effect paid off on both insured and uninsured deposits. Hence uninsured depositors came to assume that their deposits were safe and absolved themselves from monitoring the risk-taking behaviour of their depository.

In the United States during the 1980s, the way insurers and regulators chose to resolve insolvent institutions also ended up in a situation where both insured and uninsured deposits were compensated. Instead of resolving an insolvent institution by liquidation, regulators attempted to merge it with another institution. When a failed depository is liquidated, its doors are closed and the insured depositors are reimbursed. The institution's assets are placed into receivership and the proceeds are shared by the insurer, the uninsured depositors, and other creditors. Under a merger, however, both insured and some or all of the uninsured deposits are transferred to the acquirer and thereby remain safe. The deposit insurer compensates the acquirer of failed institutions for any difference between the value of transferred liabilities and the estimated value of the failed institution's assets. The merger method, referred to as purchase and assumption, can only be used if it is less expensive than a liquidation. Recently in Canada, the CDIC has begun to use purchase and assumptions to resolve failures of large trust and loan companies.

BANK EXAMINATION AND SUPERVISION

Regulators use both on-site and off-site methods to supervise institutions. The United States has the most intensive system of on-site examination of depository institutions in the world. Canada, on the other hand, has not used on-site examination to the same extent probably because of the much smaller number of institutions to be supervised. Until the 1980s, the Office of the Inspector General of Banks (OIGB), which employed a staff of fewer than ten persons, implicitly relied on self-regulation by the chartered banks. The OIGB conducted no on-site examinations but analyzed financial statements and conducted on-site interviews with senior bank executives. This system of supervision broke down in the mid-1980s with the troubles of the new regional banks. The Estey Commission, which examined the causes of regional bank failures, characterized the examination process as a "wink and nod system." The system of prudential regulation, supervision, and examination was reformed in the late 1980s. The federal regulator of the nearbanks, which had more personnel and used limited on-site examinations, was merged with the OIGB into the Office of the Superintendent of Financial Institutions (OSFI). Both the OSFI and the CDIC subsequently were provided with stronger disciplinary tools to deal with institutions that do not follow sound business and financial practices.

In both countries regulatory laxity has been a contributing factor to the high cost of depository failures. In retrospect, much of the cost of financial institutional failures since the early 1980s might have been averted if timely regulatory action had been taken. It has also been argued that some failures might have been avoided through stronger regulatory action because owners and managers of some troubled institutions would have had the incentive to behave prudently.

A policy of regulatory forbearance was mistakenly undertaken by American thrift regulators in the 1980s. Forbearance is the discretionary practice by regulators of not enforcing an existing rule. Regulators did not violate statutes; rather, in altering agency regulations they interpreted those statutes in the most liberal way possible, thereby avoiding closing insolvent institutions. The forbearance policy in part grew out of hope that the combined effect of economic recovery, lower interest rates, and statutory deregulation could allow the thrifts to "grow out of their problems." Another reason for granting forbearance was that the government deposit insurers did not have sufficient cash resources to close the large number of insolvent institutions. Unfortunately forbearance gave institutions an incentive to gamble for resurrection which resulted in rampant investment speculation and fraudulent practices, all of which added to the ultimate cost of resolving the thrift crisis.

CAPITAL ADEQUACY

Depository institutions hold capital funds to absorb losses that can result in failure and ultimately insolvency.[8] Capital consists of equity and borrowed funds. Equity represents the shareholders' or owners' stake in an institution. The larger this stake, the greater their incentive to run their institutions soundly because their own money is at risk in case of insolvency.

Capital can also be viewed as a buffer protecting depositors. While depositors have first claim on a depository institution's assets, in case of insolvency they usually have insufficient information on the quality and consequently the value of these assets. Hence capital is a way of compensating depositors for lack of information. Moreover, insofar as capital funds can be used to meet shortfalls between depositors' claims and the value of assets, they serve to bolster depositors' confidence in the safety of their deposits. Adequate capital is also a concern for deposit insurers because it protects them from loss in case of insolvency.

Canadian and American regulators have adopted international risk-based capital adequacy standards first proposed in the early 1990s for their banks. According to these standards, the amount of capital a bank is required to hold is determined by the riskiness of its assets. The Canadian banks as well as the trust and loan companies already meet these standards. However, as yet this is not so for many of the American banks and thrifts. However, under the FDICIA of 1991, bank supervisors are mandated to take progressively stricter supervisory actions against banks as their capital positions deteriorate.

OWNERSHIP

As already discussed, one feature which distinguishes the American and Canadian banking systems is the number of institutions. There are only six major domestically chartered Canadian banks as opposed to more than 11,000 American banks. Implicitly, Canadians permit a highly concentrated industry — which is typically associated with limited competition — for the efficiencies of nationwide banking and the benefits of having banks large enough to compete with foreign banks. This tradeoff may also have contributed to the stability of the Canadian banking system. Because a highly concentrated industry can extract higher profits than one which is more competitive, chartered banks have a unique ownership requirement — they must be widely held.

A provision in the Bank Act limits any one individual or group of individuals from holding more than 10% of any class of shares of a Schedule I bank. The 1980 amendments to the Bank Act permitted narrow domestic ownership of newly chartered banks as well as narrow ownership of foreign bank subsidiaries.[9] These Schedule II charters were limited with respect to their size; foreign-owned Schedule II banks were limited as a group in terms of their share of Canadian bank assets and lending. Domestically-owned Schedule II banks are required to convert to a Schedule I charter after ten years.

The notion behind the 1980 amendment to the Bank Act was that the established Schedule I banks needed more competition. It was argued that newly established domestic banks would need narrow ownership in order to raise capital and appropriately compensate new owners. Although this may have been true, the competitive presence of the established Schedule I banks — as well as unforeseen regional economic problems of the early 1980s — hampered the establishment of domestically chartered Schedule II banks. Most of them failed. Foreign-owned Schedule II banks fared better because they were backed by their foreign parent banks.

Until recently, ownership by banks of other financial institutions was also restricted. Until 1987, the chartered banks were not permitted to own securities dealers as bank subsidiaries. Federal legislative reform in 1992 now allows cross-ownership between the banks and other government-regulated financial institutions.

Trust and mortgage loan companies were generally also widely held until the early 1980s. Thereafter, the major companies were brought into common ownership with other non-bank institutions to form diversified financial conglomerates that typically had significant ownership interests in non-financial corporations. This development raised public policy concerns about the concentration of assets and powers, the potential for solvency-threatening, self-dealing transactions, and conflicts of interest. There was also the concern that any problems in non-financial affiliates of a conglomerate could spill over and undermine confidence in the soundness of its affiliated financial institutions. Such spill-overs could in effect extend government financial safety nets to commercial firms.

In light of the presence of cross-ownership, closely held ownership, and commercial-financial links, permitted by the federal financial legislative reforms in 1992, the above potential problems had to be addressed. A general ban now applies to transactions between a financial institution and its related parties. Related parties include those persons or entities who, directly or indirectly, are significant shareholders of the financial institutions, or who are in positions of influence or control over the institution. Potential conflict of interest problems are to be controlled by stronger corporate governance and internal procedures with regulatory oversight. To control financial concentration, changes in ownership of federally regulated institutions are subject to ministerial review and approval.

The issue of ownership of American financial institutions has not been as much of a concern as in Canada. Because American banks are chartered at both the state and federal level, and because interstate branching and banking is limited, American banking is less concentrated than Canadian. This does not necessarily mean that American banking is more competitive. Separation of powers among financial institutions and geographic restrictions on branching protected smaller institutions from full competitive forces. Deposit insurance, moreover, provides a benefit to smaller banks in their competition with larger banks for insured deposits. Deposit insurance partially offsets the belief that larger banks are safer than smaller ones.[10]

American banks do not have ownership restrictions such as exist in Canada. Although small institutions are typically narrowly held and larger institutions are typically widely held, this is a result of market forces and not regulation. Narrow ownership provides owners greater control and can lead to the bank being managed more efficiently, but it can present problems to regulators. Narrowly held thrifts may have been more susceptible to problems associated with moral hazard during the thrift crisis. Faced with great incentives to gamble or speculate with or simply plunder their depositors' funds, it was simpler for owners of narrowly held institutions to do so.

In the United States, commercial ownership of banks is prohibited, but commercial firms can own financial institution subsidiaries that collectively perform many banking functions. Indeed, the major auto companies operate major finance companies that are direct competitors with banks and other depositories.

Depository institutions are restricted in the types of financial subsidiaries that they may own and operate. Over the past decade, however, some restrictions have been lifted on bank and thrift holding company ownership rights. Although some commingling of financial services can take place either through the depository institution or through its holding company, there are still restrictions that limit the commingling of banking, insurance, and securities underwriting.

CONCLUSIONS

We have provided an overview of the differences and similarities between Canadian and American financial and regulatory structures. We have shown that government safety nets to keep our deposits safe have created costly moral hazard problems in that they have given depository institutions the incentive to take on excessive risk. These costs have been exacerbated by the way regulators have prudentially regulated and supervised depositories and the methods used to resolve failed institutions. The costs of keeping our money safe calls for better incentives for financial institutions to control their risks. Risk-based capital adequacy standards and other regulatory reforms have already been introduced in both countries. However, the implementation of risk-based deposit insurance premiums and other methods to prevent moral hazard problems associated with government deposit insurance remains an important financial policy issue in both countries.

NOTES

1. Nearbanks are depository institutions that perform many of the traditional banking functions. However, they are not chartered or incorporated as banks, and in Canada are not allowed to refer to themselves as banks. In Canada the trust and mortgage loan companies are the major nearbanks and in the United States the thrifts (savings and loan associations known as the S&Ls and savings banks). In both countries the credit unions, and in Canada the *caisses populaires* are also nearbanks.

2. Resolution of failed institutions refers to their closure through liquidation or by merger with, or acquisition by, another institution.

3. These were Central Guaranty Trust Company and Royal Trust Company.

4. Federal funds refers to American banks borrowing cash reserves on a short-term basis from other banks. Loan produc-

tion offices are set up by American banks in states where they are not allowed branches to solicit loans which are booked with their head offices.

5.	Securitization is the conversion of loans into saleable assets in secondary markets.

6.	Liquidity is the property of being convertible to cash at short notice and without significant cost to the lender. Deposits at banks and nearbanks are liabilities to these institutions since they represent cash claims by the public.

7.	The money market is a wholesale market in which short-term (usually less than one year and as short as overnight) highly liquid financial assets are traded in large quantities.

8.	An institution is considered to be insolvent when it has negative net worth. This occurs when the value of its assets (variously measured) exceeds that of its liabilities.

9.	Narrow ownership implies that any one individual or group of individuals owns more than 10% of any class of shares in a bank.

10.	The benefit provided by deposit insurance to smaller institutions is offset in part by the American policy of "Too-big-to-fail." Under this policy, first made explicit by regulators in 1984 when they dealt with Continental Illinois Bank, some institutions are considered to be too large or too important to close. This policy can also be effected when the regulators fully compensate uninsured creditors under the pretence that not doing so would cause contagious bank runs.

REFERENCES

Barth, James R. *The Great Savings and Loan Debate*, Washington, DC, AEI Press, 1991.

Barth, James R. and R. Dan Brumbaugh Jr., eds., *The Reform of Federal Deposit Insurance: Protecting the Taxpayers and Disciplining the Government*. New York, NY, Harper Business, 1992

Bartholomew, P.F. and J.A. Galbraith. "The U.S. and Canadian Deposit-Taking Institutions." In *Prospects for Canadian-United States Economic Relations Under Free Trade*, edited by W. Milberg and P.F. Bartholomew, Greenwich, CT, JAJ Press, pp. 179-202.

Bartholomew, Philip F. "The Cost of Forbearance During the Thrift Crisis". CBO Staff Memorandum, Washington, DC, Congressional Budget Office. June 1991.

Benston, George J. et al. *Perspectives on Safe and Sound Banking: Past, Present and Future,* Cambridge, MA, MIT Press 1986.

Binhammer, H.H., *Money, Banking and the Canadian Financial System,* 6th ed. Toronto: Nelson Press, 1993.

Congressional Budget Office. *Reforming Federal Deposit Insurance,* Washington, D.C., September 1990.

Daniel, Fred, Charles Freedman and Clyde Goodlet, "Restructuring Canadian Financial Industry", *Bank of Canada Review.* Winter 1992-93, pp. 21-44.

Dybvig, Philip H. "Bank Runs," *The New Palgrave Dictionary of Money and Finance,* New York, NY The Stockton Press, 1992 pp. 171-73

Flood, Mark D. "The Great Deposit Insurance Debate." Federal Reserve Bank of St. Louis, *Review,* July/August 1992, pp. 51-77.

Friedman, Milton "Has Government Any Role in Money" *Journal of Monetary Economics,* January 1986, pp. 37-62

Hetzel, Robert L. "Too Big to Fail: Origins, Consequences and Outlook." Federal Reserve Bank of Richmond, *Economic Review.* November/December 1991, pp. 3-15.

Kane, Edward J. *The S&L Insurance Mess: How Did it Happen?* Washington, D.C.. Urban Institute Press, 1989.

Thomson, James B. "Using Market Incentives to Reform Bank Regulation and Federal Deposit Insurance." Federal Reserve Bank of Cleveland, *Economic Review,* Vol. 26, No. 1, 1990, pp. 28-40.

Schwartz, Anna J. "The Misuse of the Fed's Discount Window" *Federal Reserve Bank of St. Louis Review*, September/October 1992 pp. 58-69

U.S. Department of Treasury, *Modernizing The Financial System; Recommendations for Safer, More Competitive Banks* Washington, United States Government Printing Office, 1991

GEORGE HOBERG

Comparing Canadian Performance in Environmental Policy*

When then Environment Minister Lucien Bouchard introduced the *Green Plan* discussion paper in early 1990, he proclaimed that the primary goal of the government's effort was "to make Canada, by the year 2000, the industrial world's most environmentally friendly country."[1] How much work must be done to achieve this goal? This chapter evaluates the performance of Canadian environmental policy by comparing it to other advanced industrial democracies, focusing especially on the United States. The comparative perspective is a valuable one, because rather than comparing performance with some abstract standard, we can compare Canada's activities to what other countries have done within similar constraints, be they technical, economic, social, or political. The focus on the US is also particularly relevant to Canada. Perhaps because Canadian perceptions of US environmental policy have been dominated by acid rain, many Canadians seem to have adopted an attitude of environmental superiority towards the giant neighbour to the south. This chapter will explore whether that attitude is justified.

A substantial body of literature on comparative environmental policy exists, although it has focused on comparisons between the US and Europe, and to a lesser extent Japan, and largely overlooked Canada.[2] If there is one theme pervading this literature, it is that the regulatory processes differ significantly in different countries, a variance that David Vogel has aptly characterized as 'national styles of regulation.' Most studies have focused on these differences in process, and have shied away from rigorous analyses of policy outcomes.

---

*   Originally published in Robert Boardman, ed., *Canadian Environmental Policy: Ecosystems, Politics and Process* (Don Mills: Oxford, 1992), pp. 246-263.

The studies that have looked at policy outcomes have come up with a surprising conclusion: despite these widely divergent regulatory styles, there is a surprising amount of policy convergence. Can the same be said of Canada?

The focus of this comparison is on the content and consequences of environmental policy, and not on an evaluation of Canada's regulatory style or an examination of the reasons for Canada's performance. After a brief survey of the methodological problems involved, the financial resources, both public and private, that Canada has committed to environmental protection will be evaluated. Then the analysis turns to a detailed examination of four important areas of environmental policy: air pollution, water pollution, pesticides, and environmental impact assessment. For each policy area, the analysis will compare the applicable laws and regulations, and then whatever data are available on actual policy outcomes and their consequences. The concluding section will provide a summary assessment of Canada's environmental performance in comparative perspective. While an explanation for the observed patterns is beyond the scope of this chapter, several important explanatory forces will be given brief mention because they shed valuable light on Canada's regulatory performance to date.

METHODOLOGICAL OVERVIEW

This type of analysis is fraught with methodological pitfalls. The first difficulty is the choice of criteria for evaluation — how do we decide whether one country has a better environmental record than another? For the purpose of this analysis, we are concerned with how much environmental protection is provided, not with some more complex notion of net social welfare. But even this more narrow concern creates difficulties, in large part because different nations confront different environmental problems. The objective of environmental policy is of course to provide a desirable level of environmetal quality in terms of clean air, clean water, etc. But because different nations confront different problems, it may not be appropriate merely to compare indices of environmental quality. For instance, because of Canada's relatively low population and industrial density, it can more easily take advantage of the assimilative capacities of the environment than a country with greater density. Thus, Canadians could pollute far more per capita and still have better environmental quality than their American neighbours. If Canada's regulations are weaker, that may reflect the presence of a less serious environmental threat rather than lack of environmental concern.

While taking this problem into account, this chapter will use the criteria of the *amount of environmental protection provided.* In principle, this would be measured by the difference between actual levels of environmental quality and what those levels would be in the absence of environmental protection measures. Unfortunately, such measures are simply not available. We must rely instead on the proxy indicators that are available, but even then much of the relevant data are scarce and difficult to interpret. Nations use different regulatory approaches that are frequently difficult to compare, and they frequently measure the implementation and consequences of regulations differently, if at all.

But this comparative task is too important to surrender to methodological difficulties. The analysis proceeds in the spirit of making the best of the data that are available, bearing in mind these dilemmas of comparison. The availability of data limits the scope of the analysis in two important ways. First, the analysis focuses on a comparison between Canada and the United States. Only occasional references, when comparable data are readily available, are made to other nations. Second, only four areas of environmental policy are considered, excluding such important areas as hazardous waste management, toxic substance control, endangered species protection, wilderness preservation, and policies towards global environmental problems. While the four areas surveyed here cover a broad range of environmental policy problems, there is no guarantee that these areas are representative of environmental policy generally.

RESOURCE COMMITMENTS

When we examine the level of financial resources Canada and the United States commit to environmental protection, the two countries appear to have similar levels of commitment. For purposes of our analysis, data for the fiscal year 1985-86 have been chosen. As shown in Table 1, at the federal level the Canadian commitment at first appears larger. Environment Canada spending was 0.46% of the total federal budget, whereas US Environmental Protection Agency spending was 0.32% of the total US federal budget.[3] But the analysis is complicated by the fact that Environment Canada's jurisdiction is more expansive than EPA's — for instance, it includes the parks branch, which in the US is included in another department.[4] When the parks branch is removed from Environment Canada's budget, environmental spending makes up 0.21% of total federal spending, less than the US amount. If, however, we leave the parks branch in

Environment Canada, and add the National Park Service to EPA's budget, Canada's fraction is slightly higher, 0.46% vs 0.41%.

The analysis of government spending is greatly complicated by the fact that much of it occurs at the sub-national level. Here the problem of consistent jurisdiction is magnified, because it is impractical to compare the scope of responsibilities of so many sub-national agencies. In the United States, the state governments spent 1.46% of their total budgets on the environment during the 1986 fiscal year. In the same year, the four largest Canadian provinces spent 0.89% of their total budgets on the environment. This difference is quite surprising, given Canada's reputation for being more decentralized. Again, these figures must be qualified by possible jurisdictional differences similar to those mentioned above, between Environment Canada and EPA.

When added together, the federal and state/provincial totals give us a better idea of total financial commitments of each government. In the US, environmental spending comprises 0.65% of total government spending if you exclude the National Park Service. In Canada, it comprises 0.49% if you exclude parks at the federal level. If federal parks programs are included in both estimates, US environmental spending is 0.68% of total government spending, and Canadian environmental spending is 0.64%. Thus, the comparison is highly sensitive to how you measure budgetary commitments, but whatever differences there are, they are relatively small.

However, government spending is an extremely indirect indicator of society's commitment to environmental protection. When governments rely on the instrument of regulation to protect the environment, government expenditures are only a weak reflection of environmental concern because the costs of environmental protection are borne by the private sector, and the administrative costs to government are quite small in comparison. For that reason, a more appropriate measure of commitment is how much business spends on environment clean-up. For instance, in the US, government regulation and monitoring makes up only 2% of total pollution control expenditures. When direct government pollution abatement is included, such as municipal sewage treatment, the fraction increases to 22%.[5]

While they are done with different methodologies, and care must therefore be taken in how they can be compared, both nations have developed estimates for the fraction of new capital investment that is spent on pollution control. In the US, approximately 2.0% of new plant and equipment expenditures by US non-farm business was dedicated to pollution abatement over the period 1985-1987. In Canada, about 0.7% of total capital expenditures over the period 1985-1987 was spent on pollution control. Comparing these two measures, the US resource commitment to the environment is nearly three times greater than that in Canada. When the analysis is restricted to the manufacturing sector, the gap narrows somewhat – 4.0% for the US and 1.9% for Canada – but it is still substantial.[6]

AIR POLLUTION

Our first substantive area of environmental policy for comparison is air pollution. There are two types of air pollution regulations: ambient air quality standards, which place limts on the concentration of various pollutants in the air, and emission standards, which place limits on the amount of various pollutants emitted by a particular source, such as smoke-stacks or cars.

There are significant differences between the two countries' regulatory frameworks for air pollution controls. In the US, air pollution control occurs largely through the federal Clean Air Act of 1970, amended in 1977 and 1990.[7] The Clean Air Act requires the federal government to establish binding National Ambient Air Quality Standards (NAAQS) for a specified list of important pollutants. These standards are supplemented by the Prevention of Significant Deterioration (PSD) program, which is designed to maintain air quality in areas where the air is already cleaner than national standards. In effect, the combination of NAAQS and PSD creates a bewildering patchwork of air quality standards, in which the NAAQS provides a national maximum, but the PSD limits impose more stringent standards in clean air areas. The states are responsible for implementing regulations to achieve the standards, but they do so under close federal supervision, backed by the threat of financial sanction. In its most stringent section, the US Clean Air Act directly establishes federal emission standards for cars and trucks. The Act also requires EPA to establish stringent federal emission standards for new sources of pollution, called New Source Performance Standards, and emission standards for new and existing sources of especially toxic air pollutants.

In Canada, the federal government plays a much smaller role in air pollution control. The Canadian Clean Air Act, passed in 1971, gives the federal government authority to set non-binding guidelines;[8] binding air quality standards and the regulations to achieve them are issued by provinces. However, the federal statute does authorize the federal government to establish national emission standards for pollutants that "pose a significant danger to the health of persons," but this provision has only been used four times in 20 years.[9] Virtually all emission standards are set by the provinces. The major exception is standards for automobile emissions from new vehicles, which are established by the federal Minister of Transportation under the Motor Vehicle Safety Act.[10]

Thus, American air pollution regulation is far more centralized than it is in Canada, and far more of the substance of the regulations is specified in US legislation. When combining provincial and federal statutes, however, there is little difference in the extent of regulatory authority over air pollution in the two countries.

The record on policy outcomes in the air pollution area is quite mixed, but it seems that Canada has had marginally more success than the US. A comparison of four provinces shows that Canadian ambient air quality standards are either equivalent to or more stringent than American National Ambient Air Quality standards.[11] However, when the US Prevention of Significant Deterioration program is included, the US air quality standards could be considered more stringent.

In the case of emissions from automobiles, the US government has been a world leader, but just recently Canada has caught up. Prior to the 1988 model year when new Canadian regulations took effect, Canadian emission standards had been between three and seven times less stringent, depending on the pollutant in question.[12] Both governments are currently in the process of tightening their regulations significantly. The 1990 amendments to the US Clean Air Act require much more stringent standards to be implemented between 1994 and 1996. In Canada, an intergovernmental agreement announced in 1989 would tighten Canadian auto emission standards to a comparable level by about the same time.[13]

The case of acid rain involves the opposite pattern. During the 1980s acid rain was a major irritant in Canadian-American relations. While pollutants flow across the border in both directions, the greater amount of US emissions carried by prevailing winds ensures that Canada is far more affected by American-generated acid rain than vice versa. It is estimated that 50% of the acid rain falling in Canada comes from American sources, whereas a much smaller fraction, between 10% and 15%, of US acid rain originates in Canada.[14] In 1982, the Canadian government proposed an agreement whereby both nations would reduce sulphur dioxide by 50%. However, the Reagan administration, which at that time refused to formally admit that acid rain was a human-made phenomenon, adamantly rejected the proposal. Facing a recalcitrant Reagan administration, Canada shifted its strategy to emphasizing unilateral reductions. In March, 1985, Prime Minister Brian Mulroney and Eastern Canadian premiers announced that Canada would reduce its emissions of sulphur dioxide by 50% in 1994.[15]

With the 1990 amendments to its Clean Air Act, the United States finally introduced a stringent new acid rain reduction program. The statute requires that sulphur dioxide emissions be reduced by 10 million tonnes below 1980 levels by the year 2000. Both countries have presented slightly manipulated figures. Taking actual 1980 emission levels as a common baseline, the Canadian program requires a 37% reduction by 1994, and the US program requires a 39% reduction by the year 2000.[16]

Thus, while the US performance in the area of acid rain has undergone a dramatic improvement, it still lags behind the Canadian program by six years. While Canadians deserve credit for addressing the problem earlier, the American program has three features which make it somewhat more stringent than its Canadian counterpart. First, the American program is nationwide, whereas the Canadian program only includes provinces from Manitoba east. Second, the American program places a 'cap' beyond which sulphur dioxide emissions cannot rise, whereas the Canadian program permits future growth. The hard-fought reductions achieved by Canada between 1985 and 1994 could be lost as a result of future population or industrial growth. *Canada's Green Plan*, announced in December 1990, proposes to rectify both of these flaws, but that depends on provincial co-operation. Third, American officials face a more difficult task to achieve similar objectives. There are only 10 major sources of sulphur dioxide in Canada, whereas the 1990 Clean Air Act Amendments directly control emissions from 111 major sources.

When actual trends in air quality and emissions are examined, the Canadian record appears to have a marginal edge over the US one. Table 2 displays trends in air quality in Canada and the United States. Because of differences in measurement methods, the air quality measures reported cannot be directly compared across the two nations. While the methodological differences may affect the rates of change as well, the percentage change figures are a reasonably reliable comparative indicator. Canadian progress in improving air quality from the mid-1970s to the mid-1980s surpassed US progress in four out of six commonly measured pollutants. When analysing the separate measure of emissions (the amount of pollution being released, rather than its concentration in the air) over the period 1980-1986, Canada had more success in reducing emissions of sulphur dioxide, but the US has had more success than Canada in reducing nitrogen oxides.[17]

In comparison to other advanced industrial countries, both the US and Canada seem to have very strong air pollution records. For instance, the major European countries are significantly behind North America in automobile emission standards. In 1989, the European Commission finally adopted standards that would move member countries to adopt standards by 1992 that were in place in both the US and Canada by 1988. By that time, North America will be well on the way to meeting much more stringent standards. Lead in gasoline, effectively banned in North America by 1990, is still used in several European countries. Finally, European nations have not gone as far as the US and Canada in addressing acid rain. A recent British program will reduce sulphur dioxide emissions by only 14% by 1997 – both North American programs go farther faster.[18]

WATER POLLUTION

The overall regulatory frameworks for water pollution control in the two jurisdictions have some important similarities. Both are federalist in nature, involving shared responsibilities between the national and sub-national governments. The principal regulatory mechanism is basically the same: waste discharges are prohibited without a permit from the government. Despite the overall similarity in approach, however, there are important differences between the two jurisdictions' regulatory framework, reflecting each nation's institutional make-up and regulatory style.

Water pollution control in the United States is based upon the Federal Water Pollution Control Act of 1972 (FWPCA).[19] While it was amended in 1977 and 1987, the basic structure of the statute, as it applies to industrial effluents, has remained essentially the same. The 1972 statute announced extremely ambitious goals (not subsequently attained): the nation's waters were to be "fishable and swimmable" by 1983, and the discharge of pollutants into navigable waters was to be eliminated altogether by 1985.[20]

To implement these goals, two major programs were established, one for industrial sources, one for municipal sewage disposal. The US Environmental Protection Agency was charged with issuing technology-based effluent standards for industrial plants. Polluters were required to install the Best Practicable Technology in 1977 and the most stringent Best Available Technology (BAT) by 1984. In addition, new sources brought on line after 1973 were required to meet an even more stringent standard, the New Source Performance Standard.

To implement these standards, permits are issued to each source of discharge. It is this permit that formally establishes the allowable quantity and quality of effluent the plant can emit. The Act gives EPA the authority to delegate the permitting and enforcement responsibility to state governments. These authorities have been delegated to thirty-three states. These states thus have primary responsibility for permitting and enforcement, although EPA actively monitors these activities. For those states that do not have their own programs, EPA performs the permitting and enforcement functions itself.

The 1972 statute also contained an elaborate program for municipal sewage treatment. The Act required almost all municipalities to install "secondary" treatment of municipal wastes by 1977. To encourage them to do so, the federal government created an $18-billion construction grant program that would pay for 75% of the costs of constructing new sewage treatment facilities. The 1977 amendments extended the deadline to 1983 (it was later extended again to 1988), and continued the authorization of huge sums of money. The construction grant program has become America's second largest public works program, after the highway system.[21]

As in the case of air pollution, Canadian water pollution regulation is much more decentralized. There is a strong basis for federal power under the Fisheries Act, which prohibits emissions of any "deleterious substance of any type in water frequented by fish" (Section 33[2]). Exemptions are allowed if the discharge is authorized by regulation. The federal government has issued regulations for six industries, but with one exception they only apply to new plants. Enforcement of these standards has for the most part been delegated to provincial regulators, although the federal government reserves the right to take enforcement action in the case of inadequate provincial action. The principal mechanism for water pollution control is thus permits for specific facilities that are issued by provinces.[22]

Federal water pollution regulation is also authorized by the Canada Water Act of 1970. Part II of the Act authorizes unilateral federal action in "interjurisdictional waters," and only if water quality has become a matter of "urgent national concern" and efforts to reach a co-operative solution with the provinces have failed. Despite the expansive authorities for water quality management in this part of this Act, it has never been used. However, Part III of the statute, now incorporated into the Canadian Environmental Protection Act, authorized regulation of phosphates in detergents.[23]

Thus, as in the case of air pollution, water pollution control in Canada is far more decentralized than in the United States. Regulatory performance is not as easily measured in the case of water pollution. Ambient standards are not used, and while both countries monitor water quality, data have not been compiled in comparable terms. Certainly the American regulatory system seems more developed. For instance, under the FWPCA the US federal government has issued effluent standards for a mind-boggling 642 industrial subcategories. The pulp and paper mill regulations alone are divided into 25 subcategories. US leadership in water pollution is reflected

by the fact that Ontario, typically the most progressive province environmentally, is revamping its regulatory system, using the US statute as a model.[24]

The comparable measures that do exist suggest that the US has
a better record on water pollution control. For instance, the elaborate, statutory-based programs on municipal sewage treatment seem
to have paid off. By 1988, 71% of the US population was served by
municipal wastewater treatment, while only 58% of the Canadian
population was. When analysed by level of treatment, the US record
is even more favourable. Of the US population, 58% is served by
facilities with at least secondary treatment, whereas only 37% of the
Canadian population is served by similar facilities.[25] It should be
noted that Quebec has lagged far behind other provinces in this area,
and facilities currently under construction in Quebec should significantly improve the sewage treatment record in Canada.

One area where there has been substantial co-operation between
the two nations is water pollution in the Great Lakes. Both nations
signed the Great Lakes Water Quality Agreement of 1972, to be implemented under the auspices of the International Joint Commission.
Implementation of the agreement has revealed differences in the two
countries' records. As a result of its larger population and industrial
activity, the US contributes far more pollution to the Great Lakes
than does Canada. But the US has been significantly more aggressive
in trying to control its effluents. For example, the US states' limit
for phosphorus in detergents, a major source of Great Lakes pollution, is more than four times more stringent than the comparable
Canadian standard.[26] Pulp mills in the US are required to have secondary effluent treatment, whereas mills in Ontario are not. As of
April, 1989, only six of 27 Ontario mills had secondary treatment.[27]
The US has more rigorous and comprehensive requirements for the
pre-treatment of industrial wastes discharged into municipal systems.[28]

Data on water pollution also provide an opportunity to test one
of the most common criticisms of American environmental programs. Analysts have repeatedly denounced the "implementation
gap" in American regulation – the gap between regulatory requirements and the actions of polluters.[29] However, the record suggests
this characterization is more myth than fact, at least when compared
to Canada. In the Great Lakes area, US compliance rates for both
municipal and industrial sources are approximately 90%. In contrast,
Canadian municipal compliance rates are between 40% and 50%, and
industrial compliance rates are even worse, between 30% and 40%.[30]
Differences in compliance definitions make only the most general
comparisons possible with these aggregate figures. But when the

Great Lakes Water Quality Board analysed an indicator for which there was consistent data – compliance with the Agreement's phosphorus effluent benchmark – the same disparity emerged. Forty-eight per cent of US sources met the benchmark, compared to 29% in Canada.[31]

Thus, while Canada's record on air pollution seemed marginally better than the US one, the US water pollution control record surpasses Canada's by a larger margin.

PESTICIDES

The basic structure of pesticide regulation in Canada and the US is similar. In both nations, pesticides are regulated through two main approaches. The "front-end" approach is based on controlling the introduction of new products into the marketplace. In the US, the Federal Insecticide, Fungicide, and Rodenticide Act (FIFRA) prohibits the sale of pesticides unless they are registered with the federal government.[32] In Canada, a similar restriction is imposed by the Pest Control Products Act (PCPA).[33] Jurisdiction over pesticide regulation, however, is substantially different in the two countries. In the US, pesticides are regulated by the Environmental Protection Agency; in Canada, they are regulated by Agriculture Canada, although Health and Welfare Canada also plays an important role. Under a 1982 interdepartmental agreement, Health and Welfare assesses the safety of pesticides, and Agriculture determines whether the identified risks are "acceptable."[34]

Front-end statutes give both governments the authority to remove chemicals from the market when new information raises health, safety, or environmental concerns. In the US, FIFRA gives EPA the authority to remove pesticides from the market if they are found to present an unreasonable risk-benefit balance. Like the US statute, the Canadian PCPA allows the Minister of Agriculture to remove a product from the market when "the safety of the control product or its merit or value for its intended purpose is no longer acceptable to him."[35]

The second, "back-end" approach is the regulation of food quality through restrictions on food adulteration. The 1954 amendments to the Federal Food, Drug, and Cosmetic Act require EPA to set quantitative limits, called "tolerances," on the amount of pesticide residues in food. In Canada, similar restrictions are imposed by Health and Welfare Canada under the Food and Drugs Act.

While the regulatory frameworks in the two countries are very similar, two important differences give Canadian regulators a small theoretical advantage. First, the EPA must weigh the benefits of pesticide use against the risks, but Canadian regulators do not. While this difference in law is significant, in practice, Canadian regulators typically perform risk-benefit analyses anyway.[36] Second, Canadian manufacturers must demonstrate that their product is effective as well as safe, while US law has no such efficacy requirement. In some cases, this may lead to greater restrictions on pesticide use in Canada.

Policy outcomes in the area of pesticides show an appreciable amount of convergence between the two nations. In the "front end" regulation of pesticide use, the two countries have taken similar actions in eight of the ten high-profile pesticide controversies since 1970. In the other two cases, the US has gone further on one and Canada has gone further on another.[37] However, a slight edge can be granted to the US because it acted first in seven cases, with Canada responding. In one case (dinoseb) the timing was nearly identical. In the other two cases (captan and alachlor) Canada took action before the US; both cases arose early in the Reagan administration when the pesticide regulatory machinery was in its early stages.[38]

When evaluating the back-end of pesticide regulation – limits on the amount of pesticide residues in food – there is also a large amount of convergence, but in this case a definite edge for regulatory stringency goes to Canada. Of the 775 cases where the two countries limit the same pesticide in the same food, for example alar on apples, Canadian and US tolerances are equivalent in 465, or 60% of the cases. Canadian tolerances are more stringent in 298, or 38.5% of the cases, while American tolerances are more stringent in only 12, or 1.5% of the cases.[39] While the US record on front-end pesticide regulation is among the world's strongest, it is out of step with that of most other advanced countries, where residue limits are more similar to Canada's.[40]

ENVIRONMENTAL IMPACT ASSESSMENT

The US National Environmental Policy Act, enacted in 1970, is renowned throughout the developed world for its rigorous requirements for environmental impact statements (EIS), Section 102(2)(C) requires that an EIS be performed for "every recommendation or report on proposals for legislation and other major federal actions significantly affecting the quality of the human environment." Citizens have the right to sue the government to enforce compliance, and courts have rigorously enforced the requirement. In the early 1970s, the standing joke in the halls of the US bureaucracies was that when Moses needed to cross the Red Sea, God would agree to part the waters only after Moses performed an environmental assessment.[41]

Until recently, Canadian impact assessment requirements have been far less rigorous. Although attracted to the NEPA model of environmental impact assessment, Canadian governments consistently rejected the accompanying legalism. The federal government, for instance, historically opposed placing EIA requirements into a statute, because they thought it would undermine the flexibility of the process.[42] In late 1973, the federal Cabinet in Canada established the Environmental Assessment and Review Process (EARP). In response to criticisms about the informality of the process. EARP was issued as a "Guidelines Order" in 1984 under the authority of the Government Organization Act. However, the 1984 changes failed to address many of EARP's perceived shortcomings. In particular, the legal status of the Guidelines was questionable; it was generally assumed that they "had no legal force to ensure compliance from intransigent departments."[43]

As a result of a combination of events in recent years, the EARP process is undergoing profound changes. In two recent cases, at the request of environmental groups Canadian courts have intervened to block the construction of dams because the federal government did not follow its own Cabinet guidelines on environmental impact assessment. As a result of the legal uncertainty generated by these cases, and stong public pressures for more rigorous environmental assessments, the federal government tabled legislation in June 1990 to incorporate EIA into a statute. If passed, Canada's impact assessment requirements may become as stringent as those south of the border.

Comparing policy outcomes under the two systems is extremely difficult. It would seem that many more full-blown impact assessments are performed in the US than in Canada, even when taking into account the larger size of the US. US federal agencies perform approximately 424 formal environmental-impact statements each year.[44] Since 1973, Canada has completed a total of 35 panel reviews under the auspices of the Federal Environmental Assessment Review Office (FEARO).[45] Many more initial environmental assessments are performed by individual agencies in Canada, but these are typically not nearly as elaborate and formal as NEPA statements. While the impact on policy decisions of these different systems is uncertain, the American impact assessment requirements thus far certainly have been more rigorous, and appear to have generated more assessment activity.

CONCLUSION

These four areas of environmental policy reveal a complex pattern. There are no major differences in the two nations' legal authority to regulate the behaviour causing environmental problems, despite fundamental differences in regulatory style. Certainly there are important differences in regulatory frameworks, with the Canadian system being both more decentralized and discretionary. In many cases, Canadian regulators are simply granted regulatory authority, whereas American statutes specify the rules themselves, or explicitly require regulators to take particular actions. For example, Canadian auto emission standards are established by the Minister of Transport under a broad grant of authority by the Motor Vehicle Safety Act, while in the US the standards are actually written into the legislation by Congress in the Clean Air Act.

When analysing what the two nations do with the authority – the policy outcomes – the picture becomes far more complex. In the air pollution case, there has been recent convergence in auto emission standards and acid rain programs, but Canada has been marginally more successful at reducing emissions and improving air quality. In the area of water pollution, the US record appears to be substantially stronger. In the case of pesticides, the US has been slightly stronger on front-end regulation, and Canada stronger in the regulation of food residues. On environmental impact assessment, American requirements historically have been more rigorous.

Given these differences, it is hard to describe the overall pattern as one of convergence, although there are some striking examples of that phenomenon. It would be more accurate to conclude that there is an *absence of patterned divergence*. In some cases, the US has gone further, in others Canada has. Based on these four areas, on balance, the two countries' environmental records seem to be roughly comparable. Of course, there are a number of additional areas of environmental policy that need to be compared before a more confident assessment can be made. It is possible that after a more comprehensive analysis, one country's record may emerge as more favourable.

The task of this analysis was to compare records, not explain the observed patterns. But it is useful to mention briefly several of the most important explanatory forces because they do have implications for the overall assessment. First, because of Canada's lower population density and smaller number of important sources of pollution, in some respects its regulatory task is easier. For example, Canada has had more success in reducing air pollution despite the fact that its regulatory requirements have not been more stringent, and, in fact, historically have been far less stringent in the notable case of automobile emissions. Canadian regulators attribute this difference to the fact that it has been much easier for them to target the small number of large, poorly controlled sources, and even to provide them with financial assistance if necessary.[46] This difference in the severity of the environmental problem is perhaps the major reason why US industry spends far more on pollution control than Canadian industry, but has not been comparatively more successful in reducing pollution. In economic terms, the marginal costs of achieving a given level of environmental quality are apparently significantly higher in the US than in Canada.

Second, one of the most important forces behind Canadian environmental regulation is in fact the influence of American environmental regulation. Despite the fears of environmental critics of the Free Trade Agreement, US influence on Canadian environmental regulation has on notable occasions been very positive. For instance, the US-dominated North American automobile market has encouraged Canada to adopt the more stringent US emission standards, producing one of the most notable cases of convergence between the two nations. Another prominent example is the pesticide alar, used as a growth regulator on apples but found to cause cancer in laboratory animals. The product was removed from the Canadian market, against the wishes of Canadian regulators, largely because of the regulatory scandal that erupted in the US in early 1989.[47]

While there are many more explanatory factors at work, these two factors strengthen the American record. Some of Canada's notable successes come from the fact that it confronts a comparatively easier regulatory problem. If Canada committed the same level of economic resources as its neighbour to the south, its environment would be much cleaner. Moreover, some of the cases of convergence are also examples of American leadership and influence on Canadian policy. Thus, the Canadian environmental record is strong in some cases *because* the American record is strong.

One final fact should be mentioned. While the two factors noted above create a more favourable image of the American record, Canada has been forced to suffer environmental harm from pollution generated in the United States far more so than vice versa, with acid rain and Great Lakes water pollution being the most prominent cases. This is unquestionably a major flaw in the US record. However deserving of criticism, US culpability in Canadian environmental damage should not make Canadians complacent about their own contributions to the degradation of the shared environment. In particular, the US appears to have been more aggressive in addressing Great Lakes water pollution.

How does Canada's environmental performance compare with the US? Certainly, Canadians have nothing to be ashamed of; this comparison suggests that the Canadian environmental record compares favourably with the American record in some areas. But the analysis also reveals areas where the US performance exceeds Canada's. The pervasive Canadian perception of environmental superiority towards the US is clearly unjustified. Even when compared to the benchmark of US policy, there is still a great deal of room for improvement in Canada's environmental performance. Canada must redouble its efforts if it intends to become "the industrial world's most environmentally friendly country" by the turn of the century.

TABLE 1 Government Spending on the Environment
1986 Fiscal Year, Millions of Dollars

	US	Canada
Federal Environment Budget		
Parks Included	$4,451[1]	520[2]
Parks Excluded	3,446	231
Total Federal Budget	1,072,773	111,227
Per Cent Environment of Total		
Parks Included	0.41%	0.46%
Parks Excluded	0.32%	0.21%
Subnational Environment Spending	5,283[3]	699[4]
Subnational Total	361,897	78,513
Per Cent Environment of Total	1.46%	0.89%
National Environment Total		
Parks Included	9,734	1219
Parks Excluded	8,729	930
National Budget Total	1,434,670	189,740
Per Cent Environment of Total		
Parks Included	0.68%	0.64%
Parks Excluded	0.61%	0.49%

1. Figures for EPA and total US budget from Executive Office of the President, Office of Management and Budget, *Historical Tables – Budget of the U.S. Government: Fiscal Year 1988* (Washington, DC: Government Printing Office, 1987). Figures for the National Parks Service are for 1985, and are from Norman Vig and Michael Kraft, eds. *Environmental Policy in the 1990s* (Washington, DC: CQ Press, 1990), appendix 3.

2. Canadian figures for total federal budget and Environment Canada budget are from *Public Accounts of Canada*, FY 85-6. The figure for Environment Canada excludes the Atmospheric Environment Service. Amount of AES and Parks comes from *Environment Canada Annual Report, 1986*.

3. Spending by the states derived from Council of State Governments, *Resource Guide to State Environmental Management* (Lexington, KY: Council of State Governments, 1988).

4. Provincial spending on the environment includes the ministries of Environment in Ontario, Quebec, Alberta, and British Columbia. Figures derived from Public Accounts of the individual provinces.

Table 2: North American Air Quality Trends

		Canada	US
Sulphur dioxide	(ppb)		
	1975	11	15.4
	1987	5	8.4
	% change	-55%	-45%
Carbon monoxide	(ppm)		
	1975	1.9	11.96
	1987	1.0	6.88
	% change	-47%	-42%
Ozone	(ppb)		
	1979	15	142
	1987	16	129
	% change	+7%	-9%
Nitrogen dioxide	(ppm)		
	1977	31	29
	1987	21	25
	% change	-32%	-14%
Total Suspended Particulates	($\%g/m^3$)		
	1975	65.9	61.9
	1987	48.0	49.4
	% change	-27%	-20%
Lead	(mg/m^3)		
	1975	.00055	1.04
	1987	.00010	0.12
	% change	-82%	-88%

Methodological note: Different measurement methods are used. All Canadian figures, and US figures for nitrogen dioxide and sulphur dioxide, are annual arithmetic means. US figures for carbon monoxide are based on the second highest readings for 8-hour periods; those for TSP are annual geometric means; ozone counts are the second highest daily one-hour maximums; and figures for lead are maximum quarterly averages.

NOTES

Research for this chapter was funded by the Social Sciences and Humanities Research Council of Canada. I would like to thank Jeff Waatainen and Lee Tsuan Lau for research assistance, and Kathryn Harrison, Peter Nemetz, and Tony Hodge for extensive comments on an earlier draft.

1. Ministry of the Environment, *A Framework for Discussion on the Environment* (Ottawa: Ministry of Supply and Services, 1990).

2. Ronald Brickman, Sheila Jasanoff, and Thomas Ilgen, *Controlling Chemicals* (Ithaca: Cornell University Press, 1985); David Vogel, *National Styles of Regulation* (Ithaca: Cornell University Press, 1986); Joseph Badaracco, *Loading the Dice: A Five Country Case Study of Vinyl Chloride Regulation* (Cambridge: Harvard Business School Press, 1985); and Lennart Lundqvist, *The Hare and the Tortoise* (Ann Arbor: University of Michigan Press, 1980). For comparative analysis including Canada, see Thomas Ilgen, 'Between Europe and America, Ottawa and the Provinces: Regulating Toxic Substances in Canada', *Canadian Public Policy* 11 (1985): 578-90; Peter Nemetz, W.T. Stanbury, and Fred Thompson, 'Social Regulation in Canada', *Policy Studies Journal* 14 (1986): 580-603; and Peter Nemetz, 'Federal Environmental Regulation in Canada', *Natural Resources Journal* 26 (1986): 552-608.

3. It should be noted that there is environment-related spending in other federal agencies in both countries.

4. The 0.47% figure given above already excludes the Atmospheric Environment Service, which is less directly related to environmental protection.

5. David Bratton and Gary Rutledge, 'Pollution Abatement and Control Expenditures,1985-88', *Survey of Current Business* (November 1990): 37. Figures are for 1986.

6. American figures are from Gary Rutledge and Nikolaos Stergioulas, 'Plant and Equipment Expenditures by Business for Pollution Abatement, 1987 and Planned 1988', *Survey of Current Business* (November 1988): 26-9. Canadian figures are

from Statistics Canada, *Analysis of the Categories of Capital Investment, 1985 to 1987,* Discussion Paper, November 1989, 15.

7. See R. Shep Melnick, *Regulation and the Courts: The Case of the Clean Air Act* (Washington, DC: Brookings Institution, 1983).

8. In 1988, the Clean Air Act was essentially incorporated into the Canadian Environmental Protection Act.

9. These four cases are chlor-alkali plants, asbestos mining and milling operations, secondary lead smelters, and vinyl chloride plants. See Peter Nemetz, 'Federal Environmental Regulation in Canada', 557.

10. Emissions from vehicles in use are still the responsibility of the provinces.

11. M.A.H. Franson, R.T. Franson, and A.R. Lucas, *Environmental Standards*, ECA83-SP/1, Edmonton: Environment Council of Alberta, 1982, 115.

12. Nemetz, 'Federal Environmental Regulation in Canada', 559.

13. Information Release, Canadian Council of Ministers of the Environment, 830-335/022, Charlottetown, Prince Edward Island, 19 October 1989.

14. Canadian House of Commons, Subcommittee on Acid Rain, *Time Lost: A Demand for Action on Acid Rain* (Ottawa, 1984), 41.

15. Ironically, Canada made this move in part because it realized that some of its air pollution regulations were less stringent than their American counterparts. See George Hoberg, 'Sleeping With an Elephant: The American Influence on Canadian Environmental Protection," *Journal of Public Policy* 11, 1 (1991): 107-32.

16. The Canada objective was stated as a 50% reduction below allowable 1980 levels; the number below actual levels is closer to 37%. The US emitted 25.7 million tonnes of sulphur dioxide in 1980, so the statute calls for a 39% reduction below that level.

17. US Congressional Research Service, *Canada's Progress on Acid Rain Control: Shifting Gears or Stalled in Neutral?* 88-353 ENR, 20 April 1988, 5-7.

18. Information on these European programs comes from David Vogel, 'Environmental Policy in Europe and Japan', in Norman Vig and Michael Kraft, eds, *Environmental Policy in the 1990s* (Washington, DC: CQ Press, 1990), 273-4.

19. This summary is based on Helen Ingram and Dean Mann, 'Preserving the Clean Water Act: The Appearance of Environmental Victory', in Norman Vig and Michael Kraft, *Environmental Policy in the 1980s: Reagan's New Agenda* (Washington, DC: CQ Press, 1984); and Frederick Anderson, Daniel Mandelker, and A. Dan Tarlock, *Environmental Protection: Law and Policy* (Boston: Little, Brown, 1984), chapter IV.

20. Despite the expiry of the deadline and the patent infeasibility of the 1985 zero discharge goal, it was maintained in the preamble to the statute when Congress revised the law in 1987.

21. Walter Rosenbaum, *Environmental Politics and Policy* (Washington, DC: CQ Press, 1985), 167-73.

22. Nemetz, 'Federal Environmental Regulation in Canada', 554-6.

23. *Ibid.*

24. Hoberg, 'Sleeping with an Elephant'.

25. The figures are from US Council on Environmental Quality, *Environmental Quality: Twentieth Annual Report*, 454. The Canadian figures are from a memo to the author from F. Cadoret, Environment Canada, 18 January 1991.

26. Great Lakes Water Quality Board, *1989 Report on Great Lakes Water Quality*, Report to the International Joint Commission, Presented at Hamilton, Ontario, October 1989, 35, 19.

27. Ontario Ministry of the Environment, *Interim Pollution Reduction Strategy for Ontario Kraft Mills*, April 1989.

28. Great Lakes Water Quality Board, *1989 Report*, 17.

29. See for instance Keith Hawkins, *Environment and Enforcement* (Oxford: Oxford University Press, 1984), and Eugene Bardach and Robert Kagan, *Going by the Book: The Problem of Regulatory Unreasonableness* (Philadelphia: Temple University Press, 1982).

30. Great Lakes Water Quality Board, *1989 Report*, 6-12.

31. *Ibid.*

32. 7 USC. 136 *et seq.* For an overview of the US regulatory framework, see US General Accounting Office, *Pesticides: EPA's Formidable Task to Assess and Regulate their Risks*, RCED-86-125 (Washington, DC: GAO, 1986).

33. Pest Control Products Act, 1968-69, c. 50, s. 1. For an overview of the Canadian regulatory framework, see J.F. Castrilli and Toby Vigod, *Pesticides in Canada: An Examination of Federal Law and Policy*, Study Paper, Protection of Life Series (Ottawa: Law Reform Commission of Canada, 1987).

34. Alachlor Review Board, *The Report of the Alachlor Review Board* (Ottawa: 1987), 23.

35. PCP Regulations, s. 20.

36. See for instance George Hoberg, 'Risk, Science, and Politics: Alachlor Regulation in Canada and the United States', *Canadian Journal of Political Science* 23 (June 1990): 257-78.

37. The cases are alachlor, aldrin/dieldrin, captan, daminozide, DBCP, DDT, dinoseb, EDB, heptachlor/chlordane, and 2,4,5-T. Canada has banned alachlor and the US has not; the US has banned dinoseb and Canada has not. In the remaining cases the outcomes are highly similar.

38. See George Hoberg, 'Reaganism, Pluralism, and the Politics of Pesticide Regulation', *Policy Sciences* 23 (1990): 257-89.

39. Compare *US Code of Federal Regulations*, Volume 40, Section 180, with *Canadian Food and Drug Regulations*, Division 15, Table 11.

40. Based on interviews with government officials in the US and Canada.

41. William Kennedy, 'Environmental Impact Assessments in North America, Western Europe:What Has Worked Where, How, and Why', *International Environmental Reporter* 11 (13 April 1988): 257-63.

42. Terry Fenge and L. Graham Smith, 'Reforming the Environmental Assessment and Review Process', *Canadian Public Policy* 12 (1986): 596-605.

43. *Ibid.*, 603.

44. Based on the average for 1987-89, from Council on Environment Quality, *Environmental Quality–Twentieth Annual Report* (Washington, DC: Executive Office of the President, 1990), 439.

45. Interview, John Mathers, Pacific Western and Northern Region, FEARO, 29 January 1991.

46. Confidential interviews, government officials. As an example of the importance of financial assistance, see the information on the smelter modernization program in House of Commons, Special Committee on Acid Rain, Report of the Special Committee on Acid Rain, 2nd Session, 33rd Parliament, Ottawa, September 1988.

47. These two examples are indicative of a much larger pattern explored in Hoberg, 'Sleeping with an Elephant'.

References & Further Reading

Terry Fenge and L. Graham Smith, 'Reforming the Environmental Assessment and Review Process', *Canadian Public Policy* 12 (1986): 596-605.

George Hoberg, 'Reaganism, Pluralism and the Politics of Pesticide Regulation', *Policy Sciences* 23 (1990): 257-89.

—, 'Risk, Science, and Politics: Alachlor Regulation in Canada and the United States', *Canadian Journal of Political Science* 23 (June 1990): 257-78.

—, 'Sleeping with an Elephant: The American Influence on Canadian Environmental Protection', *Journal of Public Policy* 10, 1 (1991): . 107-32.

Thomas Ilgen, 'Between Europe and America, Ottawa and the Provinces: Regulating Toxic Substances in Canada', *Canadian Public Policy* 11 (1985): 578-90.

R. Shep Melnick, *Regulation and the Courts: The Case of the Clean Air Act* (Washington, DC: Brookings, 1983).

Peter Nemetz, 'Federal Environmental Regulation in Canada', *Natural Resources Journal* 26 (1986): 552-608.

Norman Vig and Michael Kraft, eds, *Environmental Policy in the 1990s* (Washington, DC: CQ Press, 1990).

David Vogel, *National Styles of Regulation* (Ithaca: Cornell University Press, 1986).

Part Two: Constitutional Architecture

FRANÇOIS ROCHER

Dividing the Spoils: American and Canadian Federalism*

Canada and the United States both have federal political systems characterized by a distribution of powers between the central order of the state (Ottawa and Washington) and local governments (provinces, states, and local bodies). As Thomas J. Anton notes,

> *Federalism* is a system of rules for the division of public responsibilities among a number of autonomous governmental agencies. These rules define the scope of authority available to the autonomous agencies — which can do what — and they provide a framework to govern relationships between and among agencies. The agencies remain autonomous in that they levy their own taxes and select their own officials, but they are also linked together by rules that govern common actions.[1]

While power is divided in all states, to a certain degree, between orders of government, federal states differ from unitary states by the fact that the division of powers is inscribed in a constitution; it cannot be unilaterally amended by one order. Hence, "the provincial/state governments are... not subordinate to the central governments; instead both levels of government are subordinate to the constitution."[2] The authority enjoyed by each order of government is inscribed in the constitution and the central order of government cannot appropriate powers which it was not initially assigned, as interpreted by the courts.

---

*   Translated by Richard Nimijean.

A federal state is therefore distinguished from unitary states by the steadfast nature — at least legally — of the division of powers between the different orders of government. It also differs from supranational bodies, like the United Nations or the European Economic Community, because of the political autonomy possessed by the central government. Decisions taken by Ottawa or Washington directly affect local bodies which must adhere to them, insofar as these decisions lie within the jurisdictions provided for in the respective constitutions of the two states.

While similarities between the American and Canadian federal systems can be detected, there are many noticeable differences. From the outset, it must be stated that the Canadian provinces are far more significant political and economic entities than most American states. Their budgets, for example, are significantly greater. The expenditures of the Ontario government, the most populated province and one of the richest, equals approximately one-quarter of the central government's expenditures. By way of comparison, South Carolina's budget at the beginning of the 1990s was about $5 billion for a population of 2.6 million people, while Alberta's was about $12 billion for a population of the same size. The total expenditures of Canadian provincial administrations are slightly less than those of the central administration. Moreover, American federalism is reputed to be more centralizing than Canadian federalism. The American states, while still possessing significant financial resources, nevertheless enjoy far less autonomy vis-à-vis the central government than do Canadian provinces. The division of powers is far less vague in Canada than in the United States. In the United States, Congress has become the representative of regional interests while in Canada this role has traditionally been played by the provincial governments. There are strong tendencies toward centralization in both countries, but this has partially been challenged in Canada, granted with mitigated success, largely but not exclusively by the Quebec government. Intergovernmental relations in the two countries are rooted in very different dynamics.

The goal of this chapter is to present the similarities and differences of these two federal states. In part they are explained by historical, political, social, and economic factors. Despite certain resemblances, these two federal systems have put forth different visions of the nature of relations which must be maintained between the central and local governments.

1. TWO FEDERAL CONSTITUTIONS

Historical developments explain the adoption of a federal regime by Canada and the United States. Thus it is worthwhile to consider the intentions and circumstances which marked the drafting of the Canadian and American constitutions, for the political conditions which led to the writing of these constitutions inform us about the relationships which were to be established between the different orders of government.

It was the United States which first adopted federalism as a means of governance. The experience of American confederation was characterized by its progressiveness and by the explicit desire to neutralise Great Britain's vague aspirations for American territory.[3] Well before 1781, the majority of states were in a position to carry out important political and social reforms allowing for the reorganization of their own political institutions. From the moment of the Declaration of Independence in 1776, almost all adopted new constitutions which replaced colonial charters. In effect, this did not establish a federal regime. Rather, the principle of autonomy for each of the thirteen American colonies from Great Britain was asserted. Each state maintained its sovereignty, independence, and all powers which were not formally delegated to the continental Congress. The latter had significant room to manoeuvre in areas of prime importance — like defense, foreign policy, treaty-making — but the operations of Congress required the unanimous approval of the independent states.[4] It took until 1789 for the Confederation of 1781 to be replaced by a truly federal regime.

The adopted system of government was a compromise between two visions of what would become the new American state: a loose association of sovereign states or a unitary state. One of the most important criticisms directed towards the confederal experience concerned the absence of coercive powers, that is the power to establish laws and sanctions. These were to be accompanied by the possibility of raising financial resources via taxes collected directly from citizens. Another deficiency of confederation was its inability to regulate trade, to prevent trade wars between states, to establish common external tariffs, and to establish a common currency.[5]

Problems relating to defense and foreign affairs dominated the debates of the Fathers of Confederation. The final compromise established the supremacy of the national government over the different states. The political imperatives of the time favoured the centralization of powers, given the fact that the national government was better situated than each state to act in face of a common threat. It was also agreed to grant the central government important economic levers, including the power to issue money and establish its value, to take loans against the national credit, to set and collect taxes, to regulate internal and external trade, etc. It must be noted that the American constitution did not explicitly establish the base principles of federalism, for the division of powers was not exhaustive. According to Anton, "the most important reason for the persistence of federalism as a political issue in the United States is that spheres of autonomous action lack precise definition."[6] Hence, the powers of the states are poorly defined insofar as residual powers are concerned. The consequence of this imprecision is that the demarcation of powers belonging respectively to the central government and the states is difficult to establish. Nevertheless, it is the states which control local governments. This is also the case for health and welfare, notably public assistance, unemployment insurance, and family allowances, even though the central government largely administers social security. The states also have responsibility to administer police and justice, transportation, communications, and many areas related to the protection of the environment.

While at first glance it appears that the American constitution clearly defines the jurisdictions of the central government, the Tenth Amendment adopted in 1791 specified that the powers not delegated to the United States were reserved for the states respectively or for the people. Even though its wording is quite straightforward, it opened the door to many disputes. Thus the meaning of the initial division of powers remains highly ambiguous. On the other hand, several constitutional amendments helped limit the power of the states: the Fourteenth, which constitutionalized citizens' rights in matters of freedom, property, legal procedures and the protection of law; the Fifteenth, which prevented racial discrimination in elections; and the Nineteenth, which gave women the right to vote.[7] Moreover, despite the fact that article I, section 8 lists the powers of Congress, it also opens the door to all extensions of these, destroying in one fell swoop the significance of the enumeration. It in fact specified that Congress is empowered to make all laws which it deems "necessary and proper" to execute the listed powers, reserving the other areas for the states.[8]

All in all, the American constitution identifies the powers of the central government without doing so for local governments. The only precision concerns that which they are not authorized to do. In that way, the powers of Congress are not exclusive and states can legislate as long as their actions do not conflict with decisions taken by a superior authority. Thus there does not exist a clear demarcation of responsibilities.

Canadian federalism, for its part, has different origins from that of the United States. It dates back to the constitution of 1867, the British North America Act. While conceptualized in Canada, it was a law of the United Kingdom and, indeed, constituted the first federal experience of the British Empire. The base principles of federalism are clearly established in the constitutional document. Thus the word "federally" is mentioned in the first paragraph of the preamble to the 1867 Act.[9] It was only in 1931, following the Statute of Westminster, that Canada attained true political sovereignty. As was the case with the United States, Canadian federalism was the result of a compromise between those wishing to establish a unitary state and those wishing to preserve the autonomy of the constituent units of the new state. Adopting the federal form responded to several necessities.

The new political structure sought to meet the economic and political needs of the dominant economic groups as much in the colonies as in the imperial metropolis. In economic terms, the creation of the new state was perceived as an instrument to consolidate public finances and to allow the investments necessary for the integrated economic development of the British colonies in North America, notably with respect to the creation of railways. Many would have preferred that Canada adopt a unitary political system. In not being able to do so, Sir John A. Macdonald, the first Canadian Prime Minister, favoured a strong central government which he hoped would ultimately reduce the provincial governments to the status of administrative bodies comparable to municipalities. At the other extreme, there were those who did not share Macdonald's views and who considered the provinces to be important political communities which should maintain a maximum of autonomy. Canadian federalism was initially justified and debated in terms of the necessity to preserve and develop provinces defined as communities. The necessity of federalism was thus imposed in order to assure the collaboration of the already constituted bodies, notably Lower Canada, where the majority of French Canadians resided, and the Maritime colonies, which had a strong attachment to the United Kingdom.[10]

Canada thus became a state for pragmatic reasons, adopting the federal form on the grounds that it was necessary to come to terms with diverse regional, national, and economic entities. The political and institutional choices which guided the fathers of the federation (falsely labelled confederation) were inspired at once by tradition and the American experience. The constitution took up principles imported from the United Kingdom, namely the necessity to maintain strong executive power and to assign the residual powers to the Crown. Canada, a constitutional monarchy, is governed by a British parliamentary system based on the principles of parliamentary majority, responsible government and the effective control of authority by a Cabinet led by the Prime Minister. The federal form was adopted to reduce the problem created by the presence of profound linguistic and cultural differences in Canada. The idea of using federalism as a system of government was borrowed from the American experience.[11] Nevertheless, having in mind the recent American Civil War, the drafters of the constitution wanted to better demarcate the powers granted to each order of government by favouring a federal model which was much more centralized than that of the United States.

As Donald Smiley noted, during the debates on the adoption of the Canadian constitution, the division of powers did not seem as important an issue as it became afterwards. The Fathers of Confederation rapidly agreed on a division of responsibilities between the Dominion and the provinces which was compatible with the goals of the time, namely military defense, the integrated development of British North America and the maintenance of harmony between English- and French-speaking citizens.[12]

Contrary to the American constitution, Canada's defined the powers granted to the provinces. Hence, articles 91 to 95 established the legislative jurisdictions of each order of government. In general, the principal economic levers were granted to the central government, as was the case with the United States. In this spirit, the central government can use all means of taxation it wishes while provinces only have recourse to direct taxation. The financial needs of the provinces are in part met through federal grants. It must also be noted that many powers are exclusive to each order of government, although articles 94A and 95 establish a few concurrent powers, particularly in the areas of old age pensions, agriculture, and immigration. The provinces can exercise their exclusive authority in the fields, among others, of education, health, municipal institutions, works of a local nature, property and civil rights, natural resources, and the administration of justice. On the other hand, the residual power, that is to say jurisdiction in areas not initially foreseen, belongs to the central government and not the provinces, contrary to the American experience. Moreover, the central government reserved itself the right to establish regulations in accordance with the principle of "peace, order, and good government," particularly with the goal of reacting to situations similar to those which led to the American Civil War. Finally, in aiming to clearly ensure the predominance of the central government and to limit the autonomy of provincial legislation, the constitution conferred upon the former the powers of reservation and disallowance, although today these powers have fallen into disuse. This is how the Canadian constitution, through the multiple limitations on the ability of the provinces to act, established the supremacy of the federal government over the other orders of government.[13]

All in all, while the Canadian and American constitutions differ as to the general organization of the two states, they have in common the establishment of two federal regimes. The federal character is much better defined in the Canadian constitution and the jurisdictions are better defined. Even though a cursory analysis of the constitutional documents could lead one to believe that Canada lives under a much more centralized regime, the practice of federalism has led the two countries to follow rather divergent tendencies. This will now be examined.

2. ON THE PRACTICE OF FEDERALISM

Several factors can explain the opposing tendencies which have characterized the American and Canadian federal experiences and which saw to it that Canada lives in a much more decentralized regime than the drafters of the constitution foresaw, while the opposite applies to the United States.

i) The evolution of constitutional law

A first explanation resides partially in the interpretation of the constitutions by the courts. Until 1949 a British court, the Judicial Committee of the Privy Council, was the final court of appeal for settling disputes between Ottawa and the provinces. It largely ignored the centralizing intentions of the drafters of the constitution, gradually transforming the range of the general and residual powers by interpreting them as an emergency power. It also put forth a narrow interpretation of the central government's power to regulate trade and commerce. In the same way, provincial powers concerning property and civil rights were used to limit Ottawa's efforts to regulate the economy, work conditions, and the stabilisation of personal income.[14] The federation's decentralized nature was accompanied by a judicial recognition of the sovereignty of provincial governments, as well as the federal government, in the spheres of exclusive jurisdiction granted by the constitution. In 1883, the Privy Council adopted the view that provincial governments were not subordinate to the central government, but rather should act in coordination with it. A series of cases gradually put to rest Macdonald's vision of an omnipotent central government. These decisions, however, cannot alone explain the tendency towards decentralization. This was in part also due to the absence of strong political support for the centralist vision. In other words, an important transfer of loyalty on the part of the old communities to the new Dominion created in 1867 never took place.[15] For reasons of a political nature, Canada adopted the classical model of federalism privileging watertight jurisdictions, notably with the goal of reducing national tensions between English and French Canadians. Up to the mid-1940s, a decentralized version of classical federalism evolved.

The increase in state intervention which followed World War II and the establishment of the Supreme Court of Canada as Canada's final court of appeal[16] contributed to the development of a highly centralized vision of the federation. The Supreme Court tended to support federal initiatives, especially in the areas of work laws, trade and commerce, taxation, criminal law, and economic planning. As Kenneth M. Holland notes, "in fact, the Court emerged as the principal institutional brake on province-building, which threatened increasingly to distort the original design of the Constitution Act, 1867."[17] The adoption of the Canadian Charter of Rights and Freedoms at the time of the repatriation of the constitution in 1982 helped reinforce this centralizing tendency, as was the case with the Bill of Rights in the United States, by seeking to increase national integration in part by altering the balance of power in favour of the federal government and in part by developing uniform judicial norms with respect to rights and freedoms.

The situation was considerably different in the United States, as periods of centralization and decentralization varied according to the composition of the Supreme Court. The first judicial interpretations of the American constitution, under the leadership of Chief Justice John Marshall (1801-1835), confirmed the predominance of the central government over the states. The Court opposed state actions and supported federal action, citing the need to unify the country. The fundamental principle justifying this approach was established by the Court and rested upon an interpretation of article I, s.8, which defines the powers of Congress, and which effectively established the supremacy of the latter over the states. As was already mentioned, several amendments followed which reduced the states' ability to act. The majority of guarantees in the Bill of Rights saw to it that the states were submitted to the same constitutional requirements as the federal government. From a federalist perspective, this evolution favoured centralization and the uniformization of law for the states.[18] Subsequent interpretations instead tended to favour the states. Under Chief Justice Roger Taney (1836-64), the Court noticeably supported the states in the areas of inter-state and external trade, police, and health and welfare. Following and up to the mid-1930s, the Court rather put forth a dualist vision of federalism. As Holland notes, "the Tenth Amendment became analogous to the First Amendment, and was read by the Court as saying: 'Congress shall make no law destroying powers that states exercised before ratification of the Constitution.'"[19] While it is difficult to generalize, the Court then oscillated between centralized interpretations, particularly from 1938 to 1975 and from 1985 onward, and decentralized interpretations from 1976 to 1984. As a general rule of thumb, Republican Presidents, as will be seen below, have been favourable to decentralization, contrary to Democratic Presidents. These back-and-forth movements demonstrate the importance of politics and the preferences of the day in the nomination of judges to the Supreme Court, and also reflect the ambiguity of the constitution in the area of the division of powers and the divergent interpretations of the Tenth Amendment.

The different practices of federalism are not due solely to successive judicial interpretations. On the contrary, they also reflect the adoption of much deeper orientations, as much in Canada as in the United States, than specific institutional rearrangements in each land.

ii) The American experience

The two world wars and especially the crisis of the 1930s led the central government to mobilize considerable resources for the restoration of economic growth and to ensure that full employment was reached. Washington thus could occupy areas by arguing that it was better equipped both economically and judicially to effectively and judiciously act. The increase in American state intervention after WW II favoured the reaching of cooperative agreements between Washington and subordinate governments. Broad goals were articulated by the central government while the implementation of programs, their organization, and management were performed by the states in exchange for grants. The central government adopted a series of laws allowing it to regulate numerous fields (transportation, environmental protection, workplace safety, health, education, energy, etc.) which were traditionally reserved for the states. The United States government thus subscribed to a "Regulatory Federalism" view, which is less compatible with cooperative federalism and even less so with dualist federalism.[20]

In this context, it is not surprising to note that grants to local governments increased more rapidly than any other element of the national budget. In fact, national grants constitute the greatest source of revenue for the states and municipalities, surpassing even sales

and property taxes. Numerous programs have become intergovernmental, meaning that, increasingly, fewer of them can be operated
solely by one order of government. According to Anton,

> Washington increasingly has acted as a banker for state and
> local governments operating national programs; national gov-
> ernment employment has been essentially stable for two dec-
> ades, while state and local personnel have tripled in number.
> The confluence of the social empowerment state with the com-
> ponent state has led to a practical, if not theoretical, division
> of responsibilities.[21]

That is how American federalism came to be characterized by a
great centralization of decision-making while the roles of lower levels
are confined to the management and organization of state activities,
which of course varies enormously from one state to the next.

The centralized nature of American federalism is reflected in the
distribution of government revenues. Hence, since the end of the
1940s, the different taxes and duties collected by the national government account for nearly 70% of all government revenues. This
dominant position is explained by the state activism which marked
the post-war period in the areas of social services, social security,
education, transportation, etc. From this, the increase in national
assistance to state and local governments has allowed the latter to
considerably increase their services without having to proportionately
increase their taxes.[22] As one government document notes,

> in 1987, the federal government made 57.3 percent of all direct
> expenditures and produced 56.6 percent of total own-source
> revenues. State government, on the other hand, accounted for
> 17.4 percent of direct expenditures but raised 24.7 percent of
> total own-source revenues, indicating that it was transferring a
> large share of its revenues to other governments.[23]

These multiple transfers reflect the complexity of American federalism and helped see to it that local units like municipalities have
a greater and greater tendency to directly address the central government without first going through the states.

It is important to note that compared to Canada, the federal government's grants are proportionately more conditional, which is an
indicator of centralization. Hence, there is less recourse to block
grants than formula grants, allowing the federal government to reach
a specific clientele in sectors like education, employment or transportation, or to project grants based on the principle of competition

between bidders for the realization of broad goals. The federal government was able to strengthen these mechanisms of intervention by setting indirect conditions, when grants are bestowed, which do not necessarily have any direct relation with the goals of financial aid awarded to governments. Edmond Orban notes that this technique, known as cross-cutting, was largely used in the Johnson era. For example, in the 1964 Civil Rights Bill, nobody could be excluded for reasons of race, culture or national origin from a program funded by the federal government. Washington also uses the technique of cross-over sanctions to impose financial sanctions if the recipient government does not respect the established demands. Thus, in 1974, the federal Transport Department was not allowed to approve new road projects in the states that did not respect the speed limits established for the city or county for energy conservation purposes.[24]

Moreover, the evolution of local government revenues shows that they increasingly depend on the financial aid of the central government. In effect, federal grants represented more than a quarter of state and local government expenditures at the beginning of the 1980s; however, they decreased appreciably under President Reagan, reaching about 20% by the end of the decade.[25] Federal aid to local governments (counties, municipalities, townships, school districts, and special districts) obviously varies enormously from one sector to another. Amongst the five principal state functions, federal government aid in 1987 corresponded respectively to about 13% of education expenditures, 25% for highways, 60% for health and hospitals, 66% for public welfare, and 84% for housing and community development.[26] All in all, federal grants constitute slightly more than 10% of government expenditures, a clear regression in relation to the preceding decade when they were 17%.[27]

The distribution of employment between the different orders of government can also be an indicator of centralization. In 1987 the federal government only had 20% of total government employees, versus 23% for the states and 57% for local governments.[28] This could lead one to believe that there is strong decentralization, but it is important to consider where the most important decisions are taken and by whom. Thus, many functions performed by local governments do not possess a comparable importance to those performed by the federal bureaucratic apparatus insofar as they are increasingly executed in a framework where the federal government has a growing role.[29]

Given the importance of the federal government at the financial level, the control it exerts on the other orders of government, the diversity of economic and social conditions in each state, the configuration of political institutions which allows regional interests to be adequately represented within central institutions by the Senate, and by the absence of party discipline which in effect liberates politicians from partisan constraints, American federalism has a high degree of centralization. State and local governments, while important in the distribution of services, are not significant players compared to the central government and those who sit in it.

Attempts at decentralization under the Republican administrations of Nixon and particularly Reagan, better known as the "new federalism," sought more to relieve the central administration of the budgetary weight of the programs it financed than to better respect the principles of federalism.[30] Hence, faced with the growth of the state, the Republican strategy was relatively straightforward. For Richard Nixon, it was sufficient to return power and resources to the states. This new strategy implied two major changes. First, a multitude of programs were consolidated and second, block grants were transferred to state and local governments, which then had to decide on the way to use the funds now at their disposition: "following these principles, the Nixon administration laid before Congress a series of New Federalism proposals calling for revenue sharing, consolidation, and devolution in several functional areas."[31] For Ronald Reagan, budgetary problems called for a revision in the practice of federalism. A return to the principles of classical federalism would allow for a response to the confusion caused by the intervention of the central government and of regional or local bodies. While the new federalism of Nixon sought to start up a system better suited for contemporary challenges, Reagan's was guided by his desire to reduce the role of the state and especially to fight the deficit. While Reagan's vision was not entirely followed by Congress, this new federalism still resulted in a significant reduction in the number of programs, block grants, and authorized expenditures. His desire to revise the division of responsibilities was not entirely followed up, even though the participation of the national government in the financing of social programs was clearly reduced.

Finally, in a recent article, David B. Walker describes the American system as a "permissive federalism" insofar as this expression "pretty well captures the systemic dilemma of states and localities because it underscores the basic constitutional, political, representational, and political ascendancy of the national government, its institutions, and its processes."[32] This expression clearly reminds us that American federalism is always open to certain forms of decentralization and to the initiatives of the states and local bodies, but at the discretion of, or with permission from, national authorities. Hence, "permissive federalism" reflects the centralist tendency of American federalism and the "nation-centered system."

iii) The experience of Canadian federalism

As was the case with the United States, the Great Depression and WW II forced governments to address the new roles which they would be called upon to play. The financial crisis which accompanied the economic crisis started a debate on the division of taxation powers and the federal government's ability to act. A centralizing current took shape, arguing that the allocation of powers in 1867 no longer allowed new needs to be adequately met. Nevertheless, responsibility for activities linked to public welfare was held by the provinces which, to meet their obligations, had to count on conditional grants from the central government. Some were strongly opposed to any transfer of powers to Ottawa, either claiming the autonomy of the provinces (Quebec), or refusing any redistribution of wealth from the wealthy provinces to the poor provinces (Ontario). WW II intensified the centralizing pressures, notably in the field of taxation. The reconstruction era and the new role the state was called upon to play, inspired by Keynesian principles, required a reform of Canadian federalism. Given the inability to agree on the constitutional front, the adoption of new state functions was realized by way of collaboration between the two orders of government. Thus the response to problems posed by federalism took the form of intergovernmental accords in the areas of tax collection and shared cost programs. Given this, Canadian federalism gradually abandoned the classical vision of each order of government being sovereign in its jurisdictions, to be substituted by a cooperative federalism more open to overlapping and to informal compromises. This centralizing swing was therefore undertaken for pragmatic reasons of efficiency, therefore avoiding the need for constitutional change, with the exception of two amendments allowing the federal government to start up programs for unemployment insurance (1940) and old age pensions (1951).

In the post-war period, fiscal agreements on tax collection in exchange for unconditional transfers and new shared cost programs (among others in the fields of post-secondary education and health) were reached. In the end, the increase in the number of shared cost programs made the division of powers between the two orders of government less distinctive. By stipulating numerous and detailed conditions to federal grants, Ottawa was able to exercise greater control over the nature and range of provincial activities. Hence, Canadian federalism was altered less by resorting to constitutional changes, which were always difficult to achieve, than by reaching agreements of a fiscal or administrative nature. Provinces were responsible for the implementation of numerous social programs financed by shared cost programmes, leading the provinces to grow at a rate clearly superior to that of the central government. It was in 1957 that the federal government started an equalization program which sought to compensate provinces whose income per capita was inferior to the average, based on the revenue of representative provinces. With the exception of Quebec's hesitation to participate in many of these programs, this period was considered to be the golden age of Canadian federalism because of the great flexibility it showed.

From the end of the 1950s to the mid-1970s, the rapid growth in provincial government activities, associated with the dynamic of province-building, helped make federal-provincial relations more complex and thus favoured the implementation of new coordination mechanisms. At the same time, the expansion of provincial governments stimulated the formation of social groups further embracing the views of these provincial governments. Quebec experienced a profound transformation of nationalist-inspired claims which reinforced the autonomist designs of the provincial government, and Alberta promoted a more regionalist vision. Contrary to the United States, where regional interests can be adequately represented in the Senate or in the House of Representatives, it is often provincial governments which become the spokespersons and defenders of the specific needs of provincial communities. This is how cooperative federalism was replaced by executive federalism, which is characterized by frequent meetings between the Canadian Prime Minister and the provincial Premiers.[33] These meetings were particularly criticized for deepening the conflictual nature of federal-provincial relations.

The response to the Quebec government's demands for more autonomy and resources in fields of provincial jurisdiction resulted in a period of greater fiscal decentralization. Following pressures from Quebec, which sought to increase its fiscal capacity, in 1965 the federal government passed a law on established program financing allowing provinces to withdraw from several shared-cost programs (in the areas of hospital insurance, old age pensions, health, training) while receiving financial compensation through the transfer of tax points. Only Quebec chose to opt out, which de facto accorded it a special status in the federation; this option was offered to all provinces even though they had not formulated this request. This type of fiscal arrangement was not repeated; Ottawa rather sought, when new programs were implemented, to either directly address the targeted clientele (as was the case for labour market training) or to establish eligibility criteria for obtaining federal grants (as was the case for hospital insurance).

It was also in the mid 1960s that the constitutional agenda became a stumbling block between Ottawa and the provinces. The opening of this dossier resulted from pressures from the Quebec government, which wanted to revise the division of powers in order to increase its margin of manoeuvrability in economic, social, and cultural affairs. The federal government took advantage of this to put forth its own political agenda, notably the repatriation of the constitution, the adoption of an amending formula, a Charter of Rights and Freedoms, and a strengthening of its ability to intervene in the economy. The division of powers was way down on Ottawa's list of priorities, reflecting a deepening of the traditional conflict between federal capital and the government of Quebec. The height of this conflict was the 1980 Quebec referendum. The Quebec government asked the population for a mandate to negotiate a new constitutional arrangement based on the principle of associated states. This popular consultation was won by the supporters of Canadian federalism, although an analysis demonstrates that the citizens clearly favoured a decentralized form of federalism.

Repatriation and constitutional changes two years later were a diversion from the 1980 referendum results; only Quebec firmly opposed the federal initiative.[34] Far from having responded to Quebec's expectations, the constitutional changes and the new Charter reaffirmed the central government's desire to increase its ability to act in areas of provincial jurisdiction and to modify the original constitution despite lacking the agreement of one province. This unilateralism was not without repercussions in that it marked the end of the conception of the Canadian state based on the view that it was the result of a pact between the two founding peoples. This centralizing tendency continued with the Mulroney government's constitutional proposals which were never, on the other hand, ratified.[35] The double failure of the 1987 and 1992 constitutional proposals demonstrates the great difficulty of finding or creating a national consensus on the nature of Canadian federalism.

The federal form was adopted, as mentioned above, to reconcile national, linguistic, and religious differences when the Dominion was created. These differences are even more important in that they are geographically concentrated. The fact that the Quebec government wanted to further its political autonomy is not an historical anomaly, because 90% of Canadians with French as their maternal language reside in Quebec, even though French Canadians continue to represent approximately 25% of the Canadian population. In response to the inferior socio-economic status French Canadians had up to the beginning of the 1960s, the Quebec government sought to intervene more directly in the economy and to develop its social and cultural activities in order to preserve and promote the distinct nature of Quebec society. This dynamic has not been uneventful. Many Québécois see the provincial government as the only one able to play this role, the only one where francophone Québécois constitute a majority. It is in this context that Quebec is one of the few provinces to attach great importance on the one hand to the respect for provincial jurisdiction and on the other to an increase in provincial autonomy. Quebec's demands contributed to the braking of political centralization, even though they were not able to thwart it entirely. The central government's refusal to grant Quebec a special status in the federation has often brought it to offer all provinces that which only Quebec has demanded. This orientation has also, in a way, slowed down the movement towards centralization. As Stevenson notes, "efforts to deal with the 'Quebec problem' have spread provincialist tendencies, originally centered in Quebec, to other regions of the country,"[36] particularly in the West, which maintains that its interests are rarely taken into account by the central government and that politically it is poorly represented.

All in all, Canadian federalism has shown its flexibility in matters of administrative arrangements but has not been able to adjust the constitution and revise the division of powers. Nevertheless, it is important to mention that fiscal transfers represent not insignificant sources of revenue for the Canadian provinces, even if the distribution varies enormously according to the wealth of the latter. For example, transfers account for nearly 45% of New Brunswick's revenue but only approximately 10% for Alberta.[37] Globally, all types of federal grants constitute 20% of provincial revenue. This proportion is comparable to what state and local governments receive in the United States. Nevertheless, the nature of federal transfers is different given the importance of unconditional grants. However, even conditional grants are less constraining. The autonomy of Canadian provinces is thus greater than that of the American states vis-à-vis their respective central governments.

3. CONCLUSION

In summary, both Canadian and American federalism have centralizing tendencies, but they are not expressed nor articulated in the same way. In the United States, the political domination exercised by Washington was deepened, profiting from the confusion over the division of powers. It was also strengthened by a political system which allows regional interests to be expressed within central institutions. In Canada, the presence of distinct national communities which are geographically concentrated and the relatively small number of provincial governments compared to the number of American states, combined with political institutions inspired by British traditions and founded on principles like party discipline and a federalism which clearly identified the responsibilities accorded to each order of government, did not allow centralizing forces to operate with the same success. Provincial governments continue to count on the loyalty of their residents and to oppose federal initiatives which limit their ability to act. To these institutional factors can be added the increasingly incompatible visions of Quebec and English Canada on the nature of Canadian federalism, the former always defending a very decentralized form of federalism, the latter identifying with and supporting the central government more willingly.

NOTES

1. Thomas J. Anton, *American Federalism and Public Policy. How the System Works* (Philadelphia: Temple University Press, 1989), 3.

2. Garth Stevenson, "Federalism," in T.C. Pocklington (ed.), *Liberal Democracy in Canada and the United States. An Introduction to Politics and Government* (Toronto: Holt, Rinehart and Winston of Canada, 1985), 151.

3. Edmond Orban, "La dynamique du cadre constitutionnel" in E. Orban (ed.), *Le système politique des États-Unis* (Montréal / Bruxelles: Presses de l'Université de Montréal / Bruylant, 1987), 23.

4. *Ibid.,* 25.

5. Edmond Orban, *Le fédéralisme? Super état fédérale? Associations d'états souverains?* (Montréal: Hurtubise HMH, 1992), 48-53.

6. Anton, *op. cit.,* 8.

7. Edmond Orban, "Le déclin du fédéralisme dualiste", in Orban (ed.), *op. cit.,* 42.

8. F.C. Engleman and T.C. Pocklington, "Constitutions and Courts", in Pocklington (ed.), *op. cit.,* 130.

9. Gérald A. Beaudoin, *Le partage des pouvoirs* (Ottawa: Les Presses de l'Université d'Ottawa, 1982), 9.

10. R. Simeon and I. Robinson, *State, Society, and the Development of Canadian Federalism* (Toronto: University of Toronto Press, 1990), chap. 3; Stanley B. Ryerson, *Unequal Union. Roots of Crisis in the Canadas, 1815-1873* (Toronto: Progress Books, 1973), chaps 18 and 19.

11. Jennifer Smith, "Canadian Confederation and the Influence of American Federalism," *Canadian Journal of Political Science* 21:3 (1988), 443-463.

12. Donald V. Smiley, "The Two Themes of Canadian Federalism," in R.S. Blair and J.T. McLeod (eds.), *The Canadian Political Tradition. Basic Readings* (Toronto: Methuen, 1987), chap. 4.

13. Frank R. Scott, "Centralization and Decentralization in Canadian Federalism", in G. Stevenson (ed.), *Canadian Federalism. Selected Readings* (Toronto: McClelland and Stewart, 1989), chap. 2.

14. Stevenson, "Federalism", *op. cit.*, 164.

15. Simeon and Robinson, *op. cit.*, chap. 4.

16. This despite the fact that the Supreme Court was created in 1875.

17. Kenneth M. Holland, "Federalism in a North American Context: The Contribution of the Supreme Courts of Canada, the United States and Mexico", in Marian C. McKenna, *The Canadian and American Constitutions in Comparative Perspective* (Calgary: University of Calgary Press, 1993), 93-94.

18. François Chevrette, "La Cour supréme," in Orban (ed.), *op. cit.*, 221-225.

19. Holland, *op. cit.*, 89.

20. Edmond Orban, *La dynamique de la centralisation dans l'État fédéral: un processus irréversible?* (Montréal: Québec/Amérique, 1984), 367-371.

21. Anton, *op, cit.*, 44.

22. *Ibid.*, 133.

23. U.S. Advisory Commission on Intergovernmental Relations, *The Changing Public Sector: Shifts in Governmental Spending and Employment* (Washington: ACIR, December 1991), 4.

24. For these examples, see Orban, *"Le déclin du fédéralisme dualiste,"* *op. cit.*, 46.

25. P.F. Peterson, B.G. Rabe and K.K. Wong, *When Federalism Works* (Washington: The Brookings Institution, 1986), 2.

26. ACIR, *op. cit.*, 6.

27. Richard P. Nathan and Fred C. Doolittle, *Reagan and the States* (Princeton: Princeton University Press, 1987), 12.

28. *Ibid.*, 79.

29. Orban, "Le déclin du fédéralisme dualiste," *op. cit.*, 49.

30. On this issue, see Timothy Conlan, *New Federalism: Intergovernmental Reform from Nixon to Reagan* (Washington: The Brookings Institution, 1988) and Richard S. Williamson, *Reagan's Federalism: His Efforts to Decentralize Government* (Lanham: University Press of America, 1990).

31. Anton, *op. cit.*, 217.

32. David B. Walker, "American Federalism from Johnson to Bush," in *Publius: The Journal of Federalism* 21 (Winter 1991), 118.

33. Donald V. Smiley, *The Federal Condition in Canada* (Toronto: McGraw-Hill Ryerson, 1987), 83.

34. François Rocher, "Québec's Historical Agenda," in Duncan Cameron and Miriam Smith (eds), *Constitutional Politics* (Toronto: Lorimer, 1992), 23-36.

35. This view clearly runs counter to the standard interpretations of the Accord which fail to discern its centralizing features. For more details, see François Rocher and Gérard Boismenu, "New Constitutional Signposts: Distinct Society, Lin-

guistic Duality and Institutional Changes", in A.-G. Gagnon and J. P. Bickerton (eds.), *Canadian Politics: An Introduction to the Discipline* (Peterborough: Broadview Press, 1990), 222-245; F. Rocher, "Le Québec et la Constitution: une valse á mille temps", in François Rocher (ed.) *Bilan québécois du fédéralisme canadien* (Montréal: VLB éditeur, 1992), 20-57; and F. Rocher and Alain-G. Gagnon, "Multilateral Agreement: The Betrayal of the Federal Spirit," in Douglas Brown and Robert Young (eds), *Canada: The State of the Federation 1992* (Kingston: Institute of Intergovernmental Relations, 1992), 117-127.

36. Stevenson, "Federalism," *op. cit.,* 170.

37. Allan M. Maslove, "Budgeting in Provincial Governments", in A.M. Maslove (ed.), *Budgeting in the Provinces. Leadership and the Premiers* (Toronto: The Institute of Public Administration of Canada, 1989), 11.

FURTHER READING

Alfred H. Kelly, Winfred A. Harbison, and Herman Beltz. *The American Constitution: Its Origins and Development.* New York; W.W. Norton, 1983)

T.C. Pocklington (ed.). *Liberal Democracy in Canada and the United States. An Introduction to Politics and Government.* Toronto: Holt, Rinehart and Winston of Canada, 1985.

Daniel Elazar. *Exploring Federalism.* Atlanta, University of Alabama Press, 1987.

Donald V. Smiley. *The Federal Condition in Canada.* Toronto: McGraw-Hill Ryerson Limited, 1987.

David C. Nice. *Federalism. The Politics of Intergovernmental Relations.* New York: St. Martin's Press, 1987.

Thomas J. Anton. *American Federalism and Public Policy. How the System Works.* Philadelphia: Temple University Press, 1989.

Richard Simeon and Ian Robinson. *State, Society, and the Development of Canadian Federalism.* Toronto: University of Toronto Press, 1990.

Marian C. McKenna (ed.). *The Canadian and American Constitutions in Comparative Perspective*. Calgary: University of Calgary Press, 1993.

JENNIFER SMITH

The Grass is Always Greener: Prime Ministerial vs Presidential Government

INTRODUCTION

The word *execute* is derived from the Latin *exsequor*, which means "follow out." And so the political executive is understood to follow out something, namely, the will of the legislators as expressed in the laws. This is stated clearly in the American constitution, which requires that the president take care to execute the laws faithfully. But there must be more to the executive than that, otherwise the American philosopher of pragmatism, George Dewey, was rightfully dismissive of the American exemplar of a chief executive. Interviewed on the point at the turn of the century, Dewey responded with disdain: "I am convinced that the office of the president is not such a very difficult one to fill, his duties being mainly to execute the laws of Congress."[1]

The American constitution supplies some clues about the more formidable side of the executive. For instance, the president is commander-in-chief of the army and navy, and of the militia of the states. Here we have the executive in armour, the military might of the entire nation at his disposal. Thus the modern executive is not merely the servant of the legislature but a powerful initiator of action in his own right.

It is instructive that in both cases — the executive as follower and the executive as initiator — mention is made of the legislature. The story of the modern executive in constitutional governments is largely about the executive-legislative relationship, and at bottom it revolves around the question of which is dominant. Obviously the answer will vary from one system of government to the next, but there are two main models: presidential and parliamentary. And there are two neighbouring countries — the United States and Canada respectively — which are leading examples of each.

Since the two models are so different, it might seem that to compare them is like comparing apples and oranges — not very fruitful, so to speak. Yet people do compare them in order to better understand them, indeed, often to determine which is the better, an endeavour normally inspired by a "grass is greener" sentiment and a pre-established standard of judgement. One of the most sensational examples in the history of political science is an essay published in 1884 by Woodrow Wilson, long before he became president of the United States. Wilson was troubled by the "clumsy misrule" of an overbearing Congress, and sought to make Congress more amenable to direction by the president. He thought he saw an answer in the parliamentary model, which often enables a prime minister and his cabinet to control the legislature.[2]

How ought we to compare the presidential apple and the prime ministerial orange? There are a number of possibilities, ranging from an historical account of the origins of the offices to a description of the way each functions today. In a short essay like this, the more direct approach is to begin with the obvious yet fundamental questions of political science: Who qualifies? How long? How chosen? What constitutional powers and limits? To simplify, we will consider these questions under the following headings: selection; term and removal; powers.

1) SELECTION

The selection of a president and the selection of a prime minister are as different as night and day. In the case of the American president, the process is nightmarishly complicated and insufferably long. In the case of the Canadian prime minister, it is uncomplicated and short — although occasionally nasty and brutish. There are other differences. The American process is older; it is watched by the world; and it is governed by written rules. The Canadian event is watched only by Canadians, and there are almost no written rules. Let us give seniority its due and begin with the Americans.

For a non-American, the rules of selection outlined in the constitution seem to belong to another era, as indeed they do, and it is hard to see how they square with what actually transpires. Yet they still provide the constitutional framework of the selection process. The framers of the American constitution were not happy with the idea of the Congress electing the president, since that would make for a weak executive dependent upon the favour of the legislative branch. But they were just as troubled by the idea of direct election by the people, since that would mean another kind of dependence — dependence on the whim of popular opinion. Moreover, they doubted that voters would know enough about the candidates to be able to exercise good judgement in choosing among them. In the end, they hit upon the expedient of the Electoral College.

The Electoral College is basically a method of indirect election, and it is state-based. Each state's membership is equal to its share of senators and members of the House of Representatives. Voters in the states elect their Electoral College representatives, who in turn meet to elect a president and vice-president. The framers of the constitution thought that voters would choose politically knowledgeable electors who could be counted on to make better choices than the voters themselves. It was a sensible enough scheme that went awry with the development of political parties.

The ideal of independent electors quickly turned into the reality of partisan electors as political parties soon came to dominate the presidential selection process. Once electors became partisans who could be counted on to register their respective parties' choices, their role in the process no longer mattered. What does matter is the outcome of the vote in each state, particularly since a winner-take-all system is in effect. The winning candidate in a state almost always takes all of the state's Electoral College votes.[3] Thus presidential hopefuls normally face a two-phase process. The first is to gain the nomination of a political party, which today means the Republican Party or the Democratic Party. As Ross Perot's participation in the 1992 presidential election demonstrates, it is possible to run as an independent — but also very difficult to win that way. The second phase is the presidential campaign proper.

The race to gain the party's nomination is long, expensive, and arduous. It takes over a year and is marked by a series of electoral contests, state by state. More than two-thirds of the states hold primaries, and the remainder hold caucus conventions.[4] The primaries and the caucus conventions serve two functions, one of which is to choose delegates to the national convention that each party holds in the summer months before the November election. At the national convention, delegates choose the party's presidential and vice-presidential candidates, but since most of them are committed, the outcome in recent years has been predictable. This points to the real function of the primary and caucus contests, which is to test the field of candidates.

At the beginning of the "presidential sweepstakes," the field of candidates tends to be large, since the main criteria for entry are skill at fundraising and overweening ambition, more or less in that order. Money — lots of it — is an absolute *sine qua non*, since American campaigns rely heavily on media advertising. There is matching public financing available to candidates — the government will match individuals' contributions up to a limit of $250 — but if they decide to accept it, they must follow spending limitations. In 1992 the spending limit for the nomination phase was $33 million.[5]

Prospective candidates work hard to win the early contests because, as the saying goes, money follows power. The losers tend to drop out, and as the contests draw to a close, a winner emerges. Technically, the winner has accumulated a majority of committed delegates, which is why the choice of the party convention is normally a foregone conclusion. Once the parties have nominated their presidential and vice-presidential candidates at the conventions, the second phase of the campaign opens, and the contenders face one another in the general election. Public financing is available again, a flat amount with no matching requirements. In 1992 it was $55.2 million for each of the major party candidates. Other candidates for president qualify if they receive at least 5% of the vote and do not spend more than $50,000 of their own money on the campaign. However, if they turn down public financing, there is no limit on the amount of money that they can raise and spend. This was precisely the option chosen by the independent candidate, Ross Perot, who spent a staggering $60 million of his own money on his 1992 campaign.[6]

It is worth pausing to consider the implications of the primary, which is a unique American institution. Primaries vary in kind from state to state, but essentially they are open electoral contests. They test the candidates' popular appeal among registered voters of the party, not just the party notables. As a result, they encourage "outsiders," candidates whose main assets are financial and organizational, not long years of faithful party service. Moreover, because the primaries are so closely watched, they also favour candidates who play well to the world's most sophisticated media. The incumbent president, Bill Clinton, is a good example of a long-shot candidate with the right stuff. When the race began, he was a little-known governor of an obscure state, certainly not a Washington insider or a Democrat with national experience and a national profile. But he had a strong organization and demonstrated skill in communicating to voters through the media. As president, of course, he is learning on the job, which is another way of saying that the selection process is no guarantee of quality in office.

The fact that the primary system is so wide open to prospective candidates points to a significant difference between the American and Canadian systems. Whatever else it is, the Canadian route to the prime ministership is still very much a party process dominated by party notables and party activists. As in the American case, the nomination phase is capped by a party leadership convention, but en route to it there is nothing like a primary system in operation. Instead, delegate-selection meetings are held in each riding, a riding being the Canadian equivalent of a congressional district. The meetings are open to party members only, and the purpose is to select a slate of delegates to the convention. For the most part these delegates are committed to a particular candidate.

Skirmishes among the candidates and their supporters at the riding meetings are not unknown. Organizers work hard to get their supporters out, some of them newly minted partisans, and unregulated amounts of money are spent to this end. However, in the Canadian case the amounts are in the range of thousands of dollars, not millions of dollars. Setting aside transportation and organization costs, there is little to spend money on at the riding meetings, and not much time to spend it in, since this phase of the process is completed within two or three months. Moreover, in addition to riding delegates, there are a significant number of *ex officio* delegates who attend the leadership conventions of the national parties. Generally speaking, they include party officials, all former and serving elected representatives at both levels of government, and senators. The New Democratic Party sets aside a share of delegate seats for union representatives.

The divergence between the two systems widens at the convention itself, for often there is nothing predictable about the Canadian event at all, one reason being the significant number of *ex officio* delegates, many of whom are uncommitted. The decision-making rules at the convention require the lowest candidate after each ballot to drop off, and balloting continues until one of the candidates gains a majority of the votes cast. Finally, and again in contrast to the American system, at the conclusion there are two prizes — the party leadership *and* an obedient party. For the party in power — the governing party — there is an additional prize: the office of prime minister.

This last point was demonstrated by the 1993 leadership convention of the federal Progressive Conservative party. Prime Minister Brian Mulroney indicated his intention not to run again early in the year, an announcement that immediately set the stage for a convention to choose his successor. In accordance with the unwritten rules of parliamentary government, Governor General Raymon Hnatyshyn, the vice-regal substitute for the Queen of Canada, appointed the new Conservative leader chosen at the party convention, Kim Campbell, to be the monarch's chief counsellor, and asked her to form a government, that is, to name a new cabinet. Canadians had an opportunity to decide the fate of the new prime minister some months later; she and her party went down to a crushing defeat, and the Liberals under Jean Chretien then formed a new majority government.

2) TERM AND REMOVAL

For Americans, the constitution issues some clear guidelines on the term of office and the removal of a president. Looking to fix the president's term differently from those of members of Congress,[7] the framers decided on four years. Initially this was accompanied by unlimited re-eligibility, and then an understanding, based on the precedent set by the first president, George Washington, that an incumbent would seek to serve no more than two terms. The precedent held until Franklin Roosevelt won re-election to a third (1940) and then a fourth term (1944), arguing wartime exigencies. An unhappy Republican Congress passed a constitutional amendment imposing a two-term limitation, and the twenty-second amendment was ratified in 1951.

To impeach an official means to bring charges against him in what amounts to a political trial. The eighteenth century was the heyday of impeachment trials in England, so it is understandable that the framers would turn to the practice for a method of early removal from office. It is applicable to the president, vice-president, and civil officers of the United States, and the grounds are "Treason, Bribery, or other high Crimes and Misdemeanors." Congress does the impeaching. The House of Representatives is empowered to decide whether to proceed against an individual, and should it so decide, the trial is prosecuted before the Senate, where a conviction requires a vote of two-thirds of the members present.

The constitutional provisions on impeachment have an antique ring to them, and in the case of a president have been triggered only once, when the House of Representatives voted to impeach Andrew Johnson, who had assumed the presidency when Abraham Lincoln was assassinated. Johnson, a recalcitrant southerner from the point of view of the northern-dominated "Radical Congress," escaped impeachment in the Senate by exactly one vote. In our century, Richard Nixon skated rather close to an impeachment in the wake of the

Watergate scandal, since the House Judiciary Committee began work on impeachment proceedings. However, Nixon resigned before anything could come of them.[8]

The Twenty-Fifth Amendment, ratified in 1967, establishes rules governing the succession in the event of presidential death, resignation or disability. Essentially the vice-president assumes the office, which is the major purpose of the position of vice-president. The tricky part of the amendment is the determination of presidential disability, particularly if there is disagreement among the principals themselves. The rules are cumbersome, and seem to have been neglected altogether in the confusion immediately following the attempted assassination of President Reagan in 1981. Secretary of State Haig thought he was in charge and said so in a White House press conference, a claim dismissed by others in the administration. In the end, with the president recovering nicely in hospital from the gunshot wound, the rules of the Twenty-Fifth were never invoked.

Where the Americans rely on written rules, the Canadians rely largely on unwritten ones, and the result is a startling contrast. What prime ministerial term? The only applicable written rule stipulates that no House of Commons shall continue longer than five years, which fixes the outer boundary of a government's term. But a prime minister can call an election anytime within the five years. At least he can if he is in control. The other side of the equation is the House of Commons, and it is important to remember that in parliamentary systems, a prime minister and his government must have the confidence of the chamber, that is, the support of a majority of the members. If the prime minister's party forms the majority, which is often the case, there is no problem of confidence. The practice of party discipline ensures majority support. However, if his party is in a minority, he needs the support of members of other parties, which renders his position and that of his government less secure.

On the question of removal, guiding precedents are lacking and legal rules are non-existent. In Canada, no sitting prime minister has been forced openly by his party to resign. It could happen, of course, but probably only if the senior ministers resigned en masse in order to force the issue. Prime Minister Mulroney's decision not to lead his party in a third general election illustrates the usual practice followed when a prime minister becomes an electoral liability — in the party's eyes if not his own. He decides to leave, possibly after some encouragement, and the party gets an opportunity to choose a successor who, it is hoped, will lead the troops to another election victory.

3) POWERS

On the question of powers, the contrast between the two executives deepens. In the American case, the applicable constitutional provisions are brief but certainly clear. Article II, which is devoted to the office and powers of the president, opens by vesting executive power in him. What this might mean is amplified later in the article, when the president is named Commander-in-Chief of the army and navy, and of the militia of the constituent states. He is assigned a power to make treaties, and to appoint ambassadors, senior officers of government, and Supreme Court judges, but only with the agreement of the Senate. He is empowered to receive ambassadors and officials from other countries.

In addition to these war and foreign policy powers, there are important domestic powers. The president heads the "executive Departments" (the public service) because he is empowered to appoint (with the agreement of the Senate), remove, and supervise senior officials. He appoints federal judges, again with the Senate's agreement. And in the elegant eighteenth-century prose characteristic of the constitution, he is required to "take Care that the Laws be faithfully executed." He also has a power to grant pardons to individuals convicted of offences. On the legislative front, he is assigned the duty of addressing the Congress on the state of the union and recommending to it legislative measures that he finds necessary. Finally, his signature is required for bills to become law, which means that he has a veto power. The Congress can override the veto, but only by a two-thirds vote in each chamber.

A striking feature of the president's executive power is that the Congress manages to share in it, even in the foreign affairs field. Morever, in Article I, which deals with the legislative branch, we find that Congress is assigned the power to declare war, as well as having the all-important taxing and spending powers. The upshot is that Congress and the president need to cooperate in some fashion in order to govern.

Few presidents can be said to have dominated Congress, even when, as in the case of the current president, their party has a majority of the seats in both houses. Still, most observers agree that in this century there has been a shift from a Congress-centred government to a president-centred government.[9] One reason is that Congress delegated significant legislative powers to the executive branch during the "New Deal" era of the 1930s, when President Franklin Roosevelt introduced major programmes to counteract the effects of the Great Depression. Another is the impressive array of management resources available to the modern president: the White House Staff;

the Executive Office of the President, which includes permanent agencies like the National Security Council and the Office of Management and Budget; and the departments of cabinet.

It is worth pausing here to consider the American cabinet. It includes the heads of all the major federal government departments[10] who, as mentioned above, are appointed by the president with the agreement of the Senate. Although the word denotes a collective, in fact the cabinet is not a collective body because it does not make decisions collectively. Indeed, presidents are not much inclined to hold cabinet meetings. Nor is the cabinet responsible to the Congress, although its members individually appear before congressional committees to answer questions about their respective departments, just as they answer to the president. Occasionally presidents arrive in office determined to work a "cabinet government" — President Jimmy Carter is an example — but the effort has always come to nothing. Instead, presidents seem to end up relying on the advice of a small number of individuals, perhaps cabinet secretaries of key departments like the State Department and the Treasury Department, perhaps senior White House staffers.

By contrast, in Canada the cabinet, of which the prime minister is the leading member, is very much a collective. As a result, it is not possible to talk about the "powers of the prime minister" without reviewing cabinet government. To begin, the constitution vests executive power in the Queen of Canada, who is the head of state. She is represented by the Governor General when she is not here, and she rarely is. The "real" executive is the cabinet, on whose advice the Governor General always acts.[11] The cabinet is responsible to the House of Commons for the advice that it tenders to the Governor General. It is important to notice that the advice covers purely executive matters as well as legislative matters. For example, since cabinet members are usually heads of government departments, they oversee the administration of the laws. Thus they exercise purely executive powers. But they also hold seats in the Commons, which means that they participate in the legislative branch as well. Thus they advise the Crown on proposed laws, and shepherd them through the House of Commons. The convention of party discipline, particularly when the cabinet's party is in the majority, permits the cabinet to dominate the legislature.

How does the prime minister fit into this picture? Since the written constitution is silent on the powers of the prime minister, it is essential to recall the selection process as described above. Asked by the Governor General to form a government because she[12] is the leader of the party with the most seats in the House of Commons — not necessarily a majority — the prime minister's first notable power is in evidence in the construction of a cabinet. She not only appoints ministers — almost always from among party colleagues elected to the House of Commons — she can dismiss them at any time and without offering any reasons for doing so. She is in charge of the organization of the cabinet and the agenda of the cabinet. She controls senior civil servant appointments, and appointments to central agencies. The latter include the Prime Minister's Office, the counterpart of the White House Staff, and the Privy Council Office, which assists the cabinet. The prime minister also monopolizes the considerable patronage available to the government, unlike an American president who, as noted earlier, must share so many senior appointments with the Senate.

The timing of elections is an especially important decision that the Canadian prime minister makes, subject to the five-year limitation noted earlier in the essay. Obviously, she will try to time the election to suit her party's prospects and her own. By contrast, an American president has to fight an election at a prescribed time, and it may not suit him at all. Consider the example of President Clinton's predecessor, George Bush. Between September 1990 and March 1991, polls recorded that approval rates of President Bush reached record highs, at one point over 90% of those polled. This was the period when the United States prosecuted the Gulf War against Iraq. Any prime minister in a comparable situation would want to take advantage of it by calling an election after an appropriate interval. President Bush had no such option. He watched his popularity sink from an all-time high in March, 1992, to a low in November, 1992, precisely when he had to fight the election.[13]

CONCLUSION

At first glance the American presidency seems to be an immensely powerful office, a perception linked to the country's military and economic strength and fed by the omnipresent American media. On closer examination, it is evident that there are significant constraints on a president's powers. At bottom, these constraints arise out of the fact that the president faces institutional rivals whose political careers are not dependent on his. This is a result of the design of the American system of government, which is often described as one of separate branches (executive, legislative and judicial) with shared powers.

The framers of the constitution found many ways to separate the branches, some of which we have noted, like term of office and selection. Members of the House of Representatives, senators, and the president have different terms of office, and are elected by different constituencies. For a member of the House it is a congressional district, for a senator it is a state, and for the president, the nation. Even age requirements differ. For a representative it is twenty-five, for a senator it is thirty, and for a president, thirty-five. We might expect that political parties would hook these politicians together, and to some extent they do, but not in the fashion of parliamentary parties. And separateness is the reason. American representatives, senators, and candidates for president do not stand or fall together in electoral terms. Put another way, few presidents have "coat-tails" that congressional candidates can ride to office. Yet they share powers.

The constitutional fact of shared powers means that cooperation between the branches is required in order for the government to function. Power is diffused. The president needs to exercise powers of persuasion, not just over members from the opposing party, but sometimes over members from his own. A Canadian prime minister at the head of a majority party faces nothing remotely comparable to this so long as she takes care to keep her caucus united behind her. Power is centralized, not diffused. So it is easy to see why Woodrow Wilson, looking for ways to enhance the office of president in relation to the Congress, was tempted by the parliamentary model.

How should we judge these two offices? As always, it depends on the standard of judgement. Wilson's standard was executive effectiveness, and in that race the office of prime minister is the clear winner. But if we use a democratic standard that emphasizes openness and consultation, the office of president is the clear winner.

NOTES

1. John Bartlett, *Familiar Quotations*, 12th ed. (Boston: Little, Brown and Company, 1951), p. 638.

2. Woodrow Wilson, "Committee or Cabinet Government?" in Ray Stannard Baker and William E. Dodd, eds., *The Public Papers of Woodrow Wilson: College and State*, Vol. 1 (New York and London: Harper and Brothers, 1925), p. 128. See also Wilson's famous book, *Congressional Government: A Study in American Politics* (Boston and New York: Houghton Mifflin Company, 1885 and 1913).

3. It is up to the states to decide how their electors are chosen, and the general practice is a state-wide system. In other words, in each state the party chooses a slate of electors

who are committed to the party's presidential and vice-presidental candidates. Occasionally states have devised systems allowing for a split vote, which Maine did in 1972 by requiring that electors be chosen by congressional district. That year the Republicans carried the districts and therefore the whole of the state's electoral votes anyway. Electors still meet in their respective state capitals about six weeks after the election to cast their votes formally. At this stage, there is always the possibility of the "faithless" elector. This occurred in the 1976 presidential election, when a Washington state elector pledged to Gerald Ford, the Republican party's candidate for president, voted instead for Ronald Reagan.

4. The caucus convention is a traditional method of choosing delegates to a party's national convention, and it is simply a meeting of party members, usually at the county level, to choose delegates to a state convention, who in turn will select delegates to the national convention. The states which use it hold open party caucuses at the local level, that is, caucuses open to registered party voters who wish to attend. The widely watched "Iowa caucuses", which come early in the schedule of primaries and caucuses, are an example of the genre. For a fuller discussion see Theodore J. Lowi and Benjamin Ginsberg, *American Government: Freedom and Power*, 2nd ed. (New York and London: W.W.Norton & Company, 1993), pp. 527-32.

5. Susan Welch, John Gruhl, Michael Steinman, John Comer, *Understanding American Government*, 2nd ed., (Minneapolis/St.Paul: West Publishing Company, 1993), p.247.

6. *Ibid.*, p.247. The amount of public financing available to presidential candidates is only a portion of the amount spent during the presidential campaign. This is because there is no limit on the amount of money that individuals and organizations, particularly the PACs (political action committees), can spend independently in support of particular candidates. The 1988 presidential campaign is estimated to have cost $500 million. Estimates of the 1992 campaign are not available, although the figure is expected to be higher again. By comparison, in the 1988 general election in Canada, the political parties and eligible independent candidates received just under $20 million in public financing. Independent spending on advertising by individuals, business and labour

organizations is estimated to have been $4.7 million. For figures in the Canadian case, see the Report of the Royal Commission on Electoral Reform and Party Financing, *Reforming Electoral Democracy*, Vol.1 (Minister of Supply and Services Canada, 1991), p.337, 371.

7.   The Congress is the Senate and the House of Representatives. The phrase "member of Congress" is confusing because it might refer to a senator or a member of the House.

8.   The phrase, "civil officers", includes federal judges, including judges of the Supreme Court, and cabinet officers. It excludes members of Congress and military and naval officers. Only one Supreme Court justice has been the subject of impeachment proceedings. Samuel Chase was the target of the victorious Jeffersonians in 1894, but they failed to get a conviction against him in the Senate. For a full discussion of impeachment see Raoul Berger, *Impeachment: The Constitutional Problems* (Cambridge: Harvard University Press, 1973).

9.   Theodore J. Lowi and Benjamin Ginsberg, *American Government: Freedom and Power*, 2nd ed. (New York: W.W. Norton & Company, 1993), pp. 247-309.

10. There are fourteen departments, listed here in order of their establishment: State (1789); Treasury (1789); Defense (1789); Interior (1849); Agriculture (1862); Justice (1870); Commerce (1903); Labor (1913); Health and Human Services (1953); Housing and Urban Development (1965); Transportation (1966); Energy (1977); Education (1979); Veterans Affairs (1989).

11. The issue of the Governor General's "prerogative" is debated occasionally, and essentially revolves about the question of whether he has any prerogative power left, that is, an independent sphere of power not taken over and regulated by Parliament. Most observers say no, but Canada's late, great constitutional expert, Senator Eugene Forsey, vigorously refuted the "rubber stamp theory of the Crown". See "Crown and Cabinet" in his *Freedom and Order: Collected Essays* (Toronto: McClelland and Stewart Limited, 1974), pp. 21-72.

12.   Given the gender of Canada's last prime minister, Kim Camp-
      bell, the pronoun "she" is used in the remainder of the essay.

13.   Lowi & Ginsberg, pp.306-7.

FURTHER READING:

It is worth plumbing contemporary literature on the subject of executive power, itself. An entertaining and instructive example is An-
drei S. Markovits and Mark Silverstein, eds. *The Politics of Scandal:
Power and Process in Liberal Democracies* (New York: Homes and Meier,
1988).

As might be expected, there is a wealth of literature on Canadian
and American executive structures and powers, and the suggestions
made here amount to a way of getting started. On the American
side, there is Robert E. DiClerico's *The American President*, 3rd ed.
(Englewood Cliffs, NJ: Prentice Hall, 1990]; Michael Nelson, ed. *The
Presidency and the Political System*, 2nd ed. (Washington, DC: Congressional Quarterly Press, 1988); and Theodore Lowi, *The Personal Presidency* (Ithaca, NY: Cornell University Press, 1985).

The student of the Canadian executive should begin by consulting
J.R. Mallory, *The Structure of Canadian Government*, rev. ed. (Toronto:
Gage Publishing Limited, 1984). Two new books of readings that
contain useful articles are Michael M. Atkinson, ed. *Governing Can-
ada; Institutions and Public Policy* (Toronto; HBJ-Holt Canada, 1993),
and R.S. Blair and J.T. McLeod, eds. *The Canadian Political Tradition:
Basic Readings*, 2nd ed. (Scarborough: Nelson Canada, 1993). An ex-
cellent book on the cabinet and the role of regional ministers is
Herman Bakvis, *Regional Ministers: Power and Influence in the Canadian
Cabinet* (Toronto: University of Toronto Press, 1991).

A Tale of Two Senates

It is not coincidental that Canada and the United States both have bicameral national legislatures, with lower chambers designed to provide representation by population and upper chambers designed to provide regional representation. After all, the two countries are federal states and the creation of the Canadian Senate in 1867 was done very much with an eye on the American Senate, albeit a sceptical eye that found much at fault with the American model. However, this is not to say that the two Senates have a great deal in common, for they are in fact very different creatures. Nor is it to suggest that the American model provides a solution to the ongoing Canadian angst over Senate reform.

In order to explore the American and Canadian Senate experiences, and to assess the Canadian potential of the American model, it is useful to compare the two Senates on three interrelated dimensions: the power they exercise, the representational principles upon which they are based, and the means by which they are staffed. This comparison parallels in some important respects the quest by some Canadians for a Triple-E Senate — one that is effective, equal, and elected.

THE POWER OF THE TWO SENATES

The two Senates occupy an almost identical formal, constitutional position in the legislative process in that for a bill to become an Act of Parliament (in the Canadian case) or an Act of Congress (in the American case) it must pass by a majority vote in the Senate. In each country, therefore, the Senate possesses an absolute veto; legislation cannot be passed without its consent. It should also be noted that the American Senate possesses some special powers that the Canadian Senate does not. Perhaps the most important of these on an ongoing basis is the power to approve major presidential appointments including those to the cabinet, to federal courts including the Supreme Court, and to administrative bodies such as the Environmental Protection Agency. The last few years have witnessed some high profile and in many respects unsavory battles as presidential nominations have been grilled and, in a number of instances, rejected by the Senate. Perhaps the most memorable case was the nomination of Clarence Thomas to the Supreme Court, a nomination that was approved only after an exhaustive public debate over allegations of sexual harassment.

In practice, however, the two Senates do not play similar roles in the legislative process; their powers differ as night from day. The American Senate is the most important legislative institution in the country; it lies at the centre of the congressional system and American senators are the country's most powerful legislative players. The Senate's compliance with the policy and budgetary initiatives of the president can never be assumed. Even in the most favourable circumstances, when the same party controls the Senate and presidency, senatorial support cannot be taken for granted, as incoming President Bill Clinton found in 1993. Here it should also be noted that the Senate is far more than a reactive legislative arena, supporting or rejecting legislative initiatives crafted by the administration. It is the initial source of much legislation and plays an aggressive role in amending legislative initiatives from the president or House of Representatives to bring them into line with its own particular and sometimes peculiar definition of the national interest.

By contrast, the Canadian Senate has rarely been anything more than a rubber stamp for legislation passed by the House of Commons, and is not an autonomous source of legislative initiatives. While there were significant clashes between the Senate and the House of Commons in the last few years over the Free Trade Agreement and the Goods and Services Tax, these largely partisan disputes erupted from an unusual set of circumstances in which a Liberal-dominated Senate confronted a Conservative-dominated House. What was even more unusual, however, was that the Liberal senators seized this opportunity to confront the elected House in violation of long-standing parliamentary convention. The appointed senators justified their actions on the grounds of widespread popular discontent with the legislative proposals and, incredulously, portrayed themselves as defenders of the public interest against the elected government of the day! Yet the point to stress is that these clashes have been rare exceptions to a more general rule of senatorial acquiescence, although they may portend conflict to come if the now-Conservative dominated Senate — Brian Mulroney appointed 57 senators in his nine years in office, including 15 in the time between his public decision to retire and his replacement by Kim Campbell — confronts a new partisan majority in the House.

How, then, do we explain why American senators employ their constitutional powers to the full, and perhaps beyond, whereas Canadian senators have all but abdicated the exercise of their constitutional powers? The explanation comes only in part from the fact that American Senators are elected and their Canadian counterparts appointed, an admittedly critical difference to which I will return shortly. It also stems from a more fundamental national difference in institutional principles; the American Senate is embedded in an institutional architecture based on the separation of powers and the rejection of party government, whereas the Canadian Senate is embedded in one based on the fusion of powers and the acceptance of party government.

When Americans were designing the institutions of their new national government in the years following the Revolution, they were determined to avoid the concentration of political power in one branch or institution of government. After all, what would be the sense of throwing off the British tyrant only to create a new tyrant in Washington? The American founding fathers therefore separated or divided power among a number of institutions in the hope that power divided, including the power of the electorate, was less threatening to individual liberty. Thus the various branches of government — legislative, executive, and judicial — have distinct institutional homes and methods of appointment or election. Legislative power resides in the Congress, but is divided between the House and the Senate and is subject to a presidential veto. Executive power rests with the presidency, but presidential appointments must be approved by the Senate. The Supreme Court is independent of the executive and legislative branches, but Supreme Court justices are nominated by the president and approved by the Senate. Power, then, is not only divided but also overlaps in a way that provides a host of checks and balances among the various institutions of the national government who must cooperate if government is to be possible, much less effective. The founding fathers set out to create an institutional framework that would make it difficult for government to act, and they succeeded beyond their wildest expectations.

The Canadian founding fathers approached the design of their national institutions from a very different perspective. Their Westminster framework, adopted almost holus-bolus from the United Kingdom, was the parliamentary fusion of powers in which administrative and legislative responsibility came to rest in the same hands. Where Americans divided and separated power, Canadians fused it in the federal cabinet which served as the "buckle" between the administrative and legislative branches of government. Where Americans built in checks and balances, Canadians opted for party government which all but stripped Parliament and even the courts (prior to the Charter) of any effective power to check a determined cabinet in the exercise of its executive and legislative authority. In short, the Canadian and American approaches to institutional design were close to polar opposites.

It is also worth noting, because of its relevance to the two Senates, that the federal division of powers in the United States complemented the separation of powers within the national government. Power was simply chopped up once more, government was made even more difficult and thus liberty, it was hoped, was even further protected. In Canada, however, the federal division of powers ran at cross-purposes to the parliamentary fusion of powers. Canadians tried to divide and fuse at the same time, and not surprisingly became confused in the half-hearted attempt to build federal principles into parliamentary institutions. Canadians ended up with powerful governments at both the national and provincial level, but with impaired regional representation at the centre; Americans ended up with weak governments, at least in the domestic sphere, at both the national and state level, but with highly visible and effective regional representation at the centre.

The two very different institutional perspectives led in turn to very different expectations for the respective Senates. The American Senate has a constitutionally defined role and mandate; it is expected to be a thorn in the side of the presidential administration. The Canadian Senate, however, is denied an autonomous legislative role by the very principles of British parliamentary democracy, principles to which Canadians showed an abiding faith despite the awkward fact that Canada was a federal community and Britain was not. A Senate which might challenge the power of the cabinet and House made no sense within the norms of parliamentary government. Given that it made no sense, there was also no sense in having senators elected. The role of the Canadian Senate — to provide a sober second look at legislation passed by the House — was meant from the outset to be subordinate, and appointed senators have fulfilled this role to perfection. Thus it is not surprising that the two Senates today are such different institutions, one powerful and the other clinging to the margins of political life. The two have simply been faithful to their original architectural design.

REPRESENTATIONAL PRINCIPLES

The American Senate is based on a very simple representational formula; regardless of population, each state has two and only two senators. It matters not that more than 60 times as many people live in the largest state (California) as the smallest (Alaska); Senate representation reflects the constitutional equality of the states whereas the House of Representatives reflects the constitutional equality of individuals. In this sense, then, the American Senate is a truly federal chamber in which the constituent territorial components of the national community are represented as equals. The congressional compromise between the equality of states and the equality of individuals goes back to the very roots of the American constitution when state representatives met to fashion a new federal government in the late 1780s.

Canadians settled for a very different representational formula, one that appeared to make sense at the time of Confederation but has become increasingly nonsensical with the passage of time. Equal representation by province — the American model — was rejected in favour of equal representation by section or region; Ontario, Quebec, and the Maritimes each received 24 Senate seats. The fact that two of the three "regions" were provinces became increasingly problematic as the Maritime seats were divided among three provinces (10 each to Nova Scotia and New Brunswick, 4 to Prince Edward Island) and, after the turn of the century, as the 24 western Canadian seats were divided equally among the four western provinces. Newfoundland then received an additional 6 seats in 1949, giving the "Atlantic" region 30 seats, and the northern territories each received one seat.

Provincial representation thus ranges from 4 to 24 seats, which might make some democratic although not federal sense if the range was based on population size. However, there is little rhyme or reason to the present arrangement. Admittedly the smallest province has the greatest proportionate weight in the Senate — there is one senator for every 32,000 residents of Prince Edward Island — but the largest provinces do not have the least weight. While there is one senator for every 287,000 Quebec and 420,000 Ontario residents respectively, there is one for every 424,000 Alberta and 527,000 British Columbia residents respectively. The Senate does not compensate for the relatively light weight that the two western-most provinces have in the House, but further penalizes them! Here it should also be noted that western Canada, with 29% of the Canadian population, has only 23% of the Senate seats. Only Atlantic Canada fares well as a region, with 29% of the Senate seats and 9% of the national population.

The bottom line is that the representational foundation of the Canadian Senate no longer makes any sense. The fact that the weird distribution of seats has not been a major political issue shows only how marginal the Senate is to Canadian political life. If the Senate actually mattered, if it were seen to do things that had some impact on the lives of Canadians, then the current distribution of seats would be intolerable and untenable.

METHOD OF ELECTION/APPOINTMENT

American senators are elected directly by the people of their states whereas Canadian senators are appointed by the federal government, a fundamental difference that goes a long way in explaining the very different roles played by the two Senates in their respective political systems. Indeed, it is difficult to imagine a more dramatic institutional contrast.

American senators were originally selected by state legislatures, a form of indirect election which the Seventeenth Amendment to the American Constitution replaced by direct popular election in 1913. They are now elected for six-year terms from state-wide constituencies and thus enjoy a broad electoral mandate. By contrast, Canadian senators are appointed by the prime minister of the day and lack even the regional legitimacy which might come from appointment by their respective provincial governments. Rather than enjoying any democratic legitimacy or electoral mandate, Canadian senators are seen by the public as aging party warhorses, fund-raisers and cronies of the prime minister. This reputation comes in large part because senators are more often than not aging party warhorses, fund-raisers, and cronies of the prime minister.

It should be noted that the legislative power of American senators is reinforced by a number of factors related to their direct popular election. With the sole exception of the presidency, the United States Senate lies at the top of the career hierarchy for American politicians. There is no position apart from the presidency with as much power and prestige, and there is no political position with greater job security. (Senators enjoy remarkable longevity; incumbents have a success rate of close to 95% in congressional elections and this, combined with the six-year term, all but ensures that senators once elected have a secure legislative career.) Ambitious politicians move up from the states to the House of Representatives and then to the Senate, or from state governorships to the Senate. It is a rare event indeed for someone to resign from the Senate to run for state governor, and it is unheard-of for someone to resign from the Senate to run for the House. Although this career hierarchy is not constitutionally defined it is real nonetheless; senators are at the top of the legislative totem pole. Even for those individuals with an eye on the presidency, the Senate provides about as good a launching pad as one can get, although admittedly a number of recent presidents (Carter, Reagan, and Clinton) have jumped from the state governor's office to the presidency. Finally, the power of United States senators is further reinforced by extensive staff support; senatorial staffs numbering between 50 and 100 individuals, many of them drawing top salaries, are not uncommon. As a consequence, a United States senator is not merely an individual legislator; he or she is an impressive political machine with enough resources to reach well into the legislative and bureaucratic operations of the national government.

The case of Canadian senators is different in all these respects except one. They do not sit at the top of the career totem pole, for a Senate appointment comes *after* a successful career elsewhere. It is more an obituary than a recognition of existing status. Indeed, Senators exercise far less influence than do provincial premiers or cabinet ministers, or for that matter MPs. An American governor might well resign to seek election to the Senate but a Canadian premier would almost never resign to accept a Senate appointment; only defeat at the polls or failing health would drive a Canadian premier into the Senate. Canadian senators, moreover, have but a tiny fraction of the staff resources at the disposal of American senators; they are not formidable political machines in their own right but only bit players on the national political stage. Canadian senators rival their American counterparts in only one respect; because they are appointed until age 75, Canadian senators would appear to have even more secure tenure. In practice, however, the difference is slight; death is more likely than electoral defeat to remove from office American senators, who do not even face mandatory retirement.

In summary, the two Senates differ dramatically. The American Senate is effective in practice as well as on constitutional paper, is equal with respect to state representation, and is elected directly by the people of the states. The Canadian Senate is effective on paper but of little significance in practice, is based on an antiquated and increasingly bizarre system of regional representation, and is appointed by the prime minister without input from provincial governments or electorates. True, they are both Senates, but then Madonna and Willie Nelson are both singers.

THE UTILITY OF THE AMERICAN MODEL?

The last decade has witnessed growing Canadian pressure for Senate reform or abolition, pressure that springs in the first case from regional unrest with the representative character of parliamentary institutions and in the second case from increasing democratic unease with senatorial challenges to the elected House of Commons, unease which is likely to increase. The supporters of Senate reform have been successful in grafting their quest onto the broader national search for constitutional renewal, and the supporters of abolition are provided with new ammunition each time a Senate seat is handed out on the basis of patronage. The country appears split between Senate reformers and abolitionists, with defenders of the status quo restricted to a small band of senators and senators-in-waiting.

The dominant reform model in recent years has been the Triple-E, a Senate that would be effective, equal and elected. As we have seen, the Americans have a true Triple-E Senate and it is therefore not surprising that Senate reformers look to the American model with some appetite if not lust. Thus we might ask what light the American experience sheds on the Canadian Senate reform debate. Would the American model or a close approximation fly in Canada? What price would Canadians pay if their Senate was reformed along the lines of its American counterpart?

In addressing these questions it is not my intent to rehash the entire Senate reform debate but rather to reflect for a moment on the American experience. The Americans started in 1789 with a Senate that was effective and equal. All that remained to achieve a full "Triple-E" Senate was the introduction of direct popular election for senators, an inevitable step in a country so firmly wedded to democratic principles. Canadians, however, would have to move simultaneously on all three fronts. We would have to create an effective Senate by removing the hesitation senators normally feel in exercising the Senate's full range of existing constitutional powers. We would have to move from the existing representational mish-mash to an equal Senate, a move which recent experience has shown will be extremely difficult if the Senate is also to be effective. (The barriers in this respect include not only resistance in Ontario but, more emphatically, resistance in Quebec where an equal Senate would quite accurately be seen as a direct challenge to the influence of both Quebec and francophones within the national legislative environment.) One might think that the least contentious change would be the move to an elected Senate. Democratic values are deeply embedded and widely shared in the Canadian political culture, and undoubtedly the ill-repute of the existing Senate comes primarily from its appointed character. Yet the American experience shows that even here Senate reform would pose a serious threat to some of the most basic virtues of parliamentary government.

In short, an elected Senate would be difficult to reconcile with the principle of responsible government whereby the government of the day remains in office only so long as it can command majority support in the House of Commons. Such majority support is ensured in turn by party discipline, by the willingness of MPs to support their party even in the face of conflicting regional loyalties and personal beliefs. The American Senate works so well as a representative institution because its members are elected independently of the president and House of Representatives, and because party discipline imposes a very light constraint on the representational activities of senators. They can be effective regional representatives because they have real institutional clout and because there are few institutional incentives to compromise regional representation, to put the interests of party and country ahead of the interests of one's state. The Senate, unlike the Canadian House of Commons, is not a "confidence house" and because the president is not forced to resign if his legislative or budgetary initiatives fail in the Senate, there is no compulsion for senators to support the president. It should be noted, however, that the Senate does not function primarily as a states' house; senators have sufficient power and tenure to pursue interests which reach well beyond their state's boundaries. It should also be noted that the elected American Senate is a less faithful mirror of society than is the appointed Canadian Senate where there is a much greater representation of women, ethnic minorities, and aboriginal peoples.

The representational strengths of the American Senate come at a price, and the price is the virtual absence of responsible government. Voters cannot hold individual senators, or indeed the president responsible because, as individuals, they could not control the direction of national public policy. The president can blame Congress for his failings, and legislators can blame both the president and one another. There is no party mechanism to enforce responsible government because there is no effective party discipline within the Senate or within Congress more broadly defined. Fairly or not, Canadians can blame the government of the day, the incumbent party, when things go wrong, and they can enforce that responsibility through a highly partisan ballot. Americans have lost this option and it is by no means clear that they have fared well as a consequence. The prize they have won is a system of government that can best be described as chaotic and which is only loosely subjected to popular control.

Although the American Senate is effective as a representative institution, its contribution to responsible and effective government can only be described as negative. The Canadian Senate may be ineffective as a representative institution but at least it rarely impairs the responsible government that comes from cabinet control and party discipline in the House. A reformed and elected Canadian Senate could only be effective if it had the capacity to successfully challenge the cabinet and House. Thus the price of an effective Senate would be weakened responsible government, and here the American experience should give Canadians pause. If democracy means effective popular control of elected officials, if it means responsible government enforced through the ballot, then the appointed Canadian Senate may serve democracy well by staying out of the legislative fray. A reformed Senate would provide more effective regional representation but not necessarily more democratic government.

The basic question is whether the cost of impaired regional representation is so great that Canadians should pay the price of an American-style, Triple-E Senate. As an alienated western Canadian, someone who feels that parliamentary institutions are fundamentally flawed in their ability to provide visible and effective regional representation, I must conclude that the price would be too high. Canadian parliamentary institutions do provide responsible and reasonably effective government, and if the trade-off for this is impaired regional representation, then this may be a price worth paying. This does not mean that we should abandon the search for institutional reform, that the Senate status quo can or should prevail, or that a reformed Senate will not play a role in a new set of political institutions designed for the twenty-first century. However, it does mean that the American Senate provides an inappropriate model for Canadian institutional reform; the American model is too deeply embedded in a very different philosophy of government to provide much useful guidance for Canadians.

FURTHER READING:

Roger Gibbins. *Regionalism: Territorial Politics in Canada and the United States.* Toronto: Butterworths, 1982.

Randall White. *Voice of Region: The Long Journey to Senate Reform in Canada.* Toronto: Dundurn, 1990.

PETER McCORMICK

The Will of the People: Democratic Practice in Canada and the United States

The casual juxtaposition of the two assertions seems paradoxical: few countries on earth are more alike in their politics than the United States and Canada, and yet the differences between them are profound and important. Rather than exploring these generalizations for the total sweep of democratic politics in the two countries, this discussion will focus arbitrarily on three much more specific topics within these broad parameters: *first*, regulating election campaign financing; *second*, drawing electoral boundaries; and *third*, the recall of elected officials.

CHOOSING HOW? MODERN DEMOCRACY AND THE DILEMMA OF ELECTORAL FINANCING

The core image of democracy is comfortably homey, conjuring up cohesive communities choosing which of their neighbours will represent them in the legislature. But population growth and a widening right to vote make this image increasingly anachronistic; today, democracy means asking thousands of voters to decide which of several strangers should represent them. The mathematics are simple but compelling: each member of the United States House of Representatives represents more than half-a-million people; each member of the House of Commons represents about 100,000. This puts a high premium on using the mass media to make candidates known and attractive to voters, the problem being that not all candidates enjoy equal access. The mixture of money and democratic elections has always been problematic; in the modern context this is less a question of direct corruption (rich candidates literally buying votes) than of unfair advantage (rich candidates overwhelming their opponents by dominating the media).

The problem is exacerbated by the escalating costs of "state of the art" technology. In 1990, without a presidential race, the total spending on Congressional contests was $777 million, averaging $1 million per Senatorial candidate and $200,000 for each candidate for the House of Representatives; some Senate races cost as much as $20 million. In Canada in 1988, the election expenses of the three major parties totalled just over $50 million, and each candidate in a typical riding spent $40,000. But regulating campaign spending is a juggling act which struggles to keep three balls in the air: (1) preventing the rich from controlling parties and buying politicians; (2) preventing established parties from monopolizing the process; and (3) allowing independent individuals and groups to participate without running afoul of (1).

Logically, the problem has four major components which have generated four different strategies for containing the electoral impact of wealth. These are:

1. reporting the sources of campaign funds — if voters know who has contributed to a particular candidate or party, they know who might be the recipient of privilege or favour.

2. limiting expenditures by candidates and parties — if none can spend more than a set amount, the advantages of wealth are reduced.

3. (partial) public subsidy of candidates and parties — public funds guarantee a minimum voice to any credible party, and reduce the advantage of wealth to the gap between subsidy limits and expenditure limits.

4. limits on expenditures by non-party actors — to prevent wealth from evading the implications of spending limits, and to limit the leverage of single-issue groups who target vulnerable opponents and/or subsidize sympathetic allies.

The timing and trajectory of legislative response in Canada and the United States has been very similar. In the United States, legislation prohibiting contributions by corporations, and requiring the disclosure of campaign contributions to election committees and to individual candidates, was passed in 1910 and revised in 1925; the curious omission of trade unions was corrected in 1943. In practice, however, the legislation was a complete failure. Corporations circumvented restrictions by having corporate executives and employees make contributions in their own names; and spending limits were routinely evaded by a proliferation of purportedly independent committees supporting the same candidate. So perfunctory were the rules and their enforcement that not a single candidate for House or Senate was ever charged (let alone convicted) under the 1925 legislation.

Serious reform began in the 1970s, prompted by growing public awareness of the extent and blatancy of evasions, and reinforced by the excesses of the 1972 Presidential campaign. The *Federal Election Campaign Act* of 1971 set media spending limits for House and Senate races, required reporting of spending and contributions over stated amounts, and instituted an income tax check-off for presidential campaigns. Amendments in 1974 established a Federal Election Commission to monitor compliance, a prohibition on spending of sums over $1,000 by individuals (or by committees not authorized by the candidate) advocating the election or defeat of specific candidates, and limited provision for public funding for presidential elections.

Reform was partially but effectively checked by a constitutional challenge, the critical case being *Buckley v. Valeo* decided by the United States Supreme Court in 1976. The argument was that the spending restrictions violated First Amendment rights to free speech, and by and large the Supreme Court agreed. It upheld the reporting and disclosure requirements[1] as serving a valuable public purpose, and the limitation on contributions by any single individual. The Court also accepted a linkage between public funding and spending limitations — any candidate accepting the funding implicitly accepted the conditions and had the option of refusing — although subsequent decisions on related matters rendered these limits largely ineffective. However, the setting of general limits on expenditures by candidates, or on expenditures by an individual supporting or opposing a candidate, was unacceptable; it was the equivalent, the Court said, to allowing a person to speak in a large hall but denying her the use of the public address system.

Since *Buckley*, the activities of Political Action Committees (PACs) have become increasingly significant. These committees, which in the late 1980s numbered in the thousands, are created by unions, corporations, trade associations, and ideological interests to support clusters of favoured candidates, and are estimated to be responsible for about half of all the money spent during American national elections. The United States Supreme Court has stood by its view that these committees are entitled to full First Amendment protection, following up *Buckley* with more explicit victory for the PACs in *Federal Election Commission v. National Conservative PAC* in 1985. Subsequently, in *Federal Election Commission v. Massachusetts Citizens for Life, Inc.* in 1986, the Supreme Court struck down the restrictions on contributions and expenditures by corporations. The legislative efforts to reform election financing have been largely, although not completely, frustrated by the Supreme Court's interpretation of the constitutional guarantees.

Similarly in Canada, despite episodes like the Pacific Scandal that embarrassed the Conservatives in the 1870s and the Beauharnais Power Scandal that embarrassed the Liberals in the 1930s, early efforts at regulation were perfunctory and largely ineffective. Canada had long-standing federal legislation (since 1874) that required the reporting of over all campaign contributions and expenses (but not of individual contributions), fatally flawed by its failure to acknowledge the importance of political parties. 1908 rules to prohibit campaign contributions by corporations (and, in 1920, by unions as well) were undermined by this same flaw — contributions to candidates were prohibited, but not contributions to parties. Unsurprisingly, this section of the act never resulted in legal proceedings against any corporation or candidate, and enforcement of the reporting provisions, in Ottawa as in the provinces, was lax and casual.

In Canada, as in the United States, the late 1960s and early 1970s saw renewed interest in campaign expense regulation. The Barbeau Committee (an advisory group of former parliamentarians) reported in 1966, followed by the Chappell Committee (a Special Commons Committee) in 1970. During the same period, Nova Scotia, Manitoba, and Saskatchewan introduced reforms of their own campaign finance legislation, and in Ontario the Camp Commission was established to investigate alleged campaign financing abuses. The first attempts at drafting new federal legislation failed, but the minority Parliament after the 1972 election passed the 1974 *Election Expenses Act* — a major overhaul of national campaign finance regulation still largely in place two decades later.

The 1974 legislation comprised several major elements. The first was the requirement for full disclosure of individual campaign contributions in cash, goods, or services to political parties as well as candidates. The second was government assistance to political parties for campaign expenses, including a tax credit system, partial reimbursement of the eligible expenses of candidates receiving more than 15% of the constituency vote, and new rules for political broadcasting including a limited subsidy from public funds. The third was limits on the expenditures by candidates and parties, and a limit on the period over which political advertising was permitted. Fourth and finally, there were restrictions on any person other than a candidate incurring election expenses, extended to a total prohibition by

Table 1: Campaign Finance Regulation, Canadian Jurisdictions

Province	Disclosure Cand./Party	Limit Contribution	Limit Spending Cand./ Party	Reimburse Cand./Party	Tax Credit /Deduction
CANADA	yes/yes	no	yes/yes	yes/no	yes/no
Alberta	yes/yes	yes	no/no	no/no	yes/no
B.C.	yes/yes	no	no/no	no/no	yes/no
Manitoba	yes/yes	no	yes/yes	yes/yes	no/yes
N.B.	yes/yes	yes	yes/yes	yes/yes	no/yes
Nfld.	yes/no	no	no/no	no/no	no/no
N.W.T.	yes/no	yes	yes/no	no/no	no/yes
N.S.	yes/yes	no	yes/no	yes/no	no/yes
Ontario	yes/yes	yes	no/yes	yes/yes	yes/no
P.E.I.	yes/yes	no	no/yes	yes/yes	no/yes
Quebec	yes/yes	yes	yes/yes	yes/no	yes/no
Sask.	yes/yes	no	yes/yes	yes/yes	no/no
Yukon	yes/no	no	no/no	yes/no	yes/no

amendments in 1983. As Table 1 indicates, comparable measures apply in the provinces and territories.

Just as in the United States, so in post-Charter Canada, the legislation has been the target of constitutional challenges, although so far none have reached the Supreme Court; their combined impact is an echo of *Buckley v. Valeo* (discussed above) which supported public funding, undercut contribution limits, and opened the door to interest groups. In 1986, in *Re Mackay and Government of Manitoba*, a divided Manitoba Court of Appeal upheld the provisions of the *Manitoba Election Finances Act* providing public funding for political parties in the form of limited reimbursements for eligible expenses; the Supreme Court of Canada refused leave to appeal. More significantly in the same year, in *National Citizens' Coalition Inc. v. Attorney General of Canada*, a trial judge in Alberta agreed that the limitations on non-party spending were an unconstitutional violation of the *Charter* right to freedom of expression; the government did not appeal. Technically this ruling applied only to Alberta but the Chief Electoral Officer declined to enforce the provisions elsewhere in Canada. Consequently, advertising by groups other than political parties was widespread and extremely effective in the 1988 federal election, and the $5 million spent by supporters of Free Trade may well have tipped the result in favour of the Conservatives, especially in Ontario. The

Table 2: Provisions for Recall of State Officials

State	Year Adopted	Officials affected	Petition requirements
Oregon*	1908	all elected	15% votes
California*	1911	all elected	12%/20% votes
Arizona	1912	all elected	25% votes
Colorado	1912	all elected	25% votes
Nevada	1912	all elected	25% voters
Washington	1912	all elected, except judges	25-35% voters**
Michigan*	1913	all elected, except judges	25% votes
Kansas	1914	all elected, except judges	40% votes
Louisiana	1914	all elected, except judges	25% voters
North Dakota*	1920	all elected	25% votes
Wisconsin	1926	all elected	25% votes
Idaho*	1933	all elected, except judges	20% voters
Alaska	1959	all elected, except judges	25% voters
Montana	1976	all elected, all appointed	10%/15% voters
Georgia	1978	all elected	15%/30% voters

Note: votes = votes cast at previous election
voters = eligible voters at previous election
10%/15% = requirement for statewide/district elections
* = successful use of recall
** = varies for different offices/officials

Source: adapted from Table 5.16: Provisions for Recall of state Officials, *The Book of the States*, Vol. 26 (Lexington; Council of State Governments; 1986), p.217

resulting situation is very similar to that of the United States — valid and somewhat effective legislation on the disclosure of contributions, judicial support for limited public funding for political parties, but invalidation of limits to non-party spending — although Canadian legislators have been more successful in imposing candidate and party spending limits.

Both Canada and the United States have had strikingly similar experiences with regard to regulating election campaign finances. In both countries, long-standing but ineffective legislation persisted for decades despite growing concerns, escalating costs, and occasional evidence of widespread abuse. By the 1970s, legislators in both countries became convinced that reform was necessary, and both acted against a similar spectrum of regulatory targets; again in both countries, parallel reforms at the state or provincial level echoed (and to some extent anticipated) the national reforms. However, in both countries the legislative intent was partially but significantly frustrated by constitutional challenges, this particular impact occurring in Canada only after the entrenchment of the *Charter*.

Both countries therefore demonstrate the difficulties that contemporary governments face in developing an effective policy response to emerging problems in changing circumstances, unless they can persuade the judiciary to accept a similar definition of the urgency of the problem and the appropriate way of responding to it — something which they have so far failed to do on election spending. At the time of writing, the federal government has introduced new amendments to the *Election Expenditures Act* limiting non-party spending, largely a response to the perceived impact on the 1988 election of interest group advertising on the Free Trade issue. A *Charter* challenge seems inevitable, its outcome difficult to anticipate.

REPRESENTING WHAT?: THE SINGLE MEMBER CONSTITUENCY AND THE POLITICS OF ELECTORAL BOUNDARIES

Canada and the United States are among the minority of democratic countries, using the single-member plurality-vote electoral system. That is: the country (or the province/state) is divided into discrete geographical divisions, each electing a single representative; and the winner is the candidate receiving the largest number of votes, whether or not that is an absolute majority of votes cast. Such an electoral system has important side effects — such as the fact that a party can win a majority of seats without receiving a majority of the vote; or the way votes for candidates other than the single winner receive no representation. However, one striking implication is that it turns a "national" election into a series of individual contests, each decided without reference to the outcome of any other. Because the way the lines are drawn will unavoidably affect the way voter preferences are translated into elected representatives,[2] the process which creates electoral boundaries is critical.

There are two major temptations built into the line-drawing process. The first is *maldistribution*, which means giving some electoral divisions many more eligible voters than others. If you are the party in power, and you know that one segment of the population (say, rural areas) gives you high levels of support, you create rural ridings with fewer voters per riding; if you know that another segment of the population (say, urban areas) gives you much less support, you create urban electoral divisions much larger than average. This violates the democratic principle that votes should be weighted equally — should all have the same chance of contributing to the election of a representative — but the practice is older than the principle. It survives in provinces like Alberta where the 50% of the population in the two largest cities has fewer seats than the 30% living in rural areas, just as it used to be widespread in the U.S. where (to use the Georgia example from the famous case of *Baker v. Carr*) votes in rural counties could be worth from 11 to 120 times as much as votes in urban counties.

The second temptation is *gerrymandering*, a term that will explain itself by the end of this paragraph. If the voting preferences of many citizens are consistent from one election to the next, then the party drawing the lines can combine all the neighbourhoods that heavily support the opposition into a single constituency which returns their candidate by a massive majority, while several surrounding ridings elect government members by modest but comfortable margins. As an extreme example: imagine a bloc of nine seats, one returning an opposition member by 90-10, while eight others vote 55-45 to return government members — although overall the two parties received the samé number of votes. Sir John A. Macdonald referred to this practice as "hiving the Grits" (that is: piling the Liberal voters into a few ridings). The general term derives from a Governor Gerry of nineteenth-century Massachusetts, whose creative drawing of electoral boundaries resulted in a constituency whose shape suggested the head, legs and sinuous tail of a salamander: hence, "Gerry-mander."

In the United States, the judiciary had long used its "political questions" doctrine[3] to avoid involvement with redistricting issues, a self-imposed reluctance it abandoned in the 1962 case of *Baker v. Carr* (where the Supreme Court declared a constitutional requirement for regular redistribution to accommodate population growth and movement), and even more decisively in the 1964 case of *Reynolds v. Sims* (where it required justification for any departure from "one person, one vote" principles). Since that time, American courts have been constantly involved in controversies over electoral boundaries for state elections and for Congressional districts (which, in American practice, are set by state legislatures). These standards have recently become very exacting, sometimes striking down redistribution schemes for departures from pure mathematical equality on the order of 1%.

There has been ongoing concern with the impact of redistribution schemes on representation opportunities for ethnic minorities — blacks, Hispanics and Asians. The conceptual labels that describe these concerns are "racial gerrymandering" and "vote dilution"; they have (as yet) no counterpart in Canadian jurisprudence[4]. There have also been cases alleging partisan gerrymandering — dominant parties drawing electoral boundaries to favour their own candidates — but no redistribution scheme has been struck down on these grounds, and the evidentiary barriers are daunting. In general, American standards of review support any proposed redistribution where all districts fall within a narrow range of an overall average figure (typically plus or minus 10%) unless it violates other constitutional or statutory standards; this is referred to as a *de minimis* approach.

In Canada, the reform of redistribution processes also dates back to the 1960s, although here the initial impetus was legislative rather than judicial. At the national level, legislation establishing non-partisan redistribution commissions was introduced, but not enacted, by the Diefenbaker government in 1962; the Liberals followed through shortly after their victory in 1963. With some revisions, the 1964 legislation has remained the basis for subsequent federal redistributions.

The *Act* set up independent boundaries commissions for each province, directed to create electoral boundaries to correspond as closely as possible to the electoral quota for the province, with a normal variation of 25% that could be exceeded in unusual circumstances.[5] This standard, which has served as the jump-off point for recent court rulings on redistribution, seems generous when compared with the exacting standards that have evolved in the United States, but it should be understood within its own context. Compared with the enormous variations in riding sizes in and before the 1960s, it was positively revolutionary; and the 25% limit is permissive, disguising a general movement toward increasingly rigorous approximations of equality in most provinces.

Some inequality is unavoidable because Commons seats must be assigned to provinces and territories and cannot straddle provincial boundaries in the pursuit of voting equality. Further inequality is built in by "floors" to the Commons representation of several provinces and both territories. As a result, some provinces (Alberta, British Columbia, and especially Ontario) have been clearly under-represented in the Commons — that is, their percentage share of seats is significantly lower than their percentage share of the Canadian population. These structural factors aside, the last quarter-century has seen growing egalitarianism and impartiality in the drawing of electoral boundaries, especially within each province.

The practices of redistribution and the drawing of electoral boundaries in the provinces can be thought of as variations on a roughly similar general theme. Provincial reforms also began in the early 1960s. Indeed, some provinces anticipated federal changes just as clearly as other provinces followed them; for example, Manitoba's non-partisan electoral boundaries commission provided a model for the 1964 federal legislation.

As a brief summary: six provinces redistribute at fixed intervals (ten years for Manitoba and Newfoundland, eight years for Saskatchewan, every second election for Alberta, every election for Quebec, and every second election or every six years for British Columbia); others do so on an *ad hoc* basis. In most provinces boundaries are drawn by independent and impartial commissions, although only Quebec lets them act without opportunity for legislative intervention; only Alberta assigns the actual drawing of electoral boundaries to a legislative committee. Four provinces (Newfoundland, Manitoba, Saskatchewan, and British Columbia since 1984) have created non-partisan commissions with three or four members, one of whom is a judge and none of whom are members of the assembly. Quebec has a bureaucratic commission with independent members enjoying security of tenure. Ontario, New Brunswick and Nova Scotia have used non-partisan *ad hoc* committees of varying size, typically headed by a judge.

Most boundary commissions work within strict limits as to the number of constituencies. Alberta is the only province with a persisting practice of creating formally different types of constituencies with different electoral quotas. Manitoba did the same thing for a decade before 1968, as did Saskatchewan for its 1989 redistribution, and the practice was upheld by the Supreme Court in *Carter v. Saskatchewan* (1991). Ontario and Saskatchewan both single out northern constituencies for differential treatment.

At the core of Canada's "electoral boundaries revolution" was the depoliticization of the drawing of electoral boundaries. However, most provinces with statutory redistribution schemes have also made marked progress toward "one person, one vote." In three provinces (Quebec, Manitoba, and Saskatchewan), provincial apportionment has been as or more equal than federal apportionment within the province. For those provinces employing more *ad hoc* procedures, progress in this direction has been more modest and in some cases (such as Prince Edward Island and Alberta) virtually non-existent.

During the last thirty years, the process of redrawing electoral boundaries in Canada has undergone major changes at both the federal and provincial level, constituting nothing less than "a revolution in electoral mapmaking." (Carty, 1985, 273). Although this period coincides with the transformation of American redistricting practices, there are two important differences between the two countries' experiences:

1.   in the United States, the process was begun and the pace set by the courts, beginning with the landmark cases of *Baker v. Carr* in 1962 and *Reynold v. Sims* in 1964. In Canada, the reform impulse started in Parliament and the legislatures, with the courts playing no role. This may simply reflect the recency of Canada's entrenched *Charter*; recent cases[6] suggest that the non-involvement of the Canadian judiciary can no longer be assumed.

2.   in the United States, the initial concern was with "one person one vote" and the more recent focus is non-discriminatory boundary-drawing in the hands of a neutral (or at least bipartisan) committee; in Canada, the initial concern was the depoliticization of the drawing of boundaries, and the more recent focus has been "one person, one vote."

In both countries, electoral redistricting has since the 1960s become much more equal, and the process has been rendered much more neutral and impartial. However, problems remain and complaints periodically surface regarding partisan manipulation of electoral boundaries. In the Canadian redistribution following the 1981 census, a New Democratic Party seat in Vancouver was carved into unrecognizable pieces, an outcome no different from the 1940s when the Liberals orchestrated the disappearance of Saskatchewan Conservative John Diefenbaker's Lake Center riding. The reforms of the last three decades have significantly reduced, but hardly eliminated, the politicization of the redistricting process. However, public concern with political equality was convincingly demonstrated during the constitutional reform process leading up to the defeat of the Charlottetown Accord in 1992, and the astonishing popular hostility to the measure that would have guaranteed Quebec 25% of the seats in the Commons even should that province's share of the Canadian population fall below its current level.

ACCOUNTABLE WHEN? THE RECALL OF ELECTED OFFICIALS

The notion that elected legislators represent citizens is unconvincing unless some form of accountability is built into the process. In the normal course of events, this is accomplished by requiring periodic elections: representatives are elected for a fixed period of time (as in the United States), or for a period of time that must not exceed a constitutional maximum (as in Canada), at the end of which time they must return to the citizens to seek re-election; in the process they can be held to account, and either rewarded or punished, for their actions.[7]

But a considerable time can elapse between elections. The term of a member of the United States House of Representatives is only two years, but Senators are elected for six years at a time, and Canadian MPs (and members of provincial legislatures) serve terms that are seldom less than four years and may be as long as five. A great deal can happen during these longer terms, and the accountability inherent in periodic elections can seem remote to citizens whose representative does things they disapprove of early in the term. In a democracy, voters have the power to "throw the rascals out," but the opportunity doesn't come very often.

One answer to this problem is *the recall* (or, as its nineteenth century proponents called it, the "imperative mandate"). This process makes elected officials subject, potentially at any time the voters choose, to the direct review of the citizens who put them in office. Review is triggered by a petition calling for a recall election which if successful leads to a special election to fill the now-vacant office. It resembles impeachment, which also removes a representative in mid-term, but lacks the overtones of legal impropriety; one is *impeached* for crimes and misdemeanours, but *recalled* simply for ignoring the wishes of the electors.

Although historical allusions are sometimes made to the eighteenth-century American Articles of Confederation, the ideological context of the recall in North America was clearly the populist (or "progressive") movement.[8] The "we/they" dichotomy at the core of populist rhetoric — "we" the common people *versus* "they" the special interests — implies a focus on the democratic franchise as the weapon of choice for reform, and fuels outrage at any perceived blockage of the popular will. In the United States, the movements built on these sentiments tended to be regional in their origin — typically the rural areas of the American midwest and south. The organizational core was usually a farmers' movement (the Grangers or the Farmers' Alliance) often with tenuous connections to an urban labour movement. Populism was a significant political force in the late nineteenth century, culminating in the People's Party of the 1890s. By the turn of the century, it had been largely replaced by the Progressive movement which made major inroads in the western and mid-western states. Populism/progressivism advocated a wide range of direct democratic devices, and the particular attraction of the recall grew from its usefulness as a weapon against corrupt elected officials, or more generally against the control of state legislatures by monied special interests.

In most of the states where it exists, the recall is the enduring legacy of the Progressives. The geographical sweep of recall measures adopted before World War I and during the inter-war period clearly reflects the regional concentration of Progressive strength. The revival of popular interest in the recall in the 1970s is harder to explain; in addition to the adoption of the recall in Montana and Georgia in 1976 and 1978 respectively, a recall provision was narrowly defeated by the voters in Utah and another was narrowly rejected by a 1978 state constitutional convention in Hawaii. Fifteen states have adopted the recall for elected state officials, and a majority allow it for municipal officials; no state has ever repealed such a provision once enacted. (See Table 2 for a summary of data.) Six states exempt elected state judges while one (Montana) makes appointed state officials subject to the recall. The recall is not in effect for any federal officials, although Arizona has established a procedure which is called the "advisory recall." Under this process, a candidate seeking election to Congress is invited to file an optional statement indicating a willingness to resign if not re-elected at a recall election, although this commitment cannot be enforced.

There are three basic patterns of recall procedure. The first and by far the most common requires two votes, the first on the question of removal; if successful, this results in a second election to choose a replacement. The second, used in Colorado and Wisconsin, calls for citizens to vote simultaneously on removal and replacement (the latter counting only if the first vote is affirmative). In a third variation (used in Arizona and Nevada — and in Oregon until a 1914 State Supreme Court decision required the two questions be separated) the successful recall petition itself triggers a special election.

The proportion of voter signatures necessary for a petition varies from 10% (for state-wide officials in Montana) to 40% (in Kansas). The most common figure, used in nine of the fifteen jurisdictions, is 25%. Nine states base the requirement on the eligible voters for the office in question; six base it on the number of votes actually cast in the most recent election. Given the low turnout in state elections, the latter is more permissive. Some states limit the time for the circulation of the petition, from 60 days in Wisconsin to 270 days in Washington; most have no such limit, although the two-year term of most state legislators is as effective as any formal regulation. Several states will not allow a recall petition at the beginning of a term, the immune period varying from two months (Montana) to 90 days (California) to six months (Arizona, Colorado, Oregon) to one year (Wisconsin). An official is also immune after an unsuccessful recall election for a period varying from three months (Wisconsin) to 18 months (Louisiana), although some states will waive this if the new petitioners reimburse the state for the costs of the previous unsuccessful recall vote. Michigan is the only state that bars the recalled officer from running again in the special replacement election; more typically, recalled officials are *automatically* candidates for their own replacement unless they formally indicate otherwise. It is not infrequent (but neither is it the normal outcome) for the recallee to be elected as his/her own replacement. Some local charters stipulate a minimum turnout (typically 50%) for a recall election; no state has a comparable provision.

Successful uses of the recall have been infrequent. The only removal of officials elected on a state-wide basis came in North Dakota in 1921, when the governor, attorney general and secretary of agriculture were all recalled.[9] The removal of state legislators has not been much more common: two in California in 1913, two in Idaho in 1971, two in Michigan in 1983, and one in Oregon in 1988; and a California state senator was successfully recalled in 1919. Most recall petitions (on some estimates, more than 90%) fail to gain the necessary signatures, although the success rate for recall elections seems to be closer to 50%, an estimate including local as well as state experiences.

Canada's recall experience has been more limited, arguably because of the differences between the American Congressional system and the more centralized dynamics of parliamentary government. As in the United States, demands for the recall in Canada have been connected with waves of populism, the first of which occurred after World War I. In federal politics, the Progressives briefly held more Commons seats than the Conservatives, but faded steadily as a political force after 1921. In provincial politics (under the United Farmer label), they formed governments in Alberta, Manitoba and (briefly) Ontario. The rhetoric of the Progressives stressed grass roots democracy, delegate control, and the devices of direct democracy. In practice, the demands of office meant that little was done, and the tension between responsible government and delegate democracy was fought out within the organization of the movement.[10] Adoption of the recall did not occur until the second wave of Canadian populism, in the form of the Social Credit and Cooperative Commonwealth Federation movements of the 1930s.[11] In Alberta, stressing its continuity with the progressive movement, the Aberhart Social Credit government passed a Recall Act in April 1936. The legislation was closely modelled on the American examples of the third model described above, although the signatures required for a petition (two thirds of eligible voters) were almost triple the normal American state requirement. This seems prohibitively high, but the voters in the Premier's own riding were soon well on the way to having the necessary signatures. The Premier responded by retroactively repealing the legislation in October 1937, and running in a different riding in the next general election. Premier Aberhart believed that oil company executives ("Eastern big-shots") were bribing and intimidating their workers to support his recall, although more prosaic factors such as his flamboyant indifference to the idea of constituency service clearly played a role. Canada's only provincial experiment with the recall ended auspiciously, and dramatically demonstrates the special vulnerability of cabinet ministers — a major problem for the recall in a Parliamentary system.

Historically, the recall as a way of making elected representatives more accountable has been marginal in the United States and negligible in Canada. This makes the perennial interest it arouses perplexing; perhaps the answer lies in the transparent simplicity of the device ("Angry with your representative? Fire him!") and in the fact that its local focus makes it easier to understand and more practical to operationalize than such grander components of the populist scheme as initiative and referendum. As well, the recall device might well be more attractive in a parliamentary system than in the more fragmented Congressional system. First, cabinet members, as local members with higher profiles and wider responsibilities than their back-bench colleagues, provide particularly tempting recall targets (as Aberhart discovered). Second, a narrow government majority could be progressively eroded through selective use of the recall. Third, the rigid party discipline of Canadian parliamentary practices exposes back-bench members to the outrage of local majorities. And fourth and finally, the longer terms of Canadian parliamentarians (four or five years, compared with the United States norm of two years) offers greater scope for bad feelings and recall signatures to accumulate.

Certainly the idea of the recall has not died on either side of the border. It has recently been on the constitutional agenda in Utah and Hawaii, and two Canadian provinces (Saskatchewan and British Columbia) conducted referendums on the recall in conjunction with their 1992 provincial elections; the "yes" vote was very high, and the British Columbia government has indicated an intention to introduce enabling legislation. In federal politics, the regionally based Reform Party is the strongest advocate of the recall.

CONCLUSION

These closer investigations of three selected aspects of Canadian and American democratic practices have more than confirmed the initial suggestion of significant similarities between the two countries. If anything, they suggest a border that is extremely permeable to political ideas, as the electoral boundaries revolution and the attempts to regulate campaign financing have occurred more or less simultaneously both north and south of the 49th parallel, following similar strategies in the process. The words and phrases of the United States Supreme Court echo in Canadian court decisions and political speeches; even the "effective representation" phrase which our Supreme Court coined to distance itself from some of the detailed implications of American doctrine is in fact drawn from the representation debate in that country. The enduring exception is the populist device of the recall, widespread if seldom invoked in the United States but (with a single brief and abortive exception) absent from Canadian politics. If the current agitation for the concept proves fruitful, if recall moves in the immediate future from slogan to practical policy in one or more provinces, this will demonstrate even more dramatically the permeability of the United States-Canadian border. It may not even be stretching the point to see the two countries as conducting a joint experiment in the adaptation of Western democracy to the twentieth century, which makes the comparative perspective of this volume all the more relevant and important.

NOTES

1. Except where evidence was presented to demonstrate that compelled disclosure of names would expose contributors to harassment.

2. For example: consider a four-riding city, comprising an urban core with 25% of the population which votes heavily (say, 80%) for Party A, and a large suburban fringe with 75% of the population which slightly (say, 55%) prefers party B. If we draw the electoral boundaries as if we were slicing a pie, party A will take all four seats; if we make three seats of the suburban donut and a fourth out of the central core, party A will win only one seat. Both outcomes are intuitively unfair.

3. The United States Supreme Court has long held that it is not empowered to deal with "political questions," and although the Court has never provided a definition Prof. Edward S. Corwin has attempted one: "a political question relates to the possession of political power, of sovereignty, of

government, the determination of which is vested in Congress and the President, and whose decisions are binding on the courts." Many commentators are far more cynical about the concept, arguing that "political questions" is a label for those cases the judges have chosen not to decide, not a reason for that choice.

4.   For example: let us restructure the previous example, so that we now have one-quarter of the population in an urban core which is 90% black, and three-quarters in a suburban fringe which is 90% white. If we draw electoral boundaries as if we were slicing a pie, we make the election of black representatives unlikely; if we make a single seat of the urban core, we virtually guarantee them one representative. Less hypothetically: in the 1993 Nova Scotia general election, the boundaries were drawn to include in a single electoral division the province's most substantial concentrations of black voters and all three of the major parties nominated black candidates to give the Nova Scotia legislature its first black member. If future redistribution were to carve that riding into pieces and combine each piece with a different neighbouring riding, this could be challenged as "vote dilution" harmful to the black minority's representation prospects.

5.   The typical American *de minimis* standard is 10%, less permissive than Canada's 25%. If the average is 100,000, the American standard implies that no riding can have fewer than 90,000 or more than 110,000, but the Canadian standard accepts as little as 75,000 and as much as 125,000. The largest U.S. electoral division is 122%, and the largest Canadian 167%, of the smallest.

6.   Such as *Dixon v. A-G B.C.* (B.C. Supreme Court 1989) *Carter v. A-G Saskatchewan [the Saskatchewan Reference]* (Supreme Court of Canada 1991); and the *Alberta Boundaries Reference* (Alberta Court of Appeal 1992). Another electoral boundaries reference was before the Alberta Court of Appeal when the Alberta government called the 1993 provincial election.

7.   Of course, a representative can avoid this accounting simply by not running again; however, in modern practice, the party will supply another candidate to receive the gratitude or the annoyance of the voters. In this sense, the existence of party enhances accountability; it is an open question

whether this balances the problem of representatives caught between party discipline on the one hand and local sentiment on the other.

8. Populism is often described as being as much a mood or syndrome as a systematic philosophy. It is built on a number of factors: a common-sense celebration of the average citizen, a preference for direct democracy devices (recall, referendum, initiative) to allow direct ongoing influence by the electors, an identification with small-scale business capitalism (family farms and small business), a tendency to blame outside forces (sometimes sinister in nature) for economic and social problems and to see solutions in simple or even simplistic terms (such as the recurrent conspiracy theories), a strong feeling of community and traditional values that borders on nativism and xenophobia, a project of reform rather than revolution to solve economic and social ills, and a distrust of parties leading to a preference for non-partisanship that usually co-exists with strong support for a dominant leader.

9. More recently, in the 1980s, a strong recall attempt in Arizona was forestalled when the state legislature successfully impeached the governor.

10. For example, through the requirement that populist candidates sign an undated resignation and leave it in the hands of their constituency association; as a reaction to the progressive assault on the party system, this practice has been illegal in Canadian elections since the 1930s.

11. The casual juxtaposition of Social Credit and CCF may seem anomalous in contemporary politics, but the description is apt for the 1930s; the transformation of Social Credit into a right-of-centre good-business party took place in the 1940s and 1950s under Manning, and should not be read back into the origins of the party.

FURTHER READING:

On Redistribution Issues:

K.C. Carty. "The Electoral Boundary Revolution in Canada." *American Review of Canadian Studies* 15 (1985).

John Courtney. "Parliament and Representation: The Unfinished Agenda of Electoral Redistributions" *Canadian Journal of Political Science* 21 (1988).

John C. Courtney, Peter MacKinnon & David E. Smith (eds.). *Drawing Boundaries: Legislatures, Courts and Electoral Values.* Saskatoon, Saskatchewan: Fifth House Publishers, 1992.

Nelson Polsby (ed.). *Reapportionment in the 1970s.* Berkeley: University of California Press, 1971.

David Small (ed). *Drawing the Map: Equality and Efficacy of the Vote in Canadian Electoral Boundary Reform.* Lortie Commission Research Studies. Toronto & Oxford: Dundurn Press, 1992.

Norman Ward. "A Century of Constituencies" *Canadian Public Administration* 10 (1967).

On Campaign Spending Regulation:

Ontario Commission on Election Finances. *A Comparative Survey of Election Finance Legislation 1988.* Ontario: Queen's Printer, 1988.

J. Patrick Boyer. *Money and Message: The Law Governing Election Financing, Advertising, Broadcasting and Campaigning in Canada.* Toronto: Butterworths, 1983.

K.D. Ewing. *Money, Politics and Law: A Study of Electoral Campaign Finance Reform in Canada.* Oxford: Clarendon Press, 1992.

Leslie Seidle (ed.). *Comparative Issues in Party and Election Finance.* Lortie Commission Research Studies. Toronto & Oxford: Dundurn Press, 1992.

Leslie Seidle (ed). *Issues in Party and Election Finance in Canada.* Lortie Commission Research Studies. Toronto & Oxford: Dundurn Press, 1992.

Leslie Seidle (ed.). *Provincial Party and Election Finance in Canada.* Lortie Commission Research Studies. Toronto & Oxford: Dundurn Press, 1992.

On the Recall:

Michael Cassidy (ed.). *Democratic Rights and Electoral Reform in Canada.* Lortie Commission Research Studies. Toronto & Oxford: Dundurn Press, 1992.

Thomas E. Cronin. *Direct Democracy: The Politics of Initiative, Referendum and Recall.* Cambridge & London: Harvard University Press, 1989.

Laura Tallian. *Direct Democracy: An Historical Analysis of Initiative, Referendum and Recall Processes.* Los Angeles: People's Lobby, 1977.

Joseph P. Zimmerman. *Participatory Democracy: Populism Revived.* New York: Praeger, 1986.

DAVID THOMAS

Checkmate and Stalemate: Formal Constitutional Change in Canada and The United States

Canada's 1867 constitutional arrangements were deliberately intended to avoid what were perceived to be weaknesses in the American system of government and, in much the same way, the constitution of the United States had deliberately not been rooted in the traditions of the British parliament and crown. Canada has, nevertheless, been deeply influenced by American examples and experience and, it can be argued, has "had a habit of accepting things American whilst claiming to reject them."[1] Even so, both constitutions have not only grown a long way from their roots — a modern President has powers undreamt of by the founders, and Sir John A. Macdonald would roll in his grave at the thought of the power of the provinces — they have also developed in accord with the inexorable logic of their original constitutional architecture.

Other chapters in this volume show how important these institutional differences still are. To say this is not to attempt to minimize, or ignore, the existence of significant social and cultural variations. Nor is it to downplay the continuing appeal for many Canadians of the American constitutional model, at least in theory.[2] It is simply to recognize that constitutional arrangements are politically constraining, symbolically powerful, and, in the Canadian case, a matter of considerable, ongoing controversy. This above all is what distinguishes the Canadian and American situations: in Canada constitutional difficulties have been the focal point of a debate about the country itself. The enormous pressures of the late twentieth century, which tear at the old fabric of the state and the assumptions on which it was based, find their expression in Canada in demands for new constitutional arrangements. Old battles over representation, French/English duality, regionalism, provincial powers and citizens' "rights" have taken on new forms, and are subject to the effects of the erosion and global destabilization of traditional economic, political, social, and constitutional assumptions.

The United States also faces startling internal and external challenges; its vision of itself, the great collective narrative of American progress, is going to be difficult to sustain. But the Constitution will not be seen as either the cause of the problems or as a radical cure for what ails America.

The thesis of this chapter is that Canada's recent experiences with constitutional change have, paradoxically, served to both further differentiate the two political systems and have also brought them closer together. The chapter is in three parts: it outlines the rules for change and the ways in which these reflect very different constitutional origins and problems; it next compares and contrasts the American experience with the Equal Rights Amendment with the Canadian turmoil over the Meech Lake and Charlottetown Accords; finally it discusses the paradox of divergence and convergence and where this leaves the Canadian process.

THE RULES FOR FORMAL CHANGE

Constitutions encompass far more than formal-legal rules. They reflect "habits of the heart"; they are often silent on key questions or, if taken literally, would instantly become inoperable (and in Canada's case the Governor General would be a good deal busier). Federalism as an ideal and idea involves far more than constitutional arrangements; nevertheless, institutions and rules are important and take on a life of their own — and formal alterations to the distributions of powers are invariably serious matters, made worse in Canada by the still problematic nature of the amending procedures.[3]

If we think of Canada as a medical patient, she would recently have suffered a series of constitutional heart attacks. Rest, plus a change of constitutional lifestyle, are called for. The United States, on the other hand, would not be a patient: she would be a reasonably healthy senior citizen, albeit set in her ways. Differences in the approach taken to constitutional change can therefore reveal a great deal about our respective histories. We can analyze the principles and underlying assumptions upon which a constitution was based, consider how these have mutated, and assess the extent to which there is still consensus on, and acceptance of, our constitutional "philosophies" — and the rules for change.

American amending procedures are cumbersome, the rules archaic. They are set out in Article V of the constitution and have remained unchanged since 1787. There are two different ways to initiate an amendment and two different ways to ratify it. A proposal must be **initiated** either by a two-thirds vote (of the members present) in each of the Houses of Congress, or by a special convention which must be called by Congress if two-thirds of the states so demand. This latter procedure has never been used although the states have, on several occasions, come very close to the two-thirds required. The composition, powers and role of such a convention are a mystery and the constitution provides no guidance whatsoever on the subject. The danger is that if one were held it might open the Pandora's box of wholesale constitutional change, just as the Constitutional Convention did in 1787. **Ratification** is to take place either by successful passage through three-quarters of the state legislatures (i.e., 38 of 50) or by special conventions called for this purpose in each state. This latter approach, where, once again, the rules are not clear at all, has been used but once: the Twenty-First amendment (repeal of prohibition) was ratified in this manner. Conventions varied in size from three members in New Mexico to 329 in Indiana. A time limit for the passage of an amendment may, or may not, be set, and if it is, it has usually been seven years. This limit may be extended, as was the case with the Equal Rights Amendment (ERA) which passed the congressional hurdle in 1972 but by the 1979 deadline had not achieved the necessary votes in the states. The deadline was then controversially extended until 1982.

Other interesting aspects of the American process, particularly from a Canadian standpoint, are that a state legislature cannot rescind (revoke) its assent once given, yet can ratify even after a previous rejection. One noted authority has pithily commented, "this seems wise in view of the confusion that would otherwise result."[4] (Ex-Prime Minister Brian Mulroney would undoubtedly agree: the province of Newfoundland ratified the package of changes known as the Meech Lake Accord, only to rescind later with the arrival in office of a premier who was intransigently opposed to parts of the agreement.) The President's consent is not required. There is no provision for a national referendum, and the Supreme Court has ruled that binding state referendums are unconstitutional — they must be advisory or consultative only.

It is thus theoretically possible for the 13 states that have in total a mere 4% of the American popular vote to block an amendment, or for an amendment to be ratified by 38 of the smallest states containing only 40% of the population. However, these are hypothetical, worst-case scenarios, and the requirement for congressional initiation is always there as a check. Over the years, thousands of amendments have been proposed to the Congress. Each year they predictably appear (protect the flag, authorize prayers, balance the budget) and just as automatically they will fail. They are usually proposed in order to make a political point: to show the voters back home that their representative stands for whatever happens to be the political and social flavour of the times. The very fact that the Constitution is so venerated gives reformers (recently often conservatives) the incentive to see their pet solutions entrenched and placed beyond the reach of opponents.

The American amending formula is thus highly federalized. The majority of the founding fathers had a healthy mistrust of direct democracy and of majority rule. Article V reflects the federal principle that the states, not the people as such, should play a key role. The Courts have had to step in on occasion, and the unused sections remain unclear. The court ruling that a state cannot rescind its ratification is still controversial, and states attempt to defy it.

Nevertheless, Americans do accept their process of constitutional change, warts and all: it has the virtues of longevity and mere existence. It is so federalized that making it work is exceptionally difficult; luckily it does not need to work very often. It may take decades between the time a change is proposed and an amendment is adopted. There have been, in all, only twenty-six amendments.[5] It works in a negative way in that it really provides a mechanism for the states not to propose but to oppose. To attempt to change it would open the debate as to where, ultimately, sovereign power in a federal state should reside. Should it rest with "the people" and if so, how many? Should it be the states? Congress? The President? And how is consent to be obtained? The permutations are endless, the results of change uncertain. And so Article V remains as it was written in 1787, and the need for a workable mechanism of constitutional change has been met by the Supreme Court which acts as a constitutional backstop.

The Court's role is crucial. It fills a constitutional vacuum and is able to legitimize, deflect, and obscure political debate over the constitution and its meaning. The Court's political and constitutional importance is to be seen not only in the substantive effect of its rulings but also in the debate over Presidential nominees, the constitutional outlook they hold, and what this would do to the "balance" on the court. Robert Bork was rejected by the Senate (in 1987) because he was seen as a "constitutional radical" and because of fears that President Reagan was trying to bring the court directly into the political arena.

Americans — of otherwise widely diverse views — regard much of the [resulting] system of constitutional liberty as a fundamental part of our legal heritage. And this system is a product, not merely of the Constitution's framers, but more fundamentally of the interpretive practices of the modern Supreme Court, apparently doing its work above the battles of ordinary politics.[6]

Canada, on the other hand, has been suffering under the delusion that all sorts of political, legal, social, and even economic problems can be solved via constitutional change, and has demonstrated a naive, perhaps a foolhardy, willingness to contemplate sweeping reforms. At the same time, the extremely complicated amending procedures that were put in place in 1982 *in themselves* create serious difficulties — and have never been accepted or ratified by the government of Quebec. (Although it was negotiated by federal political leaders who were themselves from Quebec, notably Pierre Elliot Trudeau and Jean Chretien, the entire package of changes was rejected by all the parties in Quebec's National Assembly.)

Prior to 1982 Canadians had been unable to agree on the basic rules for constitutional change and matters had therefore been left where, officially, they rested in 1867. Canada had a constitution without an amending formula as such, and formal change could only come via a resolution of the British (i.e., Imperial) parliament. This was a situation that should have changed as the country attained dominion status and legislative autonomy, but there was no agreement on the role of the provinces in the process and unwritten political "conventions" emerged. Although these proved reasonably flexible the lack of an amending formula became an abeyance, a matter not to be raised because it was too fraught with danger.

There was no consensus "on the underlying question of nationhood" or on the "desired level of unity."[7] Ottawa, Quebec, and the other provinces simply could not agree on the rules of the constitutional game. In practice, after 1907, the provinces were consulted on all amendments that affected their powers directly and a convention of the need for unanimity settled into place. Provincial agreement, it should be noted, meant the consent of the premiers, not the legislatures or the population as a whole.

The 1960s saw the debate over the constitution, and how to change it, re-opened under the impetus of Quebec nationalism. To cut a very tangled tale extremely short, when a new amending formula arrived in 1982 it was still a matter of considerable disagreement. The 1982 arrangements resembled the American in that they were highly federalized and did not involve citizens directly.

The amending formula (really formulae), plus the right to "opt out," may perhaps be seen as a fine balance reflecting Canada's constitutional historical realities. Or it can be viewed as a surrender by a federal government which had previously proposed a radically different approach based upon the need to acquire legislative approval in all four "regions" (the Maritimes, Quebec, Ontario, and the West) and, failing this, would have authorized Ottawa to hold a national referendum.[8] One problem with the regional approach was that it did not treat all the provinces as equal: Quebec and Ontario each had a veto, whereas other provinces did not. The American model of state equality was held up as a counter example, and the idea that Ottawa could by-pass provincial governments and appeal directly to citizens was, ironically in view of later events, anathema to the premiers.

What emerged instead was a far more elitist and provincialist (and complicated) amending procedure, negotiated by a federal government concerned primarily with the Charter of Rights and by provinces willing to agree without Quebec being a part of the deal. The unintended consequences of these arrangements have come to haunt those who wish to bring about change by formal amendment.

The procedures for amendment may be initiated by the Senate, the House of Commons or by the legislative assembly of a province. As things now stand, some changes require **unanimity**. The federal parliament (including the Senate which has, however, only a suspensory 180-day veto) must agree. So must a majority in each of the ten provincial legislatures. The five areas covered by this section include any changes to: the office of Queen, Governor General, and Lieutenant-Governor; the composition of the Supreme Court; and the methods of, and rules for, amendment. Other matters, including the division of federal-provincial powers, most of the Charter of Rights and Freedoms, the powers of the Senate, the methods of selecting Senators, and the creation of new provinces come under the general formula, as does anything not specifically covered by the other rules for change. The **general formula** requires the consent of the legislatures in two-thirds (7) of the provinces containing 50% of the population, plus resolutions of the Senate and the House of Commons. To these can be added both federal and provincial rights to amend certain things **unilaterally**, and Ottawa's right to make **bilateral** arrangements with a province or provinces. (Some experts now see this latter as a way to solve the constitutional impass with Quebec.)

Finally, the provinces are also given the right to **opt out** of an amendment that diminishes their "legislative powers, proprietary rights or any other rights and privileges." If this opt-out is over the transfer of powers involving "education or other cultural matters" to

Ottawa, the province opting out is to be provided with "reasonable compensation." This was a clause designed primarily to protect Quebec's interests.[9]

But it was not enough. The government of Quebec would accept neither the loss of its hitherto assumed constitutional veto, nor certain key sections of the accompanying Charter of Rights and Freedoms, particularly those relating to language. (These were not, it must be remembered, to be subject to the legislative override clause. American observers of the Canadian scene must find it passing strange that contentious linguistic rights have more protection than "fundamental freedoms," and that there is an override clause at all.) Flags in Quebec were ordered to be flown at half-mast on the day that the Queen signed the Constitution Act in 1982.

After the agreement, one view was that the constitution should be left alone and given time to fit the new mould, but what looked like an excellent opportunity to reach an understanding with Quebec arose in the mid-1980s. The attempt to find a new consensus led to a continuing and broadening constitutional debate, first over the Meech Lake Accord signed by all the premiers and Ottawa in 1987. This was intended to "reintegrate Quebec into the constitutional family." When it failed to be ratified within the three-year limit, it was followed by a protracted constitutional crisis, which led to the Charlottetown Accord and the resulting referendum of October 26, 1992.

The details of these debates cannot be revisited here. What has to be noted first is that the amending procedures and processes, especially the unanimity rule, the right of a province to rescind, the role of the First Ministers' Conferences, and the uncertainty surrounding public participation, all created grave difficulties. At the heart of the matter was Quebec's lack of a clear veto over major change and the mismatch between public and interest group expectations and the realities of the amending formulae. Most Canadians simply did not understand the complexities of such things as what required unanimity and what did not — and who can blame them? Even political scientists and Mordecai Richler could get it wrong. And, just as importantly, constitutional politics is symbolic politics. It deals with values; it is seen as "playing for keeps."[10]

Quebec understandably saw the rejection of the Meech Lake Accord as a humiliation; others saw it as standing up for Canada, or as finally having to face up to aboriginal issues. What could be more emotional? Americans have not had to experience anything like this in this century.

Those who created Canada's 1982 arrangements had always assumed that proposed amendments would emerge through debate at annual First Ministers' Conferences. It is hard to even imagine the president of the United States sitting down, on a regular basis, with state governors to discuss ongoing constitutional changes. The president's constitutional problem is choosing the appointee to the Supreme Court. A presidential nightmare is the Senate's rejection of his choice. Far more than the sad affair of Clarence Thomas, the recent Clinton appointment of Ruth Ginsberg illustrates the complexity of the search for the "right" candidate and the ease of appointment once someone clearly meets the requirements of the times. In the Canadian case, executive domination, elite agreement, public deference, and legislative control were assumed, wrongly, as it turned out. The nature of the problems on the table (e.g., the distinct society status of Quebec, the future of the senate, aboriginal claims, women's rights) and an increasing sense of group and public ownership of certain parts of the constitution, notably the Charter of Rights and Freedoms, ensured that the prime minister and the premiers could no longer get away with private deal making. At the same time there was no other game in town; public involvement would have to be invented somehow, under ad hoc rules. The non-democratic character of the formulae had become an essential part of the debate over change.

At the end of the twentieth century, tampering with constitutions means raising not only the old questions that were extensively debated at Philadelphia in 1787 or at Charlottetown in 1864. It means dealing with non-federal, pluralistic, rights-oriented forces claiming economic, social and legal justice and/or equality; with demands for historical redress and future considerations; with the realization that the very process of change itself is a central part of the debate as to where power resides. Change must be seen to be "democratic" especially when there appear to be no limits to the demands for the redefinition of constitutional rights in general. Peace, order, good government, and individual protection are not the only points at issue.

In the United States these problems of "post-traditional" constitution-making are illustrated by the battle over the ERA — which also, in terms of strategy, tactics, and outcome presage, in numerous ways, the Canadian struggles over the Meech and Charlottetown Accords.

UNUSUAL AND ILLUSTRATIVE: THE ERA, MEECH, AND CHARLOTTETOWN

Canadians, if they think of it at all, must still be puzzled by the failure of the ERA in the United States and will attribute it to the antics of the Republicans and the religious right. Equality of the sexes is accorded powerful protection under the Canadian Charter of Rights and Freedoms, and the wording of the American proposal seems innocuous enough:

> Equality of rights under the law shall not be denied or abridged by the United States or by any state on account of sex.

Canadian women did benefit from American constitutional experience; feminists' failure in the United States helped to focus the strategy used to secure the entrenchment of gender equality in Canada. Even so, broader lessons might have been learned about the difficulties of federalized amending formulas by studying the actual process of non-ratification of the ERA.[11]

An equal rights amendment was introduced to Congress first in 1923 when it was defeated by a coalition of progressives and conservatives. This is the sort of coalition now familiar to Canadians who watched Jacques Parizeau, the leader of the indépendantist Parti Québécois, and Preston Manning of the Reform Party, both fight the Charlottetown Accord. It was not until 1972 that the ERA finally escaped Congressional clutches, passing the House in 1971 (354 to 23) and the Senate in 1972 (84 to 8) with resounding majorities. A mere 25 minutes after the Senate vote, the first state ratification took place (Hawaii). By early 1973, 30 states had ratified. The ERA's future seemed rosy.

In June 1982 the extended deadline came and went, and the ERA failed, three states short of the required total. This failure may not seem surprising to Canadians who witnessed an even more impressive display of solidarity fall apart after the Meech Lake Accord was signed. The ERA campaign unravelled for a great many reasons. There was no widespread agreement on the nature of the problem being remedied or on the need to further constitutionalize matters, especially when the Supreme Court and state courts had already made significant progress enforcing equality rights under the Fourteenth Amendment.

The Supreme Court itself was part of the debate; it was seen by the ERA's opponents as too progressive and already far too powerful. Giving it an expanded role could lead, it was argued, to unintended, unanticipated, and unwanted consequences. In practice, according to a number of scholars, it seems far more likely that the Court's use of the amendment would have been restrained and conservative. The absolutely central constitutional role of the United States' Supreme Court has already been noted.

Judicial decisions can have an enormous impact upon the distribution of power within a federal system as well as upon rights in general.[12] Americans have come to live with judicial supremacy of this kind even though in many ways it undermines more democratic venues for constitutional deliberation and alteration. In Canada the situation has, until now, been very different. Which brings us back to recent events.

In Canada, during both the Meech and Charlottetown debates, Canadians were also divided over the nature of the problems, the need for haste, and the role of the Supreme Court in interpreting, for example, the clause that entrenched Quebec's right to be considered a "distinct society." Some argued this clause meant virtually nothing and was largely symbolic. Others held that it could and would be used to attack and erode individual rights and values. Many could not see why Quebec had a "problem," and what was wrong with the status quo. And they worried that the Charter of Rights and Freedoms would be undermined.

ERA's proponents are seen as having done too little, too late. Opponents, in contrast, soon became focused, well-organized, well-rehearsed, and highly vocal. The same was true of both Meech and Charlottetown. The pro-Charlottetown campaign, even after the Meech experience, got off to a dreadful start. Once the decision to hold a national referendum was made, supporters had trouble working together. They were, after, all, more used to being party workers and adversaries. Advertising was ineffectual. Opponents were able to exaggerate and pick on specific problems; defenders had trouble singing from the same hymn-book. The ERA's opponents said, amongst other things, that it would mean state-funded abortion on demand, unsegregated public washrooms, an end to boys' and girls' clubs, no all-male sports teams, homosexual marriages, economic penalties in the workplace, and women drafted for combat. Supporters could not agree on its merits and its real intent. In the case of the Charlottetown Accord there were exaggerations on all sides and a similar "parade of the imaginary horribles." If it failed Canada would "fall apart." If it passed, the country was on its way to being "dismantled." Its unanticipated consequences — and there would have been many — were feared. In all three situations, to be effective, opponents simply had to pick a section or aspect of the proposal, throw some dirt, and hope some would stick.

It is certainly true that in Canada the debate was over what Peter Russell, in a widely quoted essay, has called "macro-constitutional politics." Such politics "address the very nature of the political community" and are "exceptionally emotional and intense."[13] Nonetheless, the ERA campaign too was highly charged and it took on, in many ways, the characteristics of a referendum. Indeed, it has been said that "it became a referendum on many of the cultural changes that had been under way since the 1960s — on feminism, especially, and on anti-war protest, civil rights and federal social engineering, the loss of status of housewives, the sexual revolution, gay liberation."[14] The ERA touched issues that went deep into the heart of conservative America. Meech and Charlottetown also became judgements on what Canadians thought had gone wrong with the country: free trade, bilingualism, central Canada's dominance, taxation, Quebec's complaints and power, government spending, multiculturalism, immigration, affirmative action, the Nationa Energy Policy, and Brian Mulroney's leadership. These things, and more, were part of the subtext of the debate over the Meech and Charlottetown agreements. It mattered not that many of these issues had precious little to do with the actual proposals in the texts. Proponents in each case seem to have dismissed objections too readily.

Finally, and perhaps most important of all, the ERA, Meech and Charlottetown were crippled by the process of amendment itself. Canada has chosen to copy in large part the American approach, which is, as noted previously, highly federalized and complex. Thus even successful American amendments have often taken years to pass. The three-year rule in Canada (the clock starts ticking once the first legislature has passed the amendment) has exactly the same effect as the prolonged American process, because opposition can develop and it is likely to be regionalized. The ERA failed in the southern and Mormon states; Meech and Charlottetown were deeply unpopular in the West (although the latter was also unacceptable in Quebec). Canada now has an even more complicated version of this state- (or province-) dominated formula. The extra Canadian bells and whistles include, it must be remembered, the need for unanimity on some matters and the right to rescind.

One should not push these ERA similarities too far. There were differences. Accident and chance played a vital part. Senator Sam Ervin, a leading ERA opponent, had also become famous for his role in the Watergate hearings. New Brunswick and Manitoba did not pass the Meech Lake Accord immediately, their governments changed, and the new premiers were opponents. Meech Lake was far more complex than the ERA; Charlottetown infinitely more so: its table of contents alone was two pages of small type: "It was complicated, tentative, ambiguous and entangled."[15] In the American debate there was no-one with the status of a Pierre Elliott Trudeau. It is unlikely that any former American president could have had as dramatic an effect, unless one came back from the grave. Trudeau's polemical dismissal of, and contempt for, the "weaklings" who negotiated the Accords, and his insistence that "Quebec's bluff" be called, sent the anti-Charlottetown poll figures up by a startling 16-18%.

The most obvious difference between Charlottetown and the ERA, apart from the Accord's complexities, is that Canada chose to hold a referendum. A federal referendum was not required under Canadian law and could only be "consultative" in any event. Formal power to amend rests with parliament and the legislatures. Mulroney and his cabinet were pushed into a referendum by some uniquely Canadian pressures, most importantly the deadline set by Quebec for its own referendum under Bill 150. Passed in June 1991 after the failure of the Meech Lake Accord, it required that a referendum be held in Quebec in either June or October 1992 and, in any event, by October 26 at the latest. This was to be a referendum on sovereignty or, it was assumed, could also be on "any offer of a new constitutional partnership."

The federal government's referendum decision was thus driven by this deadline and the need to legitimize and democratize the whole amending process. The federal government could argue, as it had done in the past, that it needed a mechanism to end-run the provincial premiers. An American president has no such need because the "dynamic constitutional tension" in the system is so different. The Canadian government wanted to be able to appeal to citizens as Canadians, not merely as residents of specific provinces. It needed to ensure speedy ratification in all provinces to avoid the problems that had befallen Meech. However, an even more pressing reason was that two provinces, Alberta and British Columbia, had put in place referendum legislation of their own.[16] With unanimity achieved at a First Ministers' Conference the federal government belatedly gambled on a national vote: Quebecers were to vote on the same question but under different campaign rules. It would have been odd, to say the least, to have had the citizens of some provinces voting on the proposal, while others did not. Quebec had to face the reality that it was no longer just dealing with Ottawa and the provincial premiers; Ottawa had to face the fact that if it held a national referendum it would still have to pass in every province to be assured of success (or a provincial legislature would have to disregard the wishes of its electorate).

DIVERGENCE AND CONVERGENCE

Once the referendum was over, it was almost as if it had never happened. Canadians seemed to realize how high the stakes had been and how difficult and draining the process. (Perhaps it was like having been in a brawl; you may have won but you don't want to admit that you were a part of it.) The winners — those who had opposed

— did not reap the fruits of victory. The Reform Party went down in the polls; the Parti Québécois did not gain. The losers did not seem to be as upset as they had been over the failure of the Meech Lake Accord. This was undoubtedly because in the Charlottetown Accord so much had remained uncertain. It was also due to the unequivocal nature of the results.[17] Two of the worst scenarios had been avoided: Quebec had not accepted whilst 'English' Canada rejected, nor had the reverse happened. Even aboriginal peoples had rejected what many non-aboriginals had considered an offer that was too rich.

A referendum can bring into the open the political forces that modern governments and societies have helped create and unleash, but such forces are there anyway, as the ERA shows. It will always be difficult for those in favour of some general "common good" to organize successfully against the power of specific and entrenched interests. If an amendment is specific, it will be attacked as too limiting. If vague, it will be seen as too general. The easiest way of rounding up supporters and volunteers, on either side, is to exaggerate the issues and to move to a black versus white approach, which in turn creates even more opposition and ironically, as Jane Mansbridge has pointed out, distorts the very interest that is being pursued.[18] All of this can and will happen with, or without, a referendum. Yet Canada would seem, in using such a device nationally, to have leapfrogged over the United States in the democratic stakes. For once, Canada appears to have been constitutionally more open, empowering, and populist, which is a clear variation on traditional Canadian "distrust of democratic institutions" and respect for authority.

That Canada had held a referendum at all may, in part, be attributable to American influences. The Reform Party has, since its inception, advocated referendums. Reform's roots are in the populist West where, on the American side of the border, public participation via referendums, the initiative, and the recall are widespread. Western Canadians could look to California and all its numerous ballots on major public issues, and did not have to worry unduly whether or not they understood the complexities and pitfalls of such mechanisms. Even so, an American would surely find a number of aspects of the whole affair distinctively Canadian.

Above all else it is Quebec that makes the Canadian situation unique. No American state has remotely the clout and veto power of Quebec. What American state could prevent, for two years, the imposition of conscription in wartime; precipitate a constitutional crisis all on its own; or seriously threaten to secede? In 1980, when the Quebec population voted on the famous "sovereignty-association" question and rejected the idea, the rest of the country stood by. If it too had voted it would have been rather like asking the English their views on independence for Scotland.[19] The Quebec referendum would appear to have had the very important effect of legitimizing popular sovereignty; it also showed that a clear majority in Quebec were in favour of a greater decentralization of powers. In 1992 the notion of a "people's veto" was extended to the populations of all of the other provinces; the package involved far more than Quebec's concerns. Meech had produced such a backlash, the idea of a referendum as a constitutional option had begun to take root. This was another case of an unanticipated consequence.

As noted previously, the process that led to the Meech Lake Agreement had been widely held to be unacceptable, whereas congressional debate is not open to similar charges. In the United States powerful Senators can protect and speak for state and regional interests. Canada's Senate has only a suspensive constitutional veto and its members can hardly be said to exercise any effective political power outside the chamber itself. In Canada, governments had to go to extraordinary lengths to open up the process and the debate over what was to come next. It is hard to imagine United States' citizens ever being subjected to as many opportunities for participation as were Canadians. There was everything from the Citizens' Forum on Canada's Future to six national conferences on constitutional renewal, and much, much more. The size alone of the American population would seem to preclude these kinds of state-sponsored constitutional road-shows.[20]

On this basis, one could argue that the events of 1992 have left Canada looking less like the United States than before and are yet another example of a situation where Canada's political institutions are a major source of distinctiveness. Not only has Canada "been loathe to borrow from the United States even when the American political experience may be of some immediate relevance"[21] but it continues to add new features. There are a number of reasons why this line of argument must be treated cautiously; there has been convergence as well as divergence.

Canada, like the United States, appears to be stuck with the constitutional status quo in terms of major, formal change, unless the federal government is prepared to make bilateral arrangements with Quebec — and these would be challenged. The two countries' amending formulae are so federalized, decentralized, and complex that obtaining the necessary levels of consensus and approval are extraordinarily difficult. Constitutions are not supposed to be easily amendable, but Canada's case borders on the pathological.[22] Barring yet another Canadian crisis precipitated by the drive for Quebec sovereignty, alterations to the federal system of both countries will be brought about by more "normal" forces such as fiscal policies, deregulation, tax changes, delegation, the political balance of power, the party system, and, let us not forget, through the courts. It is in this respect above all, that Canada may have moved closer to the United States. The failure of constitutional politics will place increased pressure on the Canadian Supreme Court as an agent of change. Even Section 1 of the Canadian Charter, although it subjects rights to "such reasonable limits...as can be demonstrably justified in a free and democratic society" is, in the words of one justice "tantamount to a directive to engage in a comparative exercise and research the position in other jurisdictions."[23] There are no prizes for guessing which jurisdiction will be watched most closely. Courts are at best imperfect and uncertain instruments of change. Canada's court is quite capable of making jarring judgements. If it is to perform an American-style role it will have to earn and maintain the public's confidence; there will need to be some level where popular political, debate about its composition and outlook takes place, particularly because, it must be remembered, the Court's decisions do not have to be unanimous. Reforming the Court along American lines will prove difficult indeed given provincial pressures, current practice, and Canada's institutional arrangements.

CONCLUSION: BACK TO THE FUTURE

The failure of the referendum was Pyrrhic victory for those who opposed it on the grounds that it did not go far enough. Democratic approval via a consultative referendum may have become, de facto, a new constitutional requirement if any major change is proposed in Canada. An important precedent has been set, and referendums could be here to stay. There may not be many of them held (they are not necessarily addictive)[24] but they would have the effect of making constitutional change significantly more difficult, and the rules for future referendums will still be the subject of extensive debate. Even a proposal involving only one substantive item could give rise to ERA-type difficulties.

Thus the peculiar amending arrangements of 1982, plus the experiences of Meech, Charlottetown, and the referendum, will all ensure that the 1982 settlement is even more deeply entrenched into the constitution. Canada may therefore have to move back to incremental processes of change led by traditional forces — the prime minister, the federal cabinet, and the premiers. Canadians may have decided, as is the case in the United States, that some matters have to be left unresolved and in a state of "suspended irresolution" rather than face again the daunting prospect of opening up the debate on first principles.

Will Canadians come to respect their constitution in the way that Americans respect theirs? This could be asking too much, in Quebec particularly but also elsewhere. If the search for constitutional panaceas resumes it may be because Canadians are optimists as well as gluttons for punishment, or it will be because the old issues just cannot be laid to rest. Part of any ongoing desire for constitutional change stems from the view that American constitutional arrangements provide a clarity to be admired and emulated. This is the view from off-shore or from above the 49th parallel. Americans know differently, for they live not with clarity but with complexity. If the American example starts to tarnish — if medicare reform fails utterly, gun control remains a joke, and racial violence explodes — the desire for more American-style institutions would diminish. Canadians, if push comes to shove, are likely as before to settle for efficiency and order before democracy and "freedom." But can they resolve, or shelve, the questions surrounding the future of Quebec?

Canadians have made a much more concerted effort to inform themselves on the subject of the constitution. Just as the ERA campaign, though it failed, raised the political consciousness of American women (and men), so the referendum campaign helped educate Canadians and, one hopes, has made them far more realistic in their expectations. And should have made them, and their leaders, realize how complex constitutional questions are. The difficulties of running a binational Canadian state will not go away, nor will aboriginal issues, but the pressure for constitutional reform could die down enabling the country to refocus its energies on the serious economic, social, political and moral problems of the late twentieth century. Neither Canada nor the United States can afford to let its constitutional architecture stand in the way of internal co-operation, reform, co-ordination, management, and planning.

NOTES

1. Robert C. Vipond, "1787 and 1867: The Federal Principle and Canadian Confederation Reconsidered," *Canadian Journal of Political Science*. XX11:1 (March 1989), 5.

2. For a recent example of this problem see "The Report of the Liaison Committee on Committee Effectiveness," *Parliamentary Government*. No. 43 (June 1993), 13. The Report

states explicitly that "The dilemma in Canada is that the political culture expects parliamentary committees to behave like U.S. committees and to be as influential."

3. See David Howes, "In the Balance: The Art of Norman Rockwell and Alex Colville as Discourses on the Constitution of the United States and Canada," *Alberta Law Review* Volume XXIX, No. 2, (1991). p.70. For a recent discussion of federalism and federation, see Michael Burgess and Alain-G. Gagnon (eds.) *Comparative Federalism and Federation* (Toronto: University of Toronto Press, 1993).

4. See William S. Livingston, *Federalism and Constitutional Change* (Westport: Greenwood Publisher, 1974), 232.

5. The first ten amendments adopted comprise the Bill of Rights. The Eleventh and Twelfth are little known. Then came the civil war and, as a result, the Thirteenth (abolishing slavery); the Fourteenth (long, complex and extremely important: it guaranteed citizenship and civil/legal rights); and the Fifteenth (forbidding the denial of the right to vote on grounds of race or colour). Later amendments include provisions for income tax, direct election of senators; prohibition and its later repeal; limitation of the President to two terms; presidential succession; and in 1971 the Twenty-Sixth Amendment gave the right to vote to 18-year-olds.

6. Cass R. Sunstein, "How Independent is the Court" *New York Review of Books* XXXIX, No. 17 (Oct. 22, 1992), 47-50.

7. See Walter Dellinger, "The Amending Process in Canada and the United States: A Comparative Perspective" in Davenport and Leach (eds.), *Reshaping Confederation: the 1982 Reform of the Constitution* (Durham: Duke University Centre for International Studies, 1984), 286.

8. For details on this and other key problems, see Alan C. Cairns, *Charter versus Federalism: The Dilemmas of Constitutional Reform* (Montreal: McGill-Queen's University Press, 1992), Ch. 3.

9. The details are too lengthy and complex to list. They are to be found in the *Constitution Act 1982* as follows: Unanimity rules — S.41; General Formulae S.38 and 42; Unilateral for-

mulas — S.44 and 45; Bilateral formula — S.43; Opting out — S.38(3); with Compensation — S.40; Right to rescind — S.46(2); Right to initiate — S.46(1). It is interesting to note that while the three year time is specified for the general formula, there is even disagreement as to whether this applies to S.41. See *The Report of the Special Joint Committees of the Senate and the House of Commons on the Process for Amending the Constitution of Canada* (Ottawa: Queen's Printers, 1991), 31.

10. See Peter H. Russell, "Can the Canadians be a Sovereign People," *Canadian Journal of Political Science*, XXIV: 4 (1991), 691-709.

11. See Mary Frances Berry, *Why ERA Failed: Politics, Women's Rights, and the Amending Process of the Constitution* (Bloomington: Indian University Press, 1986), also Jane J. Mansbridge, *Why We Lost the ERA* (Chicago: University of Chicago Press, 1986).

12. Note in particular the 1985 decision in *Garcia v. San Antonio Trust* as a result of which "The states must rely on the political process, not the Constitution or the Supreme Court, to preserve their historic role..." See Kenneth M. Holland "Federalism in a North American Context: The Contribution of the Supreme Court of Canada, the United States and Mexico" in Marian C. McKenna (ed.) *The Canadian and American Constitution in Comparative Perspective* (Calgary: University of Calgary Press, 1993), 90.

13. See Russell, "Sovereign People", *op. cit.*

14. See DeHart-Matthews, quoted in *The Chronicle of Higher Education* Dec. 3, (1986), 10.

15. Leslie H. Pal and F. Leslie Seidle, "Constitutional Politics 1990-92. The Paradox of Participation" in Susan D. Phillips (ed.) *How Ottawa Spends 1993-94* (Ottawa: Carleton University Press, 1993).

16. Their example was likely to have been followed by others and the federal government was thus facing the prospect of staggered, provincially administered, referenda.

17. 55.4% had said no, 44.6% said yes. Overall turnout was 74.4% and in Quebec it was 82.8%. The Accord was rejected by five provinces and one territory, and Ontario had split 50% — 50%.

18. Mansbridge, *op, cit.*, 6.

19. There would be merit in this; English interests are clearly involved and it might be important for the Scots to know what the English think. Yet when all is said and done, the Scots would be voting for self-determination, which is *not* the same as the English giving their opinions on the matter. The Quebec/Rest of Canada situation in 1980 was much like this, and does not have an American parallel. There is nothing unusual about asking a population its views on self-determination. This was done as early as 1791 in the Papal territories around Avignon.

20. For an excellent recent account see Pal and Seidle, *op. cit.* By the time it was all over $300 million had been spent, not including millions of dollars in time and travel costs. $25 million alone was spent on campaign advertising.

21. See Roger Gibbins, "The Impact of the American Constitution on Contemporary Canadian Constitutional Politics" in McKenna (ed.) *op. cit.*, 133.

22. See Peter H. Russell, "Attempting Macro Constitutional Change in Australia and Canada: The Politics of Frustration" *International Journal of Canadian Studies*, special issue on "The Charter, Federalism and the Constitution" Spring-Fall (1993) 7-8.

23. The words are those of Hon. Madame Justice Claire L'Heureux-Dubé of the Supreme Court of Canada. See McKenna (ed), *op. cit.*, 164. For a recent analysis of Canadians naivety regarding the political role of the Court, see David Milne, "Politics and the Constitution" in Alain-G. Gagnon and James P. Bickerton (eds.), *Canadian Politics an introduction to the discipline* (Peterborough: Broadview Press, 1990).

24. See David Butler "The World Experience" in Austin Ranney (ed.), *The Referendum Device* (Washington: American Enterprize Institute, 1981), 79-80.

FURTHER READING:

Berry, Mary Frances. *Why ERA Failed: Politics, Women's Rights, and the Amending Process of the Constitution.* Bloomington: Indiana University Press, 1986.

Cairns, Alan C. *Charter versus Federalism: The Dilemmas of Constitutional Reform.* Montreal: McGill-Queen's University Press, 1992.

Foley, Michael. *The Silence of Constitutions.* New York: Routledge, 1989.

Livingston, William S. *Federalism and Consitutional Change.* Oxford: Clarendon Press, 1974.

Mansbridge, Jane J. *Why We Lost the ERA.* Chicago: University of Chicago Press, 1986.

McKenna, Marian C. *The Canadian and American Constitutions in Comparative Perspective.* Calgary: University of Calgary Press, 1993.

Monahan, Patrick J. *Meech Lake: The Inside Story.* Toronto: University of Toronto Press, 1991.

Pal, Leslie A. and F. Leslie Seidle. "Constitutional Politics 1990-1992: The Paradox of Participation," in Susan D. Philips (ed.), *How Ottawa Spends 1993-1994.* Ottawa: Carleton University Press, 1993.

Pritchett, Herman C. *Constitutional Law of the Federal System.* New Jersey: Prentice Hall, 1984.

Swinton, Katherin E. and C.J. Rogerson (eds.). *Competing Constitutional Visions: The Meech Lake Accord.* Toronto: Carswell, 1988.

Part Three: Rules, Rights, and Roles

HON. MR. JUSTICE R. P. KERANS

Two Nations Under Law

What interests people about the way the law works? The prevalence of crime, and its treatment, tops every list. Litigation expense, long trials, and delay probably gain a high rating, as does the phenomenon, troubling to many, of a judiciary dominated by middle-aged men who were successful lawyers.

These problems, however, exist in both Canada and the United States, and this essay primarily aims at differences. If, then, I ask what Canadians consider special or unique about American justice, I think I would produce this list: almost all would mention the death penalty; they would add high, almost bizarre, damage awards; and they would nervously raise the issues of racism and corruption. A few would wonder whether Americans are more litigation-prone than Canadians, and if American courts encourage this. More than a few would query the impact of television in the courtroom. Some might say they hear that judges are too "activist" or "soft on crime." And how, they would ask, do courts get into curious issues like whether a child can divorce his parents, or who is the mother of a test-tube baby?

And can I ask a mythical American audience what they think of the Canadian system? I am hard-pressed to guess at any answer. Perhaps they would see the Canadian system as they seem to see the British: they would ask if judges are old and learned but out of touch with the real world. The voyage for the American reader is into more uncharted waters.

Let us begin by a visit to a courtroom. Expect to be a little perplexed. A few supposed differences are mere myths. American judges do not constantly hammer gavels, and Canadian judges do not wear wigs. If you fail to notice a flag display or a camera, you might not know whether the room is in Canada or the United States. A television camera would give away the answer, because many American state courts now allow them. All Canadian courts, except the Supreme Court of Canada, have stood against that tide.

The garb of the lawyers might stand out. If they are in business suits, it may or may not be a Canadian courtroom. But, if they wear barristers' gowns, the visitors can be sure they are in a Canadian setting. Americans never wear them, but all Canadian lawyers wear them for trials. Like school children, they are reduced, old and young, male and female, to dreary similarity in their crow-like costumes. Americans, on the other hand, must buy a more elaborate wardrobe. One might wear blue pinstripe in tax court, but not to defend a tax cheat before a jury of blue-collar stalwarts!

Beyond sartorial slavery, there is little to choose between American and Canadian lawyers or attorneys. Both belong to a merged profession, and so each is at once a barrister, who goes to court for clients, and a solicitor, who prepares documents for clients. Despite that, both tend increasingly to specialize. Some are excellent, most are competent, and a few are cheats. Most (not in Ontario) are free to work on a contingency, which means the client pays by advance assignment of part of the winnings. They have similar codes of ethics. Both now can advertise. Both must pass a standardized bar exam, and, usually, both must have a degree in law from an approved school. Canadian lawyers are licensed by province, as are Americans by state. The chief difference is that all Canadian lawyers are licensed, de-licensed, and regulated by an organization of their professional peers, the law societies. In most American states judges perform some of these tasks.

The visitors may well notice that the trial has been in occupation of the courtroom for several days. In both countries, trials once took only a day or two. Now, they often take more than a week, and can drag on for months. This curse came first to the United States, but now also has spread to Canada. There are several causes, but they come down to this: one party or another wants too much to win. Trials, and trial preparation, are expensive because clients are willing to pay for all that effort.

The courts are hard put to intervene where both sides prefer not to be sensible. But they can be faulted if they fail to respond adequately when one side compared with the other has little or nothing to lose by running up expenses. This happens when one side is either very poor or very rich. A rich litigant will "deep-pocket" the case, spinning it out until the other side is near ruin. In a similar but rarer technique, the needy litigant, who has a lawyer paid from the public purse, has nothing to lose.

To date, few Canadian courts have come to grips with these problems. On the other hand, some American courts have begun to experiment with an abandonment of the adversary system for pre-trial activity by having judges or judicial officers manage the entire process.

On the other hand, many lawyers in the past 30 years have advocated a loosening of some procedural rules with the idea that the courts might become a more effective instrument for redress. But things have not worked out as well as some hoped, and the class action is a good example.[1] Originally, this was a means to save money by joining all suits where the claimants had identical allegations against the same defendant. If not carefully regulated, this can lead to abuse. An example will best explain: a lawyer will sue a toothpaste manufacturer for, say, $9 million. This is serious stuff for the manufacturer, of course. The lawyer asserts that the label contained misleading statements, and the customer bought the wrong product. The customer had to return the product, at a cost for travel and nuisance of $3. How did the suit get to be for $9 million? Simple. The lawyer says he sues for a class, namely the three million people who bought the toothpaste that year! His only named client may be himself, and his liability for costs may be minimal.

On the criminal side both countries now have protracted pretrial hearings. They will look into how the police came by evidence for fear it is "poisoned fruit," which means it was the result of police illegality. Canadians also probe the history of the case to see if the prosecution is guilty of unreasonable delay.

But these stories again include shared problems. In what way do the trial processes vary? Here are some notable differences.

THE GAG ORDER

The American media treatment of exciting cases stuns Canadian lawyers. Not only do lawyers and others comment freely on the case before and during the trial, but so do jurors afterwards. Free speech is an admirable thing, but so also are other things, like a fair trial. A conflict between the two can arise when the police chief, with his "arrest report," proclaims the guilt of the accused. Or when the media, in their breathless on-the-spot interviews, proclaim or assume guilt. Or when the defence lawyer declaims, on the courthouse steps, his client's innocence. Almost none of this occurs in Canada.

The desperate American judge, anxious to protect the jurors from this influence during a trial, has little option but to sequester them. In other words, she locks them up in guarded hotel rooms every night of the trial, where they watch expurgated television and read edited newspapers. In Canada, the Courts protect the juries by direct action. They issue gag orders to stop excessive publicity before or during a trial. And the law forbids jurors from revealing any of their deliberations.

How did this difference arise? Revolutionary America suffered under the printing licence required by law in those days. The revolutionary complaint against "prior restraint" of free speech echoes to this day. As a result, judges prevent hardly anybody from sounding off. Canada has no similar history, and Canadians see sequestration as an awesome price for a jury to pay for all this talk.

COMMENT BY THE JUDGE

In most American jurisdictions, the judge almost never comments on the facts of case to the jury. Instead, she only offers standard directions on the law applicable in all like cases. A Canadian judge can and will. She will routinely suggest to them what are the key issues, and often expresses that issue in terms of the evidence in the case. She will also express her views about the merit of some of the arguments, and emphasize the answering arguments. She may well say what testimony impressed her, and what did not.

One result of all this is that dubious experts beset American juries.[2] In Canada, judges routinely scorn that sort of testimony. I also see a tie between the judge's commentary and three other uniquely Canadian phenomena. First, jury deliberations are not usually lengthy. Second, the bizarre verdict is rare. Third, many litigants choose a trial before a judge without a jury.

In some states the judge does not comment on the amount of the possible jury award for any loss, like pain and suffering, not susceptible to mathematical calculation. The idea is that the jury is the conscience of the community, and will decide what is fair. The same rule applies to extra awards to condemn the shocking immorality of the defendant's conduct, or to deter others from similar conduct. Because of the lack of guidance from the judge, the risk of an inordinately high award is real.[3] In Canada, by comparison, the courts have not only set limits for some common forms of general damages, but have moved away from the rule against comment about amount. Judges often now will suggest a "range" for the jury to consider.

Those troubled by excessive damage awards, and the role of lawyers in that process, will take some comfort from a recent case in San Diego.[4] A lawyer in that city who had for a decade advertised his prowess at gaining big settlements was successfully sued by a former client for incompetent handling of a claim. A jury imposed on him an award of $5 million as punitive damages!

JURY SELECTION

American jury selection is often as long as the trial itself. And it can produce dubious results. For the first "Rodney King" trial[5] in Los Angeles, over 200 prospects were rejected because they had seen the famous videotapes on television, and formed an opinion. The 12 who produced the result that rocked the country were those who asserted either that they had never seen the tape or they had not formed an opinion when they did. When one recalls the notoriety of the tape, the kindest thing to say is that they were not typical citizens.[6]

How did this happen? Both countries started with the old English rule: the accused have a right of trial near the place of the crime, and before a jury of their peers. The assumption was that an accused comes from the district where the crime occurred, and his peers will be his neighbours, certainly not some duded-up judge from London! This idea predates the idea of the presumption of innocence, and the two notions are a little contradictory. After all, to presume innocence means to have no preset ideas about the accused or the charge. The mind of each juror should offer what lawyers smilingly call a blank slate. But a trial before neighbours raises the suggestion, or at least the danger, that the jury will know a thing or two of the case or the accused.[7]

The problem for courts in the past century has been to reconcile these principles. The Canadians, following the English, do it by saying that the jurors no doubt will know something of the case. It is only in extreme cases, however, that previous knowledge will disqualify the juror. These extremes include being an actual participant, or being related to one. But not much more than that. A predisposition one way or the other because of talk the prospective jurors have heard will not disqualify them. The oath of office, the instructions and warnings of the judge, and the solemnity of the occasion, will together suffice to open the mind of the juror. In response to the suggestion that some people are bigots, the judge responds that, except in the clearest case, fear of that is not enough. After all, the accused wants trial by his peers, not by angels. In the result, Canadian courts are not only slow to disqualify, they are slow to allow even a disqualification challenge. In the result, jury selection often takes less than one hour. The result may be a prejudiced jury.

American jurists found this approach repugnant. They complained that a trial is not fair if a juror is, at the outset, partial. An enquiry must take place, they decided. A juror must be disqualified, many courts held, if, during questioning of the prospective juror, a doubt arises whether the juror is or will be impartial. Finally, some courts held that a juror who admits to any previous opinion *is* doubtfully partial, and the "King" case is the result.

OVERLAPPING JURISDICTION

Let us stay for a moment with the story of the officers who arrested Rodney King. After the acquittals in state court they faced new charges in Federal Court, and were convicted.

The technical explanation is that the accused officers were first charged in state court under state criminal law, and then in federal court under federal civil-rights law. To beat a man, one must agree, is to interfere with his civil rights. And so there is a dual and overlapping jurisdiction. In Canada, the two charges would have come before the same court, and in the same trial. In this way, the Canadian system succeeds in avoiding double jeopardy and the scandal of inconsistent verdicts.

LEGAL CULTURE

How to explain differences like these? The structural differences between the two systems are important, and I will come to them. But the legal culture is another element at work. This is a package of shared, and often unquestioned, attitudes about the law and the way it should work. Common experience shapes the culture, and the lack of a totally shared history has produced interesting differences between the Canadian and American systems.

The United States was born in revolution against established authority, but Canada proceeded from an affirmation of the establishment. Canadians do not greatly partake in the American mistrust of authority. Content with less, and suspicious of change, they do not pursue excellence with American vigour.

American rules about jury selection arguably illustrate these differences. If Canadians lean to complacency, perhaps Americans lean to the opposite extreme, the fastidious if nonetheless admirable pursuit of perfection. It may be pure accident that one works better than the other.

The same Canadian trust of authority permits judges to comment to juries on the testimony, and to exercise powers like prior restraint on free speech.

This also accounts, I think, for other notable contrasts. American courts and lawyers are dedicated to reform. They are constantly changing the rules, studying reforms, starting pilot projects, and introducing new ideas. Canadians are more comfortable, and, to an American, almost maddeningly complacent. There is nothing in Canada like the Restatement project, a massive endeavour where lawyers and judges work constantly to tidy and improve the body of judge-made law. Nor is there anything remotely like the American Judicature Society, a widely supported organization dedicated to the improvement of courts.

The culture also accounts for a different approach to the role of precedent in the work of courts. Forty years ago, most Canadian lawyers would have pointed to the American lack of respect for precedent as the single most remarkable contrast. Precedent, which is the record of previous judicial decisions, had come almost to be ignored in some American jurisdictions. I see this as an illustration of the American instinct away from authority and towards change. Canadian lawyers and judges, by comparison, had for too long a colonial's awe of English precedent. They felt compelled to find a precisely similar previous decision to legitimize a current one. (Today, embarrassed by silly but opposite extremes in the past, many appellate courts in both countries tend to accept, with Justice Harlan Jr.,[8] that ". . . the task of the law is to reform and project, as well as mirror and reflect . . . ").

Diverse experience has had impact on the two legal systems in many other subtle and important ways. For example, the two countries do not totally share a history of mistrust of local institutions. True, in the 1930s and 1940s, both developed a considerable reliance on national as opposed to local, provincial, or state government. These were the years of a Great Depression and a World War. Both countries then saw a need for the exercise of strong national will and the subservience of local interests.[9] In the United States, the scandals associated with Prohibition and institutionalized racism exacerbated the trend. The results of this massive shift in attitude were many, and included an impact on legal systems in both countries. People accepted the notion of the aggressive application of constitutional rights against local governments, and local judges, by nationally appointed judges. This attitude, encouraged also by a sense of paralysis of congressional government, went so far in the United States, to allow what some critics call government by judges.[10]

Respect for local institutions, on the other hand, tempers the work of the Canadian judiciary.[11] But then the new attitude about the role of the local governments never went so far in Canada, and ended much earlier.[12] A key difference was the role of Quebec in Canadian life. It never accepted those exigencies as adequate excuse to interfere with provincial rights. And the judges have no sense that Parliament cannot act; on the contrary, they often comment how legislators are better able to deal with problems than judges.[13] Most Canadian judges are very uncomfortable about limiting the power of government.[14]

Whatever the reasoning, the undeniable fact is that the United States Supreme Court, during almost two decades, made stunning changes in the law. Perhaps not every change was a wise exercise of judicial power, but one cannot deny that all the famous changes were intended to improve the lot of the underclass. This sensitivity to the plight of the oppressed has earned for the American judiciary the admiration of the world.

STRUCTURE

The legal systems of Canada and the United States have a common British ancestor, and share some essential characteristics. Indeed, the fact that both are federal states makes our structures more alike than are those of Canada and England. But both in the main follow the English or common-law system. Judges make no independent investigation into a dispute but rely on the "case," the testimony and argument, put by each side to the dispute. Both have a strong tradition against private or outside influence on the persons deciding the case. We believe this is the best bulwark against corruption. Also, neither has the continental system of a judicial profession. Instead we rely on ex-lawyers to act as judges, and on citizen-juries to decide facts.

But the commonality between the two is more like the shared ancestry of the redwood and the tamarack. The rugged Canadian tree stands just as straight, but is shorter and less well-adorned. It is not merely that there are 50 states and but ten provinces. Provinces, excepting always Quebec, offer little systemic variation. States, on the other hand, offer an almost unmanageable array of contrasts, including, in Louisiana, a remnant not unlike Quebec of the civil code system in colonial France. The variations are such that any general comment becomes dangerous.

Each country has dual judicial structures to reflect the federated state. Both demonstrate, albeit in different ways, the competition for dominance between the two levels of government. The constitutional peculiarities of each country have a considerable bearing on court structure, and lead to problems. Both strive, without total success, to keep the judiciary both of high quality and removed from the rest of the governmental apparatus. I shall explain some of this in detail.

The following chart explains, in a comparative way, the two judicial structures.

CANADA

SUPREME COURT OF CANADA
Nine judges
Appointed by the Federal Cabinet
Hears appeals from the provincial appeal courts and the
Federal Court appellate division. Final court of appeal for
Canada in all cases. Controls workload by requirement for
leave to appeal.

Federal Court
Federal appointment.
Trial and Appeal Division.
Assisted by Tax Court.
Judges travel but live in Ottawa.
Jurisdiction limited to cases involving Government of Can-
ada, e.g., income tax.
No criminal cases.

APPEAL COURTS
One in each province. Size varies.
Appointed by Federal Cabinet.
Sit in panels. Hear appeals for all provincial trial courts
and tribunals.

Provincial Superior Courts
Federal appointments. One court in each province.
Size varies.
Judges sit anywhere in province and on all sorts of
cases, including jury trials and both civil and criminal
cases.
Often hears appeals from Provincial courts.
Called Queen's Bench, or Superior Court, or Supreme
Court. In Ontario called Ontario Court General Division.

Provincial Court, Family Court, Youth Court, Magistrates Court,
(and others, including some kinds of tribunal, or system
of tribunals for the resolution of labour disputes, a court
to supervise the estates of deceased persons, and the
like)
In Quebec *Cours de Québec*.
Appointed by Provincial Cabinet.
Jurisdiction limited.
Hear about 80% of all cases.

USA

SUPREME COURT OF THE UNITED STATES
Nine Judges appointed by the president with the advice
and consent of Senate.
Hears appeals from circuit courts, and in special cases,
state supreme courts.
Controls docket with leave to appeal, called "cert."

Circuit Courts of Appeal.
Presidential appointments
10 Courts in Washington and spread around the country.

Federal District Court
Presidential appointment
A trial court. Judges sit in assigned districts and hear
cases arising under federal laws and where it is unclear
which state law should apply.
Applies U.S. Constitution to state institutions, including
state courts.
Assisted by masters and magistrates.

STATE SUPREME COURTS
One in each state. Usually elected. Sits *en banc*.
Is final court of appeal in most cases from all state
courts and tribunals.
In larger states, assisted by an intermediate Court of Ap-
peal.

State Superior Courts
Usually elected. Usually one in each state.
Usually called Superior Court.
Jurisdiction similar to provincial superior courts in Canada.

State, County, and Magistrates Courts
Created by state.
Sometimes elected.
Sometimes no requirement for legal training.
Variety of courts and tribunals exercising specialized and
limited jurisdiction, including petty crimes and small civil
disputes.

FEDERAL INFLUENCE

As the chart shows, Canada has a tidy and tight hierarchical system for judicial review. Although the provinces create their appeal courts, they do not appoint the judges of these or other "superior" courts, and the Canadian constitution permits the federal government to establish a "general court of appeal," and appoint its judges. This broad jurisdiction of the Supreme Court of Canada is the principal means by which Canada influences judicial work at the provincial level. Despite its limited caseload, that court, working in a country the size of Canada, offers detailed, some say smothering, direction. This is partly also because of its penchant for broadly worded decisions, which tend to go much further than the case before it.

The United States Supreme Court, on the other hand, does not operate as a general court of appeal from all American courts. It hears appeals from state supreme courts only when they, on national constitutional grounds, invalidate federal statutes or validate state statutes.

Nevertheless, state courts are not free from considerable federal influence. The citizen can *sue* (for an injunction or *habeas corpus*) a state court in United States Federal Court, and allege against it a breach of constitutional rights. That rule had little effect until, in this century, the United States Supreme Court decided that the entire national Bill of Rights governed state governments and state courts. This made the state courts subject to the writ of the federal courts on many grounds.

Until then, the work of the United States Federal Court, not unlike its Canadian counterpart, had limited scope. It had heard suits against the government and its many agencies, which continue today to be its principal activity in terms of volume. It also heard suits between citizens when they lived in different states. But federal review of state courts had a momentous impact on American society. It led to landmark cases like those ordering integration of state-run schools and the rewriting of state electoral boundaries.[15]

This form of interference has produced a serious problem of duplicated litigation. Death penalty disputes already delayed at the state level produce almost endless movement back and forth between the two systems. To keep the system from collapse, the United States Supreme Court has adopted several new rules.[16]

Canada avoided this sort of problem by its hierarchical review. But she pays a price. Many provinces complain that Ottawa tends to appoint judges to the Supreme Court who show a slant its way on disputes that arise between the two levels of government. Observers quickly dub judges of that court as "centralizers" or "balkanizers," the two most popular epithets for the differing views. In any event, a restructuring of the systems of appointment to the Supreme Court has been on the Canadian constitutional agenda for two decades.

The American failure to have a consolidated system accounts for the second trial of the accused in the "Rodney King" affair. As we already noted, the Americans have not avoided overlapping law. Nor have the Canadians, where overlapping federal and provincial laws are also not uncommon. In the result, in Canada also, an accused might be charged under both federal and provincial law, but both charges can go to trial simultaneously before one court. The Canadian government gives jurisdiction over much of its law, including bankruptcy and criminal law, to provincial courts. This, as I have said previously, avoids the scandal of duplicate and contradictory verdicts.

Ottawa gives jurisdiction to provincial courts because it also names most judges in that provincial system. The Fathers of Confederation accepted the now-discredited legal opinion that only the federal cabinet could exercise the power of appointment of a superior-court judge.[17] Thus, Canada names, and pays, those judges in each province, and the provincial governments who create the jobs need not pay the job-holders. This has proved a boon to the poorer provinces, who can and do put people on the federal payroll with a stroke of the pen. The American system has no similar rule allowing the staffing by one government of the courts created by another.

But federal appointment to a provincial institution has been a curse upon the logical and efficient ordering of the judicial structure, in large provinces and in small. Many provinces, not just Quebec, have for many years sought to increase the jurisdiction of those courts and tribunals to which *they* name the judges. Some also want to give "their" judges as much power as possible and pull tight on the purse strings for the others. Debates about reform are usually about which government gets the appointment power, not about a sensible structure that will get the job done. No government has offered to ease the problem by giving up its appointment power. Worse, Canada now has a curious and unique body of law regarding what is a "superior" court and what is not. These rules arise from the pushing and shoving between the two levels of government.

In sum, both systems have had difficulty getting a balance between the two levels of government, and suffer as a result.

JUDICIAL INDEPENDENCE

Canadian courts are at the mercy of the creating governments, who pay the piper. The government, usually provincial, hires all the staff, builds all the courthouses, and pays all the bills to run the courts, except perhaps the judicial salary. Worse, the administrative arm of the court is, typically, a branch of government headed not by a judge but a politician. It is not unusual for the judges, even the Chief Justice of a Canadian court, never to see, or be permitted to see, the budget for the administration of the court. No doubt being on the federal payroll insulates judges from improper pressures from these provincial governments who have considerable business before them. But it also isolates them from the increasingly important administrative side of court business. Canadian judges now speak of the need for administrative, not just decisional, independence.

Unlike Canada, each American state has adopted its own constitution. The details vary strikingly from one to another, but most prescribe in detail the structure of the courts in the state. Changes to the courts thus need changes to the constitution. Moreover, the constitutional status of the courts permits them to assert administrative independence as a matter of constitutional right.

Many states have adopted the Vanderbilt reforms.[18] They feature unitary trial courts, where all limited jurisdiction and general jurisdiction courts become part of one big, centrally administered apparatus. A similar system operates at the federal level. The newest state, Alaska, created the ultimate modern system. That state has a "single-line" budget for the courts' administration, with little interference from the state legislature. The office of Chief Justice in Alaska is elective, but the electors are fellow judges. Canada has nothing like this, and modern court reform has passed it by.

JUDICIAL SELECTION

Judicial selection offers the greatest difference between the two systems.

The older states started with the colonial system, and followed the English model of appointed judges. Delaware to this day appoints judges. But many states, particularly those who joined the union in the nineteenth century, fell under the influence of the ideals of Jacksonian democracy. They chose to have all judicial offices localized and elective. Many judges, despite seeking a statewide office, must run for election in, and sometimes must live in, this county or that.

This rule sometimes applies to the judges of the state Supreme Court, the highest court of appeal in a state.

For a Canadian, the most disquieting aspect of the American system is the election of judges. This seems to thrust them into the middle of the political thicket. Americans respond that they have, in many states, built up ethics codes to deal with these problems. These describe what is improper in campaign activity and offer rules for raising campaign funds. Essentially, they seek to insulate the judge from the process.

Many states have also modified the elective process. Judicial elections are often not partisan and equally often nobody opposes the judge. Local, broadly-based bar groups without ties to political parties will publicly support a judge for re-election, and raise campaign funds if necessary.

Many states have adopted some variant of the Missouri system, which relies on the rule that the governor fills, by appointment, vacancies that arise between elections. That appointment lasts until the next election, but nobody then ordinarily challenges the new judge. An essential part of that system is that the appointment is non-partisan, and subject to some form of merit selection. Usually a blue-ribbon committee approves a short list of names from which the governor chooses.

In Canada, and in the American federal system, the national government appoints judges. Everybody remembers the Senate hearings for Judge Clarence Thomas, and the dramatic allegation of sexual harassment he faced. But what most people do not know is that the president names *all* the judges in the American federal system. The Senate must then approve his choice. Few are subject, however, to the same scrutiny as candidates for the Supreme Court. Some assert that the real choice lay in the past with the two senators for the state in which the judge would live and work. The other senators and the president would defer to them. As a result, those two each could veto, and perhaps name, the candidates. That system may have broken down, but, in the view of some, no close Senate examination yet occurs for circuit and district nominations.[19]

In Canada, the federal cabinet makes all appointments without any intervention by parliament. This is true of all federal appointments, whether to the Supreme Court, Federal Court, or to the provincial superior courts. Similarly, the provincial cabinets appoint judges for provincial courts and tribunals.

The curiosity in Canada is the selection process for the Supreme Court of Canada. Critics note the total absence of any known screening process. While many individuals and pressure groups presumably attempt to influence the process, nobody knows which names are under consideration, or why one is chosen or passed over. It is also not clear who does the assessment. The cabinet makes the appointment on the recommendation of the prime minister. It is obvious that the prime minister delegates that task, except perhaps for selection from a short list. But to whom? What consultation occurs, if any? Rumours abound, but the matter remains a mystery.

Most provinces have established blue-ribbon reviews for candidates for provincial judicial office. But most do not make public their deliberations, or their recommendations. On occasion, these have been criticized, usually on the basis that the review panel recommends lawyers who meet a restricted ideal of professional "success": big-city, big-firm, rich, male, and grey-haired.

At the federal level, Canada has since 1989 also named blue-ribbon committees to pass on the fitness of candidates for all judicial offices *except* the Supreme Court. The difficulty is that most candidates, who are all lawyers, win approval as qualified. The choice thus left is wide, too wide in the view of some. More recently, the committees can opine who is "highly" qualified as opposed to merely qualified. It remains to be seen, however, whether government will limit choices to the shorter list. It is difficult to discover what happens because the entire process is conducted in the deepest secrecy. Officials of the provincial governments seem content with consultation about candidates, and most Canadian governments offer that as a courtesy.

Everybody in every system asserts a commitment to merit selection. Yet the process everywhere traditionally accepts claims to geographical, linguistic, religious or ethnic representation on the bench. These "trophy" demands limit the scope of merit review. Some groups argue for "quota" appointments: they demand that the numbers from their group in the judiciary be in the same proportion to the entire court that their total group bears to the larger society. Few are content to limit this to the proportion that exists among lawyers of appropriate age. They contend for a form of affirmative action, and would use judicial office to improve the lot of their group in society. These are, assuming the group is in fact disadvantaged, understandable ambitions. But they get in the way of merit selection.

These issues have not earned any serious examination in Canada by governments, lawyers, or judges[20] and certainly not by the groups who think they can influence the political process. In the United States, by contrast, serious efforts are underway to establish standards for merit selection acceptable to all.

In sum, neither the elective nor the appointive system is free of difficulty in terms of producing a competent, respected, sensitive, and independent judiciary. As a result, questions about removal[21] have arisen in both lands.

These difficulties emphasize the related matter of judicial formation. How does one train a judge to be a better judge? Much more aware of their possible shortcomings than the public supposes, judges are now committed devotees of the professional seminar. They go to share ideas about procedure, to join voices to complain of job conditions, to learn the recent developments in the law, to understand their jobs better, and to be taught more about the minority groups of whom they may not have learned much in their previous careers. In Canada, they also go to learn to speak, and understand, French or English.

Another facet of formation is ethical review. Of course, all decisions of judges are subject to scrutiny by appellate courts, egged on by losing parties. But some issues, mostly about behaviour off the court, do not naturally come before appeal courts. American judges have established detailed codes of ethics, and a system of prior peer review. In other words, they encourage a judge, before embarking on a certain course of conduct, to consult more senior and experienced colleagues regarding the fitness of it. Canadian judges have left this to informal consultation, so that those who need the advice the most might not seek it or get it.

I should, to keep a sense of balance, observe that the two systems seem to be the envy of the world. They have, with all their warts, succeeded in one critical way where others have failed: this is in the most basic sense of judicial independence, the idea that tribunals decide cases without being told how by the local political power. Most of the world suffers from some version of what, in the old Soviet Union, a jurist frankly described to me as "telephone justice," where the local party people privately told the judge and jury what to do. The first item on the shopping list of most recent revolutions throughout the world has been "independent judges and juries." For all their sins, and they may be many, the systems under review share, in the main, that achievement.

The problems faced by judges and the judicial process in both countries as we end the twentieth-century are substantial, and sometimes daunting. Most transcend the differences between the two legal systems. I have attempted to point out some problems and to compare methods of solution. Legal culture or structural arrangements usually explain the different responses. In short, they are a reflection of differences in the larger societies in which they work. The lesson is that, while comparisons are instructive, what will work well in one society might not work at all in another.

NOTES

1. Walter Kolson, *The Litigation Explosion: What happened when America unleashed the Lawsuit.* (New York: Dutton, 1991).

2. Peter Huber, *Galileo's Revenge: Junk Science in the Courtroom.* (New York: Basic Books, 1991). See also *Daubert v. Merrell Dow Pharmaceuticals Inc.* 61 L.W. 4805 (June 29, 1993 S.C.U.S.).

3. Many American states now permit the trial judge to refuse to enter unreasonable awards, an after-the-fact brake not always as well reported as the original jury decision.

4. "Jury charges Spital a $2.6 million fee" *San Diego Union-Tribune*, March 5, 1993 and "Jury tells Spital to pay $5 million more," *San Diego Union-Tribune*, March 9, 1993.

5. A citizen videotaped several city police officers making an arrest. After the tapes were aired, the officers were charged. When they were acquitted, outraged citizens rioted.

6. This system has also produced an opportunity for an accused to obtain a jury partial to him. A well-funded defence can have secret and sophisticated public opinion studies done in advance of trial. These can tell not only which kinds of people are partial against him, but also which kind are partial *towards* his defence. He can then, by using the results as a guide at jury selection, challenge the first group and identify the second. Except in the unlikely event that the prosecution is equally resourceful, the accused will tend to start the trial with at least some jurors partial to him, which, given the need for unanimity, is enough to protect him from conviction.

7. As indeed they did in the early cases. And do today in any situation where the community is too small to achieve anonymity, as is the case for jury trials in the Inuit settlements in northern Canada.

8. *U.S. v. White.* 401 U.S. 745 at 786 (1971).

9. *New York v. The United States* (1946), 326 U.S. 572.

10. Neeley, *How Courts Govern America* (Yale, 1981), 221.

11. Compare, for example, the approach in *Baker v. Carr* (1962), 369 U.S. 186 to that in *Reference Re: Electoral Boundaries Commission Act (Sask.)*, [1991] 3 W.W.R. 593 (Sask. C.A.).

12. *Alberta Natural Gas Tax Reference* (1981), 28 A.R. 11 (C.A.).

13. *R. v. Schwartz*, [1988] 2 S.C.R. 443, at p. 488.

14. In the past, the greatest difference between the two systems turned on the power of the American judge to enforce against an unwilling government the constitutional rights of the citizen expressed in the Bill of Rights or its state equivalent. But, 10 years ago, Canada adopted its equivalent, the Charter of Rights and Freedoms, and that difference evaporated.

    In Canada, particularly after the introduction of the *Charter*, issues about interpretive approaches, and the legitimacy of judicial interpretation, also arose. They have not, however, been much acknowledged. But, after an expansive first phase, the interpretive policy of the Supreme Court has moved into a cautious, limited, and very Canadian mode.

15. *Brown v. Board of Education* (1954), 347 U.S. 483, and *Baker v. Carr [supra]*.

16. *Stone v. Powell*, 428 U.S. 465 (1976), for example.

17. *Re Adoption Act*, [1938] S.C.R. 398.

18. Vanderbilt, "Minimum Standards of Judicial Administration" (A.B.A. 1949).

19. . *The New Yorker*, January 18, 1993, p. 31-32.

20. Another controversial aspect of merit selection is the legal philosophy of the candidate. Traditionally, lawyers protest a "litmus test," a close scrutiny of the political views of the candidate, because that can lead to "stacking," the appointment of judges committed to a specific decision agenda. This is, of course, exactly what others want. This issue came to a head yet again when President Reagan nominated Judge

Bork, whose professional credentials were above reproach but who wanted to roll back some decisions of the United States Supreme Court. He was denied the nomination on that account. Most candidates refuse to say what they will do as judges. And presidents recently have been careful not to appoint people who, like Bork, have published views in a "paper trail." President Clinton has asserted his right to nominate judges of a satisfactory "record" while at the same time disavowing a "litmus test."

21. Judges named by a province may be removed by the province. Most, but not all, provinces have put in place schemes for an independent inquiry into allegations before dismissal occurs. Judges named by Canada cannot be removed except by a joint resolution of both the House of Commons and the Senate, which has never happened. Currently, the government may refer any accusation to the assembled Chief Justices of all the Courts, who may and have ordered their own inquiry.

An American federal judge can only be removed from office by an act of impeachment, which results in a trial before the Senate. This can and does happen. State judges also can be impeached, or defeated in an election.

FURTHER READING:

About the organization of courts and selection of judges:

United States:

Henry J. Abraham, *The Judicial Process* (Oxford) 1980

Walter F. Murphy and C. Herman Pritchett, *Courts, Judges and Politics: An Introduction to the Judical Process,* 3rd edition (Random House), 1979

Canada:

Peter H. Russell, *The Judiciary in Canada: The Third Branch of Government* (McGraw Hill) 1987

On the American tradition of no prior restraint of free speech:

Anthony Lewis, *Make No Law* (Random House) 1991

On the jury selection process:

United States:

Ann Fagan Finger, *Jury Selection in Civil and Criminal Trials* (Tiburn, CA: Lawyers Corp.) 1984

Canada:

Seminar on the Conduct of the Jury Trial, *The Conduct of the Jury Trial* (Edmonton: Criminal Trial Lawyers Association of Edmonton, 1980)

CHRISTOPHER P. MANFREDI

Inalienable Rights and Reasonable Limits: The US Bill of Rights and the Charter of Rights and Freedoms

In his 1990 book *Continental Divide*, the American sociologist Seymour Martin Lipset argued that Canada's adoption of a constitutionally entrenched Charter of Rights and Freedoms represented the most important "Americanization" of Canadian politics and society in our history. The purpose of this chapter is to explore this claim by comparing the structure and text of the Charter with the US Bill of Rights, and by assessing the impact that US constitutional jurisprudence has had on Canadian law in the post-Charter era.

At first glance, Lipset's claim appears to be a strong one, since there are important similarities between the Charter and the Bill of Rights. Both documents protect important aspects of individual liberty such as freedom of religion, freedom of expression and of the press, and freedom of assembly. Like the Bill of Rights, a significant portion of the Charter concerns the general legal rights of Canadians and the specific procedural rights of accused persons. Moreover, since the Charter's drafters were acutely aware of the Bill of Rights and its interpretation by American courts, they consciously attempted to articulate certain rights and freedoms in ways that would take advantage of the positive elements of the US experience while avoiding some of its more problematic aspects.

Despite these similarities, the Charter is nevertheless a politically indigenous document. It protects some uniquely Canadian rights, such as general language rights and minority language educational rights. It also contains an explicit limitations clause (section 1), as well as a legislative check on judicial power (section 33, the "notwithstanding" clause) that is more far-reaching than anything found in the US Constitution. Moreover, unlike the US Bill of Rights, the Charter does not expressly protect private property rights. Finally, the Charter differs from the US document in granting explicit constitutional legitimacy and protection to affirmative action programs.

This combination of similarities and differences has led many commentators to speculate and comment on the potential impact of American civil rights jurisprudence on Charter adjudication. Although some commentators have praised the US experience and urged Canadian judges to follow it, others have issued warnings about the nature of that experience and how its adoption might affect Canadian politics. Perhaps more importantly, however, the justices of the Canadian Supreme Court have been cautiously optimistic that American decisions might guide their own judgements. As Chief Justice Brian Dickson wrote in 1988, "American courts have the benefit of 200 years of experience in constitutional interpretation. This wealth of experience may offer guidance to the judiciary in this country."

THE ORIGINS OF THE CHARTER AND THE US BILL OF RIGHTS

The list of similarities and differences between the Canadian Charter and the US Bill of Rights begins with the origins of the two documents. In neither country was it considered necessary to include explicit protection for individual rights and freedoms in their original constitutions. According to Alexander Hamilton (a participant at the 1787 Constitutional Convention and one of the authors of the *Federalist Papers*), it was both unnecessary and dangerous to include a bill of rights in the US Constitution: unnecessary, because these documents are superfluous in nations characterized by popular sovereignty and a constitutional structure embracing federalism and the separation of executive, legislative and judicial power; dangerous, because restrictions on government power could be understood as implicit grants of power.[1] Indeed, Hamilton argued in *Federalist No. 84* that "the Constitution is itself, in every rational sense, and to every useful purpose, a Bill of Rights."

Hamilton's arguments failed to persuade opponents of the constitution framed in Philadelphia in 1787. According to these opponents, known as the Anti-Federalists, the constitution did not adequately protect local self-government from the tyranny of national majorities. Consequently, they insisted on a statement of rights that would bind the national government and prevent it from violating the liberties of state citizens. The proponents of the new constitution reluctantly agreed to this condition, and one of its most important authors —

James Madison — shepherded the Bill of Rights through the US Congress. Nevertheless, in its origins the Bill did not apply to majority rule *per se*, but only to majority rule as exercised through the institutions of the national government. Indeed, the US Supreme Court did not consistently enforce the Bill of Rights against the states until 1925.

In contrast to the US Bill of Rights, the Canadian Charter originated as an important component of an explicit strategy to enhance national unity and the status of the central government. As part of its plan for renewing federalism in the aftermath of Quebec's 1980 referendum on sovereignty-association, the federal government expected the Charter to contribute to national unity in three ways. First, some provisions of the Charter, particularly in the area of language rights, targeted specific Quebec policies considered inconsistent with national unity (which helps to explain Quebec's reluctance to endorse the Charter in the same way that the rest of Canada has). Second, the government hoped that the Charter would shift national political debate from regional issues to universal questions concerning human rights. Third, by subordinating provincial legislation to a set of rights ultimately enforced by a predominantly national political institution (the Supreme Court), the Charter could act as a "unifying counter to decentralizing provincial demands in the Canadian constitutional debate."[2]

In view of this federal strategy, it is hardly surprising that only two provinces (Ontario and New Brunswick) initially supported the patriation project of which the Charter was a part. What eventually convinced seven of the remaining eight provinces to agree to the project was Prime Minister Trudeau's willingness to include a legislative override provision in the Charter. Section 33 of the Charter allows the federal Parliament or any provincial legislature to declare for renewable five-year periods that statutes "shall operate notwithstanding a provision included in section 2 [fundamental freedoms] or sections 7 to 15 [legal and equality rights] of this Charter." This so-called "notwithstanding clause" saved the November 1981 First Ministers' Conference from complete deadlock.

What is intriguing about these divergent origins is that both the Charter and the US Bill of Rights have come to serve the same purpose. The Charter's principal impact has been on provincial legislation and on provincial administration of federal statutes. Moreover, as Alan Cairns has forcefully argued, the Charter has created a new set of constitutional actors that now competes with provincial governments for space at the constitutional negotiating table. Similarly, despite its initial objectives, the US Bill of Rights has been overwhelmingly used as an instrument to control state legislation.

Indeed, since 1930 the US Supreme Court has overturned six times as many state statutes as federal laws. From abortion to capital punishment to criminal justice policy to education and voting rights, the Bill of Rights has become an instrument for limiting the traditional policy discretion of the states. Different intentions, in other words, have produced similar results.

QUESTIONS OF INTERPRETATION

Since rights-protecting documents must necessarily be written in broad, indeterminate language, their impact is largely determined by judicial interpretation. Should judges provide restrictive definitions that are consistent with the meaning intended by the document's framers, or should they be more expansive and creative by looking for meaning outside of the constitution and its historical context? What is the correct balance between individual rights and the community's need to pursue the collective good? These are only two of the questions that underlie constitutional interpretation of the Charter and the US Bill of Rights.

Canadian judges have been greatly assisted by the structure of the Charter in their attempt to answer these questions in a way that is consistent with liberal democratic principles. Section 1 of the Charter, which provides that the rights and freedoms set out in the document are "subject only to such reasonable limits prescribed by law as can be demonstrably justified in a free and democratic society," allows courts to define rights expansively while simultaneously avoiding the political consequences of those broad definitions.

Charter decision-making thus takes place in two stages. First, the court determines whether the legislation or government action in question limits a Charter right, which almost always produces an affirmative answer. Second, the court must determine whether the limit is reasonable. This second step embraces two elements. One element is that the government defending the limit must show that its legislative objective relates "to concerns that are pressing and substantial in a free and democratic society." The second element is that the limit must be proportionate to the legislative objective, which courts determine through a three-pronged test. To pass the first prong of this test, the limit must be rationally connected to the legislative objective. Next, the government must show that the limit represents the least restrictive means of achieving this objective. Finally, the benefits gained from limiting the right or freedom must outweigh the costs of the impairment.

The pragmatism embodied in section 1 stands in stark contrast to the deep theoretical divisions over judicial review that exist in the United States. On one side of this theoretical divide stands the theory of *non-interpretivism*, which holds that judges should be creative in formulating and applying novel definitions of rights in order to determine the constitutionality of legislation and other government action. In this way, the theory asserts, constitutional law can become an engine of moral progress. This theory is opposed by *interpretivism*, which argues that legislation and government action should only be measured against specific constitutional provisions, or interpretations of those provisions that are clearly inferable from the document's language or history. According to this theory, constitutional law must provide a set of relatively fixed constraints on government power; and whatever the constitution does not explicitly prohibit, it permits.

Two points of clarification about these theories are perhaps useful. First, the technical meanings of the terms *non-interpretivism* and *interpretivism* are precisely the opposite of their common sense meaning. This divergence from common sense is explained by the fact that the process of interpretation assumes the existence of a text with a relatively fixed and discoverable meaning. Interpretivists want to *find* the constitution's meaning, while non-interpretivists want to *give* the constitution meaning. This accounts for the priority that interpretivists give to constitutional documents, as well as for the use of the term non-interpretivist to describe those who consider the document to be without any inherently relevant meaning. The second point of clarification is that these terms are not synonymous with political conservatism and liberalism. For example, a non-interpretivist could also promote a conservative political philosophy by giving the constitution a meaning that prohibits progressive legislation.[3]

For the most part, the Canadian Supreme Court has followed its modern US counterpart in developing an expansive non-interpretive approach to judicial review under the Charter. This trend began in the Supreme Court's first Charter decision, *Law Society of Upper Canada v. Skapinker* (1984), when Justice Willard Estey repeated US Chief Justice John Marshall's assertion in *McCulloch v. Maryland* (1819) that judges "must never forget, that it is *a constitution* [they] are expounding." Chief Justice Brian Dickson later relied on what he called the "classical principles of American constitutional construction" to declare in *Hunter v. Southam* (1984) that the Charter calls for a "broad, purposive analysis, which interprets specific provisions of a constitutional document in the light of its larger objects." Dickson further defined this approach in *R. v. Big M Drug Mart* (1985); however, echoing one of Marshall's principal concerns, he argued that courts should not "overshoot the actual purpose of the right or freedom in question."

As in the United States, however, the Canadian Court soon began to abandon the more cautious elements of Marshall's interpretive principles. In *Reference re Section 94(2) of the Motor Vehicle Act (B.C.)* (1985) Justice Antonio Lamer implicitly associated Marshall's principles with the "living tree" metaphor of Canadian constitutional interpretation articulated in *Edwards v. A.-G. Canada* (1930). Lamer argued that the Court could not allow historical materials to determine its interpretation of the Charter, since this would cause the Charter's meaning to become "frozen in time to the moment of adoption with little or no possibility of growth, development and adjustment to changing societal needs." Citing *Edwards*, Lamer offered the following warning: "If the newly planted 'living tree' which is the Charter is to have the possibility of growth and adjustment over time care must be taken to ensure that historical materials...do not stunt its growth."

By embracing, and even extending, the principles of the modern era of US judicial review — whose most celebrated decisions have been the products of non-interpretivism — the Canadian Court has carved out a theory of constitutional interpretation that envisions a strong and creative judicial role in defining the norms embedded in the Charter. As Chief Justice Dickson said in the Court's 1988 abortion decision, *Morgentaler, Smoling and Scott v. The Queen*, the Court is now "charged with the crucial obligation of ensuring that the legislative initiatives of our Parliament and legislatures conform to the democratic values expressed in the Canadian Charter of Rights and Freedoms." One of the key issues raised by this approach concerns the source of these unenumerated democratic rights and values. As the American constitutional theorist John Hart Ely has argued, discovering the fundamental values implicitly protected by constitutions is a problematic enterprise, since there is a danger that this exercise will simply lead to the imposition of the individual policy preferences of judges. Although the Canadian Supreme Court has attempted to deal with this problem by identifying the "basic tenets of our legal system" as the source of the values it intends to uphold, the precise content of these "basic tenets" remains to be defined. Consequently, non-interpretivism raises the same normative question in the Canadian context as it does in the American: on what grounds do unelected judges overturn the decisions of democratically-accountable decision-makers?

Of particular interest to Canadian commentators is whether the adoption of US-inspired non-interpretive review will lead the Canadian Court to define democratic values in a manner consistent with the philosophical assumptions of US constitutional jurisprudence, or whether non-interpretivism will acquire a uniquely Canadian character. Consequently, the debate between interpretivism and non-interpretivism is accompanied in Canada by a debate between liberal-individualist and communitarian theories of constitutional interpretation. Communitarianism asserts that the "good of the individual is not conceivable apart from some regard for the good of the whole"; that "restraints on individuals are natural rather than contractual, flowing from the very duties and rights which are implicit in membership in a larger community"; and that there is no "necessary tension between the state and freedom."[4] While recognizing the influence of liberal individualism on both the Charter and Canadian political culture, communitarians argue that Canada's commitment to "collectivist, organic values" is embodied in the protection the Charter provides for the collective rights of linguistic groups, aboriginal peoples, and cultural communities.[5] If Canadian courts use judicial review under the Charter to promote the predominantly American value of individualism, communitarians argue, the result will be a further erosion of Canada's distinctive political character.

According to these communitarian critics, Canadian judges "must regard attempts by the community to embody its fundamental beliefs in law as something more than the imposition of one person's 'external preferences' on another." Judicial review, in other words, should not protect individual rights at the cost of reducing the capacity of communities "to define their common identity [and] enrich the lives of individuals in those communities." This requires an approach to judicial review which ensures that the Charter does not adversely affect communities and which broadens the scope of the collective rights of communities and other groups that are already entrenched in the Charter.[6] What communitarian critics fear is that the profoundly individualistic assumptions of US constitutional theory will prevent the emergence of a collectivist-oriented Canadian theory of judicial review. Or, to use a more familiar metaphor, that Canadian judicial review will simply become "another branch-plant operation of an American head office."[7]

QUESTIONS OF APPLICATION

How do Canadian and US Supreme Court justices compare in their application of similarly-worded sections of the nations' respective rights documents? In order to provide a preliminary answer to this question, this section compares important decisions concerning freedom of religion and expression (section 2 of the Charter; US First

Amendment), criminal procedure (sections 7 to 14 of the Charter; US Fourth to Eighth Amendments), and equality (section 15 of the Charter; US Fourteenth Amendment).

Freedom of Religion and Expression

Although the Canadian Supreme Court has found First Amendment jurisprudence useful in Charter cases, it has also held that Canadian constitutional doctrine and the structure of the Charter mandate a somewhat different approach in specific cases. Certain section 2 freedoms, for example, are more broadly worded than their US equivalents (e.g. expression, conscience); and there is express protection under the Charter for freedoms that are only protected in the US by inference from other First Amendment rights (e.g. association). Moreover, as we saw above, section 1 of the Charter explicitly authorizes the Court to limit fundamental liberties like freedom of religion and expression.

These differences were apparent in the Court's two Sunday-closing decisions, *R. v. Big M Drug Mart* (1985) and *Edwards Books and Art v. The Queen* (1986). At issue in *Big M Drug Mart* was the constitutionality of the federal *Lord's Day Act*, which prohibited the performance of most forms of work and commercial activity on Sunday. In majority decisions authored by Chief Justice Earl Warren, the US Supreme Court had upheld the constitutionality under the First Amendment of state legislation requiring Sunday closing. What saved the legislation was Warren's view that the laws in question no longer had a religious purpose, but were secular measures aimed solely at regulating labour.

Dickson refused to follow Warren's approach, and instead characterized the *Lord's Day Act* as a law designed to compel "sabbatical observance." Since this legislative purpose directly conflicted with religious freedom, Dickson declared the *Act* unconstitutional. Dickson also accepted the proposition that legislation enacted in pursuit of constitutionally valid purposes might nevertheless be invalid because of its effects. However, if the violation is a function of legislative effects, he declared, the statute may be upheld by reference to section 1 of the Charter. The Court's duty at this stage of analysis would be to balance the importance of the legislation's purpose against its constitutionally harmful effects.

The opportunity to apply this second mode of analysis to legislation similar to the *Lord's Day Act* arose in *Edwards Books and Art*, where Dickson considered Ontario's *Retail Business Holidays Act*. After affirming the constitutional validity of the *Act*'s objective of providing a common day of rest from labour, Dickson shifted his focus to the effects of the Ontario statute. Dickson's survey of similar American cases revealed unanimous agreement among US Supreme Court justices that such laws impose an economic burden on retailers whose religion requires a day of rest other than Sunday. The Chief Justice's analysis of the impact of Ontario's law produced roughly the same conclusion. In his judgement, the legislation imposed a competitive disadvantage on Saturday-observing retailers, as well as burdens on Saturday-observing consumers.

Was this burden on Saturday-observing retailers and consumers sufficient to invalidate the *Act*? Dickson adopted the US-style reasonable accommodation doctrine, since it most closely resembled the balancing process called for by section 1 of the Charter. For Dickson, the question in *Edwards Books and Art* became whether the *Retail Business Holidays Act* sufficiently accommodated the right of Saturday-observing retailers to freedom of religion, thereby satisfying the criteria necessary to justify limits on Charter guarantees under section 1. In his view, the law made sufficient allowances for non-Sunday observing retailers as to be constitutionally valid.

This case illustrates the important practical difference between judicial review under the Canadian Charter and the US Bill of Rights that is attributable to section 1. The absence of a "reasonable limits" clause in the US Bill of Rights forces American courts to build limits into the substantive definition of rights. Section 1 of the Charter allows Canadian courts to balance the rights and freedoms guaranteed by the Charter against other considerations without necessarily restricting the substantive scope of the Charter's provisions.

The Charter's balancing process played an important role in two important cases concerning freedom of expression (s.2(b)): *Retail, Wholesale and Dept. Store Union v. Dolphin Delivery Ltd.* (1986) and *Ford v. Quebec* (1988). In *Dolphin Delivery*, the Court considered whether the term "expression" was broad enough to encompass picketing during labor disputes. In answering this question, Justice William McIntyre accepted the use of American cases to support the assertion that picketing is a form of expression entitled to constitutional protection. Finding the US jurisprudence persuasive on this point, McIntyre concluded "that the picketing sought to be restrained would have involved the exercise of the right of freedom of expression." According to McIntyre, however, the social cost of industrial conflict is sufficiently high to justify regulating the right to picket. He held, therefore, that the injunction issued against secondary picketing in *Dolphin Delivery* constituted a reasonable limit on the right to picket under section 1 of the Charter. McIntyre reached this result without restricting the definition of expression; by contrast, the US

Supreme Court has been able to uphold similar state picketing regulations only by distinguishing between speech and conduct.[8]

In *Ford*, the principal question was whether "freedom of expression" protects commercial expression, as well as political expression. This question had been litigated in the US Court, which found that commercial expression deserves First Amendment protection because of the benefits it confers on consumers. In a unanimous, unsigned opinion, the Canadian justices adopted their US counterparts' general principle that commercial expression merits at least some constitutional protection. Consequently, the Court agreed with retailers who objected to Quebec's language regulations, holding that section 2(b) includes a right to engage in commercial expression in the language of one's choice. The Court thus found that the impugned legislation violated the Charter, bringing into consideration section 1. Although the Court found that the objective of the legislation at issue in *Ford* — to preserve and promote the French language in Quebec — was serious and legitimate, it held that Quebec had not demonstrated "that the requirement of the use of French only is either necessary for the achievement of the legislative objective or proportionate to it." The Court indicated that it would be more favourably disposed to a statute that required predominancy of French without excluding other languages.

Quebec's response to the Court's decision in *Ford* was to enact Bill 178, which relaxed the French-only requirement for interior commercial signs while continuing the requirement for exterior signs. Under Bill 178, other languages could be used on interior signs as long as French remained the predominant language inside commercial establishments. In order to immunize Bill 178 from further judicial review, Quebec exercised its power under section 33 of the Charter (the "notwithstanding clause") to override the Charter's fundamental freedoms, legal rights, and equality rights. The public and political reaction to Quebec's move was extremely negative, and the province's decision to invoke the notwithstanding clause dealt a fatal blow to the chances for ratification of the Meech Lake constitutional accord.

Perhaps in no other freedom of expression case is the impact of section 1 more apparent than in *R. v. Keegstra* (1990), where the Court considered the constitutionality of the *Criminal Code*'s hate literature provisions. James Keegstra served as a high school teacher and principal in Eckville, Alberta for nearly ten years, during which time he used this position to disseminate anti-Semitic conspiracy theories to his students. In 1984, the Crown charged Keegstra with unlawfully promoting hatred against an "identifiable group." The case eventually came before the Supreme Court, which narrowly upheld the constitutionality of the law according to which an Alberta jury had convicted Keegstra.[9] Although the Court unanimously agreed that the "hate propaganda" law infringed freedom of expression, a majority found this infringement reasonable under section 1. It is highly unlikely that such a law would pass constitutional muster in the United States, where courts have upheld the constitutional right of neo-nazis to march through predominantly Jewish neighbourhoods. The Canadian Court, however, was able simultaneously to declare the importance of freedom of expression and uphold an important law. In this instance, the collective rights of politically vulnerable groups overrode the individual right to express certain opinions.

Criminal Procedure

In contrast to the United States, where both the federal and state governments exercise jurisdiction over criminal law and procedure, these matters are largely within the exclusive jurisdiction of the federal government in Canada. Prior to the enactment of the Charter, common law rules that Parliament could easily modify determined the rules of criminal procedure. To a large degree, this approach to criminal procedure reflected the values of what Herbert S. Packer called in his book *The Limits of the Criminal Sanction* (1968) the *crime control* model of criminal procedure.[10] The crime control model de-emphasizes the formal adversary components of the criminal process in favour of the pre-adjudicative, investigative phase of the process. Police, prosecutors, defence lawyers, and judges work together to ensure the efficient administration of criminal justice and the rapid processing of criminal cases.

The principal effect of the Charter is to impose constitutional limits on the traditionally unfettered legislative power to alter criminal procedure. The Charter accomplishes this in two ways: first, by virtue of sections 8 to 11, the Charter grants courts extended supervisory powers over criminal procedure; second, section 24(2) explicitly authorizes courts to enforce these constitutional guarantees by excluding evidence from trial. In so doing, the Charter embraces elements of the *due process* model of criminal procedure that Packer contrasted with the crime control model.[11] The due process model is skeptical about the motivations and fact-determining skills of law enforcement agencies and prosecutors: rigorous procedures are considered to be the best instruments for guaranteeing correct outcomes. The best place to begin evaluating the extent to which the Supreme Court has operationalized the Charter's conceptual shift to the due process model is with its use of American jurisprudence in this area. As in the case of the Charter's fundamental freedoms provisions, US criminal procedure decisions have been frequently cited in Canada since 1982.

The basic assumptions underlying the due process model were at the core of the US Court's incorporation of the Bill of Rights into state criminal proceedings under the leadership of Chief Justice Earl Warren during the 1960s. Indeed, the Warren Court's concern with maintaining the factual integrity of the criminal process led it to extend the protections of the Bill of Rights to the earliest stages of criminal investigation. Indeed, what the US Court created was an entirely new code of conduct for police officers. For example, in order to ensure that the fact-finding process would not be tainted by evidence gathered illegally, the Court applied the federal exclusionary rule to state criminal proceedings as a way of deterring law enforcement officers from violating the Fourth Amendment's prohibition against unreasonable searches and seizures by excluding from trial all evidence obtained in violation of a defendant's constitutional rights.

The Canadian exclusionary rule found in section 24(2) of the Charter is textually more limited, and has been aimed at different purposes, than the modern American rule. These two differences are both a product of the instruction to Canadian judges in section 24(2) that evidence should be excluded only if its admission "would bring the administration of justice into disrepute." Consequently, the implementation of section 24(2) has not been concerned with deterring illegal police behaviour, but with maintaining the integrity of the criminal justice system. In fact, some courts have admitted evidence on the grounds that *excluding* it would bring the administration of justice into disrepute. The result is that the Court attempts to determine whether a "reasonable person" would view admission of the evidence as impeding the fairness of the trial. Nevertheless, despite these textual and judicial qualifications, the Charter's exclusionary rule has revolutionized the law of evidence in Canada. Indeed, in several cases the Court has excluded evidence that would have been admitted prior to the Charter.

By broadening the supervisory powers of the Canadian Supreme Court in the area of criminal procedure, and especially by explicitly entrenching the exclusionary rule (albeit in a qualified form), the Charter has clearly created the potential that Canadian criminal procedure will converge with the American procedural jurisprudence inspired by the due process model. That the Supreme Court of Canada is gradually realizing this potential is evident in the fact that the Charter's impact on criminal justice has been greatest with respect to the pre-adjudication, investigatory phase of the criminal process. By the end of 1989, the Court had upheld eight of seventeen challenges to government conduct brought under the section 8 prohibition against unreasonable searches and seizures. More dramatically, challenges brought under section 10(b) (guaranteeing the right on arrest or detention to retain and instruct counsel without delay and to be informed of that right) were successful in thirteen of sixteen cases. Finally, the Court found that evidence should have been excluded in eleven of the 36 cases in which section 24(2) was invoked.

Although the Court has rejected specific components of the American version of the due process model, particularly in the area of controlling impaired driving, it has accepted several aspects of it. For example, Chief Justice Dickson's understanding of the relationship between the presumption of innocence and the state's burden of proving guilt beyond a reasonable doubt relied in large part on the US Supreme Court's decision in *In re Winship* (1970). The Court also followed a series of US decisions in holding that a valid waiver of rights must be premised on a true appreciation of the consequences of the waiver. In addition, the Court has at times been even more restrictive than its US counterpart. It has nullified the constructive murder provisions of the Criminal Code, which continue to exist as "felony" murder provisions in some states' criminal statutes;[12] it has also required that suspects be informed of their rights to counsel and protection from self-incrimination in circumstances that would not require such notification in the US. Unfortunately, the Court has sometimes misused the US jurisprudence by, for example, applying Sixth Amendment (right to counsel) jurisprudence to a situation actually covered by the Fifth Amendment (right against self-incrimination).[13]

The Canadian Supreme Court has also experienced one of the hard lessons the US Court learned in the 1960s: unpopular criminal justice decisions can leave the Court politically vulnerable. The Court first faced this lesson as a result of its 1990 decision on unreasonable trial delays (*Askov v. The Queen*). In this decision, the Court suggested that delays of more than six to eight months violated the accused's rights, and should be remedied by a stay of proceedings. Although the Court anticipated that this would have little impact on the administration of criminal justice, the ruling resulted in thousands of dismissals, severe public criticism by elected officials, and unprecedented public comments by a sitting justice about the unexpected consequences of the decision. The Court was finally forced to "correct" itself in a later case. Similarly, in *Seaboyer v. The Queen* (1991) the Court's image suffered after it struck down evidentiary rules designed to protect complainants in sexual assault trials from being questioned about their past sexual conduct. Indeed, an outer wall of the Supreme Court building was defaced by red paint to symbolize the Court's complicity in continuing violence against women.

Equality

The major difference in this area is that equality in the US Constitution is protected by a nineteenth-century provision the limited purpose of which was to prohibit racial discrimination, while equality in Canada is protected by a late-twentieth-century provision that explicitly prohibits several forms of discrimination and recognizes the legitimacy of affirmative action. This is not to say that the American Supreme Court has been unable to expand the meaning of the Fourteenth Amendment's guarantee of equal protection of the laws. Discrimination on the basis of citizenship, legitimacy, age, indigency, and sex have all been limited under the Fourteenth Amendment. However, the US Court has also developed different levels of scrutiny that make some forms of discrimination easier to justify than others. For example, while racial classifications are virtually unconstitutional by definition, gender classifications are only subject to intermediate scrutiny, which means that the classification is permissible if it is substantially related to important governmental objectives.

The text of section 15 of the Charter not only offers more extensive protection than the Fourteenth Amendment, the Canadian Court has been willing to expand these protections even further. Consequently, it has invited groups who are not explicitly listed in section 15 to seek protection under the equality rights umbrella, and it has adopted an effects-oriented approach to equality rights adjudication. More generally, the Court has embraced a doctrine of substantive equality, in which more than just the equal application of neutral laws is necessary to satisfy the government's responsibility under section 15. Although Canadian feminists have expressed dissatisfaction with the practical consequences of certain elements of the Court's interpretation of equality, section 15 clearly offers the potential for far-reaching reform of legislation and social practices in Canada. The most recent example of this is the constitutional attack against laws that discriminate, whether intentionally or not, on the basis of sexual orientation.

CONCLUSION

Has the Charter of Rights contributed to a further "Americanization" of Canadian politics and society? To some degree, the answer to this question must be answered in the affirmative. Most obviously, the Charter has elevated the Supreme Court of Canada to the same political status enjoyed by the US Supreme Court. In the words of Rainer Knopff and Ted Morton, the Court has become the "oracle" of the Charter, and hence the principal arbiter of the political, moral, and social issues encompassed by the various rights and freedoms the Charter purports to protect. The status of the Court and the Charter is so high that disagreement with judicial pronouncements about rights, even through the exercise of legislative power constitutionally authorized by the notwithstanding clause of section 33, is bound to generate severe criticism. Indeed, in 1989 Prime Minister Brian Mulroney told the House of Commons that section 33 "holds rights hostage" and makes the entire constitution "not worth the paper it is written on." As in the United States, the Charter appears to have transformed the discourse of Canadian politics into a discourse about rights.

The predominance of "rights discourse" is perhaps most clearly evident in Canada's two most recent attempts to amend its constitution. The opposition to the Meech Lake Accord's "distinct society" clause and to the Charlottetown Accord's "Canada clause" were in large part motivated by concerns about how these clauses might limit the impact of the Charter. Women's groups, for example, were concerned that their quest for equality through the courts might be derailed by these clauses. In general, some opponents, like former Prime Minister Pierre Trudeau, worried that these clauses would create a hierarchy of rights and give precedence to collective rights over individual rights. What this suggests is that the Charter has changed the currency of Canadian politics from interests to rights.

In addition to this cultural shift, the Charter has had an important "Americanizing" effect in several areas of public policy. In the area of criminal justice, police practices that were once permissible are now prohibited as in the United States. The use of confessions and other statements by accused persons is now subject to more restrictions than in the past. Defense counsel can seek to exclude otherwise reliable and relevant evidence on the grounds that investigators obtained it in violation of an accused's rights. In general, it is now more difficult for legislatures to control private behaviour in the interests of broader collective objectives. While this may in the balance represent a change for the better, it is a change of which Canadians should be aware. Moreover, Canadians should also be aware that the experience with individual rights-based judicial review in the United States is not unqualifiedly positive.

The three most important differences between the Charter and the US Bill of Rights are the reasonable limits clause in section 1, the protection of the collective rights of certain groups, and the notwithstanding clause in section 33. The reasonable limits clause allows judges to define rights in the broadest possible terms while still upholding legislation that limits those rights. Perhaps the best example of how this works is the Canadian Court's decision with respect to hate literature, which upheld criminal sanctions against some forms of expression despite finding that those sanctions limited freedom of expression. Collective rights find their expression in such provisions as section 15's affirmative action clause and section 23's guarantee of minority language educational rights. Section 33, of course, gives the federal and provincial governments the constitutional power to override judicial interpretations of certain Charter rights. Although the political legitimacy of this power is in doubt, and a convention of non-usage appears to be emerging, section 33 does provide one possible remedy for a problem that Canada now shares with the United States: the transformation of constitutional supremacy into judicial supremacy. As others have noted, by preserving this power, Canada may make a unique contribution to the theory and practice of liberal constitutionalism.

NOTES

1. Hamilton argued, for example, that, by restricting government regulation of expression, a bill of rights would imply that such regulation was legitimate under certain circumstances.

2. Peter H. Russell, "The Political Purposes of the Canadian Charter of Rights and Freedoms," *Canadian Bar Review* 61 (1983): 1-33.

3. This is precisely what the US Supreme Court did in the early twentieth century.

4. Patrick Monahan, *Politics and the Constitution: The Charter, Federalism and the Supreme Court of Canada* (Toronto: Carswell/Methuen, 1987), 92, 109.

5. David J. Elkins, "Facing Our Destiny: Rights and Canadian Distinctiveness," *Canadian Journal of Political Science* 22 (1989), 699, 703-704.

6. Monahan, *Politics and the Constitution*, 96, 98, 104, 111-120.

7. *Ibid.*, 96.

8. *Dolphin Delivery* also raised the question of whether court orders could be considered government action for purposes of Charter review. On this question, the Canadian Court reached a conclusion precisely the opposite of that reached by the US Court, which held in 1948 that court orders should be considered state action. The Canadian Court decided that this should not be the case.

9. Although convicted in his original trial, Keegstra regained his freedom when the Alberta Court of Appeal declared the "hate propaganda" law unconstitutional. It was this ruling that the federal government appealed to the Supreme Court.

10. Herbert L. Packer, *The Limits of the Criminal Sanction* (Stanford, CA: Stanford University Press, 1968). According to Packer, this model views "the repression of criminal conduct [as] the most important function to be performed by the criminal process." In order to achieve this purpose, it focuses attention on "the efficiency with which the criminal process operates to screen suspects, determine guilt, and secure appropriate dispositions of persons convicted of crime."

11. This approach to criminal procedure is concerned with the factual integrity and accuracy of the criminal process, and aims at eliminating the possibility of erroneous fact-finding.

12. Under these laws, individuals may be found guilty of first degree murder if they cause death during the commission of another offence.

13. Robert Harvie and Hamar Foster, "Ties That Bind? The Supreme Court of Canada, American Jurisprudence, and the Revision of Canadian Criminal Law Under The Charter," *Osgoode Hall Law Journal* 28 (1990), 750.

REFERENCES & FURTHER READING:

Aleinikoff, T. Alexander. "Constitutional Law in the Age of Balancing," *Yale Law Journal* 96 (1987): 943-1005.

Elkins, David J. "Facing Our Destiny: Rights and Canadian Distinctiveness," *Canadian Journal of Political Science* 22 (1989): 699-716.

Ely, John Hart. *Democracy and Distrust: A Theory of Judicial Review.* Cambridge, MA: Harvard, 1980.

Harvie, Robert and Foster, Hamar. "Ties That Bind? The Supreme Court of Canada, American Jurisprudence, and the Revision of Canadian Criminal Law Under The Charter," *Osgoode Hall Law Journal* 28 (1990): 729-87.

Knopff, Rainer and Morton, F.L. *Charter Politics.* Toronto: Nelson Canada, 1992.

Lipset, Seymour Martin. *Continental Divide.* New York: Routledge, 1990.

Manfredi, Christopher P. "The Use of United States Decisions By The Supreme Court of Canada Under The Charter of Rights and Freedoms," *Canadian Journal of Political Science* 23 (1990): 499-518.

Manfredi, Christopher P. *Judicial Power and the Charter: Canada and the Paradox of Liberal Constitutionalism.* Toronto: McClelland and Stewart, 1993.

Monahan, Patrick. *Politics and the Constitution: The Charter, Federalism and the Supreme Court of Canada.* Toronto: Carswell/Methuen, 1987.

Morton, F.L. "The Politics of Rights: What Canadians Should Know About the American Bill of Rights," *Windsor Review of Legal and Social Issues* 1 (1989): 61-96.

Packer, Herbert L. *The Limits of the Criminal Sanction.* Stanford, CA: Stanford University Press, 1968.

Russell, Peter H. "The Political Purposes of the Canadian Charter of Rights and Freedoms," *Canadian Bar Review* 61 (1983): 1-33.

KATHY BROCK

The Issue of Self-Government: Canadian and American Aboriginal Policy Compared

As the issue of Aboriginal self-government unfolds in Canada, the temptation to look to the United States for a model of how to structure relations between federal, provincial or state, and First Nation governments becomes stronger. The long history of Indian self-government in the United States seems to provide Canadian policy-makers with working examples of arrangements which balance the interests of the broader society with those of the First Nation communities. However, upon closer examination, the American example may be a chimera which does not deliver on its initial promises. Even more seriously, grafting American solutions onto a Canadian political framework may result in the creation of a governing system which is complex and antithetical to the needs of First Nation communities. If the American model is to be used, it must be used with caution and careful consideration of the special Canadian context.

This paper contrasts the Canadian experience with the development of Aboriginal governance through the constitutional forum with the relevant aspects of the American experience. While the similarities in policy and practices pertaining to Aboriginal self-government in the two nations are noted, the differences are stressed in order to determine the limitations inherent in the American model for Canada. This type of analysis is important for ensuring that by borrowing from American institutions and arrangements, Canadian policy-makers do not pose unnecessary obstacles to the achievement of effective and efficient self-government in Aboriginal communities. While the American examples provide guidance, Canadian structures of self-government must be consonant with Canadian and First Nation experiences and practices.

The argument is divided into four sections. The first of these contrasts aspects of the historical relations between the federal and the First Nation governments in Canada and the United States. Subsequent sections identify three important features of the recent drive towards the recognition of Aboriginal governance in Canada that emerged through the constitutional process, and illustrate how in each case they are distinct and reflective of the underlying political philosophy and institutional structures of Canada when viewed in contrast with the United States. These distinctive characteristics give rise to the need to examine carefully and adapt American models to the Canadian context.

Some brief observations should be borne in mind in any binational comparison of Aboriginal populations. In Canada the term "Aboriginal Peoples" is used to refer to First Nations, Inuit, and Métis inclusively. This term has become accepted for distinguishing these communities collectively from the rest of Canadian society. However, the preferred practice is to refer to each separately so as to avoid obscuring real differences among them. Members of First Nations prefer to be referred to as such or by the name of their First Nation. "Aboriginal" is also the term used by status-blind organisations in urban centres who deliver services to members of these communities. In the United States, the term "Aboriginal" is becoming more accepted. However, "Indian," "Eskimo," and more commonly, "Native Americans" are used.

The demographics are also significantly different in the two nations. According to the 1991 Census data, Canadian Aboriginals comprise approximately 2.3% of the total population, although this figure is disputed as underrating the actual Aboriginal population size. The percentages by province vary from a low of 0.5% in P.E.I. to a high of 9.2% in Manitoba and 8.9% in Saskatchewan. In the Yukon and Northwest Territories, the Aboriginal components of the population are 16.3% and 60.2%.[1] According to the 1984 data on Aboriginal populations in the United States, Aboriginal peoples constitute less than 1% of the total population. In the area of heaviest concentration, the West, the Aboriginal population comprises merely 3.22% and 1.12% of the Mountain and Pacific regions. Even in Alaska, the area with the highest proportion of Aboriginal peoples, the total percentage is only 15.95%. In Canada, Aboriginal peoples experience the worst social and economic conditions of any segment of society whereas in the United States, Americans of African descent are comparatively worse off socially and economically than Aboriginal peoples. These factors work towards placing Aboriginal issues more directly on the agenda of governments in Canada than in the United States. However, as the following history and highlights of Aboriginal relations in the two nations reveal, other factors have resulted in a different treatment of issues in the two nations.

ONE SOURCE, TWO TRIBUTARIES

The source of Canadian and American Aboriginal policy is the Royal Proclamation of 1763. Embedded in the Proclamation is an ambivalence which gave rise to two very different histories with Aboriginal governance in Canada and the United States. On the one hand, the Proclamation recognised that Indian nations were independent and should be dealt with through treaties by central authorities. The document established the basis of treaty and reservation land systems, and provided a basis for current land claims. On the other hand, the Proclamation confirmed that Indian tribes possessed a limited sovereignty and were subject to British rule. Thus, they were not seen as equal to European nations and as many limits were imposed on their actions as was practically possible.

Canadian and American policy with respect to Aboriginal governance diverged from the Royal Proclamation. American policy tended to regulate external aspects of tribal life while Canadian policy tended to extend into the internal life of tribes as well. This difference became particularly pronounced after the 1830s when the American legal concept of Indian tribes as domestic dependent nations was developed and offered some protection to them. Simultaneously, in Canada, the 1830s saw the transfer of authority over Indian affairs from the military to civilian authorities and a more intrusive, active policy established.

Canadian Indian policy regarding Aboriginal governance may be divided into five distinct, albeit overlapping phases. Following the Royal Proclamation to the 1830s, Indian policy was administered by the military and reflected the military, economic, and political concerns of a frontier society in the process of establishment. The First Nations were needed as allies and benefactors. The British were more interested in establishing good relations with tribes than in promulgating British rule over them, and only began to challenge the political integrity of the First Nations when the latter's military prowess weakened and the balance of power favoured the settlers. Policy goals during this alliance phase were therefore limited.

A new direction in policies respecting the First Nations and Métis characterised the second and third phases. The second phase of Canadian policy began after 1830 when civilian authorities assumed control of Indian affairs. "Civilisation" and segregation became the dominant policy themes. This entailed a direct intrusion into the internal politics and social life of First Nations. The policy placed Indians on reserves and encouraged them to be good Christians, sturdy farmers, and loyal Britons. First Nation sovereignty and self-government were impaired in effect. From 1868 to 1945, the Indian Act set the policy direction and represented an extension of the previous phase. The question of First Nation sovereignty was, for all practical purposes, laid to rest in the eyes of the Canadian government. Tribal powers of self-government were curtailed. Goals of protection and assimilation were pursued. Almost every conceivable facet of First Nation life and culture was subject to scrutiny and regulation by Indian Affairs' officials. The Act denied First Nations legitimate powers over economic resources, cultural and religious practices, and their political affairs. Provisions were made for a transfer from traditional forms of government on reserves to elected band councils subject to the control of the Indian agents. Resistance to Indian Affairs control was quickly squelched. During this phase, Métis were offered some recognition of their rights and status as a distinct people with the land entitlement process. However, the quashing of Métis attempts to establish a provisional government at the Red River Resistance in 1869 and the defeat of the 1885 Rebellion in the Battle of Batoche, show that the Canadian government never doubted its sovereign authority over the Métis. During these periods, the effect of government policy was to erode traditional structures and community bonds and to fail to replace them with substantive alternatives which would provide the means for First Nation and Métis communities to become self-sufficient within the Canadian system.

The fourth phase of Aboriginal policy signalled a shift in the policy paradigm. Postwar reactions against totalitarianism and recognition of human rights internationally forced a rethinking of policies for Aboriginal peoples. Hearings on the Indian Act from 1946 to 1948 ushered in a new understanding of the role of First Nations in governing their affairs. Limited self-government was endorsed and band consultation by Indian officials was introduced. The right to vote in federal elections was extended to Indians in 1960. In 1968 Indian policy reached a crisis point with the tabling of a termination proposal in the guise of a White Paper on Indian policy. This paper proposed abolishing the special status accorded Indians under Canadian law and integrating them into Canadian society upon the same terms as other Canadians. This policy denied the historical rights of Aboriginal peoples and elicited a quick and vehement response from the First Nation communities. As a result, the period since 1968 has been one of new beginnings and reflections. Aboriginal title has been accorded formal legal recognition in the Canadian courts. A greater scope of authority has been recognised for bands under the Indian Act. Aboriginal rights have been recognised for Indian, Inuit, and Métis peoples. Negotiations on Aboriginal self-government have begun and continue. The new attitudes born in the fourth phase are bearing fruit in the final phase.

In contrast to Canada, tribal governments with inherent powers have been recognised historically in the United States. Unlike Canada where Indian legislation tends to be centralised and systematic, in the United States Indian legislation comprises over 5,000 federal statutes, 2,000 federal court opinions, and nearly 400 ratified treaties and agreements. Although Canadian policy is moving in this direction, it in no way approximates the sheer volume and complexity of the American case. This cumbersome attribute of the American model is worth noting and avoiding in the present era which emphasises objectives of government efficiency and responsiveness.

Despite the complexity, American Indian policy is centrally administered by the Bureau of Indian Affairs, and six phases or patterns in policy development are generally recognised. In the first period from 1776 to 1817, American policy built upon the Royal Proclamation of 1763 and was premised upon a theme of stabilisation. Like Canadians, Americans viewed Indian tribes as potential allies and as peoples to be assimilated eventually. Unlike Canadians, Americans recognised tribal sovereignty in law as well as practice. The tentative position and vulnerability of the American state caused its government to enter into treaties, respect land, and recognise tribal authority and right of self-governance. Once recognised, tribal sovereignty was difficult to retract.

The legal foundation of self-government followed during the second phase, which saw a policy of removal and reservation creation from 1817 to 1887. This period saw the encroachment of European settlers on Indian territory and the forced removal of Indian Nations from their lands. The treaty process was terminated. Eventually Congress passed legislation establishing the authority of American courts over crimes committed within Indian communities. These actions hampered the practice of Indian self-government. However, it was during this phase that the Supreme Court recognised the status of tribes as "domestic dependent nations" whose internal powers of self-government were not restricted by treaties or by the trade and intercourse acts. The only limit was that the external affairs powers of tribal governments were subject to Congressional authority and the prospects of further limits were implied.

In the period following removal and reservation, from 1887 to 1934, Indian self-government and sovereignty were assaulted primarily on two fronts. The first attack was made through the land tenure system. The Allotment Act of 1887 provided for the division of Indian lands among individuals with the possibility of "alienation" (i.e. the land could be sold privately). This policy was extended to Alaska in 1906. This struck at the communal basis of Indian governments. The second blow came with legislation conferring citizenship unilaterally upon Indians in 1924. Overtures of assimilation were undeniable. No longer content with separating Indians, policy-makers began to interfere directly in the internal affairs of tribes and the basis of their system of government, and to "recast" the Indian character along liberal principles. Unlike the situation in Canada, American Indians were viewed as both citizens (with full participatory rights) and as subjects (under state authority). And because land could be alienated, reservations were "checkerboarded." Canadian reservations remained largely intact.

A new direction in policy commenced in 1934 under the direction of a new Commissioner of Indian Affairs, John Collier. He oversaw the reversal of the trend towards the erosion of self-government and the expansion of tribal powers but at the expense of traditional forms of government. Indian sovereignty and self-government were rejuvenated during this phase but still subject to the plenary final and binding power of Congress. The tribal constitutions passed in this phase incorporated liberal principles into the tribal communities. This policy direction was briefly interrupted by the fifth phase of policy when the termination legislation was passed. The objective of this legislation was to assimilate Indians into American society as equals and full tax-payers. Similarly, the extension of civil rights to Indian communities further imposed liberal assumptions on Indian communities. Although termination was shortlived, the trend towards the liberalisation of Indian tribes and the erosion of communitarian and collective principles of government continued.

The final phase of Indian policy was ushered in with the pronouncement on Indian Self-determination in 1970. President Nixon introduced this change with his reconceptualisation of the relationship with tribes as autonomous entities. He favoured greater tribal control over education and economic development on reservations. He also sponsored the creation of a special body to represent Indian interests exclusively within the national government. His policy set the tone for the 1970s and was reinforced in the 1980s by Reagan's recognition of the relationship between the national and tribal authorities as "government-to-government."

These policy shifts were prompted by a strong and activist leadership among the First Nations, just as in Canada during the 1970s and 1980s. In the face of stiff resistance and skilled leadership, the

Canadian and American governments have been forced to redirect their policies. However, in the United States, tribal government powers continue to be subject to limit through the Congressional plenary power and to be challenged and limited in the courts. The Canadian right of self-government has not yet been encumbered by this history.

The two histories reveal qualitative differences in the treatment of Aboriginal government in the two nations. In Canada, the right to self-government was suppressed and denied early in history. In the United States, it was recognised. However, it has been subject to increasing restrictions and the imposition of liberal principles and practices ever since. The erosion of tribal sovereignty has been incremental but steady. Canada stands poised with the formal recognition of Aboriginal rights in 1982 to integrate Aboriginal government into the Canadian federal system. In the process of restructuring relations, it is tempting to look to the long American tradition but the effect of this action may be to accept the limits incorporated into their relationship. To understand why this may be undesirable, it is useful to highlight three distinct features of the development of self-government in Canada in the 1980s and 1990s.

WAYS AND MEANS

The means of achieving Aboriginal self-government in Canada and the United States were significantly different throughout the 1980s and into the 1990s. The means are important because they affect the perception, outcome, and structure of self-government initiatives. In Canada, the primary vehicle for achieving self-government has been through constitutional negotiations. While this has by no means been the only vehicle used, it has received a disproportionate amount of attention. It reflects the Canadian obsession with constitutional tinkering which has characterised Canadian intergovernmental negotiations but has become more pronounced in the last three decades. In contrast, in the United States, the First Nations have relied on the courts to reinforce their traditional right of self-government. Again, this is consistent with that nation's tendencies. Formal constitutional change is difficult to achieve in the United States, and thus, traditionally, groups have relied on the courts and the process of judicial review to update the constitution. While the Canadian action then becomes constructive, the American action has been protective and conservative. This contrast requires explanation.

The drive for Aboriginal self-government has been intimately connected with the Canadian constitutional exercise of the 1980s and 1990s. In 1982, after intensive and prolonged lobbying by representatives of the First Nations, Inuit, and Métis, Aboriginal and treaty rights were entrenched in the constitution under a new section 35(1) of the Canada Act, 1982. This formal affirmation and recognition of the existence of Aboriginal and Treaty rights gave rise to the need to define what specific rights were contained in the guarantee. The Aboriginal perspective was that section 35 constituted a "full box"; that is, it implied recognition of all rights unless otherwise specified. In contrast, the federal and provincial governments tended to assert that the section had to be defined before it could be operationalised. The new section 37 of the Canada Act, 1982, mandated a constitutional conference attended by the first ministers and representatives of the four national Aboriginal organisations — the Assembly of First Nations, the Native Council of Canada, the Métis National Council, and the Inuit Committee on National Issues — to identify and define those rights implicit in section 35(1).

At this first First Ministers' Conference (FMC) on Aboriginal Matters held in 1983, section 37 was amended to provide for at least two more constitutional conferences within five years of April 17, 1982. In fact, three more conferences were held in 1984, 1985, and 1987. Between the 1983 and 1984 conferences, through the choice of the Aboriginal organisations, and aided by the release of the House of Commons Special Committee Report on Indian Self-Government in Canada (Penner Report), the focus of the talks became Aboriginal self-government. The Aboriginal organisations were united in their demands that the right to self-government be recognised as inherent, and that it contain a clause committing the governments to providing adequate resources for the realisation of the aims of Aboriginal government in communities. In contrast, the majority of governments wanted self-government recognised as a more limited power delegated by them to the First Nation, Métis and Aboriginal communities. They were vague on the commitment for resources.

No amendment for self-government was achieved during the 1982-87 constitutional talks on Aboriginal matters. However, the talks had at least two important effects upon the development of Aboriginal self-government. First, they mobilised and focused Aboriginal organisations. The four national organisations continued to pursue the goal of achieving recognition of the inherent right of self-government despite funding cutbacks and changes in leadership. Second, the discussions had introduced the Canadian general public to the concept of self-government and placed the item squarely on the table for governments to deal with in the future. Canadians had watched while governments expended significant resources on these talks and had seen an impressive array of talent among Aboriginal leaders. As the talks wore on and the logic of allowing First Nations in particular and Aboriginal peoples more generally the same right of self-determination within Canada became compelling, Canadians became more receptive to the policy proposal. Similarly, governments began to calculate the economic costs and savings. While governments such as Alberta, B.C., Saskatchewan, and Newfoundland were most opposed to the policy idea and most likely to bear the highest costs with the possible exception of Manitoba, other governments, particularly the federal government, began to realise the benefits of Aboriginal governments assuming more responsibilities and revenue-raising burdens.

The change in thinking on Aboriginal issues became abundantly apparent during the 1987-1990 constitutional round. Initially, the Meech Lake Accord did not contain any mention of the right to self-government, or of any Aboriginal rights generally. However, during the drafting of the legal text at Langevin, a clause was added providing protection for Aboriginal rights against any changes made to the constitution by the list of proposed amendments. There were still no positive measures to advance Aboriginal rights contained in the Meech Lake Accord. This oversight galvanised Aboriginal opposition to the Accord and became one of the main instruments in its death. Given that the Accord proposed recognising Quebec as a distinct society and provided formal recognition to the English and French components of Canada without acknowledging the status of First Nations and Aboriginal peoples, it was viewed as an incomplete and offensive document. The four national organisations, as well as various groups, individuals, and interests within the general public, argued that recognition should be extended to the most distinct component of Canadian society, the First Nations, and that Canada had three original founding nations, not two. This was not the only reason for the rejection of the Meech Lake Accord but it was one of the most significant. This perception was reinforced by the death of the Meech Lake Accord in the Manitoba Legislative Assembly when the lone representative of a First Nation, Elijah Harper, stood holding an eagle's feather and denied the government the unanimous consent of the members required to amend the motion paper and introduce the Accord into the house for passage. The symbolism was poignant.[2]

In contrast to the Meech Lake process, representatives of the Aboriginal constituency were included in the drafting of the Charlottetown Accord.[3] In response to the circumstances surrounding the demise of the Meech Lake Accord, the 1990-92 constitutional process was intended to be more inclusive of the various interests and groups within Canada. In particular, Aboriginal participation was deemed necessary because of the legitimacy their cause had gained during

Meech, the proactive stance of Aboriginal leaders, the support their cause received in Constitutional committee reports issued in the 1990-91 rounds of hearings, and the attention drawn to their concerns by the stand-off between the Mohawk Warriors and the Quebec government and police at Oka.[4] Aboriginal organisations played an integral role in drafting the sections of the Charlottetown Accord on Aboriginal rights and Aboriginal self-government. As Mary Ellen Turpel explains,

> The Charlottetown Accord contained the most comprehensive set of reform proposals on Aboriginal issues in the history of Canada. The inherent right of self-government was recognised and Aboriginal governments were described as one of the three orders of government in Canada. The Accord recognised the need for a treaty review of process and committed the federal government to dealing with treaty grievances in good faith. The reform package was sweeping but its real significance stemmed from the fact that unanimous political agreement was reached on these hitherto contentious areas.[5]

The change in perception and status of Aboriginal matters was underscored by the refusal of some of the provincial governments to support the "Aboriginal package" of amendments unless the leaders of the Aboriginal communities endorsed them. The right to self-government had gone from being a disputed item in 1983 to an accepted direction of policy and negotiated constitutional clause in 1992. However, these clauses met considerable opposition within the Aboriginal communities from women who desired more Charter protection, the Treaty First Nations who desired more secure recognition of their treaty guarantees, and other Chiefs who viewed the package as not providing adequate guarantees of funding. Still, the point had been made: Aboriginal leaders were a force to be reckoned with and Aboriginal self-government was a necessary element of constitutional reform.

The involvement of Aboriginal peoples in the constitutional process has not been replicated in the United States. There is no talk of constitutional entrenchment of the right to self-government. First, it is unnecessary given that the Supreme Court under Chief Justice John Marshall in the early 1830s recognised the tribal right of self-government.[6] This conceptualisation of the American Indian nations as sovereign established the relationship between the federal and tribal governments as "nation-to-nation." Significantly then, tribes possessed all the powers of self-government subject only to defeasance (i.e., being declared null and void) by the American Congress. Second, although judicial protection of the tribal right to self-government has waxed and waned over time, the operation of the American legal and political system discourages American Indians from attempting to secure better protection for their rights through constitutional change. Formal constitutional change is difficult to achieve since the American constitution requires an amendment to be passed by two-thirds majorities in both houses of Congress as well as by three-quarters of the states. By 1988, the constitution had been amended only 26 times. Third, Americans tend to view their constitution as immutable and are less receptive to the prospects of amendments than their Canadian cousins.[7]

Thus, in the United States, Aboriginal peoples are less likely to resort to formal constitutional change as a means of securing their rights. Originally, it was the courts which recognised and reinforced the right of First Nations to self-government. This provided an extra-constitutional base for the right of tribal self-determination. In Canada, Aboriginal peoples are looking to anchor their rights in the constitution in much the same way as Quebec is, in order to provide a more secure foundation for their governments.

LEGALISATION OF A POLITICAL RELATIONSHIP

The development of Aboriginal self-government in Canada has reflected Canada's distinct constitutional history in another way. Just as the entrenchment of the Canadian Charter of Rights and Freedoms has encouraged interest groups and minorities to resort more to the courts to challenge restrictive or discriminatory policy and practices, the entrenchment of Aboriginal rights has resulted in Aboriginal challenges to restrictive or discriminatory policy and practice. The courts have provided a fall-back strategy to both Aboriginal and non-Aboriginal communities when regular policy channels fail them.

One of the most significant effects of the constitutional discussions leading to the Canada Act, 1982 was that Aboriginal issues were recast as rights and entrenched in the constitution as such. Although the process of recognising Aboriginal rights had begun with the Calder case in 1973,[8] entrenchment of Aboriginal rights in 1982 provided the formal legal basis for adjudication of disputes in the courts. By transforming Aboriginal claims into constitutional rights, the politicians allowed the judiciary the greater involvement in the final determination of the definition of those rights.[9]

The repeated breakdowns in constitutional negotiations have resulted in Aboriginal organisations and communities resorting to the courts to affirm their rights, albeit with reluctance. Bands across

Canada have filed suits to have their rights recognised, including the right to self-government. At the forefront of this action has been *Delgamuukw v. the Queen* which is an action brought by the Gitskan and Wet'suwet'en First Nations in B.C. to establish Aboriginal title over their lands and the right of self-government.[10] (The Manitoba Métis Federation has also resorted to the courts.) The courts have thus become a viable alternative to the regular policy process.

This development means that the relationship between Aboriginal communities and the federal and provincial governments is being fought out and shaped in a legal environment. The first cases before the courts will set the general principles and parameters of the new relationship. The decisions could circumscribe the room for negotiation and definition of self-government. Even the recent gains in cases such as Guerin, Simon, Sioui, and Sparrow have affirmed Aboriginal rights and jurisdiction but also affirmed Canadian sovereignty and may have limited the prospects for self-government under section 35(1).[11] While the political arena allows for compromise and negotiation, the legal forum forces issues into a zero sum situation with winners and losers. As a result, judicialisation of political issues tends to cause polarisation of views and positions with a more limited range of solutions considered.

The American experience may be informative here. In the United States, as mentioned, the formal legal basis for the recognition of tribal self-government was provided through the courts. Marshall's decision in Worcester (amending his decision in Cherokee Nation) established the legal convention of tribal sovereignty. Politicians followed the lead of the courts reluctantly. As the history of American policy highlighted, many of the policies have been aimed at restricting this convention and right. However, despite this history and despite the fact that the Supreme Court has retreated from a strict enforcement of tribal sovereignty in the 1980s, the American courts have remained integral to the fight of American tribal governments to maintain their powers and rights.[12] The courts set the limits of federal and state government intrusion on tribal powers. Thus the courts have played an active role in defining and defending the basis of tribal government in the United States.

While the initial interactions of the American courts and Aboriginal peoples may prove instructive to Canadian Aboriginal peoples, two important implications must be borne in mind. First, the legal doctrine of tribal sovereignty and terms such as "domestic, dependent nations," or the legal conceptualisation of the relationship between the American federal government and tribal governments as "nation-to-nation" have been exclusive of Aboriginal peoples other than Indians living within recognised communities. This legal construct does not apply to "Métis" loosely defined, urban Indians living off-reserve, or other Aboriginal peoples. Even Aleuts and Eskimos in Alaska are excluded from this relationship.[13] The variety and richness of Aboriginal traditions in Canada precludes a similarly restrictive definition being desirable in Canada.

Second, over time, the relationship between American tribes and the courts has evolved into one where tribes resort to the courts to fend off encroachments by the states on their rights, or to force recognition of their powers by the other governments. Because the courts had recognised a comprehensive power of tribal self-determination but one that was subject to defeasance by Congress, the action of tribes in the courts has tended to become defensive and reactive. Despite the grand rhetoric in the legal realm, the definition of tribal government has placed Indians historically in a position of fighting to stave off federal and state encroachments through recourse to the courts. In contrast, in Canada the First Nations have begun to use the courts more since the Calder case in 1973 which signalled a change in the judicial attitude towards Aboriginal rights, and especially since the entrenchment of rights in 1982, to expand and recognise their right to self-government. This is a more proactive and positive use of the courts. The two traditions are opposite in this respect. This difference should be borne in mind when importing American legal fictions and concepts into Canadian cases to argue the right of self-government. The different contexts may not provide the same results or American limitations on the concept may be inadvertently imported and only realised in future litigation.

MORE THAN WORDS CAN SAY

As authors such as Noam Chomsky have reminded us, language is important because it shapes the political perception of an issue. The nature of the debate over self-government in Canada and the United States has been very different. The language and rhetoric used to couch the development of self-government can affect its acceptance in the larger culture. Thus, the importation of American terminology must be done carefully.

In Canada, the rhetoric of Aboriginal self-government has differed at the local and national levels of government. Many First Nations are in negotiations with the federal and provincial governments for the transfer of the development and delivery of services to their communities. Demands centre on health care, language, child care, educational, cultural and other programs, business, capital and labour development, and other issues of a more local nature such as gambling and gaming. Similarly, in Manitoba the Métis federation is attempting to effect a transfer of authority from the provincial and federal government over such areas as labour market development, social programs, education, property, and housing. These powers are consonant with community development. In this way, the negotiations for powers and jurisdiction reflect the provincial demands for local control over local affairs which became part of the constitutional deal struck in 1867. This was the argument used for the establishment of a federal system in Canada. More currently, the areas under negotiation parallel the provincial demands for more control over areas such as labour market training, business development, and immigration. Aboriginal land claims are also consistent with this pattern. What is striking about the negotiations is the sheer pragmatism of the discourse. The objective is to improve the living conditions of the communities in the shortest time possible.

At the national level, the rhetoric is more aggressive and idealistic, and yet consistent with the rhetorical interplay of provincial and federal governments throughout Canadian history. Terms such as "sovereignty," "inherent rights," "nation-to-nation negotiations," and so on pepper the national Aboriginal discourse. While these terms are and have been adopted at the local level, they are used more directly in negotiations at the broader provincial or national level to help forge a more comprehensive picture of self-government and to elevate the status of First Nations within Canada. The national Aboriginal organisations refer to their participation in the constitutional negotiations as "completing the circle of Confederation," and to themselves as founding nations. Like Quebec, they demand recognition of their special status. Like the western provinces, they demand that the Canadian political system become more responsive to their needs. Like the Atlantic provinces, they argue for the necessary support to become economically self-sustaining. In short, the debate and negotiations over self-government have a uniquely Canadian flavour to them and thus are less threatening to citizens.

While the difference in language and focus of the debates at the local and national or provincial levels should be complementary, some problems have arisen. During Charlottetown, Aboriginal leaders were accused of being out of touch with their community needs. This conflict was most heightened with the exchange between the Chiefs and native women over whether the Canadian Charter of Rights and Freedoms should apply to Aboriginal governments. The Chiefs were held to be placing principles above community concerns by holding that the Charter should be limited in application. The women were seen to be placing the needs of children and women above trust in their traditions by asserting that the Charter must apply. Since Charlottetown, the question of the representativeness of national and provincial organisations has been raised and used to justify provincial and federal negotiations with local community governments over issues instead of with the organisations who tend to maintain harder positions on questions involving larger issues of sovereignty or control. These perceptions and actions have split the Aboriginal communities.

In contrast to the Canadian debate, the American debate over tribal sovereignty has a more legalistic flavour. The primary locus of the debate is in the courts, not in the intergovernmental forum. In this issue as in other important political questions, Americans have tended to look to the courts for guidance. The terms of the debate were set by the courts. Similarly, land claims in the United States are determined through legal forums instead of through a negotiating procedure first, as in Canada. The legal doctrines of "native sovereignty" and "domestic, dependent nations" were manufactured by the courts in an endeavour to reconcile the continued existence of Indian tribes with the fragile and new American system of government. As the American system gained strength and Indian nations became weaker, the notion of the defeasance of tribal powers by Congress acquired prominence and authority and the powers of Indian tribes have been nibbled away through continued challenges. The gulf between reality and rhetoric is becoming larger as time proceeds.

CONCLUSION

This brief review of the development of Aboriginal self-government reveals some important differences in the Canadian and American cases. In Canada, Aboriginal self-government is anticipatory. While the development of self-government reflects the richness and diversity of Aboriginal traditions, they are only beginning to be recognised, and the extent and possibilities of their contributions to Canadian culture and politics is yet to be realised. In the United States, Indian nations have had their right to self-determination realised but they must fight continually to retain its core and to stave off intrusive actions by other governments. The courts offer the best avenue of protection. In Canada, the political arenas of constitutional and intergovernmental negotiations still offer the best prospects for the realisation of the aims of self-government with the courts providing a means of prodding the governments to action or reinforcing their rights. In the United States, the courts have led the Aboriginal fight; in Canada, the politicians have led the way to self-government, albeit reluctantly at times.

These differences are important for two reasons. First, Canadians must be cognizant of the advantages as well as the disadvantages of their process for the development of Aboriginal self-government. The American case provides both positive and negative lessons. For example, the courts can be useful in advancing the cause of self-government but may become limiting if overused. Political negotiations, although frustrating at times, may provide more workable compromises.

Second, the differences illuminate an important feature in the development of Aboriginal self-government in Canada. Despite the frustrations and failure of the constitutional negotiations, Aboriginal self-government is being realised in Canada. The constitutional negotiations prepared the way for negotiations at the community level. The rhetoric at the national and provincial levels prepared federal and provincial governments for the negotiations at the local levels. The political negotiations of the 1970s and early 1980s led to the constitutional entrenchment of Aboriginal and treaty rights. This has strengthened the position and bargaining powers of Aboriginal peoples in Canada and has given them another weapon in the pursuit of the realisation of self-government — the courts. However, the American example is useful in revealing the pitfalls of resorting to the courts. In sum, the Canadian experiences, when viewed in contrast to the American experiences, reveal that the opportunities exist for the realisation of the aspirations of the First Nations, Inuit, Non-Status, and Métis within Canada. When looking across the border for models of government, we must be careful not to import their limitations and to stultify the prospects at home.

NOTES

1. It is argued that a working model of Aboriginal self-government exists in the NWT since the majority of the population is Aboriginal and the majority of representatives in the legislative body are Aboriginal.

2. For a review of Meech Lake and the actions taken by Aboriginal peoples in Manitoba, see Ovide Mercredi, "Aboriginal Peoples and the Constitution," David E. Smith, Peter MacKinnon and John C. Courtney (eds.), *After Meech Lake: Lessons for the Future*, (Saskatoon: Fifth House Publishers, 1991), 219-222; and Donna Greschner, "Selected Documents from the Assembly of Manitoba Chiefs on the Meech Lake Accord," *Native Studies Review*, 6:1 (1990), 119-52.

3. For accounts of Aboriginal participation in the 1990-1992 constitutional exercise, see Ovide Mercredi and Mary Ellen Turpel, *In the Rapids: Navigating the Future of First Nations* (Toronto: Viking, 1993); and, Susan Delacourt, *United We Fall; The Crisis of Democracy in Canada* (Toronto: Viking, 1993).

4. Material on this confrontation is growing. For different perspectives on the encounter, see for example, Kahn-Tineta Horn, "Interview: Oka and Mohawk Sovereignty," *Studies in Political Economy* 35 (Summer 1991), 29-41; Rick Hornung, *One Nation Under the Gun* (Toronto: Stoddart Publishing, 1991); Maurice Tugwell and John Thompson, *The Legacy of Oka* (Toronto: Mackenzie Institute, 1991); and Geoffrey York and Loreen Pindera, *People of the Pines: The Warriors and the Legacy of Oka* (Toronto: Little, Brown and Co., 1991).

5. Ovide Mercredi and Mary Ellen Turpel, *In the Rapids: Navigating the Future of First Nations* (Toronto: Viking, 1993), 208.

6. *Worcester v. Georgia*, 31 U.S. (6 Pet.) 536 (1832). For a discussion of the courts' involvement in Indian policy development see Vine Deloria Jr. and Clifford Lyttle, *The Nations Within*, (New York: Pantheon, 1984); and Russell Lawrence Barsh and James Youngblood Henderson, *The Road: Indian Tribes and Political Liberty*, (Berkeley: University of California Press, 1980).

7. The American attitude towards constitutional change is captured in Archibald Cox, *The Court and the Constitution* (Boston: Houghton Mifflin Co., 1987), 378; and Eric Black, *Our Constitution: The Myth that Binds Us*, (Boulder: Westview Press, 1988).

8. *Calder et al. v. Attorney General of British Columbia* [1973] S.C.R. 313 (SCC).

9. This is part of a larger trend given that First Nations were precluded from bringing actions against the state for the first half of this century.

10. One of the most informative sources on this case is Frank Cassidy (ed.), *Aboriginal title in British Columbia: Delgamuukw*

v. the Queen (Lantzville, B.C. and Montreal: Oolichan Books and Institute for Research on Public Policy, 1992).

11. For a discussion of this view, see Michael Asch and Patrick Macklem, "Aboriginal Rights and Canadian Sovereignty: An Essay on R. v. Sparrow," *Alberta Law Review* XXIX:2 (1991), 498-517.

12. For accounts of these fights, see S.L. Cadwalader and Vine Deloria Jr., *The Aggressions of Civilization*, (Arizona: Temple University Press, 1984); and Vine Deloria Jr., *American Indian Policy in the Twentieth Century* (Norman: University of Oklahoma Press, 1985).

13. See Thomas Berger, *Village Journey* (New York: Hill and Wang, 1985).

FURTHER READING:

Boldt, Menno. *Surviving as Indians: The Challenge of Self-Government.* Toronto: University of Toronto Press, 1993.

Corrigan, Samuel W. and Lawrence J. Barkwell (eds.). *The Struggle for Recognition: Canadian Justice and the Métis Nation.* Winnipeg: Pemmican Publications, 1991.

Deloria Jr., Vine and Clifford Lyttle. *The Nations Within: The Past and Future of American Indian Sovereignty.* New York: Pantheon Books, 1984.

Fleras, Augie, and J.L. Elliot. *The Nations Within: Aboriginal-State Relations in Canada, the United States and New Zealand.* Toronto: University of Toronto Press, 1992.

Johansen, Bruce E. *Forgotten Founders: How the American Indian Helped Shape Democracy.* Harvard and Boston: Harvard Common Press, 1982.

Lyden and Lyman H. Legters (eds.). *Native Americans and Public Policy.* Pittsburgh: University of Pittsburgh Press, 1992.

Mercredi, Ovide and Mary Ellen Turpel. *In the Rapids: Navigating the Future of First Nations.* Toronto: Viking Books, 1993.

Richardson, Boyce (ed). *Drumbeat: Anger and Renewal in Indian Country*. Toronto: Summerhill Press and the AFN, 1989.

York, Geoffrey. *The Dispossessed: Life and Death in Native Canada*. London: Vintage U.K., 1990.

MANON TREMBLAY

Gender and Society: Rights and Realities

INTRODUCTION

Whenever the United States and Canada are compared, there is a certain misapprehension: it seems as though the United States is the leader in the area of feminism and women's rights, while the words and actions of Canadian feminists are but a pale reflection of those of their southern neighbours. The American women's movement appears to be more worthy of attention than the Canadian one – even in the eyes of Canadians themselves. Granted, the American movement is one of the oldest[1] and most active. The first conference on women's rights dates back to 1848 in Seneca Falls, New York, where, in something of a paraphrase of the U.S. Declaration of Independence, resolutions concerning the equality of women in, among others, the areas of education, property and inheritance, and divorce, were adopted. Also associated with this are major struggles for the right to vote and for the recognition of gender equality within the Constitution. Moreover, the American women's liberation movement embodies both awareness[2] and mobilization.[3]

However, beyond a community of thought and struggle, the women's movement in Canada can be proud of its own originality, and has achieved victories which its southern neighbours have good reason to envy. I do not wish to imply through this that the situation of Canadian women is without its problems or that feminism has lost its *raison d'être* in Canada, but rather that, in many ways, the situation of Canadian women can be compared quite favourably to that of American women. Such a viewpoint comes from an examination of the rights of women in Canada, as well as the struggles and victories of the feminist movement in Canada over the course of the last few years.

The purpose of this article is to examine the rights and conditions of women in Canada and the United States, as well as women's movements in the respective countries, in order to show the limitations of conceiving the situation with the American experience as the point of reference. In a way, this paper aims to "decolonize" feminism in Canada by bringing out the uniqueness of the feminist experience, the richness of its theory and practice, and its victories and defeats. Since the women's movement in Canada exists in a broader political context because of its two founding peoples, I will spend some time dealing with the Québec situation.[4]

THE WOMEN'S MOVEMENT IN CANADA AND THE UNITED STATES

As we await the dawning of the year 2000, the women's movement is almost a century and a half old; the first women's rights activities began in the middle of the 19th century. It is customary to identify two "waves" in this movement which correspond to particular times of intense mobilization: the suffrage movement and the contemporary women's movement.[5] While the thought, organization, strategies, and methods, as well as the claims and demands characteristic of these two phases of the women's movement can vary a great deal, the movement remains driven by the single objective of changing and improving women's place in society, particularly through the achievement of gender equality. The links between the past and present forms of the women's movement can be seen not only in the philosophies adopted, the issues tackled and the strategies employed, but, in particular, in the hopes and energy invested by women in their fight to improve the conditions of their lives.

THE SUFFRAGE MOVEMENT

Historically, the Canadian and American suffrage movements date from the middle of the 19th century to around 1920. The right to vote represented an excellent way for women to attain a status equal to men; it was the key to political citizenship. For suffragettes who were inspired by a social or maternal feminism, the vote became the tool which allowed them to perform their natural social functions while participating in the creation of a better society. The vote was also seen as a way of assuring a certain domestic harmony. In the United States, the suffrage fights were to last over 70 years and would be marked by 19 battles in Congress, before the 19th Amendment to the American Constitution would be finally adopted on August 26, 1920. Canadian women, for their part, would have to wait a shorter time – about 30 years – to vote in the federal election of May 24, 1918, after only three attempts at having legislation passed.[6] The suffrage battle in Canada did not last as long as in the United States, nor was it marked by as many significant events to arouse public opinion.[7]

The unwillingness to recognize women's right to vote stemmed from the bipolar belief that society be organized with women dependent on men. Women's involvement in the public domain was seen as incompatible with their role in the family, their interests being associated with those of the family unit; the role of representing the family – and, consequently, the woman – in the public domain fell to the man. In response to feminists who argued for the moral superiority of women, those opposed to suffrage claimed that, instead of purifying political mores, women who became involved in matters of the state would see their own mores degraded. In line with the view of political citizenship based on masculinist parameters, they also felt that since women had no obligation to serve in the military, they could not obtain the privilege of voting and sitting in Parliament.[8]

Let us step aside now to focus on the particularly heated debate in Québec concerning women's right to vote. In addition to the opposition to women's demands mentioned above, Québec women had to face opposition from the Church.[9] In fact, although women in *la Belle province* had been fighting for the vote since the end of the 19th century, they were the last in Canada to obtain the vote at the provincial level, in 1940, while women in some provinces were able to vote provincially before federally.[10] The Church's resistance to allowing Québec women to vote rested largely on tradition: the survival of French-Canadian culture depended on maintaining the status quo. Lamoureux identifies two basic arguments on this issue: women's voting would go against both a "natural" gender hierarchy (based on the private/public distinction) and the best interests of society (since the state of social relations would be put in question by a new division of the roles and functions of the sexes).[11]

Following the victory in the fight for the right to vote, the women's movement in Canada and the United States seemed to enter a calmer phase. There are several explanations for this phenomenon. The suffrage movement was driven by too narrow a goal – the vote – and achieving it led all the more to demobilization because no other issue was around to crystallize the movement.[12] Moreover, dissenters abounded within the movement, as much in terms of the factors that motivated them to get the vote as in the particular strategies and methods employed in the process. We can add to this the economic crisis and the rise of the feminine mystique which emphasized the traditional gender divisions and the occupation of housewife.

However, this perception of a women's movement on its last legs from the end of the 1920s to the middle of the 1960s is not altogether realistic.[13] Granted, the movement remained somewhat depoliticized, marginal, and off the political scene, but women nonetheless remained actively involved in a number of issues and within organizations.[14] Such a narrow view rather conceals the fact that over the course of this period the contemporary women's movement (or the feminist movement) was being born.

THE CONTEMPORARY WOMEN'S MOVEMENT

Aside from major political changes (such as the advent of the Welfare State), economic changes (as in the move from manufacturing to service industries), and socio-cultural ones (like the "baby-boom" phenomenon and transformations in the structure of the family), two factors contributed to the emergence of the second wave of the women's movement in Canada and the United States: the increase in women's participation in the workforce (especially working mothers), and greater access to higher education for women. There were also various protest movements – the student movement, the peace and anti-Vietnam war campaigns, and, in Québec, the Front de libération du Québec, for example – which led to the mobilization of many women and to the politicization of their understanding of the social relations between the sexes. The first half of the 1960s also saw the publication of works which would come to symbolize feminist thought and struggle in Canada and the United States.[15] Friedan's book in particular caused quite a stir since it presented a critique of traditional roles of women in family and society.

The contemporary women's movement emerged at the end of the 1960s and the beginning of the 1970s. It can be classified as "any and all activities and organizations which have the aim of improving women's status and situation;"[16] this includes elements as diverse as consciousness-raising groups, collectives, women's centres, women's studies programmes, and feminist publishing houses. Its principal objective is to change and improve the social status of women by replacing the hierarchical relationships between men and women with those of equality. The movement is characterized by considerable ideological and organizational diversity, and by a wide range of claims and demands.

It is fashionable to identify two distinct branches of the Canadian and American women's movement: a reformist wing and a revolutionary wing. Primarily interested in the distribution of women and men in the public sphere, the reformist wing is linked to liberal and institutional feminism. This perspective does not raise the issue of the private/public dichotomy; it leaves the socio-cultural representation of the respective roles of each sex intact, seeking instead to extend to women the roles already enjoyed by men. In this context, women's equality means their assimilation into the male model. Groups associated with this wing include the National Organization of Women (NOW) and the National Women's Political Caucus in the United States, and the Fédération des femmes du Québec and the National Action Committee on the Status of Women in Canada. The revolutionary wing, on the other hand, corresponds to a whole network of autonomous and community-based women's groups which have extremely diverse ideologies (for example, radical, socialist and Marxist feminists, separatist feminists, and lesbians). Generally speaking, the desegregation of roles according to gender is their common goal; this involves the destruction of the division between the private and the public, of the traditional statuses, functions, and roles they represent, and even of the institutions of which they are a part. The groups associated with this wing include the New York Radical Women, New Feminists of Toronto, the Montreal Women's Liberation Movement, and Front de libération des femmes du Québec. These groups express a range of demands which reflect the ideological diversity of the women's movement today.[17]

At least four phases can be identified in the feminist movement in Canada and the United States.[18] First was a phase of emergence between 1967 and 1971, when the feminist movement identified and analyzed the oppression of women (the Bird Commission was set up at this time), established organizations, proposed strategies (fostering an abundance of consciousness-raising groups) and mobilized itself in a number of areas (in Canada we think of the Abortion Caravan of 1970). This was followed by a phase of expansion and consolidation which lasted throughout the 1970s. The modern woman's movement grew both from an organizational perspective and with respect to the issues it tackled. It was also at this time that the movement became institutionalized through state organizations like the Canadian Advisory Council on the Status of Women, and widened its outlook through several ideological trends.

At the end of the 1970s and the beginning of the 1980s, the women's movement underwent a strategic realignment in terms of its alliances and links. In Canada and the United States, these new involvements were most notable in the battles surrounding the addition of a gender equality clause in the Constitution.[19] Finally, over the course of the last few years, the feminist movement has devoted itself particularly to fighting to maintain what women have gained[20] in a climate of political conservatism,[21] of financial austerity,[22] and of the affirmation of a neo-conservative right wing.[23] In addition, the antifeminist undercurrent which is currently developing in the West has led to the belief that the feminist movement has lost its *raison d'être* with women now having achieved equality with men. Let us now see what is closer to the truth.

WOMEN'S RIGHTS IN CANADA AND THE UNITED STATES

In 1992, Canada earned the title of the country with the best quality of life in the world. Canadian women, like American women, have every reason to believe that they live in a privileged country: guaranteed basic liberties, a high standard of living, a high level of industrialization, a well-educated population, etc. However, upon closer inspection, the lives of Canadian and American women still have numerous weaknesses which cry out for the women's movement to continue its fight. To demonstrate this, let us review some of the indicators of the current conditions of women's lives and of their gains in recent years, keeping in mind the goal of identifying the differences between the situation of Canadian women and that of American women. I will organize my presentation around three themes – family and reproduction, work and education, and politics – since they appear to be the major areas into which the demands of the second-wave women's movement are channelled.

FAMILY AND REPRODUCTION

The women's movement has traditionally concerned itself with questions of the family and reproduction. For example, the first issues of concern to the women's rights movement in the 19th century centred on the homeless, prostitution and poverty. Even today, such issues occupy an important place on the agenda of the women's movement in Canada and the United States: the legal and economic equality of partners in a marriage, the equal division of family patrimony, alimony payments, domestic violence, the issue of abortion, and new reproductive technologies.

Over the last 30 years, Canadian and American women have undergone similar demographic and social transformations. The statistics that follow are evidence of this.[24] In Canada the synthetic fertility index dropped from four births per woman of conceiving age in 1959 to 1.7 in 1990 while in the United States this figure went from 3.4 in 1960-64 to 2.0 in 1989. At the end of the 1980s, the synthetic divorce index was 4.0 for every 1000 marriages in Canada, and 4.7 in the United States; in 1969 it was 1.4 in Canada and in 1970, 3.5 in the United States. The rise in the number of births among single women was also anything but negligible: it went from 28,000 in 1975 to 63,000 in 1986 in Canada, while in the United States it went from 398,700 in 1970 to 1,094,200 in 1989. It is worth mentioning, too, that, contrary to the way it might appear, women still have primary responsibility for parental and domestic duties.

In terms of violence against women, a recently published study[25] based on 21,200 cases of violence reported to 15 police forces across Canada in 1991 shows that the family does not necessarily provide a secure environment for women; while the wife or ex-wife was responsible for 3.0% of the incidences of violence against men, the husband or ex-husband was responsible more than 43.0% of the time in cases of violence against his present or former partner. In the United States, a similar statistic shows that 18.5% of violent crimes against women between 1979 and 1987 were perpetrated by their husband, ex-husband, or boyfriend, while 1.2% of violent crimes against men were committed by their wife, ex-wife, or girlfriend.[26] These acts of violence against women have led to the establishment of a whole network of shelters for women who are victims of violence.[27]

These changes in the relationships between women and the family and reproduction have been accompanied by poverty, particularly in single-parent mother-only families. According to a report published by the National Council for Social Welfare in the autumn of 1992.[28] 60.6% of single-parent mother-only families in Canada in 1990 had very little income; it was estimated that 27.0% of single-parent father-only families were in this position. Poverty hits women more than men regardless of age or lifestyle. In fact, if there has indeed been a reduction in poverty in Canada over the last few years, the trend has benefited father-only families more than mother-only ones.[29] By the same token, these authors also state that throughout the 1980s, American women in single-parent families were affected by poverty more than Canadian women in the same situation. They explain that this is due to cuts in social programmes during the Reagan and Bush administrations, and to the more generous social policies in Canada.

One issue that has served to mobilize the women's movement in Canada and the United States is that of abortion. In themselves, women's demands for the freedom to choose a termination of pregnancy embody the feminist ideal of gender equality and women's autonomy. Over the last 20 years, the number of therapeutic abortions has increased in Canada (from 15.5 for every 1000 women in 1975 to 19.3 in 1986) and in the United States (from 13.2 for every 1000 women in 1972 to 27.3 in 1988). In 1973, in its judgment in the Roe v. Wade case, the United States Supreme Court concluded that a woman's decision to have an abortion was an integral part of her rights.[30] In Canada, the highest tribunal in the country ruled in January 1988 that the legislative provisions contained in Article 251 of the Criminal Code were in conflict with the rights guaranteed by Article 7 of the Canadian Charter of Rights and Freedoms in a way that went against all principles of basic justice. The result of this decision was to make the abortion legislation ineffective and to decriminalize the procedure, creating at the same time – according to some – a "legal vacuum." Today, Canadian and American women's access to abortion services remains in a volatile state: the election of a new government in Ottawa could mean a recriminalization of abortion (as bill C-43, which was defeated in the Senate by a narrow majority, intended), [and legal judgments that smack of conservatism (particularly Webster v. Reproductive Health Services) have reached the same plane as the Roe v. Wade ruling.] Nevertheless, the liberal views of certain provincial governments, Québec and Ontario among them, could mean that, in the future, it will be American women who will cross the border to put an end to an unwanted pregnancy.

WORK AND EDUCATION

The image of the man as the principal breadwinner in a family where the woman stays at home as the "brownie-baking mother" to see to the education of the children (typically two or three) is hardly a realistic picture; only one in four American families fits such an image. The changes outlined above have shattered the family model, sometimes dramatically affecting women's lives. Ryan[31] writes that since the advent of no-fault divorce at the start of the 1970s in the United States, men's standard of living has increased by 42.0%, while that of women has decreased by 73.0%. The women's movement, as much in the United States as in Canada, has reacted to this impoverishment of women by taking steps to achieve pay equity, affirmative action policies, better daycare services, maternity and paternity leaves, sexual harassment policies, and a non-sexist education system, to name but a few.

Women in Canada and the United States share a certain number of problems in their education systems and in the workforce. In Canada in 1991, the average wage of women working full-time was 69.9%

of men's average earnings, this figure being 71.6% in the United States.[32] In both countries, there is still a great deal of workforce segregation. In Québec, a study conducted by Paquette gauged the weighted separation index to be 58.7% in 1981,[33] while Ferber[34] alludes to 57.0% in the United States. In both countries, there is a shortage of daycare centres: while the United States has no national policy in this area (relying instead on a network of private centres with the financial burden that accompanies it), Canadian resources can meet only around 10.0% of the need.

In terms of maternity leave, there is no national policy in the United States, although around 30 states provide some kind of coverage. Moreover, there is a lack of consensus among feminists themselves as to the potential effects of such leaves on women.[35] In Canada, since 1972, maternity leaves have been covered by unemployment insurance for a period of 15 weeks; debate has centred more on accessibility to the programme and to the arrangements it makes. I note finally that while affirmative action is subject to recognition in principle in the Canadian Charter of Rights and Freedoms,[36] it meets with vehement opposition in the United States, particularly in conservative circles.[37] In 1978, quotas in the area of affirmative action policies were judged to be illegal by the U.S. Supreme Court.

Over the last few years, women have made significant progress in the realm of education: at the beginning of the 1990s, half of the undergraduate students in Canada and the United States were women. However, although women have had access to university education since the second half of the 19th century, education remains split according to gender: at the end of the 1980s, women were still in the minority among master's and doctoral degree recipients, and boys and girls were still pursuing careers traditionally considered to be appropriate to their gender.[38] It must be noted that a significant achievement for the women's movement in the area of education has been the establishment of a large number of women's studies programmes, in Canada as well as the United States. However, in the U.S., these programmes have been subject to cuts by the Reagan and Bush administrations.[39]

POLITICS

Women have clearly been underrepresented in both Canadian and American politics: 13.6% of the seats in the Canadian House of Commons are occupied by women as of September 1993, while 9.9% of the members of the United States Congress are women at the same date – and women have only nine of the 100 Senate seats and 47 of

435 in the House of Representatives. Many elements explain this political underrepresentation of women: the single-vote electoral system which is not conducive to the election of women;[40] the reticence of political parties which nominate women for ridings where there is little hope for victory;[41] and financial difficulties,[42] to name but a few.

One dimension of politics which contributes to distinguishing between the women's movements in Canada and the United States is that of the incorporation of a gender equality principle into the Canadian and American constitutions. The year 1982 saw a victory in Canada and a defeat in the United States. The Equal Rights Amendment (ERA) was presented to the United States Congress for the first time in 1923, and was adopted almost 50 years later (in 1972). It took seven years to be ratified by 75% of the states (the delay lasted until 1982). Opposition to the amendment developed during that time, notably through Phyllis Schlafly's Stop ERA and a number of conservative and religious right-wing groups. The failure of ERA, despite favourable public opinion for its ratification, can be attributed to several factors, among which are a long and complex process of constitutional change and the ten-year delay which allowed opposition to mount and react; the interpretation of the amendment as a change of roles rather than equality of roles, with its attendant implications; the difficulty in achieving consensus within the women's movement itself as to the scope and effects of ERA; and an antifeminist undercurrent and a social climate universally unsympathetic to the demands of any social movement.[43]

In Canada in 1980, Prime Minister Trudeau announced that he wanted to "bring home" the Constitution from Great Britain. The article in the Canadian Charter of Rights and Freedoms dealing with discrimination on the basis of gender was not satisfactory to feminists; it differed little from the Canadian Declaration of Rights, which had not really done much to advance the situation of women, especially where native women, women in conjunction with their spouse, and women in the workforce were concerned. So Canadian feminists mobilized, notably through the Canadian Advisory Council on the Status of Women (CACSW) and the Ad Hoc Committee. From October 1980 to November 1981, they led studies, held a national conference on "Women and the Constitution," put pressure on the federal government, provincial premiers, and MPs. The principle of the equality of women and men was finally adopted into the Constitution and cannot be subject to a provincial notwithstanding clause. What American feminists had been fighting for in vain for nearly 60 years, Canadian feminists achieved in just a few months. Several factors help explain this success, including the willingness of the Trudeau government to bring home the Constitution; a parliamentary situation where several political groups co-existed and where women had some involvement; the lessons Canadian feminists had learned from the American experience; a political culture more attuned to collective rights and a socially interventionist state; and a more unobtrusive right-wing which had little time to organize its opposition.[44]

CONCLUSION

This paper set out to examine the struggles and the successes of the women's movement in Canada and the United States, as well as the rights of Canadian and American women, in order to draw attention to the limitations of viewing the Canadian experience as a mirror image of the precedents set south of the border. Of course, the women's movement in Canada did not develop in a vacuum, sheltered from any American influence. This is illustrated particularly well by events such as the creation of the Bird Commission a few years after the Kennedy Commission: in both cases, these commissions were able to awaken public opinion to the situation of women (and to the sexual discrimination that they went through), to prompt governments into action, and to mobilize the women's movement so that it might put the recommendations proposed in their reports into action. American women also served as a source of inspiration for Canadian women through their publications and shows of strength. The relatively easy access to abortion in the United States after 1973 – in comparison to the situation in Canada up to January 1988 – also helped to drive feminist action in Canada.

Despite this influence, the women's movement in Canada can claim an identity of its own with respect to the American movement. For example, it is a movement which reflects the political tensions that exist in Canada between the two founding cultures (which is not to say that the American movement is not divided along ethnic lines). It is also a movement that can count on financial assistance from the state, even though the recent recession has led the government to trim its commitment to women (an example would be the financing of shelters for women who are victims of violence). Canadian women can also rely on paid maternity leave, even if having a child in Canada still means that women have a higher price to pay than do men. Moreover, the women's movement in Canada has achieved victories which, in many respects, place them in a better position than their American counterparts. The most striking example is undoubtedly the success enjoyed by Canadian women with respect to Articles 15 and 28 of the Constitution, which is in stark contrast to American women's setback with ERA. Affirmative action – that temporary strategy designed to place the priority on equally competent women – remains much more accepted in Canada than in the United States.

Still, the future remains uncertain. The election of Bill Clinton to the White House is a harbinger of liberalism[45] although the resistance from the right that was put in place during the Reagan/Bush era remains influential.[46] And in Canada many of the effects of the election of a new Liberal government are unclear.[47] In this climate of uncertainty, Canadian and American women would do well to draw from the struggles they have each endured, since the oppression of women goes beyond national borders: it is indeed an international struggle.

Chronology of Events Marking the Women's Movement and Canadian and American Women's Rights During the 20th Century

UNITED STATES

1904   Establishment of *Bethune-Cook-man College*, Daytona Beach

1909   First major workers' strike

1914   *Congressional Union for Woman Suffrage* founded

Publication of the journal *Woman Rebel*

1915   Margaret Sanger imprisoned for distributing information on birth control

1916   *National Woman's Party* founded by Alice Paul

1917   Women's suffrage demonstration by *Woman's Party* in front of the White House

Jeanette Rankin elected as the first woman in Congress

1919   *League of Women Voters* formed

1920   Women obtain the right to vote in presidential elections (the 19th Amendment ratified on August 26)

Creation of the *U.S. Women's Bureau*

CANADA

1907   *Fédération nationale Saint-Jean-Baptiste* founded

1914   *National Union of Women Suffrage Societies of Canada* founded

1918   All women obtain the right to vote in federal elections

---

*   This chronology does not purport to be exhaustive; it has a strictly indicatory purpose. *Sources*: Adamson, Briskin & McPhail, 1988; Boivin, 1986; Collectif Clio 1982; Davis 1991; Hartmann 1989; Lamoreux 198; Smith & Wachtel 1992.

1921 Agnes MacPhail is first woman elected to the House of Commons

Mary Ellen Smith becomes first woman minister

1923 The *Equal Rights Amendment* is introduced for the first time in Congress, by Alice Paul and the *Woman's Party*

1925-1945 Discrimination towards women increases, particularly in education and the workforce

1929 The Privy Council of London recognizes that women are persons in the eyes of the law; they become eligible for Senate nomination

Ligue des droits de la femme founded (Québec)

1933 Frances Perkins nominated as the first woman in Cabinet

1930 Cairine Wilson becomes first woman nominated to the Senate

1937 The group *Business and Professional Women* endorses ERA

1940 Québec women are the last women to receive the vote in provincial elections

1942-1943 Women allowed into the armed forces (the *Women's Army Auxiliary Corps, Women's Reserve of the Coast Guard*, etc. formed)

1944-1960 The reign of the *Feminine Mystique*

1944 Family allowance programme established

1953 Publication of the English version of Simone de Beauvoir's book *The Second Sex*

1954 The "double standard" in cases of separation or divorce abolished

1960 *Voice of Women* founded

Canadian Declaration of Rights adopted

1961 *President's Commission on the Status of Women (Kennedy Commission)* established; report submitted in 1963

Aid to Families with Dependent Children adopted

1961 Claire Kirkland-Casgrain becomes first woman elected to the Québec legislative assembly

1962 President Kennedy prohibits
sexual discrimination in the
federal civil service

1963 *Equal Pay Act* adopted

Publication of Betty Friedan's
The Feminine Mystique

*Interdepartmental Committee on
the Status of Women* established

*Citizens' Advisory Council on the
Status of Women* established

1964 *Civil Rights Act* adopted, Article VII of which prohibits sexual discrimination in the
workplace; the *Equal Employment Opportunity Commission*
(EEOC) is formed as a result

1964 *Loi sur la capacité juridique de
la femme mariée* adopted in
Québec

1965 *Griswold v. State of Connecticut*
ruling

1966 *National Organization of Women*
(NOW) formed

Discrimination prohibited for
employers with government
contracts (Executive Order
#11246)

1966 *Fédération des femmes du Québec*
(FFQ) founded

*Association féminine d'éducation
et d'action sociale* (AFEAS)
founded in Québec

1967 First *Be-In*, San Francisco

Anti-Vietnam war demonstration by the *Jeanette Rankin Bri-
gade*

1967 *Royal Commission on the Status
of Women* (*Bird Commission*) established; report submitted in
1970

1968 Anti-Miss America pageant
demonstration, Atlantic City

Women's Equity Action League
founded

First national *Women's Liberation* conference, Chicago

1968 Women students at McGill University publish the *Birth Control Handbook*

*Toronto Women's Liberation Move-
ment* formed

First national *Women's Liberation* conference, Saskatoon

TWA air hostesses protest
their discriminatory working
conditions

Publication of the journal
*Voice of the Women's Liberation
Movement*, Chicago

*Women's International Terrorist
Conspiracy from Hell* (WITCH)
established

The Feminists established, New
York

Publication of Mary Daly's
book *The Church and the Second Sex*

1969	The EEOC declares legislation designed to protect one gender illegal	1969	Changes made to the Criminal Code: ban lifted on information on birth control, therapeutic abortion under medical supervision authorized where a woman's life or health is in danger

Publication of Kate Millett's
book *Sexual Politics*

President Nixon introduces the
Family Assistance Plan

New Feminists formed, Toronto

Redstockings formed

*Montreal Women's Liberation
Movement* formed

Bread and Roses established,
Boston

Publication of the journal *The
Pedestal*

New York Radical Feminists
formed

Boston Women's Health Collective
established, later to publish
Our Bodies, Ourselves

1970	Publication of Shulamith Firestone's book *The Dialectic of Sex*	1970	*Abortion Caravan* goes from Vancouver to Ottawa

Publication of Germaine
Greer's book *The Female Eunuch*

*Front de libération des femmes du
Québec* formed

Strike for Women's Equality held

1971   *Reed v. Reed* ruling: for the first time, the Supreme Court declares a law which is discriminatory towards women to be unconstitutional

National Women's Political Caucus formed

Women's National Abortion Coalition formed

Publication of the magazine *Ms.*

1971   Publication of *Manifeste des femmes québécoises*

Centre des femmes de Montréal founded

Demonstration for the right to abortion

Publication of *The Body Politic*

1972   Congress adopts the *Equal Rights Amendment* (ERA); 22 states ratify it

Title IX of the *Education Amendments* adopted

Equal Employment Opportunity Act adopted

The Democratic and Republican parties endorse ERA

President Nixon exercises his right of veto against the day-care bill

1972   *National Action Committee on the Status of Women* (NAC) formed

Unemployment insurance covers maternity leaves

Women's Press established

Publication of *Women Unite!*

1973   *Roe v. Wade* ruling

The EEOC deals with discrimination by AT&T towards its female employees; the company is forced to pay damages

Eight states ratify ERA

Stop ERA formed

1973   *Canadian Advisory Council on the Status of Women* formed

Conseil du statut de la femme formed in Québec

Murdoch ruling: adoption of provincial legislation on the division of family patrimony

First Morgentaler rulings in Québec

Canadian Association for the Repeal of the Abortion Law formed, later becoming the *Canadian Abortion Rights Action League*

Réseau d'action et d'information pour les femmes (RAIF) formed

1974	*Women's Educational Equity Act* adopted	1974	*Toronto Rape Crisis Centre* opens

Equal Credit Opportunity Act adopted

Housing and Community Development Act adopted

1975 *Title IX* of the *Education Amendments* takes effect, prohibiting sexual discrimination in education

1975 *Charte des droits et libertés de la personne* adopted, Québec

Publication of *Atlantis*

The Eagle Forum established

National Commission on the Observance of International Women's Year established

1976 *ERAmerica* formed

1976 Publication of *Les Têtes de Pioche*, Québec

Wage equity law adopted, Québec

The Parti québécois authorizes abortions in CLSCs

1977 *National Women's Conference*, Houston

1977 Badgley report on abortion

1978 *Pregnancy Disability Act* adopted

1978 First *Take Back the Night* march, Toronto

Delay for ratification of ERA extended to June 1982

Regroupement des femmes québécoises formed

1979   *Feminist Party of Canada* formed

1980   *Women Against Pornography March*, New York

1981   Sandra Day O'Connor becomes first woman nominated to the Supreme Court

1981   Federal conference on "Women and the Constitution"

Constitutional Act of 1982 adopted: articles 15 and 28 ensure gender equality (article 15 did not take effect until 1985)

Bertha Wilson becomes first woman nominated to the Supreme Court

R.E.A.L. Women Canada established

1982   ERA defeated on June 30; the vote was three states short of the 38 required for constitutional change to take place

1983   *Economic Equity Act* adopted

1983   Changes made to the Criminal Code: limits imposed on questions that can be put to sexual assault victims

1984   *Family Violence Prevention Services Act* adopted

Geraldine Ferraro becomes presidential candidate Walter Mondale's running mate

The state of New York rules that it is illegal for a man to rape his wife

1984   Leaders of the major political parties debate *Women's Issues*

First affirmative action programme (CN Rail)

Jeanne Sauve becomes the first woman Governor General

1985 ERA presented to Congress again	1985 Section 12(1)(b) of the *Indian Act* is repealed; native women who marry non-natives can keep their status
	1986 *Employment Equity Act* adopted
	Native women living on reserves obtain the right to vote
1987 *National Gay and Lesbians Rights March*, Washington	1987 A coalition of women's groups against the Meech Lake Accord is formed
Fund for the Feminist Majority established	Midwifery is recognized by the Ontario government
	The federal government proposes a national daycare policy, but this falls by the wayside before the 1988 election
	1988 *Morgentaler* ruling: decriminalization of abortion
1989 *Webster v. Reproductive Health Services* ruling: states can impose certain restrictions on the use of public funds for abortions	
Around half a million people attend pro-abortion march, Washington; this is one of the most important demonstrations for women's rights	
1990 Sharon Pratt becomes the first black mayoress of a large city (Washington)	1990 Audrey McLaughlin becomes first woman elected to the leadership of a major Canadian political party
Three women were elected governors (Oregon, Kansas and Texas) and two were re-elected (North Carolina and Nebraska)	

1991   Anita Hill accuses Clarence Thomas of sexual harassment; he is nevertheless nominated as a justice of the Supreme Court

1991   Rita Johnston becomes the first woman provincial premier, after the departure of the former British Columbia premier

Provisions on the protection of rape victims are invalidated (the *Seaboyer* affair)

1993   President Clinton shows himself to be favourable to the rights of women: he lifts several limitations on access to abortion, nominates several women to important executive posts, and envisages the introduction of the abortion pill RU-486.

1993   Catherine Callbeck becomes the first woman elected provincial premier in Prince Edward Island elections

Kim Campbell becomes first woman to hold the office of Prime Minister following the resignation of the former Prime Minister

NOTES

1. I shall be more specific here on the subject of mobilization, since the question of gender equality has much deeper roots in Europe. It could be found in France as early as the beginning of the 17th century, in the writings of Marie de Gournay (*Egalité des Hommes et des Femmes*, 1622, and *Grief des Dames*, 1626) and of Poulain de la Barre (*De l'égalité des sexes*, 1793), but especially in those of Olympe de Gouges (notably her *Déclaration des droits de la Femme et de la Citoyenne*, 1791), and, in Great Britain, in Mary Wollstonecraft's *Vindication of the Rights of Women*, 1792, and John Stuart Mill's *The Subjection of Women*, 1869.

2. Take, for example, the publication of such notable works in feminist thought as *The Feminine Mystique* and *Sexual Politics*.

3. As in the demonstration against the Miss America pageant in Atlantic City in 1968, where women symbolically burned their bras, an action which the media seized upon to reduce feminists to the label of "bra-burners."

4. Although anglophones and francophones have collaborated on many issues and although their objectives are the same in many respects, I feel that feminism in Québec has become a mode of expression which is very different from that found elsewhere in Canada, particularly because of its historical evolution and its ties to catholicism and nationalism, but also because Québec has seen a number of important feminist battles (we need only look at the issue of abortion). In fact, these two branches of the Canadian movement remain distinct; we recall the positions taken by francophone and anglophone feminists in the 1980 referendum, at the time of the Constitution being brought home or, again, during the Meech Lake Constitutional talks. On the women's movement in Québec, one may consult: Collectif Clio, *L'histoire des femmes au Québec depuis quatre siècles* (Montreal: Club Québec Loisirs, 1992), M. Dumont, "The Origins of the Women's Movement in Québec" in C. Backhouse and D.H. Flaherty, eds., *Challenging Times: The Women's Movement in Canada and the United States* (Montreal & Kingston: McGill-Queen's University Press, 1992), 72-89 and D. Lamoreux, *Fragments et collages. Essai sur le féminisme québécoise des années 70* (Montreal: Remue-ménage, 1986). On the split in the Canadian

women's movement due to the linguistic division between francophones and anglophones see S.B. Bashevkin, "Building a Political Voice: Women's Participation and Policy Influence in Canada" in B. Nelson and N. Chowhury, eds., *Women and Politics Worldwide* (New Haven & London: Yale University Press, forthcoming) and M. De Sève, "The Perspectives of Quebec Feminists" in C. Backhouse and D.H. Flaherty, eds., *Challenging Times*, 110-116.

5. It should be stressed that this breakdown does not in any way imply that the vote was not an issue during the 19th century; there was a resolution, in fact, on the subject at Seneca Falls, although it was not unanimously adopted. In 1876 in English Canada, the Toronto Women's Literary Club was founded, which became the Toronto Women's Suffrage Association in 1883. In Québec, women who met certain criteria of propriety could vote from 1807 to 1834. Nor does such a breakdown imply that the struggles and demands of women in Canada and the United States began with the demand for the vote. In the 19th century, the women's rights movement, which dealt with more general issues of social reform (alcohol temperance, aid for the poor, working conditions, prostitution, slum clearance, etc.), aimed to provide women with the natural rights already accorded to men. This movement provided women with real rights, notably in the area of education (the first Canadian and American universities opened their doors to women at the end of the 19th century), with regard to certain professions (Dr. Emily Stowe became the first woman to practise in Canada in 1867), in the area of property and inheritance, and with respect to children, as well as in other areas.

6. In 1885, 1898, and 1918.

7. In fact, Canadian history really does not show many "extraordinary" incidents – like great rallies, hunger strikes, arrests or imprisonments – concerning women who were fighting for the vote, unlike the members of the Woman's Party in the United States, for example.

8. See: C. Bacchi, *Liberation Deferred? The Ideas of the English-Canadian Suffragists, 1877-1918* (Toronto: University of Toronto Press, 1983), C.L. Cleverdon, *The Start of Liberation: The Woman Suffrage Movement in Canada* (Toronto: University of

Toronto Press, 1974) and N.F. Cott, *The Grounding of Modern Feminism* (New Haven & London: Yale University Press, 1987).

9.   Note that French women obtained the vote in 1944, and Italian women in 1946; the Catholic church then had a great deal of influence in these two countries. Lovenduski notes that religion can affect women's ability to associate with feminism; in Québec, Roman Catholicism contributed to women's limited participation in politics. J. Lovenduski, *Women and European Politics: Contemporary Feminism and Public Policy* (Amherst: University of Massachusetts Press, 1986).

10.   1916 for Manitoba, Saskatchewan and Alberta, and 1917 for British Columbia and Ontario. This trend can also be observed in the United States, where about 30 states had already recognized women's right to vote in presidential elections even before the 19th Amendment was adopted; B. Ryan, *Feminism and the Women's Movement: Dynamics of Change in Social Movement Ideology and Activism* (New York: Routledge, 1992), 31.

11.   Diane Lamoreux *Cityonnes? Femmes, droits de vote et démocratie* (Montreal: Remue-ménage, 1989), 56-58.

12.   Not to mention that a more global feminist perspective was completely lacking.

13.   To be convinced further, see L.J. Rupp and V. Taylor, *Survival in the Doldrums: The American Women's Rights Movement, 1945 to the 1960s* (New York: Oxford University Press, 1987).

14.   For example, during this period Canadian and American women were involved in two important battles for their political citizenship: the "Affairs des personnes" in Canada and the Equal Rights Amendment in the United States. See the chronology in the Appendix.

15.   We think here of Betty Friedan's *The Feminine Mystique* as well as other, more radical works like Kate Millett's *Sexual Politics*, Shulamith Firestone's *The Dialectic of Sex*, or *The Female Eunuch* of Germaine Greer.

      Although these works were translated into French at the beginning of the 1970s, Québec feminists are also influenced by the writings of French women, notably those of Simone de Beauvoir, through the publication of an issue of the *Partisan* periodical in 1970, and through the publication *Questions féministes*, which later became *Nouvelles questions féministes*.

16. L. Tuttle, *Encyclopedia of Feminism* (New York: Facts on File, 1986), 361.

17. For example, the equality of spouses in law, the economic rights of women at home, the share of family patrimony, and the recognition of women's work in conjunction with their spouse are issues nearer to the reformist wing of the movement. Issues such as freedom of choice in abortion, lesbian rights, or the battle against pornography and prostitution are associated with a more radical direction of the feminist movement. Nevertheless, this division remains in flux, since one single demand can come from both the reformist and the radical wings (the fight against sexual harassment, for example), but be approached in a different manner.

18. See N. Adamson, L. Briskin and M. McPhail, *Feminist Organizing for Change: The Contemporary Women's Movement in Canada* (Toronto: Oxford University Press, 1988), 42-87 and B. Ryan, *Feminism and the Women's Movement*, 54-58.

19. In Canada, the *Ad Hoc Committee of Canadian Women* was formed, and the United States saw the *ERA Ratification Council* and *ERAmerica*.

20. For example, in the area of government services and grants to women's groups.

21. Notably, the election of the Mulroney government and the Reagan and Bush administrations (for the United States, see B. Ryan, *Feminism and the Women's Movement*, 99-112).

22. Which provoked reactions on the part of women like the formation of the group *Women Against the [Bennett] Budget* in British Columbia.

23. We need only look at the Canadian group *Realistic, Equal, Active for Life (REAL) Women*, which opposes several feminist demands such as the freedom of choice in the area of abortion, and affirmative action measures, or at *Eagle Forum* in

the United States. For more details see P.J. Conover and V. Gray, *Feminism and the New Right: Conflict over the American Family* (New York: Praeger, 1983) and K. Dubinsky, *Lament for Patriarchy Lost? Anti-Feminism, Anti-Abortion, and R.E.A.L. Women in Canada* (Ottawa: Canadian Research Institute for the Advancement of Women, 1985).

24. It must be stressed that the scope of certain comparisons is limited by the difference in the parameters used by each country to establish its statistics. The information has been taken from D. Anderson, *The Unfinished Revolution: The Status of Women in Twelve Countries* (Toronto: Doubleday Canada, 1991), Bureau of the Census (Economics and Statistics Administration, U.S. Department of Commerce), *Statistical Abstract of the United States, 1992* (Washington, DC: U.S. Bureau of the Census, 1992), Statistics Canada, *Earnings of Men and Women* (Ottawa: Minister of Industry, Science and Technology, catalogue 13-217 annual, 1993), *Marriage and Conjugal Life in Canada* (Ottawa: Minister of Supply and Services Canada, catalogue 91-534E, 1992a), *Gender Differences Among Violent Crime Victims* (Service Bulletin, Canadian Centre for Justice Statistics (Ottawa: Minister of Industry, Science and Technology, catalogue 85-002, vol. 12, No. 21, 1992b), *Universities: Enrolment and Degrees, 1990* (Ottawa: Minister of Supply and Services Canada, catalogue 81-204, 1992c) and *Current Demographic Analysis: New Trends in the Family, Demographic Facts and Features* (Ottawa: Minister of Supply and Services Canada, catalogue 91-535E, 1990).

25. Statistics Canada, *Gender Differences Among Violent Crime Victims*, 8.

26. C.W. Harlow, *Female Victims of Violent Crime* (Bureau of Justice, Office of Justice Programs, US Department of Justice, January, NCJ-126826, 1991), 2.

27. Such shelters have the advantage of being publicly funded in Canada, while in the United States such subsidies simply vanished under Reagan and Bush.

28. National Council of Welfare, *Poverty Profile, 1980-1990: A Report by the National Council of Welfare* (Ottawa: Minister of Supply and Services Canada, 1992).

29. See M.J. Hanratty and R.M. Blank, "Down and Out in North America: Recent Trends in Poverty Rates in the United States and Canada," *Quarterly Journal of Economics* 107 (1992), 233-254.

30. For more details see F. Davis, *Moving the Mountain: The Women's Movement in America since 1960* (New York: Simon & Schuster, 1991), 453-470.

31. B. Ryan, *Feminism and the Women's Movement*, 101-102.

32. It is worth mentioning that for the United States, this statistic lies at the median and not at the mean.

33. This segregation index means that six out of ten workers must change jobs so that men and women might be distributed equally throughout the various professions. L. Paquette, *La situation socio-économique des femmes* (Québec: Les Publications du Québec, 1989), 51.

34. M.A. Ferber, "Women and the American Economy" in C. Backhouse and D.H. Flaherty, eds., *Challenging Times*, 208.

35. C. Backhouse, "The Contemporary Women's Movements in Canada and the United States" in C. Backhouse and D.H. Flaherty, eds., *Challenging Times*, 12-13.

36. Article 15(2) stipulates that "Subsection (1) does not preclude any law, program or activity that has as its object the amelioration of conditions of disadvantaged individuals or groups including those that are disadvantaged because of race, national or ethnic origin, colour, religion, sex, age or mental or physical disability."

37. M.A. Ferber, "Women and the American Economy" in C. Backhouse and D.H. Flaherty, eds., *Challenging Times*.

38. For example, the engineering world remains less popular among girls.

39. Almost $6 million in *Women's Education Equity Grants* were slashed in 1983.

40. R. Darcy, S. Welch and J. Clark, *Women, Elections, and Representation* (New York: Longman, 1987), 113-116 and W. Rule, "Electoral Systems, Contextual Factors and Women's Opportunity for Election to Parliament in Twenty-Three Democracies," *Western Political Quarterly* 40 (1987), 477-498.

41. S.B. Bashevkin, *Toeing the Lines: Women and Party Politics in English Canada*, 2nd edition (Toronto: Oxford University Press, 1993); S.B. Bashevkin, "Women's Participation in Political Parties" in K. Megyery, ed., *Women in Canadian Politics: Toward Equity in Representation* (Toronto: Dundurn Press, 1991), 61-79; J. Brodie (with C. Chandler), "Women and the Electoral Process in Canada" in K. Megyery, ed., *Women in Canadian Politics*, 3-59, and L. Erickson, "Women and Candidacies for the House of Commons" in K. Megyery, ed., *Women in Canadian Politics*, 101-125.

42. S.B. Bashevkin, *Toeing the Lines*, 170-171 and J. Brodie, "Women and the Electoral Process in Canada."

43. J.K. Boles, "Building Support for the ERA: A Case of Too Much, Too Late," *PS* 15 (1982), 572-577; F. Davis, *Moving the Mountain*, 385-411, M.A. Haussman, "The Personal Is Constitutional: Feminist Struggles for Equality Rights in the United States and Canada" in J.M. Bystydzienski, ed., *Women Transforming Politics: Worldwide Strategies for Empowerment* (Bloomington/Indianapolis: Indiana University Press, 1992), 108-123, J.J. Mansbridge, *Why We Lost the ERA* (Chicago: University of Chicago Press, 1986), B. Ryan, *Feminism and the Women's Movement*, 106-107.

44. N. Black, "Ripples in the Second Wave: Comparing the Contemporary Women's Movement in Canada and the United States" in C. Backhouse and D.H. Flaherty, eds., *Challenging Times*, 94-109; M.A. Haussman, "The Personal Is Constitutional"; C. Hosek, "Women and the Constitutional Process" in K. Banting and R. Simeon, eds., *And No One Cheered: Federalism, Democracy, and the Constitution Act* (Toronto: Methuen, 1983), 280-300, and P. Kome, *The Taking of Twenty-Eight: Women Challenge the Constitution* (Toronto: Women's Press, 1983).

45. Consider, for example, the steps he took on abortion as soon as he entered office, or the debate surrounding the French abortion pill, RU-486.

46. We need only look at the issue of homosexuals in the American military.

47. We must remember that nothing is assured in this respect for Canadian women, while the right to an abortion was guaranteed to American women in 1973.

FURTHER READINGS

Adamson, Nancy, Linda Briskin and Margaret McPhail (1988), *Feminist Organizing for Change: The Contemporary Women's Movement in Canada*, Toronto, Oxford University Press.

Backhouse, Constance (1992), "The Contemporary Women's Movements in Canada and the United States" in Constance BACKHOUSE and David H. Flaherty (eds.), *Challenging Times: The Women's Movement in Canada and the United States*, Montreal & Kingston, McGill-Queen's University Press: 3-15.

Bashevkin, Sylvia B. (forthcoming), "Building a Political Voice: Women's Participation and Policy Influence in Canada" in Barbara J. NELSON and Najma Chowhury (eds.), *Women and Politics Worldwide*, New Haven & London, Yale University Press.

Black, Naomi (1992), "Ripples in the Second Wave: Comparing the Contemporary Women's Movement in Canada and the United States" in Constance Backhouse and David H. Flaherty (eds), *Challenging Times: The Women's Movement in Canada and the United States*, Montreal & Kingston, McGill-Queen's University Press: 94-109.

Costain, Anne N. (1992), *Inviting Women's Rebellion: A Political Process Interpretation of the Women's Movement*, Baltimore & London: Johns Hopkins.

Davis, Flora (1991), *Moving the Mountain: The Women's Movement in America since 1960*, New York: Simon & Schuster.

Haussman, Melissa A. (1992), "The Personal Is Constitutional: Feminist Struggles for Equality Rights in the United States and Canada" in Jill M. Bystydzienski, (ed), *Women Transforming Politics: Worldwide Strategies for Empowerment*, Bloomington/Indianapolis, Indiana University Press, 1992: 108-123.

Ryan, Barbara (1992), *Feminism and the Women's Movement: Dynamics of Change in Social Movement Ideology and Activism*, New York, Routledge.

Part Four: Cultural Reflections

TAMARA PALMER SEILER

Melting Pot and Mosaic: Images and Realities

Most Canadians are proud of being different from Americans. One way they see themselves as being different is in the way they have approached nation building and the related challenge presented by an increasingly diverse population. Canadians' relatively recent adoption of the mosaic to symbolize their approach in contrast to the American symbol of the melting pot provides them further assurance that they are *not* Americans. For their part, Americans, who generally know very little about Canada, are much less aware of the mosaic image or of the differences in national experiences it embodies. In general, however, Americans continue to endorse the ideals projected in the image of the melting pot, and to assume that it captures an essential reality of American experience.

These assumptions on both sides of the 49th parallel are, if not wholly misguided, at least overly simplistic.[1] The historical experiences and the national sensibilities behind each image are in many ways quite different. But they also have much in common. The mosaic and the melting pot are profoundly similar in that they are symbols whose public purpose is to legitimate ethno-cultural diversity while at the same time affirming national unity. Both proclaim the ideal of horizontal rather than vertical ethnicity and point to an ideal balance between unity and diversity in increasingly pluralistic societies.

Further, the societies they represent are similar in that neither has fully realized the ideal embodied in its symbol. Both have complex skeletons, different, though related, ones, in their respective closets that make the ideal of horizontal ethnicity difficult to achieve. To oversimplify, Canada's skeleton is the colonial legacy of a deeply en-grained and institutionalized ethnic hierarchy. America's inter-related skeletons are its *defacto* ethnic hierarchy (not completely dissimilar to Canada's) and its closely related history of Black slavery. Nor has each symbol been universally endorsed in each country. The melting pot has been criticized from a number of perspectives in the United States, as has the mosaic in Canada. As well, in both countries, the processes and structures that have been created to promote the ideals embodied in either the melting pot or the mosaic may at times, whether intentionally or unintentionally, work to perpetuate the very tensions and inequalities they are intended to reduce.

To understand these differences and similarities, one must look both to the past and to the present, since they are deeply rooted in the historical background of each country, as well as in very contemporary events and forces. What follows, then, is a discussion first of the differences and then of the similarities between Canada and the United States with regard to their approaches to cultural diversity.

FUNDAMENTAL DIFFERENCES

Comparing Canada and the United States with regard to immigration and cultural diversity reveals fundamental differences and similarities that one can see manifested in a variety of institutions, processes, and attitudes.[2] Canada's history was profoundly counter-revolutionary and colonial. These two inter-related factors, fueled by the presence and persistence of the French Canadian culture in Quebec, along with a formidable geography and climate, have been particularly important in shaping Canada's approach to immigration and its response to diversity. Equally important in the United States have been its revolutionary origins and its early commitment to building a nation based on individual rights. Its abundant resources in combination with its (relatively) mild climate and its emergence as a major world power have also been formative. Broadly speaking, it seems clear that these two distinct impulses produced the Canadian "mosaic" on the one hand and the American "melting pot" on the other. Many if not most of the differences between the two countries with regard to immigration and diversity can be seen as products of these two sharply contrasting dynamics.

How has Canada's counter-revolutionary, colonial past affected its approach to immigration, nation building, and diversity? First, it powerfully reinforced the legitimacy of the British presence in Canada. Second, it reinforced the legitimacy of an ethnically based hierarchy, which was complicated, but generally further reinforced, by the presence of French Canadians. Third, it reinforced what Northrop Frye has called the "garrison mentality," a tendency to view the outside world, both natural and human, as threatening, and to erect barriers against it. And fourth, it accentuated what might be called a general

European predisposition to view the North-American landscape in primarily economic terms. These cornerstones of Canadian sensibility have been expressed in the country's evolving processes and institutions related to nation building and diversity.

Loyalists fleeing the American revolution, determined to avoid the excesses of republicanism, wanted to live in *British* North America, and that commitment was not in any way betrayed by Confederation in 1867. Confederation itself was in virtually every way a top-down process, from its being the brainchild of political elites to its being legally constituted by an Act of the British Parliament. Furthermore, the nationhood to which the British North American Act of 1867 gave birth was propelled not by political ideals and the blood of 'patriots,' but by a view that it was the least of several evils. Further momentum for nation building was provided by major, centrally planned economic projects and policies: the building of the railway, a protective tariff, and a centrally planned immigration policy.

The strength of the British imperial tie was not, of course, dear to the hearts of French-Canadians. Ironically, however, after the British conquest of the French on the Plains of Abraham in 1759, the British imperial connection provided the framework that enabled French-Canadian culture to persist despite its being a Gallic island in an Anglo sea. The Quebec Act of 1774, which granted greater territorial, religious and legal rights to French Canadians, was a British attempt to cement French-Canadian loyalty in the face of an American uprising. This was followed by the Constitutional Act of 1791 which created Upper and Lower Canada (Ontario and Quebec). These acts were the first in a long series of negotiations that would ultimately constitute the defining feature of Canada: the necessity for English Canadians to recognize and accommodate "the French Fact." This process played on the French-Canadian need for cultural protection and the English-Canadian desire for a bulwark against the increasingly powerful threat of Americanization.

Thus, if for English Canadians in the post-Confederation years to at least the 1920s, the key element of their national pride was the imperial connection with Britain, for French Canadians, the element that made confederation at least palatable was the concept of Two Nations. These were in some ways incompatible national visions. Nevertheless, this seeming incompatibility constituted the dynamic tension that at once held the country together as well as threatened from time to time (as during the Riel Rebellions, the Manitoba Schools debate, and the conscription crises of both World Wars) to tear it apart. It was on this foundation of a British imperial tie, which privileged British ethnicity, and a tension-ridden French-English duality that the Canadian nation was built a century after the Americans had begun to feel themselves a definable entity quite separate from Britain.

In short, devotion to the British Empire combined with a marriage contracted largely for business and political reasons did not inspire the passionate, heartfelt nationalism in Canada that the Revolution inspired in the United States. The evolution of assumptions about citizenship in each country is revealing in this regard. In the American colonies, the attempts by the British Parliament to regulate citizenship, and particularly to prevent the colonies from instituting a more open immigration policy, were among the official grievances that sparked the American Revolution. When the Revolution broke out, more than a third of the white colonial population was of origins other than British. In contrast, at Confederation in 1867, only 8% of the $3^1/_2$ million people in the Dominion were of non-British or non-French background. Thus, while Tom Paine insisted in 1776 that "Europe and not England, is the parent country of America," as late as 1928, R.B. Bennett, then Leader of the Opposition and later to become Prime Minister of Canada, stated confidently that the essence of Canadian life was "living under British institutions in that part of the Empire we call Canada."[3] Indeed, as late as the 1970s, a British citizen living in Canada could automatically become a Canadian citizen.

However, by 1928 when R.B. Bennett made the speech referred to above attacking the American melting pot and defending anglo-conformity, or the notion that immigrants should conform to British standards and institutions, the nation of 1867 was being transformed as a result of the two waves of immigration dating from 1896. In that year the federal government, under Prime Minister Sir Wilfrid Laurier, began an aggressive campaign of immigrant recruitment. This, combined with the closing of the American frontier, brought three million immigrants to Canada between 1900 and 1920, approximately one-third of them from central, eastern, and southern Europe.

During the same time, immigrants to the United States from these sources constituted as much as 71% of the total.[4] Both countries thought of this mass of "foreigners" as a "problem." However, south of the border, the solution tended to be seen as "Americanization," toward which considerable time and effort was expended. In English Canada, anglo-conformity remained the ideal most widely subscribed to until after the Second World War. Less bent than Americans on consciously building a new-world civilization, most Canadians not only had no strong notion of what would constitute Canadianization outside of anglo-conformity, but they also conceived of the value of immigrants primarily in economic terms. Their "dilemma" was to preserve the Dominion's British character while at the same time promoting its economic expansion.[5] The space in the rhetoric and mythology of nation-building occupied by non-British and non-French immigrants was much more marginal in Canada than in the United States. This, along with their low socio-economic status, their concentration in resource industries, (and in western Canada, far away from the centers of power), may have also contributed significantly to their (at least initially), "peripheral impact on Canadian institutions."[6] The impact of these immigrants, however, was increasingly significant as the century unfolded. By the time of Quebec's Quiet Revolution in the 1960s, the second and third generation descendants of the central and eastern Europeans immigrants who had pioneered western Canada, and of those who had settled in Canada's growing cities, had come of age. Many had proved themselves by participating in the Second World War, and by moving up the socio-economic ladder. Their numbers had been reinforced by new waves of post-war immigrants, many of them educated and articulate. Partly as a result of these factors, many ethnic Canadians, like French Canadians, became increasingly dissatisfied with the gap they could see between their contribution to Canadian society and what they regarded as their second-class citizenship.

Ironically, they were galvanized into political action by Quebec's Quiet Revolution and its momentum toward greater economic and political power for French Canadians. It was the Royal Commission on Bilingualism and Biculturalism, charged by the government of Lester B. Pearson in the early 1960s with the task of examining the increasingly troubled relationship between English and French in the country, that ultimately gave rise to the policy of multiculturalism instituted by the government of Pierre Trudeau in 1971. Insisting that the two-nation vision of Canada relegated their groups to insignificance, leaders of what came to be called the "third force" lobbied for inclusion. It came, first in the form of Book IV of the Bilingualism and Biculturalism Commission Report, which acknowledged the contribution of "the other ethnic groups," and later in the form of official "multiculturalism within a bilingual framework." The policy of 1971 became, with some modifications, the Canadian Multiculturalism Act of 1988, whose primary aim is "the preservation and enhancement of multiculturalism in Canada."[7]

The United States has no parallel legislation to provide an official description of the country's cultural dynamics. How do we explain this difference? Although there are doubtless a number of plausible explanations (including the one that might be favored by some Canadians; namely, that it exemplifies Canada's greater tolerance, sensitivity, and commitment to fair play), it might also be seen as evidence of the fundamental differences between the two countries.

That is, the Canadian colonial legacy of privileged British (and to a lesser extent French) ethnicity was an inadequate political, rhetorical, and mythological framework for a society as ethnically diverse as Canada had become by the late twentieth century. The United States, in contrast, had inherited a much more flexible institutional and symbolic framework for handling the pluralism of contemporary North American society: Canada needed multiculturalism and the mosaic image that accompanied it as a corrective to the rigidity of its vertical ethnicity, which had been built into its institutions and its mythologies; the United States, with its commitment to melding a new nation out of diverse peoples, did not. Rhetoric and symbolism aside, however, at the mundane level of daily experience, ethnically based inequality was and is a fact of life in both countries.

FUNDAMENTAL SIMILARITIES

The kind of analysis above, which sees significant differences between the two countries and explains them historically as the effects of two distinct political cultures, can be illuminating. However, it certainly does not tell the whole story. As well as the differences pointed out above, there have also been, and continue to be, significant similarities between the two countries with regard to immigration and diversity.

Viewed from a global perspective, Canada and the United States have played very similar roles in the centuries-old drama of the mass migration of peoples. As North American territories, the destinies of both have been shaped by their vast geographies, their abundant resources, particularly land, and the closely related dynamics of European imperialism. Together they constituted an undifferentiated "New World," a repository for European dreams of wealth and various kinds of utopias, and eventually a safety net for a variety of Europe's political, social, and demographic problems. These historical and geographic forces, while producing two quite distinct political cultures, especially when viewed close-up, have also produced similarities in political culture, particularly when viewed from afar. Thus, while Alex de Tocqueville's perceptive observations in 1837 about the profoundly democratic and individualistic nature of America would have been less true of Canada, both then and now, the phenomenon he was observing was to some considerable extent a North American one: the lives and values of Canadians as well as Americans have been irrevocably shaped by a belief in democracy and individualism. Some combination of these two ideas may be the natural ideological centre of both of these frontier societies, which were joint heirs of

British legal traditions, and in which vast numbers of people have been able to own land.

As well as sharing certain fundamental assumptions, both countries have histories that feature many nearly identical plots, characters, and themes: the exploration of rugged, largely unsettled land; the exploitation of vast resources; the pioneer settlement of an ever-expanding western frontier; the tragic destruction of indigenous peoples; the growth of a national consciousness and sensibility and of the bureaucratic structures that inevitably accompany them; the seemingly relentless march of industrialization, urbanization and technology. Of course, closely linked with all of these has been the immigration, both solicited and unsolicited, of vast numbers of increasingly diverse peoples.

Both Canada and the United States have been forced to grapple with the challenges presented by a series of mass migrations set in motion by complex economic, political, and social processes that have, over the past four hundred years, transformed the new-world countries, such as the United States, Canada, Australia, New Zealand and Argentina, to which the emigrants came. Both Canada and the United States have had to deal with similar problems, such as how to facilitate a workable fit between vast numbers of newcomers and existing economic, social, political, and cultural structures. Both have had to devise systems to deal with the recruitment, screening, settlement, adjustment, and integration of immigrants. And, as part of these processes, both have had to develop rhetoric and symbols to help promote harmony.

The history of immigration is similar in both countries, in terms of who came and how policy evolved. There are, of course, some important differences that should be noted at the outset of any such comparison, not the least of which has been the asymmetry between the two countries in terms of their ability to attract immigrants. The United States has always been a greater magnet; indeed, Canada has itself been a major source of immigrants to the United States. Also important to note is that Canada became a major receiver of immigrants much later than the United States. Canada began attracting massive numbers of immigrants only after the best land on the American frontier had been taken, while the United States was attracting migrants even before the American Revolution. This important difference helps to account for several others. For example, the consistently greater economic emphasis of Canadian immigration policy reflects Canada's greater difficulty in attracting immigrants to fill the at-times desperate demand for certain kinds of workers in an expanding frontier economy. As well, that Canada's major economic development occurred about a century later than that of the United

States helps explain the somewhat differing ethnic mix in each country.

Also important is that the proportions of immigrants to native-born at various times in each country were different. For much of the twentieth century, although the overall number of immigrants to Canada has been smaller than that to the United States, the percentage of immigrants within the total population has been larger in Canada. This is particularly true in the period following the Second World War. For example, since 1945 Toronto, Canada's largest city, has been transformed from a largely Anglo-Protestant city of less than 700,000 to a metropolis of 2,500,000. Forty percent of its people are immigrants. From the 1950s to the mid-1970s roughly half as many immigrants came to Canada as to the United States, even though Canada's population is only one-tenth that of the United States. However, this difference in proportion has become less pronounced in recent years since America has taken in greater and greater numbers of refugees, and particularly since the enactment in October 1990 of a new immigration bill which increased potential immigration to the United States significantly to approximately 700,000 annually for three years, not including refugees. Always more closely tied to economic considerations than American immigration policy, which has been somewhat more responsive to foreign policy considerations and to domestic lobbies, Canadian immigration policy has yielded slightly fewer immigrants recently. For example, more immigrants came to Canada in 1966 than in any year between 1975 and 1987.

Despite these important differences, immigration policy evolved similarly in both countries. Policies in both were closely linked to changes in the major sources of immigration. While the population of the United States was more ethnically diverse earlier than Canada's, both were gradually transformed from quite homogenous clusters of peoples from the British Isles and northern Europe to very heterogeneous populations. Immigration was largely unrestricted at first. Gradually, however, people in both countries began to think it required regulation, and eventually a federal bureaucracy. During the 1880s both countries responded to the anti-Chinese sentiment developing on their respective west coasts by enacting restrictive measures against Chinese immigrants. In the United States, the sources of immigration were shifting to southern, eastern, and central Europe (what was called the "new immigration") just as this federal regulatory apparatus was being developed. The same shift was a significant feature of Canada's first massive wave of immigration, and was also occurring just as immigration was becoming a key element in the government's "National Policy" of protective tariffs, territorial expansion, and national consolidation.

By the 1890s, the "new immigrants" constituted the majority of those coming to the United States. This, combined with the growing influence of social Darwinism and rising social and economic unrest related to rapid industrialization, urbanization, and a series of boom-bust economic cycles, nurtured the growth of nativism, or anti-foreign sentiment. An Immigration Restriction League was founded in the United States in 1894; various anti-Oriental Leagues were formed in California. A major congressional report was commissioned to look into the "problems" related to immigration, and in 1910 it produced 42 volumes on the subject. Given impetus by the First World War, this growing suspicion of immigrants culminated in the Immigration Act of 1917, which was the first in a series of restrictive acts that defined American immigration policy for the next 45 years. Canada's experience was strikingly parallel. A similar "pecking order" of preferred groups undergirded the discriminatory quotas used in each country. Furthermore, response to refugees has been similar in both countries. The extent to which they have been accepted has depended not on an unwavering national commitment to affirming human rights and/or assisting those in need, but on "prevailing political and economic conditions" within each country.[8]

The similarity of the history of immigration policies can also be seen in the liberalization that occurred in the 1960s. Although the Second World War itself was probably the most powerful catalyst for liberalization, both countries continued for a time after the war with new regulations based on the restrictive and discriminatory quota systems that had been developed in the early part of the century.[9] However, both were soon forced to deal with substantial numbers of post-war refugees, a demand for family re-unification, and a changing public mind set, one sickened by the lengths to which racism was taken in the Second World War.

These structures and pressures, together with buoyant, expanding post-war economies set the stage for liberalization. Also important, particularly in the case of the United States was the growing power of the Black civil rights movement, and the pressure exerted by a variety of players on the international stage where the United States had become a star player. Although the American Immigration Act of 1965 established an overall ceiling of 120,000 immigrants, it eliminated the old National Origins quota system. In Canada a similar total overhaul of immigration policy was effected, partly as a result of the recommendations of a government White Paper on Immigration which was released in 1966. The policy that was enacted in 1967 contained reforms very similar to those in the American policy. Ethnic or racial discrimination was eliminated, and a point system was introduced whereby immigrants were ranked according to education, employment skills, language skills and proposed destination. By this time, Canada had undergone massive urbanization. Its demographic profile had changed from the early inter-war period when it was approximately 40% urban to over 80% by the late 1960s. Consequently, the desired immigrant was no longer a prospective farmer or farm labourer, but an urban person with industrial or professional skills. Cities were the primary destinations for the new immigrants, particularly Toronto and other cities in southern Ontario's "golden horsehoe," as well as Montreal and Vancouver.

CONTEMPORARY CHALLENGES

In both countries, the impact of these changes opened the doors to yet another type of "new immigration," this time from various parts of the "third world." With the old racist quota systems gone, immigrants from various parts of Asia, Africa, and the Caribbean entered Canada and the United States in ever increasing numbers. The percentage of immigrants to Canada from Asia provides a dramatic illustration, jumping from 1.4% of the total number of immigrants in 1957 to 44% in 1987. The overall percentage of non-European immigrants increased from 15% in 1967 to 60% in 1985. Refugees formed a significant component of this "new immigration" for both countries, though the sources varied somewhat. The United States drew many more thousands of refugees from Cuba, for example, and later from Vietnam than did Canada. Illegal immigration became a more major problem during the 1970s and 1980s for the United States than for Canada, with Mexico being the major source. Since the 1950s, the American government has attempted to find solutions to the persistent and increasingly massive problem of illegal Mexican migrants. While it is impossible to provide accurate numbers with regard to illegal immigrants, by the mid 1980s, American authorities were apprehending over 1.6 million per year.

Canada, too, has a problem with illegal immigrants. Like the United States, it has been forced to deal with a mounting worldwide tide of peoples variously displaced by massive political, economic, and social problems and by war. Increasingly, both have had to wrestle with the difficulties of establishing workable criteria for defining legitimate refugees, and of preventing migrants from entering the country illegally. Nor are these urgent problems likely to go away for either country. A recent United Nations report claims that the current movement of migrants and refugees is unprecedented, and warns that the gap between rich and poor nations will precipitate "an uncontrollable tide of people" moving from the "third world" to the rich nations, including Canada and the United States. [10]

The perception around the world of Canada and the United States as highly desirable destinations for desperate migrants has created a challenge for legislators in both countries. The challenge has been to devise immigration legislation that, on the one hand, creates an orderly process of recruiting and selecting immigrants, while, on the other hand, respects the rule of law and the liberal democratic values on which each country prides itself. Each has in place legislation that attempts to force immigrants to apply for immigrant status at an overseas diplomatic post. However, illegal migrants continue to pose a problem.

In the 1985 "Singh" decision, Canada's Supreme Court ruled that anyone who claims refugee status in Canada has a right to an oral hearing in the same way that anyone charged with a criminal offence is entitled to a fair trial. This decision threw the country's refugee determination system into disorder. As many as 80,000 refugee claimants languished in Canada for years while Canadian immigration officials attempted to determine which refugee claims met the accepted United Nations definition of a genuine refugee. The backlog problem was further dramatized for Canadians in August, 1986, when a boatload of 155 Tamils arrived on the shores of Newfoundland. A year later another boatload of Sikhs arrived in Nova Scotia.[11] These two situations severely tested Canadians' generosity toward refugees and forced the Canadian government to amend the Immigration Act to create a fair process for determining the legitimacy of refugee claims. However, legal impediments continue to make it difficult for the Canadian government to remove illegal migrants. In a 1993 discussion paper, the Canadian government conceded that "irregular migration" may "threaten the strong consensus among Canadians that immigration is good for Canada."[12]

Americans, too, are becoming increasingly concerned about illegal migrants and the seeming inability of the American government to control the situation. The June 1993 landing of the *Golden Venture* with its load of 300 Chinese migrants in New York drew media attention to this problem. Americans were shocked to learn that an estimated 80,000 illegal Chinese migrants were living in the United States, many of whom paid as much as $30,000 to be smuggled into the country. This number pales in comparison to the estimated three million illegal immigrants believed to be in the United States in 1993. The case of Sheikh Omar Abdel Rahman, an Egyptian cleric who was alleged to have links to the 1993 bombing of the World Trade Centre, illustrated the legal complexities involved in deporting an illegal alien and frustrated Americans who could not understand why illegal aliens cannot be returned without delay to their countries of origin.[13] In attempting to deal with these problems, both the American and Canadian governments are examining proactive approaches such as overseas interdiction of illegals, multilateral aid, and cooperative agreements.

Another crucial similarity which a simplistic reading of the mosaic/melting pot distinction may distort is in the daily experience of immigrants in both countries. Immigrant adjustment seems to have certain almost inevitable features and stages which create similar problems regardless of place and time. For example, agrarian immigrants from Scandinavia who settled various parts of America's northern midwest, such as Minnesota and Wisconsin, in the 1840s, had to cope with many of the same problems created by isolation and pioneering conditions that Scandinavian, Ukrainian, or German immigrants faced when they settled in the Canadian Northwest Territories, what became Alberta and Saskatchewan, in the late nineteenth and early twentieth centuries.[14] Similarly, urban immigrants in both countries, whether they were Poles who, in the second half of the nineteenth century, settled in Pittsburgh to work in the coal mines, or Italians who settled in Toronto in the 1950s, had to struggle with problems of language, economic exploitation, differences between their values and those of the host society, and many other related challenges as they worked to establish themselves, their families, and their communities in an unfamiliar, North American milieu.[15]

As well, despite the economic, political, and social forces that have been moving their societies in the seemingly inexorable direction of greater universalism and hence greater equality among individuals, both countries have been, and continue to be, characterized by profound, and some would say increasingly intractable, inequalities, particularly in relation to class, race, gender and region. Blacks and Asians in both countries have been the victims of both official and unofficial prejudice and discrimination, and continue to be victimized by the latter. Both countries enacted similar discriminatory legislation against the Chinese, which was not rescinded in either case until the 1940s; both interned their Japanese populations during the Second World War; and while the treatment of Blacks in America has been both more visibly horrendous and overtly unjust, as well as more central to the nation's history and to its sense of national consciousness and of national failure than has been the case in Canada, Blacks have nevertheless experienced similar injustice in Canada. However, both their very small numbers in Canada (historically, less than 2% of the population), as well, perhaps, as certain features of Canadian political culture, have worked to mute public awareness of the degree to which Blacks have been discriminated against north of the border.[16] The degree to which there are parallel tensions surrounding racial issues in both countries was forcefully illustrated in the summer of 1991 when the not-guilty verdict in the Los Angeles-area trial of two white police officers accused of beating a black man, Rodney King, sparked a riot with strong racial overtones in Toronto.

In both countries, economic and social stratification has had close and complex links with both race and ethnicity. Not surprisingly, social analysts have been intrigued by the question of how similar or different these patterns of stratification have been in Canada and the United States and what relationship, if any, there may be between patterns of stratification in each country and the mosaic/melting pot distinction. This question was central to sociologist John Porter's classic 1965 study of social stratification in Canada, *The Vertical Mosaic* (1965):

> Speculatively, it might be said that the idea of an ethnic mosaic, as opposed to the idea of the melting pot, impedes the process of social mobility....The theme in American life of what Geoffrey Gorer has called 'Europe and the rejected father' has no counterpart in Canada...(and, further, it has been)...suggested that the strong attachments to Great Britain on the part of those of British origin, and to their former national cultures on the part of those of European origin were essential if Canada was to remain separate from the United States. The melting pot with its radical breakdown of national ties and old forms of stratification would have endangered the conservative tradition in Canadian life, a tradition which gives ideological support to the continued high status of the British charter group and continued entrance status of the later arrivals.[17]

Porter went on in this well-documented study to argue against the approach to diversity embodied in the mosaic, with its stress on preserving ethnicity, on the grounds that doing so ultimately perpetuates inequality. In contrast, proponents of the mosaic vision, on which Canada's multicultural policy is based, have argued that cultural pluralism is a fact of North American life, and that recognizing the value of ethnic diversity is the best way to break down economic and social barriers to equality. They also see it as an antidote to the potentially unhealthy psychology of minority ethnic groups who may feel their culture (and thereby themselves) devalued by approaches to nation building, such as anglo-conformity or the melting pot, which demand varying degrees of renunciation of ethnic culture.[18]

Is it possible to say that the two countries have differed markedly with regard to the socio-economic mobility of immigrants? Or to say which country's approach to diversity has been better at fostering conditions most conducive to the social and economic mobility of immigrants? Nearly thirty years after Porter asked essentially the same question we are left with no definitive answer. This reflects not only the complexity of the ongoing academic debate about how best to ask and answer the question, but it also reveals the complexity of each country's experience and the difficulty of finding crystal clear differences between them. While Porter's 1965 data is still impressive, some more recent studies have tended to contradict his thesis. Others have confirmed the persistence of the tie in Canada between ethnicity and class.[19] Similarly, one can find evidence to suggest that there has been a great degree of social mobility in American society, as well as studies that reveal the persistence of ethnic stratification.[20]

There is considerable evidence that Canadian society is more elitist than American, that in Canada political, social, and economic power is more concentrated and less accessible. This, combined with Canada's historic privileging of the English and French, has probably made certain avenues to mobility, perhaps particularly political ones, more accessible to immigrants in the United States than in Canada. Further, British immigrants had more of an advantage and central, southern, and eastern Europeans bore more of a stigma in Canada than in the United States. Nevertheless, historical analyses of the mobility of American immigrants suggest the existence of a "vertical mosaic" pattern very similar to that in Canada.

But it is also true that the descendants of the "new immigrants" who came to both Canada and the United States in the nineteenth and twentieth centuries have partaken of the general prosperity of both after the Second World War. A similar pattern can be observed in both countries in terms of which groups have "succeeded" based on various measurements of mobility, the extent to which they have done so in relation to each other, and the means used by various groups to move beyond their (economic, social, and residential) ethnic ghettos. Scandinavians and Germans, for example, have followed similar patterns in both countries, as have Italians, Jews, and Slavs.

Nevertheless, ethnic and racial hierarchies are readily apparent to observers in both countries. Ironically, in light of "melting pot" rhetoric, this is particularly true in the United States where racial hierarchies and tensions are an undeniably marked and increasingly worrisome feature of contemporary urban life. Certainly ethnic relations are significantly different in each country in so far as they have been, and continue to be, shaped by the presence of different ethnic groups in different proportions and hence with somewhat different priorities. Specifically, public debate surrounding immigration and ethnicity in Canada continues to be in many ways framed by the fact that

French Canadians constitute approximately one-quarter of the population, and that their collective agenda has for many years centered on the survival of their culture, particularly their language, and their nationalist claim to a particular territory — Quebec. This has meant that immigration has often been one of many points of contention between English and French Canadians, with the latter seeing it, if not part of an English plot to undermine their claim to special status, at least an important weapon in their struggle for survival and for power within the Canadian federation. In the United States, the large Black population, with its particular history of grievance, has profoundly affected the debate about diversity, as has the large Hispanic population, constantly reinforced by the proximity of Mexico. In a sense, however, these differences also provide parallels between the two countries: in Canada French-Canadian nationalism spurred and provided a kind of model for the rise of the "third force" and its demands for greater participation and recognition; in the United States, it was the Black civil rights and Black power movements that energized and provided a model for the resurgence of ethnic consciousness that occurred in the 1960s and 1970s. In both countries, tensions have arisen between these large groupings as they have jockeyed for power and lobbied for different visions of their countries.[21] Also, while bilingualism is official in Canada, it continues to be a somewhat contentious issue, as it is also becoming in the United States, where the growing presence of Spanish-speaking people makes it an increasingly visible public issue.

Since the late 1960s, both Canada and the United States have received yet another wave of "new immigrants," many of them members of visible minorities from third world countries. There is evidence that, while attitudes toward diversity have become more liberal in both countries since the Second World War, the response on the part of the native-born to these recent migrants is not unlike that evoked by the earlier waves of "new immigrants" who came to North America during the nineteenth century and the first half of the twentieth century. A recent poll conducted by the Canadian government found that "One-third of those polled wanted to 'keep out people who are different from most Canadians' and over one-half were 'really worried that they may become a minority if immigration is unchecked'"[22] There is little reason to suspect that attitudes are substantially different in the United States. Both countries continue to be faced by the seemingly unrelenting challenge of integrating substantial numbers of diverse people into societies that at some levels want, need, or feel obligated for humanitarian reasons, to accommodate new immigrants, and at other levels are considerably less than enthusiastic, at times even hostile to their presence.

However, unlike countries in western Europe, such as Germany and France, who have only quite recently become major destinations for migrants, Canada and the United States, as new-world nations for whom the immigrant experience is perhaps the central fact of their histories, have evolved not only a variety of regulatory mechanisms to deal with immigration, but also national mythologies and symbols to facilitate the difficult process of creating cultural as well as economic and social spaces for newcomers. The images of the melting pot and the mosaic, though different in content, have served the same symbolic and rhetorical functions in their respective national mythologies.

The United States, presided over by the Statue of Liberty beckoning "the huddled masses yearning to breathe free," has been more often idealized as a "promised land" than Canada. It has developed a more explicit "promised land" mythology, which it has adapted to the rhetoric of its civic religion. But Canada too has been the destination of huddled masses, or at least "(men) in sheepskin coats with stout (wives)," as well as gold-seekers and idealists, and it has provided the setting for a variety of utopian experiments. Since the Second World War, Canada has developed an idealistic image of itself as an international mediator and a peacemaker, as well as a kind of "peaceable kingdom": a testament to the world that it is possible for a wide variety of peoples to live together in harmony.

CONCLUSION

Clearly, there are some very real differences between the Canadian and American experiences with immigration and diversity — differences that reflect the ways in which the two countries are, at their very cores, different. Paradoxically, the also very real similarities between their respective experiences with immigration and ethnicity reflect parallels between them that are perhaps equally fundamental.

That the American ethos, with its roots in a liberal revolution — an ethos that was reinforced, at least to some extent, by the selective migration to America of people with liberal sympathies — should have produced the melting pot to symbolize its attitude toward diversity and nation building is not surprising. The melting pot is, after all, an inclusive, optimistic symbol, one that validates equally (at least at the symbolic level) a variety of cultures, not just the Anglo-Celtic. Evoking images of steel plants, it is also dynamic and future-oriented, suggesting the value of process and what is yet to come, rather than stasis and what has been. Nor is it surprising that the Canadian ethos, with its strongly counter-revolutionary origins, its long and dual colonial inheritance, and its closely related conservative habit of mind, should have produced the mosaic as its symbol of the relationship between diversity and nation building. Evoking associations with the windows of medieval cathedrals, the mosaic points to the past, to the beauty and stability of tradition, and, while not exactly embodying hierarchy, it certainly suggests the importance of boundaries even as it suggests that ethnicity is more horizontal than vertical. Thus, while America boldly proclaims a cultural vision of unity (although perhaps with an increasing number of caveats), Canada inserts the present into the past with its official policy of "multiculturalism within a bilingual framework," thereby continuing to acknowledge an old hierarchy, while cautiously validating a new, if somewhat static, alignment.

However, despite the admittedly quite striking differences suggested by these two symbols, the realities they each point to, in characteristically contrasting ways, may be much more similar than the images themselves suggest. Each image, in its own way, may be seen as a kind of iconization of a Machiavellian "state lie." Each is useful to the collective civic life of the nation it represents: as an egalitarian ideal toward which to strive, as a vision of national identity and a source of pride; as a shorthand (if erroneous) rendering of national history. Also, and perhaps on a more sinister level, each is useful as a means of covering up both historical and present realities. But overall, if one understands that a gap between the ideal and the real is an inevitable feature of human life, and that the mosaic and the melting pot constitute different metaphorical visions of very similar, though not identical, scenes, each, viewed separately, and in relation to the other, is an illuminating symbol of national experience and perhaps most of all, of national aspiration.

ACKNOWLEDGEMENTS

I am indebted to Herman Van Reekum for his contribution to my understanding of current immigration regulations and problems.

NOTES

1. For an earlier discussion of this topic, particularly vis-à-vis attitudes toward immigrants, see Howard Palmer, "Mosaic vs. Melting Pot?: Immigration and Ethnicity in Canada and the United States," *International Journal* (Summer 1976), pp. 488-528. An abridged version of this article appears in Eli Man-

del, David Taras and Beverly Rasporich, eds., *A Passion for Identity, An Introduction to Canadian Studies* (Scarborough, Ont.: Nelson Canada, 1993.)

All further references will be to the latter version unless otherwise indicated.

2.   The American sociologist, S.M. Lipset, has written widely on the subject of Canadian/American differences. See, for example, his classic article "Revolution and Counterrevolution: The United States and Canada", in Thomas Ford, ed., *The Revolutionary Theme in Contemporary America*. Lexington: The University Press of Kentucky, 1965, pp. 21-64.

3.   R.B. Bennett, House of Commons *Debates*, June 7, 1928, pp. 3925-7 as anthologized in Howard Palmer, ed. *Immigration and the Rise of Multiculturalism*, Vancouver,Calgary, Toronto, Montreal: Copp Clark, 1975, p. 120.

4.   See H. Palmer, "Mosaic vs. Melting Pot," p. 84. This suggests another significant difference in the immigration history of each country: differing proportions of immigrants from particular sources and differing patterns of settlement. Because the United States was settled and developed earlier than Canada, immigration to the United States during the second half of the 19th century and the 20th was primarily to the urban centres of burgeoning industrialization. Canada, however, was still expanding its agricultural frontier, so agrarian immigrants were sought, and their destination was primarily the newly opened lands of western Canada.

5.   Bruno Ramirez, "The Perils of Assimilation: Toward a Comparative Analysis of Immigration, Ethnicity and National Identity in North America," in Valeria Lerda, ed., *From 'Melting Pot' to Multiculturalism, The Evolution of Ethnic Relations in the United States and Canada*. Rome: Bulzone Editore, 1990. p. 150.

6.   Ramirez, p. 150.

7.   Canadian Multiculturalism Act R.S.C. 1985, Chap. 24 (4th Supp.); {1988, c. 31, assented to 21st July, 1988). The quoted words are taken from the line that introduced the Act, appearing just below the title.

8.   Gerald E. Dirks, *Canada's Refugee Policy, Indifference or Opportunism?* Montreal and London: McGill / Queen's UP, 1977, "preface". For a fascinating discussion of the tragic response to Jewish refugees during World War II, see Irving Abella and Harold Troper, *None is Too Many: Canada and the Jews of Europe 1933-1948*. New York: Random House, 1983.

9.   The Canadian Immigration Act of 1952 was "designed to attract a continuing selective stream of immigrants...And in keeping with a longstanding practice of Canadian immigration legislation, the act allowed the minister of imigration and his officials enormous discretionary powers to institute regulations that could open or close the door against virtually any group or individual." The American McCarran-Walter Immigration Act of 1952 was similarly restrictive. (David M. Reimers and Harold Troper, "Canadian and American Immigration Policy Since 1945," in Barry R Chiswick, ed. *Immigration, Language and Ethnicity, Canada and the United States.* [Washington: AEI Press, 1992] pp.24, 28.)

10. As reported on the front page of the *Calgary Herald*, Tuesday, July 6, 1993.

11. Valerie Knowles, *Strangers at our Gates* (Toronto and Oxford: Dundurn, 1992), pp. 171-77.

12. Employment and Immigration Canada, "An Approach to International Migration," Immigration Policy Group, January, 1993, pp. 4-5.

13. See *U.S. News and World Report,* "Coming to America," June 21, 1993, pp. 26-32.

14. It is interesting to note that many immigrants actually lived in both countries. For example, many of the Scandinavian immigrants who came to Alberta during the settlement boom between 1896 and 1914 had settled first in the United States, then, for a variety of reasons, came north. For a detailed discussion, see Howard and Tamara Palmer, eds., *Peoples of Alberta: Portraits in Cultural Diversity* (Regina: Prairie Books, 1985). See also John W. Bennett and Dan S. Sherbourne, "Ethnicity, Settlement, and Adaptation in the Peopling of the Canadian-American West," in Jean Burnet, et. al., *Migration and the Transformation of Cultures,* (A Project of the

UNESCO World Decade for Cultural Development) (Toronto: Multicultural History Society of Ontario, 1992).

15. For interesting discussions of immigrant life both north and south of the border, see, for example, Billy Boyd Caroli, Robert F. Harney and Lydio F. Tomasi, eds. *The Italian Immigrant Woman in North America.* Toronto: Multicultural History Society of Ontario, 1978; Robert F. Harney and J. Vincenza Scarpaci, eds., *Little Italies in North America.* Toronto: Multicultural History Society of Ontario, 1981; and Frank Renkiewicz, ed., *The Polish Presence in Canada and America.* Toronto: Multicultural History Society of Ontario, 1982.

16. See Robin Winks, *Blacks in Canada.* (New Haven: Yale UP, 1971). See also Harold Troper, *Only Farmers Need Apply.* (Toronto: Griffin House, 1972). Also Howard and Tamara Palmer, "The Black Experience," in *Peoples of Alberta, pp. 367-393.*

17. John Porter, *The Vertical Mosaic, An Analysis of Social Class and Power in Canada* (Toronto: University of Toronto Press, 1965), pp. 70, 71.

18. For lucid discussions of this debate, see Jean Burnet, "Multiculturalism in Canada," in Leo Driedger, ed., *Ethnic Canada, Identities and Inequalities.* (Toronto: Copp Clark, 1987), pp. 65-79; and Robert F. Harney, "So Great a Heritage as Ours," *Daedalus* (Special Issue, *In Search of Canada,* No. 117, No. 4, Fall, 1988,) pp. 51-97. See also *Multiculturalism, Building the Canadian Mosaic,* Report of the Standing Committee on Multiculturalism, (House of Commons, no. 5, June, 1987), in *Minutes of Proceedings and Evidence of the Standing Committee on Multiculturalism* (Ottawa: Queen's Printer, 1987).

19. Jean Burnet in "Multiculturalism in Canada" points to Darroch (1979) and Reitz (1980) as researchers who "have presented data and arguments that throw strong doubt on the vertical mosaic interpretation. They have shown that neither the measured occupational dissimilarity between ethnic groups nor the inequality in occupational ranks of immigrant groups is very great or very stable." p. 78-9. An earlier questioning of Porter's findings is Harvey Rich, "The Vertical Mosaic revisited: toward a macrosociology of Canada," *Journal of Canadian Studies,* Vol. 11, No. 1, 1976, pp. 14-31.

For analysis that confirms Porter's thesis, see Wallace Clement, *Class, Power and Property* (Toronto: Methuen, 1983). See also Peter S. Li, *Ethnic Inequality in a Class Society* (Toronto: Thompson Educational Publishing, 1988).

20. Peter C. Pineo, "The Social Standing of Ethnic and Racial Groupings," in Leo Driedger, ed., *Ethnic Canada*, pp. 256-272 finds that Canadians and Americans produce (with a few interesting differences) a very similar ranking of ethnic groups in terms of status, and that the ranking follows quite closely the ethnic pecking order that informed the old restrictive immigration policies of both countries.

21. See Howard Palmer, "Ethnicity and Pluralism in North America, A Comparison of Canadian and American Views," in Rob Kroes and Henk-Otto Neuschafer, eds., *The Dutch in North-America, Their Immigration and Cultural Continuity.* (Amsterdam: VU University Press, 1991), pp. 441-469. (This is an update of the article referred to above as "Mosaic vs. Melting Pot?"). See esp. p. 459. For an example of the "new ethnicity" in the United States, see Michael Novak, *The Rise of the Unmeltable Ethnics* (New York: Macmillan, 1972). It is interesting to note that just one year after Canada introduced the multicultural policy in 1971, the Nixon administration passed an Ethnic Heritage Studies Act which had an annual budget of $15 million primarily for educational projects. For an insightful discussion of the French Canadian response to immigration in Canada, see Bruno Ramirez, "The Perils of Assimilation."

22. Canadian Press (1992), "Survey showed immigrants unpopular," *The Globe and Mail*, Sept. 14, p. A4, as quoted in *On Balance, Media Treatment of Public Policy Issues*, Vol. 6, No. 3, p. 1.

RECOMMENDED READING

Abella, Irving and Harold Troper. *None is Too Many: Canada and the Jews of Europe 1933-1948*. New York: Random House, 1983.

Avery, Donald. *Dangerous Foreigners: European Immigrant Workers and Labour Radicalism in Canada, 1886-1932*.

Bodnar, John. *The Transplanted, A History of Immigrants in Urban America*. Bloomington: Indiana University Press, 1985.

Burnet, Jean with Howard Palmer, *Coming Canadian: An Introduction to the History of Canada's Peoples*. Toronto: McClelland & Stewart, 1988.

Chiswick, Barry R. ed., *Immigration, Language and Ethnicity, Canada and the United States*. Washington, DC: AEI Press, 1992.

Clement, Wallace. *Class, Power and Property*. Toronto: Methuen, 1983.

Daedalus, Journal of the American Academy of Arts and Sciences, Special Issue, "In Search of Canada," Fall, 1988. Vol. 117, No.4.

Dinnerstein, Leonard and David Reimers. *Ethnic Americans, A History of Immigration and Assimilation*. New York: Dodd Mead & Co., 1975.

Dirks, Gerald E. *Canada's Refugee Policy: Indifference or Opportunism?* Montreal and London: McGill / Queen's University Press, 1977.

Driedger, Leo, *Ethnic Canada, Identities and Inequalities*. Toronto: Copp Clark Pitman Ltd., 1987.

Hascker, Andrew. *Two Nations: Black and White, Separate, Hostile, Unequal*. New York: Charles H. Scribner, 1992.

Handlin, Oscar. *The Uprooted*. Boston: Little, Brown & Co., 1951.

Hawkins, Freda. *Canada and Immigration: Public Policy and Public Concern*. Montreal: McGill Queens University Press, 1972.

Knowles, Valerie. *Strangers at Our Gates: Canadian Immigration and Immigration Policy, 1940-1990*. Toronto and Oxford: Dundurn Press, 1992.

Lerda, Valeria, ed. *From 'Melting Pot' to Multiculturalism, The Evolution of Ethnic Relations in the United States and Canada*. Rome: Bulzone Editore, 1990.

Li, Peter S. *Ethnic Inequality in a Class Society*. Toronto: Thompson Educational Publishing Inc., 1988.

Mandel, Eli, David Taras, and Beverly Rasporich, eds. *A Passion for Identity, An Introduction to Canadian Studies.* Scarborough, Ont.: Nelson Canada, 1993.

Novak, Michael. *The Rise of the Unmeltable Ethnics.* New York: Macmillan, 1972.

Palmer, Howard. *Immigration and the Rise of Multiculturalism.* Vancouver, Calgary, Toronto, Montreal: Copp Clark, 1975.

Palmer, Howard. "Mosaic vs. Melting Pot: Immigration and Ethnicity in Canada and the United States," *International Journal* (Summer, 1976), pp. 488-528.

Palmer, Howard. *Patterns of Prejudice, A History of Nativism in Alberta..* Toronto: McClelland & Stewart, 1982, 1985.

Palmer, Howard and Tamara Palmer. *Peoples of Alberta: Portrais of Cultural Diversity.* Saskatoon: Prairie Books, 1985.

Porter, John. *The Vertical Mosaic: An Analysis of Social Class and Power in Canada.* Toronto: University of Toronto Press, 1965.

Thernstrom, Stephan, ed. *Harvard Encyclopedia of American Ethnic Groups.* Cambridge, Mass. and London, England: Harvard UP, 1980.

Troper, Harold. *Only Farmers Need Apply.* Toronto: Griffin House, 1972.

Winks, Robin. *Blacks in Canada.* New Haven: Yale UP, 1971.

DAVID TARAS

A Question of Character: Political Reporting in Canada and the United States

While it may seem at first glance that the Canadian and American media report political events in essentially the same way, a closer examination reveals stark differences. It is true that in both countries, news reporting fixates on sensational events, dwells on personalities, focuses on the horse race aspects of election campaigns, and that stories are becoming shorter, snappier and less substantive. Politicians on both sides of the border play to the cameras, have handlers and spin doctors to manipulate messages and massage journalists, and use many of the same techniques to set the political agenda and bypass critical reporting by the media. In both countries politicians and journalists are drawn together by mutual need and partake in a relationship that by its very nature produces both symbiotic cooperation and sharp conflict. Yet the nature of the relationship is different in Canada. This is because Canadian journalists inhabit a different world, and play by different rules.

In the United States, journalists focus an enormous amount of attention on character issues. The search for the character flaws of national leaders has reached almost epidemic proportions. What Larry Sabato has referred to as "attack journalism" has become central to presidential elections and presidential reporting.[1] In Canada, character issues are still considered to be largely out of bounds. Investigating the backgrounds of leaders in any serious way is seen as intrusive and somehow illegitimate. The reasons for this difference are varied, but they go to the very heart of the two political systems. This essay, which is based in part on interviews conducted with journalists, will examine how different media structures, laws, and cultural attitudes have produced substantial differences in the political climates of the two countries.

In the United States, the national media have for all intents and purposes replaced political parties as the primary "screening committee" for those who aspire to high office.[2] Public figures, whether they are running for President, being nominated for cabinet positions, considered for the Supreme Court, or are simply in the orbit of presidential and congressional power, all have to endure virtually a trial by fire. It is a trial that is based on questioning about, and investigations of, their characters. Sometimes it has seemed as if the Washington media are a kind of character police administering their own special brand of justice.

One of the reasons that this task has fallen to the media is that American political parties no longer have the capacity to scrupulously examine the characters and qualifications of presidential candidates. The extensive primary system that developed in the 1970s ensured that effective power in deciding party nominees would be determined by the grassroots membership and not by the senior office holders and high party officials who could be expected to have first-hand knowledge of those running. Presidential politics became more entrepreneurial as candidates fashioned organizations and constituencies independent of party establishments. Parties were up for grabs and could be captured by whatever coalition of interests was brought together by the candidate who won a party's presidential nomination.

Those who aspire to high office can expect that their private and public lives will be placed under an intense spotlight of journalistic scrutiny. Indeed presidential elections are littered with the political corpses of those who could not withstand questioning about their characters.

During the 1988 presidential race a leading Democratic contender, Gary Hart, had to withdraw soon after a stakeout at his Washington home by reporters from *The Miami Herald* produced a flurry of stories about his affair with model Donna Rice. At a news conference, Hart was badgered with questions about whether or not he had ever committed adultery. Joseph Biden, another leading candidate for the Democratic nomination in 1988, had to withdraw following charges that he had plagiarized from a speech by British Labour party leader Neil Kinnock. The party's eventual nominee, Michael Dukakis, had to endure questioning about the state of his mental health and his wife Kitty's bouts with alcoholism. On the Republican side, one highly rated prospective candidate, Jack Kemp, faced a media "feeding frenzy" over his reputed homosexuality, rumours that remained unsubstantiated. Pat Robertson, a TV evangelist and champion of the party's right wing, lost ground and became the butt of jokes after it was revealed that his wife had become pregnant before they were married. And George Bush's vice-presidential choice, Dan Quayle, was pilloried by repeated investigations into his background: his low high school and college marks, his alleged dodging of service in Vietnam by joining the Indiana National Guard, an alleged affair with Capitol Hill lobbyist Paula Parkinson, and rumours about plagiarism and drug use. He was an easy mark for comics and the hosts of late-night talk shows for whom he became an object of almost nightly ridicule. Roger Ailes, Bush's media consultant during the 1988 campaign, described the attack on Quayle graphically when he observed that if you drop "a hot dog in a tank of 15,000 bluefish [journalists]...That hot dog goes quick, you know what I mean?"[3]

Candidates in the 1992 presidential race had to fight on a similar battlefield. If anything the in-coming fire was even more intense. Leading contender Senator Charles Robb of Virginia was hounded by media reports about allegations that he had attended parties where cocaine was used and was having an affair with beauty queen Tai Collins, later the subject of a pictorial feature in *Playboy* magazine. Robb, once the golden boy of the Democratic party, decided not to run. Independent candidate Ross Perot was the subject of highly critical investigative pieces by the *New York Times, The New Republic, The New York Review of Books, Time,* and by the three TV networks, particularly ABC. These reports depicted Perot as someone with doctrinaire views and a quirky, paranoid, and eccentric disposition. When he left the presidential race at mid-course in July 1992, it was at least in part a retreat in the face of an avalanche of negative reporting. He complained bitterly about "got-cha" journalism and his press secretary, Jim Squires, compared press coverage of his boss to the brutal beating of Rodney King by the L.A. police.[4]

Bill Clinton suffered unrelenting attacks on his character as various reports about an alleged mistress, whether or not he had smoked marijuana, tried to avoid the draft, participated in peace demonstrations during the Vietnam War or had played golf at a club that had a restricted membership made their way through the journalistic food chain (his alleged affair with Gennifer Flowers had received wide play in the tabloid press before the story was picked up by the establishment media) during the first phase of his run for the democratic nomination. He appeared on *60 Minutes* where he answered questions about the state of his marriage put to him by Mike Wallace, a celebrated media executioner, and was grilled relentlessly about his personal life during an appearance on *Donahue.* The media's hunger for scandal seemed to be so overriding that Samuel Popkin, one of Clinton's pollsters, observed that "a single comment about the draft would knock a full eighteen hours of talk about the economy right off the evening news."[5]

Even those who aspire to lesser offices have to be prepared to withstand a painstaking examination of their past actions both by congressional committees and by a scandal hungry media. John Tower, nominated by George Bush to be Secretary of Defense, was rejected by the Senate after stories about his drinking and womanizing were widely reported. Judge Douglas Ginsburg had to withdraw his name from consideration for a position on the Supreme Court after Nina Totenberg, a reporter for National Public Radio, broke the story that Ginsburg had once smoked a marijuana cigarette. Clarence Thomas's nomination to the Supreme Court barely survived charges of sexual harassment levelled against him by Anita Hill, an ex-employee. The Thomas case became a cause célèbre as his confirmation hearings before the Senate Judiciary Committee were broadcast live. Zoe Baird, Bill Clinton's nominee for attorney general, withdrew from consideration when it was reported that she had hired an illegal alien to work as a nanny.

Critics of recent American politics have argued that the media has made the pursuit of character issues into a spectacle and has gone overboard in its pursuit of scandals that may have little bearing on a candidate's public performance. They charge that gossip mongering to sell newspapers and attract viewers has replaced the reporting of the real scandals in American society: the fate of the poor and the homeless, the decline in the education system, the size of the debt and deficit, the savings and loan fiasco, the deterioration of the inner cities. News has merged with entertainment to the extent that it is designed to shock, sensationalize, and titillate as much as it informs. Nonetheless, few would disagree that attack journalism is now deeply embedded in American politics and that its effects have reverberated and can be felt throughout the American political system.

Canadian political leaders have not had to run the gauntlet of scrutiny to nearly the same degree as American politicians. It is not that Canadian politicians are any more moral or circumspect than their American counterparts. Indeed, the Canadian media would have had no shortage of meaty personal scandals to report on, had they been so inclined. A number of prime ministers and premiers let alone senior cabinet ministers have had serious drinking problems, less than wholesome lifestyles, eccentric habits, and suspicious financial dealings. Not to report such matters has been the accepted norm among Canadian journalists, a norm that is seldom broken.

In the case of Margaret Trudeau, for instance, her unseemly behavior — wearing a see-through T-shirt and appearing without underwear in Cuba, yelling "fuck you!" to Japanese dignitaries, cavorting openly with various celebrities, and engaging in heavy marijuana use — was downplayed by the media until her behavior was so public and so extreme that it could no longer be ignored.

While character has played a central role in Canadian politics and elections, journalists have been satisfied to describe the statements and actions of leaders and whatever charges or questions are raised by the opposition parties and have then left it to the public to come to its own conclusions. Journalists tend not to see themselves as assertive participants in the screening and selection of political leaders. They are there to record and comment but not to dramatically disturb the dynamics of the political process by probing behavior, applying standards, and making moral judgements.

One can only compare, for instance, the almost microscopic investigation by American journalists of Ross Perot's career with the relative absence of such scrutiny during Kim Campbell or Jean Charest's run for the prime ministership in 1993. While *Maclean's*, *The Globe and Mail*, the CBC, and *The Canadian Forum* among others all did profiles on Campbell's background, these pieces barely scratched the surface in describing how Campbell rose so quickly to the heights of power, how she arrived at her beliefs, how she conducted herself during crises, or how she was perceived by those who worked closely with her. A revealing and controversial interview with Peter C. Newman which was published by *Vancouver* magazine was an act of commission by Campbell herself and not a piece of investigative journalism. There was also little careful scrutiny of Jean Charest's career and background. Jeffrey Simpson of *The Globe and Mail* has lamented the "free ride" given Charest by the country's media: the lack of debate about his youth and inexperience, the failure to pose even elementary questions about his performance as Minister of the Environment, as well as their disinterest in providing rudimentary analysis and criticism of his basic policy proposals.[6]

Other Canadian political leaders — Jean Chretien, Lucien Bouchard, Preston Manning, and Audrey McLaughlin — have passed through the line having never faced the voracious and deep inspection that American presidential candidates have had to endure.

The wide gulf that separates the worlds of Canadian and American political reporting stems from a number of factors. These factors, which reveal a great deal about the differences in the two societies, will be discussed below.

EXPLANATIONS AND CAUSES

1.Presidents and Prime Ministers

One critical explanation is that there is a fundamental difference between electing an American president and electing a Canadian prime minister. The American president is the leader of a far more important country, a country that presides over, and to some degree dominates, economic and military relationships around the world. A president has the capacity to make war or peace and has his hand close to the nuclear trigger. He (someday she) helps to steer global economic relationships and influences the response of western nations to many of the world's problems. Given the vast weight of presidential powers, it is argued that journalists have a responsibility to ensure that someone with serious character flaws, that someone who can abuse that power, is prevented from attaining it.

The stakes aren't nearly as great for a Canadian prime minister. The prime minister is only a peripheral player on the world stage, although few would deny that he or she can have a profound affect on Canadian life. As Don Newman of the Canadian Broadcasting Corporation (CBC) has described the differences between the president and the prime minister, "the person who is president of the United States could essentially blow up the world and the more you know the better....Here it [the prime minister] is seen as not as important a job and the qualifications don't have to be quite so exacting." *The Toronto Sun*'s Bob Fife observed that, "When you are the only superpower in the world, and you are going to lead a country for four years, and your decisions are not only affecting 250 million Americans but the whole world, the tendency is for a lot deeper examination than of the political leaders we have here."

Moreover, American journalism has been deeply shaped by the experiences of Vietnam and Watergate when, to quote a famous phrase from that period, Washington was "awash with lies." Lyndon Johnson and Richard Nixon bred fear and suspicion and came to be seen as dangerous men driven by power and conceit. By the mid 1970s, a "culture of cynicism" toward political leaders had emerged among American journalists. Politicians were almost automatically viewed with distrust and their words and statements open to question. Watergate was also a boon to investigative journalism. Influenced by the celebrity status conferred on Woodward and Bernstein, the reporters who helped to break the Watergate story, investigative reporting gained credibility and seemed to have a glamorous edge to it. The professional image held up to journalists was of the crusading fighter against injustice who exposed the wrong doings of political leaders and held them accountable for their actions.

There was also the curious legacy of John F. Kennedy. During his presidency, journalists were smitten by the glamour and youthful vigour of the Kennedys, and ignored disquieting evidence about Kennedy's behavior — his habitual womanizing, his serious dependency on drugs, his medical problems, and his lack of experience and conviction. In retrospect some journalists felt guilty about having kept their silence. Craig Oliver, CTV's Ottawa bureau chief who reported for many years from Washington, observes that "a lot of Americans [journalists] felt burned by the Kennedy myth...and figured we're not going to let this happen to us again."

The American president is, in addition to being the head of government, also the head of state. There is supposedly a majestic and transcendent quality to the office; the president is expected to embody and symbolize the nation. Walter Dean Burnham, a leading student of the presidency, has argued that, "In certain important aspects, the American presidency bears some comparison with the principate of Imperial Rome....Americans vote for a political leader who, in addition to his other functions, is the pontifex maximus, not very different, perhaps, from Augustus Caesar. The president is the chief priest of the American civil religion."[7] While Burnham may be overstating the case, the presidency has a mystique and a ceremonial aspect that is completely absent from the role played by prime ministers. In fact, the partisan bitterness and leveling quality of the daily question period in the House of Commons is almost guaranteed to remove the varnish, to show up the bruises and foibles of the prime minister. Expectations are greater for a president on many levels.

Another consideration is that as the issue agenda has become increasingly complex and overloaded, and the media's reporting of issues more abbreviated and sensationalized, citizens experience great difficulty following or understanding issues. Samuel Popkin and others have argued that as voters have lost their grip on issues, the presidency has come to be viewed as a "trusteeship."[8] Voters make judgements based on who they trust to provide general leadership rather than on a candidate's stand on particular issues or because of party or ideological affiliations. As Paul Taylor of the *Washington Post* has put it, "Americans do not elect position papers to high office; they elect human beings."[9]

2.The Nature of Reporting from Washington and Ottawa

Another important difference is the sheer size of the national press corps in the United States compared to Canada and the much more intense competitive pressures that exist south of the border. With close to 10,000 news outlets in the United States, it has become almost impossible to maintain secrecy or discretion once a news organization possesses a story. Inevitably, if that news organization doesn't break the story or further it in some way, some other news organization will. A journalistic force of gravity pulls the story forward. The emergence of cable news services like C-Span and CNN and the creation of "the news cycle without end," have added further pressures. According to Larry Sabato, the advent of around-the-clock news has created "a voracious news appetite demanding to be fed constantly, increasing the pressure to include marginal bits of information and gossip and producing novel if distorting "angles" on the same news to differentiate one report from another."[10]

By comparison, the Ottawa news agenda is dominated by a relatively small number of large organizations: CBC-Radio Canada, CTV, Global TV, *The Globe and Mail*, *Maclean's*, Canadian Press, Southam News, *The Suns*, *The Toronto Star*, *La Presse*, and *Le Devoir*. The world of Ottawa reporting is still tight and intimate enough that tacit understandings are often reached among journalists about how stories will be handled. While not everybody adheres automatically to the same code of behavior, the boundaries of what is acceptable to report and what isn't are often widely shared. The existence of so few major organizations also means that enthusiasm for a story can be dampened quickly if the other news outlets decide not to pursue it.

One critical factor is that there are many more news organizations in the United States with both the resources and the space to devote to investigative reporting. A number of the Canadian journalists interviewed for this study complained that their cash-strapped news organizations were not in a position to do anything more than the most rudimentary probing of political leaders. As Bob Fife explained the situation:

> American journalists are freed up more to really do good serious background pieces....largely what you get [when you are assigned to do] profiles in Canada is at most a week, probably not that — four or five days of research. You write it in a day or two days....So you call the libraries, you make phone calls to the person's friends. That's not the kind of research these [American] reporters were doing on Ross Perot. I'm assuming these were at least month or month-and-a-half research projects.

And look at the space in those articles. What magazines in Canada — even *Saturday Night* wouldn't be able to give it that much space.... There isn't any mainstream paper that could do what the *New York Times* does.

Canadian journalism simply lacks economies of scale in terms of the size of news organizations and the number of outlets for in-depth political reporting that a much larger market makes possible. The Canadian equivalents of *The New Republic, Rolling Stone, The New Yorker, Vanity Fair, The New York Review of Books,* or *The New York Times Magazine* simply don't exist. So the limited number of outlets available and constraints on space and resources, place severe handicaps on the ability of Canadian journalists to do basic investigative work.

3.Private versus Public Broadcasting

Perhaps the most critical difference between the two media systems is the centrality given in Canada to the publicly financed CBC. The so-called "mother corp." has a special mandate to cover events of national significance and "contribute to shared national consciousness and identity." Although the CBC's marquee news program, *Prime Time News,* seems to have fallen behind the *CTV National News* in number of viewers since it was moved to 9 o'clock, the CBC is still regarded as the premier news and current affairs broadcasting institution in the country. Through its many arms — CBC Radio; CBC Newsworld; Radio-Canada; its regional news programs and its northern service; TV programs like *The Fifth Estate, Venture* and *The Nature of Things,* and its documentaries — the CBC has an immense capacity to influence the political agenda.

The American television networks are all owned by giant corporations — NBC by General Electric, CBS by Loews Corporation, ABC by Capital Cities, and the Fox network by media mogul Rupert Murdoch. Profit is the bottom line and programming is usually designed to appeal to up-scale audiences that are the most desired by prospective advertisers. The news divisions are expected to make money and this has led, some would argue, to news reporting that is highly sensationalized and entertainment driven. The old adage, "If it bleeds, it leads" seems to characterize much American TV reporting.

Public broadcasting does exist in the United States in the form of the Corporation for Public Broadcasting. The corporation is dependent on relatively small appropriations from Congress (the American government's contribution to public broadcasting amounted to $1.00

per person in 1987 compared to $22.37 per person given by the Canadian government to public broadcasting) and sponsorships by major corporations as well as charitable foundations and local viewers.[11] It has many notable achievements to its credit including such landmarks as *Sesame Street, The MacNeil/Lehrer Newshour, Mr. Roger's Neighborhood, The McLaughlin Group,* and its much-heralded series such as those on the civil rights movement (*Eyes on the Prize*) and on the American Civil War. Its viewing audience, however, remains small and peripheral.

The CBC's mandate makes it fundamentally different from the big American television networks. As is stated in Section 3(i) of the 1991 Broadcasting Act, broadcasters have an obligation to provide programming that is "varied and comprehensive, providing a balance of information, enlightenment and entertainment for men, women and children of all ages, interests, and tastes..." What this means, in effect, is that programming cannot be targeted only at up-scale, high-income audiences that are the most attractive to advertisers. Programming must be directed at a whole spectrum of viewers; the young, the old, people from different ethnic and religious backgrounds, and those living in different regions. This sometimes means that only a minority of viewers are being appealed to. While this requirement falls on all broadcasters, the CBC shoulders special responsibilities as a publically funded broadcaster. The CBC also attempts to portray societal problems as they really are. In its news reports and documentaries the network quite often focuses on the most tragic and desperate human circumstances; a graphic depiction, for instance, of the suffering of a burn victim, following someone who is dying of AIDS through the various stages of the disease, or doing features on the pain of child poverty or on the deteriorating environment.

The CBC is dependent on the government for over 75% of its funding; it received $953 million from parliament for its 1993 operating revenue, and garnered $314 million in advertising revenue in 1992.[12] This dependence places the CBC in a sometimes sensitive position when it comes to how it is to report on the actions of its political masters. The CBC has on occasion had to bend to pressure as its programs have provoked the wrath of prime ministers, been angrily denounced by members of parliament, and been investigated by parliamentary committees. From the scrapping of the controversial program *This Hour Has Seven Days* in 1966, to the tempests caused by the CBC's reporting of various constitutional struggles, to the furor over the documentary *The Valour and the Horror,* CBC has sometimes been buffeted by harsh political winds.

As one senior CBC news manager has described the difficulties experienced by government leaders, "Throughout its history there has been an inherent contradiction between independent journalistic coverage of government, and government funding. As journalism became more adversarial, the contradictions were exacerbated. You've got to be a real grown-up to say I believe in public broadcasting and I'm going to fund it, and every day walk out and get punched in the face by it." Another veteran CBC journalist believes that during Brian Mulroney's prime ministership the CBC came under intense scrutiny and refrained from controversial programming for fear of antagonizing the government:

> It's not the "being watched." You can even laugh at the being watched. You lose your ability to do your job accurately....There never was an extensive documentary report about Brian Mulroney's record. It is too politically sensitive. They [CBC executives] won't do it....I know that when the Conservatives were elected they were hostile, irrationally hostile. There were two schools of thought [within the CBC]; you can either coddle them or you can do the work that you do. The CBC takes the position that we can't offend them. We have to go asking for money and we can't offend them.

Not all CBC journalists think that governments have cast a "chill" over the corporation. Yet it is also true that Canadians rarely see hard-hitting CBC exposés on the lives and records of political leaders.

4. Canadian and American Defamation Law

American defamation law makes it exceedingly difficult for political leaders to win law suits against news organizations. As a consequence journalists almost never have to worry about whether their stories will anger politicians and bring legal action. In a landmark 1964 case, *The New York Times v. Sullivan*, the American Supreme Court ruled that as political comment was shielded by the First Amendment, the onus lay with aggrieved public officials to prove that there had been deliberate and intentional malice by journalists and news organizations. The logic behind the American approach was aptly described in a Supreme Court decision in the case of *Connick V. Myers*, "The First Amendment was fashioned to assure unfettered interchange of ideas for the bringing of political and social change desired by the people....speech concerning public affairs is more than self-expression; it is the essence of self-government."[13]

Common law practice in Canada takes a different tack. It places considerable value on the individual's right to a "good reputation," and the need to "provide citizens with a defence against the awesome power of the printed word."[14] While journalists have a right to "fair comment" on matters that are of genuine public interest, in a court action journalists and/or news organizations face the quite heavy burden of proving why their claims and accusations were thought to be accurate and free of malicious intent. News organizations complain that the law has had an intimidating effect and prevents them from undertaking the kind of exposés that are routine in the United States. According to Elly Alboim, until recently the CBC's Ottawa bureau chief:

> The Sullivan decision in the United States gave American media absolute licence to say whatever they want about a public figure. There is no such licence in Canada....Public interest is not a defence in this country, you have to prove truth and a lack of malice. We are *de jure* precluded from printing three-quarters of what American media print as a matter of course. Even if there was a desire to explore character you couldn't do it.

While a number of journalists interviewed for this study stated that they didn't give any thought to defamation laws when they prepared their stories, media executives may be becoming more conscious of the perils involved. Almost all of the major news organizations in Canada have found themselves in court at one time or another in the last few years. John Turner sued *The Toronto Sun*; former Alberta premier Don Getty has sued both the *Calgary Herald* and *The Globe and Mail*; former Tory Defence Minister Robert Coates sued *The Ottawa Citizen*; former ambassador to the United States Allan Gottlieb sued (and then withdrew the suit against) a critic of his appointment to the Canada Council; the CBC has been the subject of law suits and is suing columnist Michel Vastel; and powerful corporations and businessmen such as Hees International, the Reichmann family, and Conrad Black have all either sued or threatened to sue journalists, publishers or news organizations. Some observers contend that "libel chill" has cooled the ardour of Canadian journalists and set real limits on whom and in what ways they can report.[15]

5. Cultural Differences

While it may be trite to describe Canada as a more respectful and gentler society than the United States, there is evidence with respect to the media's treatment of the private lives of politicians that would seem to support this contention. At the very least, one can say that social conventions are more conservative. In Canada, the voyeurism of a *People* magazine and the freak show displays that often appear on Geraldo Rivera-style talk shows are still seen as unseemly. There seem to be boundaries that journalists cannot cross without touching sensitive nerves or arousing a negative response.

One of these is the rule of thumb that reporting on the private lives of political leaders is out of bounds unless the story has a direct bearing on a matter of vital interest to the public. The conventional wisdom is that exposés that cut too deep would come across as mud-raking and would not be condoned by the public. Joan Bryden of Southam News expressed it this way, "I think we just have a greater respect for privacy, in a general sense, which I personally am quite proud of. There's a tradition somewhere....I think that we've decided that if it's not affecting his job, it's nobody's business." Craig Oliver, the CTV Ottawa bureau chief, put it much the same way:

> There's a different tradition here. My criteria is a job-related criteria. If you can tell me that this is affecting this guy's performance on the job, as a public servant or as a leader of men and women, then I think we would probably do it. Otherwise I think we've left people's private lives pretty much alone, and I know all kinds of incidents when we've done that.

The prohibition against delving too deeply into the private lives of political leaders is, if anything, even stronger among francophone journalists. One argument is that francophone journalists, many of whom are sympathetic to Quebec nationalism, cloak politicians who are seen as championing Quebec's rights in a shroud of respectful adulation. They are reluctant to undermine those whom they see as natural allies. But even beyond this, there can be little doubt that the style and tenor of public life is different in Quebec. Leaders do not parade their families and their private lives on the public stage. Distance and privacy are preserved to a far greater degree than in English-speaking Canada. And journalists have understood that these proprieties must be protected unless there are behaviors that are clearly beyond the political pale. Chantal Hebert of *Le Devoir* has described the sensibilities of francophone journalists and the Quebec public:

> We don't do features on candidates' wives. Robert Bourassa's wife does not campaign with him. I wouldn't know what she looks like....People know who Jacques Parizeau's wife was because she was a well-known writer.... but there hasn't been a story: is Parizeau feeling lonely? People don't really care for

Mila Mulroney stories. I don't think I could get on radio or television with a story about Mila Mulroney spending money for clothes when she was in New York. There's character and there's character. If Robert Bourassa is being blackmailed for his sexual preferences [that would be different]....It's a small society and it's involved with what are felt to be survival issues...

Many Canadians would like to believe that Canada is a more civil society than the United States. Whether or not this is true or can ever be proven may not be as important as the perception among journalists that Canadians will react with distaste to reporting that seems to violate the norms that are expected.

In contrast, Jay Rosen has argued that in the United States journalists are expected to display their toughness, that there is almost a "cult of toughness" and a "level of shamelessness and aggression," that is intrinsic to the way that journalism has come to be practised.[16] It is so much a part of the culture that displays of journalistic machismo, regardless of how destructive they might be, are virtually routine. As Rosen explains, "Journalists are proud of their oppositional stance, especially in relation to office-seekers and office-holders. It is their willingness to be tough (on everyone, they say) that makes them valuable to the political community — or so they think. "Toughness" might even be considered the default agenda of the press, an end in itself to be pursued regardless of the consequences."[17] The American public seems to accept this role and even to admire it.

CONCLUSIONS

Differences in the structures and values of Canadian and American journalism have produced different styles of political reporting in the two countries. In the American system, journalists have assumed a central role by investigating, exposing, and passing judgement on the characters of those who aspire to high political office. In doing so they have usurped a role that once belonged to the political parties. In Canada, the news media does not intrude into the political process to nearly the same degree. The philosophy is that citizens have the capacity based on what is on the public record to judge the behavior of politicians for themselves. Journalists are obligated to present and explain the actions and statements of political leaders so the public can make those judgements. Of course, this still gives journalists and news organizations enormous power and discretion in setting the public agenda.

Which of these two models represents the better approach is a difficult question to answer. The American method of placing candidates under the glare of a magnifying glass has the benefit of producing a character check that does weed out some of those who would be unfit for office. The question is whether attack journalism reveals the most important flaws. There are those who argue that the media's fixation with character issues rarely goes beyond "gotcha" stories that are salacious and sensational. Deeper and more meaningful questions are almost never posed. Doris Kearns has compiled a list of some of the questions that reporters seldom address; How has the candidate coped with crises or setbacks? How accurate is the candidate's picture of reality? How open is the candidate to new ideas or information? How much mental and physical energy does the candidate have? Is the candidate surrounded by "yes" men or is the candidate exposed to honest assessments and criticism from close advisors?[18]

Larry Sabato contends that reporters only engage in a frenzy of attack when they are certain that there has been a history of improper behavior. There is, in his words, a "subtext" that drives the investigation.[19] Gary Hart's affair with Donna Rice was not the issue. The affair was the symptom of deeper problems: Hart's often strange behavior, his penchant for taking chances, and his flagrant dishonesty. Sabato suggests that political leaders who are seen as sound and credible will be treated in a dignified manner.

The question that Canadian journalists face is whether the decision not to act strongly on character issues actually constitutes an intervention on the side of those politicians whose behavior and characters are inappropriate. The public is then deprived of information that could be vital in making an intelligent assessment of the leaders and in weighing how to vote. Moreover, by choosing not to expose deviant behavior journalists may, in fact, be condoning it. Yet many Canadian reporters are repulsed by the ferocious brand of attack journalism practised by American journalists. It is a step into the abyss that they are unwilling to take. For Canadian journalists discretion is likely to remain the better part of valour.

NOTES

All quotations not cited are taken from interviews conducted by the author in 1992.

1. Larry Sabato, *Feeding Frenzy: How Attack Journalism Has Transformed American Politics* (New York: The Free Press, 1991).

2. *Ibid.*, p. 1.

3. Quoted in Sabato, p. 83.

4. F. Christopher Arterton, "Campaign '92: Strategies and Tactics of the Candidates" in Gerald Pomper, ed., *The Election of 1992* (Chatham, NJ: Chatham House Publishers, 1993), p. 106.

5. Quoted in Arterton, p. 76.

6. Jeffrey Simpson, "When the tortoise starts to gain, it's time to ask some questions," *The Globe and Mail*, June, 4, 1993, A20.

7. Walter Dean Burnham, "The Legacy of George Bush" in Gerald Pomper, ed., *The Election of 1992* (Chatham, NJ: Chatham House Publishers, 1993), p. 32.

8. Samuel Popkin, *The Reasoning Voter: Communication and Persuasion in Presidential Campaigns* (Chicago: The University of Chicago Press, 1991), p. 71.

9. Paul Taylor, "Political Coverage in the 1990s: Teaching the Old News New Tricks" in *The New News V. The Old News: The Press and Politics in the 1990s* (New York: The Twentieth Century Fund, 1992), p. 50.

10. Sabato, p. 53.

11. John Carey, "Public broadcasting and Federal Policy" in *New Directions in Telecommunications Policy*, Paula Newberg, ed., (Durham: Duke University Press, 1989) p. 220.

12. Harvey Enchin, "CBC seeks niche in new TV markets," *The Globe and Mail*, 12 April, 1993, A1.

13. Quoted in John Richard and Stuart Robertson, *The Charter and the Media* (Ottawa: The Canadian Bar Foundation, 1985) p. 50.

14. See David Schneiderman, ed., *Freedom of Expression and The Charter* (Toronto: Thompson Professional Publishing Canada, 1991).

15. Val Ross, "Getting the cold shoulder," *The Globe and Mail*, November 30, 1991, A11; "Bryan Schwartz isn't warming to libel chill," *The Globe and Mail*, July 7, 1992, A16.

16. Jay Rosen, "Politics, Vision and the Press: Toward a Public Agenda for Journalism," in *The New News V. The Old News: The Press and Politics in the 1990s* (New York: The Twentieth Century Fund, 1992), p. 16.

17. *Ibid.*

18. Quoted in Taylor, p. 58.

19. Sabato, p. 71.

FURTHER READING:

Frederick Fletcher. "Mass Media and Elections in Canada" in Frederick Fletcher ed., *Media Elections and Democracy*, Volume 19 of the research studies of the Royal Commission on Electoral Reform and Party Financing (Ottawa: Minister of Supply and Services Canada, 1991)

Kathleen Hall Jamieson, *Dirty Politics: Deception, Distraction and Democracy* (New York and Oxford: Oxford University Press, 1992).

Larry Sabato. *Feeding Frenzy: How Attack Journalism Has Transformed American Politics* (New York: The Free Press, 1991).

David Taras. *The Newsmakers: The Media's Influence on Canadian Politics* (Toronto: Nelson Canada, 1990).

Paul Taylor. *See How They Run: Electing the President in an Age of Mediaocracy* (New York: Alfred A. Knopf, 1990).

JAMIE PORTMAN

And Not By Bread Alone: The Battle Over Canadian Culture

"Increasingly, American mass culture is being seen by Canadians as 'normal' culture, and Canadian mass culture as 'abnormal' culture. Canadian artists have moved to the fringe of their own country. Thus, in the video rental shop I frequent, the films of Claude Jutra are classified as 'foreign' films. And, in the record store, 'Canadian' records have a special bin, along with Ukrainian dances and Flamenco guitarists."[1]

Canadian composer and playwright John Gray made these somewhat jaundiced observations on the state of Canadian culture in a speech entitled "Learning How to Fail" which he delivered in November, 1985, at the Cultural Imperatives Conference in Waterloo, Ontario. It was not a new refrain. Variations of these sentiments have echoed and re-echoed over many decades — from the Aird Commission of the 1920s to the nationalist warnings which Canada's new Conservative Prime Minister, Kim Campbell, delivered to new American President Bill Clinton at the 1993 Tokyo economic summit. But in more recent years, the message has taken on a note of new urgency, with articulate members of the cultural sector — such as Gray — leading the charge.

The central issue is that nebulous something called "cultural sovereignty." The Canadian cultural community fears for its safety in the face of the continuing dominance of the United States in such key areas of Canadian life as film, publishing, television, and sound recording. By contrast, concerns for American cultural sovereignty are almost never an issue south of the border. True, that country's performing unions are as distrustful as their counterparts in Canada of imported talent, but whereas the leadership of Canadian Actors Equity or the Alliance of Canadian Cinema, Television, and Radio Artists is concerned with both safeguarding the nation's cultural life and protecting the jobs of its members, the American counterparts of these unions are primarily concerned with jobs. Indeed, the phrase "cultural sovereignty" seems mystifying to most Americans; it is an alien philosophy to which they cannot easily relate. And although the United States can be as protectionist as the next country in many key areas of industry, it has precious few anxieties concerning its culture: here, on the contrary, expansionism seems the keynote. It is therefore in a predominantly Canadian context that this chapter addresses the issue.

As Canada moves into the mid-1990s, its cultural community continues to mistrust the commitment of federal political leadership to honour and safeguard its concerns — despite the fact that the preservation and nurturing of Canadian culture have been basic to Canadian government policy, under both Liberals and Conservatives, for decades.

That governments have sometimes wavered in these commitments is undeniably true. Yet, even during the years of Brian Mulroney's Conservative regime, from 1984 to 1993, when funding in arts and culture was being slashed drastically, major cultural initiatives were still being announced in Ottawa; that they were not always fulfilled is due to several factors, perhaps the major one ironically being the opposition of the very country — the United States — whose influence over Canadian cultural life had made them necessary.

In 1987, Conservative Communications Minister Flora MacDonald authorized the publication of *Vital Links*, an 80-page government paper which articulated the most pressing concerns facing Canadians in the area of cultural policy. "Culture is the very essence of our national identity," the document stated in a brief preamble. "Nourishing that identity are the cultural industries, whose artists are more assured than ever but whose institutions face long odds against success.... We want to shorten those odds."[2]

But shorten the odds against whom? Essentially, against the Americans. The statistics quoted in *Vital Links* have essentially not changed to any degree since its publication — an indication, perhaps, of just how thorny the challenge is:

> Canadians are avid consumers of cultural products. We are, for example, the second-highest per capita purchasers of records and tapes in the world (after the Dutch). We are also among the world's great filmgoers. We think of ourselves as being particularly sports-loving: but in 1985 more Canadians attended professional theatre, dance and musical performances than they did professional sports events.[3]

But then the Department of Communications paper places all this in a more disturbing context, noting that most of the off-stage cultural fare that Canadians consume comes from somewhere else. It finds that 76% of books sold in Canada are imported, that 97% of screen time in Canadian cinemas goes to imported films, that 89% of earnings in the sound-recording industry ends up in the coffers of 12 foreign-controlled firms that principally market imported popular music. Most ominously, "despite decades of effort to regulate broadcasting, over 90 per cent of dramatic television presentations are non-Canadian in origin."[4]

The country of "origin" most responsible? The United States of America. To keepers of Canada's cultural identity it has been the enemy for nearly seven decades. As far back as the 1920s, many Canadians were so disturbed at the dominance of American programming on Canadian radio stations that the King Liberal government finally responded with the appointment of the *Aird Commission* in 1929 to examine the problem. Two fundamental principles outlined in that report have guided Canadian broadcast policy since that time:

> That the airwaves are a public resource and should be regulated by the Government on behalf of the Canadian people; and that use of this scarce resource entails obligations in the public interest;...That a publicly owned broadcaster is necessary, within the broadcasting system, to ensure that broad cultural goals are met and public needs properly served.[5]

When the Aird Commission talked about "broad cultural goals," it was doing so within a Canadian context, emphasizing the responsibility of the broadcasting system to enhance Canadian cultural expression. The most significant and long-reaching effect of the report was the Bennett Conservative government's establishment of the publicly-owned Canadian Broadcasting Corporation. But the Aird report has also been the basis for many other essentially protectionist broadcasting policies in the ensuing years, all of them aimed at strengthening the domestic broadcasting market.

However, the most influential cultural document in Canada's history is the 1951 *Report of the Royal Commission on National Development in the Arts, Letters and Sciences* — better known as the Massey Royal Commission. This elegantly written volume examined all aspects of Canadian cultural life — education, broadcasting, the performing and visual arts, the written word, and the mass media. Under the chairmanship of Vincent Massey, the man who would later become Canada's first native-born Governor General, the committee correctly foresaw the dawning of a new era of professional "mass culture" in a country which up to then had been characterized by amateur, community-oriented activity with only small pockets of professionalism. In the eyes of many, the report's most significant achievement was that it affirmed the principle of federal arts support carried out at arm's length free of political interference; thus, it paved the way for the establishment in 1957 of the Canada Council which in turn helped touch off the explosion of performing arts activity which was to be such an important part of the country's cultural landscape over the next quarter-century until government cutbacks started diminishing the Council's ability to fulfil its mandate.

Equally significant was the underlying premise of the commission's report: as had the Aird Commission more than 20 years previously, Massey feared for Canada's cultural independence in the face of the neighboring American juggernaut.

> It issued the first clear warning about the dangers of dependence upon American culture in the post-war world and proposed a deliberate and co-ordinated strategy for state-sponsored Canadian cultural development.[6]

At the same time as the Commission lamented a lack of "defence in depth," it also acknowledged that in many areas Canadians had benefited substantially from the nearby American presence — the millions in research funding from such groups as the Carnegie Corporation and the Rockefeller Foundation, the accessibility of American educational institutions to Canadian scholars, and the vast importation of what might familiarly be called the American cultural output:

> We import newspapers, periodicals, books, maps, and endless educational equipment. We also import artistic talent, whether personally in the travelling artist or company, or on the screen, in recordings and over the air. Every Sunday, tens of thousands tacitly acknowledge their cultural indebtedness as they turn off the radio at the close of the Sunday symphony from New York and settle down to the latest American Book of the Month.[7]

But more significantly, the commission saw grave dangers in what it perceived as excessive dependence on the United States, and in particular American popular culture. Some commentators, among them Paul Litt and Frank Underhill, have questioned the report's tone of elitism and what they perceive as an underlying anti-Americanism. "In the ideology of the Canadian culture lobby, nationalism and elitism merged on an alliance aimed at developing a Canadian culture opposed to the invasion of 'American' mass culture," writes Litt. "The commissioners exploited contemporary nationalist aspirations by offering a coherent vision of a superior national identity. By brandishing the flag, they made the cause of high culture both less recognizable and more attractive to the average Canadian."[8]

It is easy to forget today that the report did receive mixed reviews from certain quarters when it was published. Harold Innis believed Canada had a duty to stave off what he feared would be cultural annexation by the United States He claimed that English Canadian culture was in jeopardy as a result of "constant hammering from American commercialism."[9] In contrast, University of Toronto historian Frank Underhill questioned whether Canadians really were different from Americans or whether Ottawa should force them to be so: "These so-called 'alien' American influences are not alien at all," Underhill asserted. "They are just the natural forces that operate in the conditions of twentieth-century civilization. It is mass consumption and the North American environment which produce these phenomena, not some sinister influences in the United States."[10]

Underhill's views, although expressed four decades ago, would still strike a chord today with those powerful American forces who have a continentalist view of culture and who see the legacy of the Massey Report as a monstrous threat to their interests. Paul Litt, although scarcely an uncritical admirer of the Massey report, notes that from a nationalist perspective, the Massey report's misgivings about mass culture reflected both a more conservative and a more collectivist outlook, and its general endorsement of state action can be seen as "a continuation of the nation-building policies of the Nineteenth Century — the National Policy adapted to the information age."[11]

How successfully has this vision been fulfilled in the Canada of the 1990s? There has been an explosion of creativity in the years since the Massey report, and particularly since the establishment of the Canada Council in 1957. Professional orchestras, theatres, and dance organizations have sprung up from coast to coast, and many enjoy international reputations. New galleries and museums have been built. Major Canadian writers have won acceptance both in their own country and abroad.

To be sure there are elements of paradox inherent in this impressive record: there are notable Canadian accomplishments that have not necessarily been due to cultural protectionism. The international reputations of pianists Glenn Gould and Oscar Peterson are the result of valuable recording contracts with foreign-owned firms. In the days when Macmillan of Canada was still British-owned, it played a crucial role in advancing the careers of major Canadian novelists such as Hugh MacLennan, W.O. Mitchell, Morley Callaghan, and Robertson

Davies. More recently, such prominent Canadian writers as Timothy Findley and Mordecai Richler have chosen to publish with foreign-owned branch-plant firms.

Notwithstanding these exceptions, it is still legitimate to argue that the Canadian cultural landscape would be barren, and that few of the accomplishments of the past three decades would have been possible without generous public subsidy from the three levels of government — and there is no doubt that the Massey report and the subsequent founding of the Canada Council were vital in legitimatizing this principle.

On the surface, it would therefore seem that Canada has been able to assert the existence of a bold, vital cultural life. Yet despite these very real achievements, the infrastructure supporting such activities is increasingly fragile. Declining government funding is one major cause. But beyond this is the continuing next-door presence of American culture. Threats to Canadian cultural sovereignty which the Massey Commission and the Aird Commission warned against continue to preoccupy Canadians today, and not without reason. "The Canadian marketplace is abnormal for two reasons," sighed *Vital Links*. "The vast majority of books, films and records available here are produced elsewhere. And the revenues generated by their distribution largely flow out of Canada to finance production industries elsewhere."[12] Yet, the United States has never been really able to understand Canada's concern in such areas, which is why Canada's determination to protect its culture was a major source of friction during the US-Canada Free Trade negotiations.

Increasingly as well, the focus of concern is not on Canada's much-admired non-profit performing and visual arts institutions but rather on broadcasting — both publicly and privately owned — and the so-called "cultural industries" which nurse the rosily optimistic hope that one day they will be able to compete on a more even commercial playing field with the Americans. It is on the English-language side that the challenges are most formidable — Quebec's cultural industries are insulated to a much larger degree from American influence by the dominant presence of the French language within that province — and it is the vulnerability of English Canada's cultural life that has triggered most nationalist concerns. An examination of some of these areas reveals a mixed record of both achievement and retreat.

PERIODICAL PUBLISHING

In contrast to book publishing and the film- and sound-recording industries, Canada's periodical industry is in general under the control of Canadians. A 1984 industry survey estimated that more than 5,000 periodicals, not including newspapers, were published in Canada, with a total annual circulation of approximately 1 billion copies. This situation, comments *Vital Links*, exists "largely because government measures have helped create a more normal market environment for periodical publishers than other industries." It cites a number of Ottawa initiatives: reduced postal rates for Canadian periodicals, fiscal incentives aimed at encouraging Canadian companies to advertise in Canadian magazines, and taxpayer support of "specialized, non-commercial publications of cultural or scholarly importance."[13]

However, in the area of mass culture, the most significant government move was in the area of taxation and the direct target of its often controversial measures was the American periodical industry. Magazines come into Canada from south of the border enjoying advantages denied to a home-grown publisher: they are essentially over-run copies of publications that have already recovered their production costs in their home market. It was this situation which made possible the creation of a so-called "Canadian" edition of *Time* magazine: while the bulk of its content continued to be editorial copy of American origin, it was nevertheless able to prosper by carrying substantial Canadian advertising. Liberal government legislation introduced in 1965 and amended in 1976 — and popularly known as Bill C-58 — altered this situation. Under this legislation, Canadian companies were able to deduct for income tax purposes the costs of advertising in Canadian periodicals, newspapers or broadcasting outlets, but they were allowed no such tax benefits for advertising in foreign publications aimed at the Canadian market. Concurrently, Ottawa also imposed new Customs rules whereby non-Canadian periodicals containing more than 5% of advertising directed at a Canadian readership would be prohibited from entry into Canada.

The effect of these actions has been dramatic. The Canadian edition of *Time* was abandoned, and the Canadian edition of *Reader's Digest* increased both the ownership and content requirements of its Canadian edition in order to meet the legislation's advertising strictures.

"This change to the Income Tax Act had the general intent of redirecting to Canadian magazines some of the considerable advertising revenues that had been flowing into multinational coffers," observes the Federal Cultural Policy Review Committee in its 1982 report to the government. Perhaps the most significant beneficiary of the new policy was *Maclean's* magazine which acknowledged that without such changes "it would not have felt able to undertake its transformation from a monthly consumer magazine to a weekly news-magazine...”[14]

However, Bill C-58 was opposed by both Washington and the American periodical industry at the time and it remains a source of friction. Had not Canadian negotiators been vigilant in keeping culture off the table during the free trade talks, this policy along with other major Ottawa cultural initiatives might well have vanished.

Furthermore, American publishers have not ceased in their efforts to circumvent this bill, seeing technology as their latest weapon. In March, 1993, the Time-Warner organization in the United States began publishing a “Canadian” edition of *Sports Illustrated* magazine which consisted mainly of recycled material from its American parent edition and whose production costs would therefore be low enough that it could lure Canadian advertisers away from Canadian publications through lower advertising costs. Because technological advances undreamed of in 1976 would enable *Sports Illustrated* to beam electronically its advertising copy directly to a Canadian printing plant, the magazine hoped it would be able to bypass customs laws preventing physical shipment of such magazines at the border.

However by July, after prodding by the Opposition parties and a worried domestic industry, Canada’s Conservative government was moving to plug this loophole — initially with new rules allowing the country’s Investment Canada watchdog to prevent the establishment of new foreign-owned magazines if they were considered detrimental to the domestic industry.

BOOK PUBLISHING

Vital Links described in this way the unique problem faced by the Canadian publishing industry:

> Canadian publishers can hardly survive on such a small domestic market unless foreign publishers let them distribute more foreign titles or bid for the rights to publish them, or unless they can expand into the lucrative educational publishing market.[15]

The total book market in Canada had an estimated wholesale value of $1.3 billion, with 83 per cent or $1.1 billion reflecting sales of books in English and 17 per cent or $213 million representing French-language sales in 1984. Yet these figures scarcely signified a thriving domestically owned industry.

Additionally, within the portion of revenues earned by the Canadian-based industry, both Canadian and foreign-owned, the foreign-owned subsidiaries do far better financially than their Canadian-owned rivals. Although only 29 of the 201 publishing companies reporting to Statistics Canada were subsidiaries of foreign publishers, they controlled 58 per cent of all book sales (both Canadian titles and imports); for English-Canadian firms this figure rose to 65 per cent.

Standard trade publishing is a risky venture in any country. In Canada it is especially so because of the competition of imported books produced in mass runs in countries like the United States. In 1984, the 37,000 titles in print in Canada were competing with the 300,000 titles available from other countries, principally the U.S. Canadian-controlled publishers are therefore concentrated in the most crowded and fragmented area of the market.

The educational publishing industry is a further problem. Provincial governments have almost exclusive responsibility for education, and are able to set the rigorous standards that are required of publishers before texts will be approved and purchased. Educational publishing itself makes unique demands: it requires a different marketing structure, and extensive research, design and testing of materials must be undertaken. All of this is expensive, and so although the market is lucrative, foreign-owned subsidiaries have been able to control two-thirds of it, because Canadian publishers lack access to adequate levels of financing.

In 1972, in the face of genuine dangers that the Canadian-owned portion of the industry could disappear, Ottawa began providing financial support to book publishers, both through the arm's-length Canada Council and in direct government grants. In additional, a postal subsidy system was instituted for mailing printed materials in Canada. By 1986, the Conservative government had committed itself to an allocation of $65 million over five years to the sector. But the overriding aim was to provide an environment for more financially strong Canadian-controlled firms. In seeking to fulfil this aim, Marcel Masse — the Conservative Communications minister during this period — forced a new policy through cabinet and in the process sparked an angry confrontation with the Americans.

Known as "the Baie Comeau policy," this 1985 measure laid down a new framework for increasing Canadian ownership of publishing firms. The principal targets were exisiting foreign-controlled branch-plant companies. Under Baie Comeau, purchase of such a company's foreign parent would require the new owner to sell control of the Canadian holding to Canadians within two years at fair market value. The American reaction was furious, and the policy began to unravel almost immediately when the giant Gulf and Western Corporation in the United States successfully defied Ottawa's efforts to force it to turn over one of its recent acquisitions — the publishing firm of Prentice Hall (Canada) — to Canadian control.

Prentice Hall (Canada) remained under American ownership, as — later on — did Canadian-based subsidiaries of other American firms whose ownership had changed hands. Although the Mulroney government continued to insist that the Baie Comeau strategy was still in place, it seemed clear to cultural nationalists that Ottawa was more concerned about pacifying the Americans than in upholding its own policy.

That the policy had touched a sensitive nerve in the US was readily apparent. Not only was a giant conglomerate like Gulf and Western declaring open warfare on the policy, but it also had political support in Washington. One of the most persistent congressional critics of Canadian cultural nationalism during the 1980s was John Dingell, a Michigan Democrat, who accused Ottawa of unfair trade practices and suggested Washington should institute a similar screening and review policy towards the massive acquisition by Canadian firms such as the Thomson organization of U.S. publishing concerns. In his submission to Congress, Dingell complained that with the Baie Comeau policy, Canada was attempting to override transactions occurring outside its borders. "That is what makes the... policy so egregious," Dingell complained. "While there may be tensions between legitimate cultural aspirations and foreign ownership, the forced exile of American investments from Canada under these circumstances was overreaching in the extreme."

Over the years, Marcel Masse's controversial policy has been quietly abandoned, and foreign control of Canada's book publishing industry remains a serious problem.

FILM

Thirty years ago, there was no real Canadian film industry, apart from the output of the publicly owned National Film Board. By the 1980s, Canadian films were being produced in increasing numbers — and in Quebec at least were starting to find an audience. But in the country as a whole, the presence of a Canadian movie was frequently so rare as to be an aberration.

Canadians do love movies, a point *Vital Links* emphasized. In 1987, the year this document was published, more than 100 million cinema tickets were being sold in Canada every year, and the total annual market for film and video in Canada was worth more than

$1 billion. In subsequent years, the market was to increase dramatically because of home video's increasing penetration of the consumer market. But the observation of *Vital Links* that "Canadian audiences have only brief and fitful opportunities to see Canadian films" is as valid today as it was then.

The reason is clear-cut: Canadian movie screens are dominated by a Hollywood studio system which for nearly 70 years has considered Canada to be a mere extension of the American market and which will even enlist the support of the president of the United States to maintain its stranglehold. Ironically, Hollywood's grip on Canadian screens has actually increased in recent years. In 1963, Canada was the sixth largest export market for American films, but by the mid-1980s it had become the first. What is more, Canada lagged behind other countries in ensuring adequate screen time for its product:

> Other countries where American films are popular have taken care to ensure that their own films are also produced, distributed and screened. Australian films usually account for over 20 per cent of all films viewed in Australia. British films normally represent 26 per cent of the British market, Italian films 44 per cent of the Italian market and French films 48 per cent of the French market. But only 3 to 4 per cent of screen time in Canadian theatres is devoted to Canadian films.[16]

This proportion has not changed appreciably since the late 1970s, despite improvements in the number and quality of productions. Without a new film policy, this situation will not change. The Canadian film industry will continue to be dominated by foreign producers and distributors.

Canadian governments both Liberal and Conservative have provided public financing machinery — initially through the Canadian Film Development Corporation and later through its successor, Telefilm Canada — to encourage production of quality theatrical movies. Various tax incentives have also been initiated from time to time. Some outstanding films have resulted from such actions, but only rarely have they been able to secure widespread exposure. The market's structural anomalies create a situation where Canadian producers cannot reach their potential audience and so a cycle of dependency on government is perpetuated.

A 1985 film industry task force established by the Canadian government concluded that the domestic industry's problems were rooted in the fact that by the mid-1920s the major Hollywood studios had established their own distribution arms both at home and abroad to ensure greater power in the release and exhibition of their films in major market. *Vital Links* was blunt in its analysis of the negative impact of this situation on the Canadian industry.

> The American film giants have used the same strategies to control the distribution process in Canada as in the United States. Canada has been considered to be integrated into the American film market since the 1920s, to the great disadvantage of Canadian distributors who are ready and able to buy separate Canadian rights to successful overseas films, as well as American ones. This has a subsequent negative effect on the development and financing of a national cinema in Canada.[17]

Major U.S. studios do not reinvest their Canadian-generated profits in Canadian productions. Such films as are made for the U.S. market are shot in Canada for reasons that have to do with scenery, climate and currency. Money flows out of the country to create yet more American products for Canadians to buy.

The task force report recommended that the "distribution of films and videos in all media in Canada be by companies owned and controlled by Canadians." The Conservative government wasn't prepared to go that far, but in 1987, Communications Minister Flora MacDonald did attempt to correct the anomaly to a degree by announcing a bill which would distinguish between Canadian-controlled and foreign film-distribution companies and allow the former to increase their share of the Canadian market by a substantial margin.

Under MacDonald's scheme, a dual licensing system would go into effect. One would allow the major Hollywood studios to continue importing movies which they themselves had produced or for which they held worldwide rights. But a second licence would be available only to Canadian distributors, giving them the sole right to bid for and import other non-Canadian films for which a Hollywood major did not own worldwide rights. Such a policy would have ensured that major box-office successes from independent filmakers — the American-made *Platoon* and the Australian-made *Crocodile Dundee* are two examples — would be distributed in Canada by a Canadian company and that the distribution earnings would remain north of the border to strengthen the domestic industry further rather than end up in the United States.

But MacDonald's film bill never made it into Parliament because of the vociferous opposition of the powerful Motion Picture Association of America and its politically connected boss, Jack Valenti. In April, 1987, U.S. President Ronald Reagan visited Ottawa and personally voiced his concerns about the proposed legislation with Prime Minister Brian Mulroney. In Washington, the Senate Finance Committee and the House Ways and Means Committee attacked the proposal. Peter Murphy, chief U.S. negotiator in the Canada-U.S. free trade talks, told the *Wall Street Journal* that Canada's film policy "would give us very considerable problems in getting a free trade agreement approved by Congress."

By 1988, when MacDonald finally did introduce her film bill in the Canadian Commons, it had been watered down considerably. No longer would Canadian-owned distributors have preference. Hollywood-owned distributors would continue to handle all movies for which they earned worldwide rights. New foreign distributors would still be permitted to set up business in Canada. As for the crucial provision giving Canadian-controlled companies the sole right to import and distribute foreign independent films, this was scrapped. Instead, the Canadians would merely be allowed to bid against their financially powerful Hollywood adversaries for the rights to such fare.

Critics of the revised bill rightly noted that such an arrangement would place Canadian companies at an automatic disadvantage. Meanwhile, American politicians continued to object to any film legislation of any kind. The bill, even in its emasculated form, went nowhere and was allowed to die by the government.

BROADCASTING

The importance of broadcast policy has already been touched on earlier. But with the impact of new technologies — particularly the emergence of the satellite dish — the international broadcasting environment has shifted and poses tough new challenges to Canadian public policy aimed at making more and better Canadian programming available for Canadian audiences. The existence of a public broadcasting system such as the CBC, the Canadian content quota rules imposed on private broadcasters by the Canadian Radio, Television and Telecommunications Commission, the Canadian Broadcast Program Development Fund administered by Telefilm Canada — these and other initiatives have one fundamental purpose: to ensure that Canadians have access to their own programming and to attempt to aid in the evolution of a viable radio and television industry.

Yet, how successful have these initiatives been? In 1986, the *Federal Task Force On Broadcasting Policy* bluntly reported that a crisis situation existed, and that the same areas of weakness pinpointed by earlier studies remained evident:

As Sir John Aird's commission reported to the government in 1929, when radio alone was at issue, Canada was fast becoming a mere satellite of American broadcasting. It is truly astonishing that in the ensuing 57 years, despite two broadcasting acts, the Board of Broadcast Governors, the CRTC, the CBC, black-and-white television, color television, public television, private television, pay television, provincial television, community broadcasting, cable . . . superstations, satellites, satellite dishes, VCRs and Telefilm — we continue to be dogged by the same overriding problem Sir John pointed to so long ago.[18]

Despite passage of a new Broadcast Act in the late 1980s aimed at defining the responsibilities of the system as a whole and at creating an improved environment for Canadian programming, pressures from south of the 49th parallel remain formidable — particularly in television — with Canadian programmers competing against American networks whose wares are now available to most Canadians via cable. But beyond this has been the sheer cost of producing Canadian fare, especially TV drama which is clearly the most popular type of television programming, representing about 60 per cent of what people watch on English television during the peak evening hours.

But despite drama's vital role in purveying cultural values, it is also the most costly to produce. It is far cheaper to import foreign drama than to produce it in Canada. Broadcasting rights to an hour of popular U.S. programming can be as low as $60,000, while it would cost $1 million or more to produce a similar drama program in Canada. Increasing the number of Canadian-produced high-quality dramatic productions for prime-time viewing has always been a "central strategic objective" — and it has always remained elusive.

Furthermore, the world of broadcasting is so volatile because of continuing technological change that the ability of Canada to fashion a meaningful broadcasting strategy remains open to question. When it came to technology, the 1986 task force was scarcely optimistic in focusing on what it perceived as the major threat to Canada's broadcasting sovereignty:

We are not naive about the potential consequences of new satellite technology. We are under no illusion as to its capacity to flood our country (and the rest of the world) with more and more American programs, obliterating cultural distinctions between countries. There is no doubt that the quantitative domination of Canadian television by American programming will remain an inexorable fact. Only our response — how we choose to cope with the inevitable onslaught — is in question.[19]

The broadcast task force's most fundamental conclusion was that — at the very least — Canadians should be guaranteed a greater choice of high-quality domestic programming. Yet, objectives such as this were to become a major bone of contention during the U.S.-Canada free trade talks. The Canadian government had pledged at the onset of negotiations that culture would be kept off the bargaining table, and that Canada's cultural sovereignty would be safeguarded at all costs. But all indications are that the U.S. negotatiors battled repeatedly to get culture into the talks. And even though Canadian officials proclaimed at the closing of the deal that culture had been safeguarded, many in the sector were not convinced.

From the American perspective, the proposed film distribution bill has not been the only provocation. Among the many other sources of aggravation:

- Canadian content regulations limiting the exposure of U.S. programming in Canada

- Bill C-58 which not only discourages Canadian firms from advertising in U.S. magazines by prohibiting them from deducting such expenditures for tax purposes, but also applies the same rules on firms wishing to buy commercial time on U.S. border stations

- The right of Canadian stations to bump U.S. signals off cable when both are simultaneously showing the same program.

- Government subsidization of Canadian television production.

- Postal subsidization of Canadian publishers

- Canadian content quotas on radio stations lead to reduced air play for U.S. recordings

Following the conclusion of the free trade talks, Canadian officials repeatedly emphasized that Canadian culture was safe under the deal. In the House of Commons, on April 7, 1988, Communications Minister Flora MacDonald declared that:

> We have a free trade agreement because this prime minister, this minister of communications and the government promised one thing: that Canada's right to determine our own culture would be respected in every degree. Without that promise, a deal was simply not possible.[20]

But most members of the cultural sector remained unconvinced of this during the 1988 federal election campaign which was fought largely on the issue of free trade and returned the Mulroney Conservatives to power. And they remain unconvinced today; indeed their suspicions have intensified as a result of the government's decision to buck Canada's Access to Information legislation by refusing to release thousands of pages of free trade documents pertaining to culture.

At the same time, Canada's cultural industries have scrutinized federal cultural policy both during and after the free trade talks and have concluded that concessions were made to the Americans. In support of this conclusion Canada's Cultural Industries Alliance cited several pieces of evidence in 1988:

- Ottawa's June, 1987, action in announcing a major reduction in the special Capital Cost Allowance for production of Canadian films and television programs. The Americans had considered this an unfair stimulus to Canadian production.

- The government's abandonment of its new film and publishing ownership policies in the face of U.S. opposition.

- The government's rejection of key Broadcast Policy recommendations made by an all-party House of Commons committee, aimed at both strengthening Canadian programming and placing firm limits on the continentalization of broadcasting through control of U.S-based satellite networks wishing to make their programming available to Canadians.

But even more ominous to guardians of Canada's cultural sovereignty was Article 2005 of the Free Trade Agreement which, while stating that cultural industries were exempt from the deal, nevertheless followed up with a "notwithstanding" clause which in effect gave the U.S. the right to retaliate against any *new* Canadian cultural initiatives deemed damaging to U.S. business interests. Later, President Ronald Reagan sent a message to Congress pledging that Washington would invoke this clause against new cultural industry initiatives by Ottawa.

The issue is clearly not dead on either side of the border. In 1991, with the arrival of a new set of trade talks involving Canada, the U.S. and Mexico, U.S. Trade Representative Carla Hills once more tried to get culture on the bargaining table. Charging that the exclusion of culture from the original U.S.-Canada agreement remained an "irritant," Hills went on to complain that Ottawa was raising unacceptable trade barriers aimed at safeguarding Canadian culture. Her comments were a masterpiece of misrepresentation. She told a satellite news conference that:

I don't think that our largest trading partner and we should have substantial barriers on such a large segment of trade, nor do I think the consumers should be deprived of the broadest range of choice, and the lowest possible price in important areas like books, films, and documentaries.

It required only the most cursory glance at statistical data to realize she was talking nonsense. But her remarks remain significant if only because they reveal the glaring gap in understanding which exists between Canada and the U.S. when it comes to culture. The truth is that the so-called "barriers" to cultural exchange of which Hills complained are not "substantial." They are, on the whole, humble. They are aimed, not at keeping American culture out, but at ensuring that Canadian creativity retains at least a modest portion of its own playing field.

When Carla Hills complained that Canadians are denied freedom of choice, she was really employing a Washington jargon meaning that Canadians do not have adequate access to the glories of American cultural expression. Obviously, it was unsatisfactory to her that — for example — Americans control only 93 per cent of Canada's video and movie business and that Hollywood movies account for 97 per cent of screen time, or that the average Canadian household is already inundated with American programming.

Again, the problem is rooted in a difference in perception. To the free-enterprise members of the U.S. Congress, the big Hollywood studios and the New York publishing interests, culture is a business just like any other business. Other countries, Canada included, see culture as a reflection of a nation's soul. American negotiators will not understand or accept this point of view. Indeed, Carla Hills's lack of comprehension became apparent when she made the patronizing suggestion that the U.S. would have no objection if Canada still wanted to protect its culture through activities such as "fairs."

People like Carla Hills or Jack Valenti, the political power broker who heads the Motion Picture Association of America, are easy targets for self-appointed keepers of Canada's cultural identity. But it can also be argued that Canadian cultural nationalism frequently invites an extremism bordering on ideological thuggery. "Continental is treason," declared Canadian nationalist S.M. Crean in her 1976 book, *Who's Afraid Of Canadian Culture?* "Like other imperialist cultures, U.S. culture conquers, by fair means or foul, chewing up whatever it comes in contact with." Crean not only called for a new national cultural policy restoring Canadian control over its cultural life but freely admitted the policy must be anti-American.[21]

At what point does cultural protectionism become xenophobic? Shortly after becoming director of the Canada Council in 1986, Peter Roberts addressed an artists' group in Toronto. I was present at this meeting. In the course of his remarks, which were clearly addressing the need to strengthen Canada's cultural life, Roberts said that he supported the U.S.-Canada free trade agreement. With that observation, Roberts lost his audience. He did go on to emphasize that he supported the agreement only if culture could be adequately safeguarded, but by this time people were not listening. They seized on one thing and one thing only — the fact that the head of a major Canadian cultural institution had dared to say something even mildly positive about the United States. "He is betraying everything we stand for" was typical of the comments heard afterwards.

Of course, Roberts was doing nothing of the sort, but the incident did highlight the extreme irrationality, not to mention blind prejudice, which can bedevil the entire debate over Canadian cultural sovereignty. Furthermore, there are senior members of the arts sector who recoil from cultural extremism. Novelist and essayist Mordecai Richler has frequently voiced his contempt for Canadian nationalism both at home and abroad. Veteran actors such as Barry Morse and Kate Reid have over the years condemned their own Canadian unions for policies aimed at keeping American performers from working in Canada. Morse once sardonically referred to the nationalists in the Canadian Actors' Equity Association as motivated by sour grapes, accusing them of coming from the ranks of "the unemployed and unemployable."

Critic Robert Fulford, who throughout his career has been an articulate spokesman for Canada's artists, also has problems with some aspects of cultural nationalism. In a 1961 *Toronto Star* article, he applied the derisory label of "Cancult" to "a Canadian cultural process by which literature and art are demoted to the status of a crutch for Canadian nationalism. It is part of a process which makes culture into an artificial historical event, a part of an unending quest for Canadian identity."[22]

But Fulford warned that Cancult exacts a price:

The price is anti-Americanism — or as some anti-American Canadians say, "pro-Canadianism." Most countries can support the arts through government simply because the arts are good things to have around and don't pay for themselves. Not Canada. Cancult demands that we justify the tax money used on the CBC, the Film Board and the Canada Council by saying it prevents something from happening. That something is the further spread of American culture in Canada... Cancult is what makes us do the right thing for the wrong reason. Essentially, Cancult — while seeming to support culture — is anti- cultural; in fact, Philistine. It is Philistine because it holds that in a contest between art and nationalism, nationalism is more important. That's Cancult.[23]

Yet, the defence of cultural nationalism can be eloquently and persuasively articulated. *Vital Links* had a point when it quoted St. Augustine's definition of Nation as "an association of reasonable beings united in a peaceful sharing of the things they cherish." There are more than territorial boundaries involved here; there is also the reality of a nation's culture. But the Massey report took this concept one step further when it argued all those years ago that a government's costly investment in national independence could become a futile exercise. The concern is no less valid today: that Canada would be an "empty shell" without a continuing commitment to the idea of a vigorous and distinctive cultural life as a key component of nationhood.

NOTES

1. From "Learning How To Fail", a speech delivered by John Gray at the Cultural Imperatives Conference, Waterloo, Ont., Nov. 2, 1985.

2. *Vital Links: Canada's Cultural Industries* (Ottawa: Federal Development of Cummunications, Ministry of Supply & Services, 1987), 5.

3. Ibid.

4. Ibid., 11.

5. Ibid, 61.

6. Paul Litt, *The Muses, the Masses, and the Massey Commission* (Toronto: University of Toronto Press. 1992), 3.

7. *Report of the Royal Commission on National Development in the Arts, Letters and Sciences,* [*1949-1951*] (The Massey Commission) (Ottawa: The King's Printer, 1951), 14.

8. Litt, op. cit., 251.

9. Quoted in Litt, op. cit., 227. See Harold Innis: *The Strategy of Culture* (Toronto, 1952).

10. See Frank Underhill, "Notes On The Massey Report" *Canadian Forum*, Aug. 1951. Reprinted in Frank Underhill, *In Search Of Canadian Liberalism* (Toronto, 1960).

11. Litt, op. cit., 5.

12. Vital Links, op. cit., 19.

13. Ibid., 35.

14. *Report of the Federal Cultural Policy Review Committee* (Ottawa: Department of Communications. Ministry of Supply and Services. 1982).

15. *Vital Links*, op. cit., 25.

16. Ibid., 43.

17. Ibid., 45.

18. *Report of the Task Force on Broadcasting Policy.* (Ottawa, Ministry of Supply and Services, 1986.) Page 691.

19. *Ibid*, 692.

20. *Hansard* (Ottawa: April 7, 1988).

21. S.M. Crean, *Who's Afraid of Canadian Culture?* (Toronto: General Publishing, 1976), 277.

22. Robert Fulford, *Crisis At The Victory Burlesk* (Toronto: Oxford University Press, 1968), 182. (Originally appeared in *Toronto Star*, Jan. 19, 1961.)

23. Ibid., 183.

FURTHER READING:

Vital Links: Canadian Cultural Industries, Minister of Supply and Services Canada, 1987.

Report of the Royal Commission on National Development in the Arts, Letters and Sciences, [*1949-1951*] (The Massey Commission) (Ottawa: The King's Printer, 1951).

Paul Litt: *The Muses The Masses and The Massey Commission.* 1992. Toronto. University of Toronto Press.

Report Of The Task Force on Broadcasting Policy. 1986. Minister Of Supply And Services Canada.

S.M. Crean: *Who's Afraid of Canadian Culture?* 1976. General Publishing.

STEPHEN J. RANDALL

Divergent Visions, Common Problems: Canadian and American Foreign Policy Traditions

Canadians are fond of believing themselves to be distinct from Americans and considering Canada a morally superior society. This volume explores a variety of areas of comparison between the two countries — their institutions, historical experiences, and values. One of the major areas of comparison is their foreign policies, the traditions which underlie those policies, and the factors which account for the divergent experiences of the two societies during the past two hundred years.

Living in the shadow of the nation that enjoyed the responsibilities and privileges of what *Time* magazine founder Henry Luce dubbed the American Century has not always been an easy task for Canada. Former Prime Minister Pierre Elliott Trudeau captured the essence of the dilemma in drawing an analogy between the relationship of our nations and an elephant and mouse attempting to co-habit; the smaller and more vulnerable must be ever alert to the slightest shift in the position of the more weighty. This essay is concerned not so much with Canadian-American relations, however, as it is with the nature of the foreign policy traditions that developed in the two countries. Is this one of the areas in which Canadian and American differences can be clearly delineated? Has Canadian foreign policy been entirely distinct from its southern neighbour in spite of their common European heritage? Has the presence of French Canada made a difference to Canadian foreign policy? Is there a tendency toward convergence or divergence in the foreign policies of the two countries? This essay seeks to explore the similarities and differences, focusing on several basic categories: constitutional provisions; historical traditions; ideology, economics, and power.

CONSTITUTIONAL FRAMEWORK:

Canada and the United States share the dilemma and advantage of remarkably vague and general constitutional provisions governing the conduct of foreign policy. In the American case, the language of the Constitution on foreign policy grew out of a concern in the 1780s with America's weakness as a new entry in the community of nations, at the same time that there remained a strong sense of distrust of potentially abusive authority — the legacy of the War of Independence. In the Canadian case, the original Canadian Constitution — the British North America Act — reflected the basic reality of 1867, that Canada was a British colony, not expected to exercise an independent voice in foreign and military affairs.

Although it may not have been the intent of the framers of the American Constitution in 1789, the Presidential-Congressional structure of the American federation has produced a strongly centralized government in the United States over the past two hundred years, especially the office of the President. The American Constitution is neither eloquent nor expansive in its foreign policy provisions. The Constitution provides (Article II, Section 2) that the President "shall be commander in chief of the army and navy of the United States, and of the militia of the several states...." The President is also empowered to make treaties and appoint ambassadors and other representatives abroad (with the advice and consent of the Senate). The President can request Congress to declare war, but only Congress is explicitly empowered to declare war. Congress has also held the power of the purse and hence the Constitutional power to "raise and support armies..." and to "provide and maintain a navy" (Article I, Section 8).

From these relatively humble beginnings, presidential power evolved by World War II into what American historian Arthur Schlesinger Jr. has referred to as the "imperial presidency." The power to make war has historically proven to be far more powerful in the American system than the power to declare war. Thus the United States has actively engaged in military hostilities with foreign powers on many occasions prior to — and in some instances without — a formal declaration of war. This was true of the naval war in the North Atlantic in 1940-41 before the United States entered World War II, of the Korean War, the Vietnam War, and the Iraq War, as well as the many instances in which the United States has used its armed forces to achieve foreign policy goals in short-term circumstances. Such was the case with President Eisenhower's deployment of marines in Lebanon in 1958, Lyndon Johnson's use of marines in the Dominican Republic in 1965, Richard Nixon's incursion into Cambodia in 1970, the Reagan and Bush administrations' role in supporting pro-American Nicaraguan and El Salvadoran forces in the 1980s, Ronald Reagan's use of force in Granada, and the Bush administration's actions against Manuel Noriega's Panama in late 1989. None of these actions involved a declaration of war by Congress.

The reality of American military power and global responsibilities in the twentieth century accounts for the increased centralization of foreign policy decision-making in the United States and the relative decline of Congressional authority. The national security state that emerged early in the Cold War accelerated the tendency toward increased centralization, bureaucratization and secrecy. In 1947 the Truman administration obtained passage of the National Security Act, establishing the Pentagon, the National Security Council and, under the NSC, the Central Intelligence Agency. Since 1947 the NSC and CIA have acquired extensive reponsibilities that impact directly on foreign policy, although their existence was certainly not anticipated by the framers of the American Constitution, who would, without doubt, be shocked by the extent to which the relative power of Congress in foreign policy affairs has diminished.

In the Canadian instance, the 1867 British North America Act was even more general than the American Constitution on foreign affairs. Section 132 stated simply that "The Parliament and Government of Canada shall have all powers necessary or proper for performing the obligations of Canada or of any province thereof, as part of the British Empire, towards foreign countries, arising under treaties between the Empire and such foreign countries."[1] As with the American Constitution, the BNA Act was silent on the bureaucratic innovations that would be required to develop a foreign policy, what the role of the Prime Minister might be relative to Parliament, or what the British North American foreign policy might actually be. Certainly the Act did not anticipate Canadian autonomy from Britain in the development of foreign policy, let alone the modern efforts of individual provinces — most significantly Quebec — to be represented abroad for trade and cultural objectives or to control their own immigration policies.

Gradually Canada acquired by default, and through steady pressure, increased autonomy in foreign policy. Conservative Prime Minister John A. Macdonald participated in the Anglo-American negotiations in 1871 that resulted in the conclusion of the Treaty of Washington, but he did so as one of the three British delegates. In 1914, as a British colony, Canada was automatically at war once Britain declared war against the Central Powers, although then as in 1939 French Canada was less than enthusiastic about the British connection, and the issue of conscription became a federal government-Quebec crisis. The status of Canada vis-à-vis Britain changed with the passage in 1931 of the Statute of Westminster, which in effect ended the application to Canada of laws passed by the Parliament of the United Kingdom, or nullification of Canadian laws by the British Parliament.[2] The Statute of Westminster recognized in law what had become essentially a reality, in domestic as well as foreign affairs. Canada by the 1930s had developed its own traditions in foreign policy, its own diplomatic service in the Department of External Affairs, and negotiated on its own behalf in the foreign realm.

HISTORICAL ROOTS AND DEVELOPMENT

Two fundamental developments have shaped the course of American and Canadian foreign policy. The first is that the United States was born in the 1770s in a revolution against British colonialism; Canada evolved toward sovereignty in the nineteenth century under the second British Empire and then as a member of the Commonwealth in the twentieth century. This "revolution rejected" by those who would become Canadians, combined with the substantial influx of American tories no longer welcome in post-revolutionary America, has been a fundamental factor in shaping Canadian political development, including its foreign policy.

The second feature was the logical corollary of the first; Canada remained a British colony when the United States fought for its independence, and until the Second World War there was little evidence that Canadians thought of themselves as an "American" nation, whose interests lay largely in the western hemisphere. Indeed, Canadians defined themselves essentially in terms of *not* being Americans, and Canadian foreign policy was conceptualized as a policy that would ensure Canadian-American cooperation without loss of sovereignty to the superpower that gradually emerged on the Canadian frontier. Ultimately in the course of the twentieth century the United States and Canada came to have what was considered a "special" relationship — non-conflictual, cooperative, institutionalized dispute settlement, the world's longest undefended border. Most, though certainly not all, disputes tended to be resolved outside the public spotlight, through quiet diplomacy, behind-the-scenes negotiations, or through various bilateral agencies — such as the International Joint Commission, the Permanent Joint Board on Defense, or, most recently, as a product of the Free Trade Agreement, the binational trade dispute settlement panels.

Differences though there are in the American and Canadian foreign policy traditions, Canadian foreign policy has never veered significantly away from the values and objectives that are shared with the United States: the promotion of democratic institutions abroad; political pluralism; capitalism and free enterprise; humanitarianism; international order. The basic difference between the two nations has been the greater power of the United States to shape the international order. Nonetheless, Canadian capitalists expanded into the Third World along with American capital; Canadian entrepreneurs abroad built railroads, ran hydroelectric facilities, opened branch banks, developed mines, and gained control of large-scale plantations in the tropics. Until the 1920s, Canada pursued such goals, however, largely as a dependency of Great Britain. Although Canadians are now proud to consider themselves a non-military nation, more inclined toward peacekeeping than the practice of war, it was not always thus. As a British colony, Canada fought in the Boer War in South Africa at the end of the nineteenth century, while the United States was preoccupied with dismantling the remnants of the declining Spanish empire in the Caribbean and Pacific. Also as a British colony, Canada entered World War I in 1914, three years before the United States Congress and people, as well as President Woodrow Wilson, were convinced that American national interests were sufficiently threatened by the war in Europe to justify an American declaration of war. The United States rejected the League of Nations at the end of World War I and the notion of collective security that lay at the heart of the League, while Canada, as a small power, threw itself with enthusiasm into an international organization that seemed at the time to hold out the promise of world stability and the taming of military aggression.

The United States clung to isolationism in the 1930s; Canada retained its faith in international organization. Prior to Pearl Harbor there was intense opposition in the United States to American involvement in the European war. Isolationist sentiment held public and Congressional opinion in a vice-like grip throughout the 1930s, and it was only the outpouring of nationalism and outrage that followed the Japanese attack on American forces at Pearl Harbor that made a declaration of war against Japan possible. Even then, it was Germany that declared war on the United States a few days later. Again the United States held back from formal involvement for more than two years while its northern neighbour assumed an important role in the military conflict on the continent. Isolationist though it may have been in official policy between 1939 and 1941, the administration of Franklin Roosevelt moved, of necessity, toward consolidating hemispheric defense, establishing the Permanent Joint Board on Defense with Canada, assuming control of British bases in the western hemisphere, convoying supply ships to the British Isles, and actively confronting the German naval threat in the North Atlantic; but still, until the Japanese attack at Pearl Harbor in December 1941, Canada but not the United States was at war.

Canadian and American hopes of a peaceful world proved illusory. With the outbreak in 1939 of what quickly became a world war, Canada, still tied politically and emotionally to Britain and more international in its outlook than the United States, once again promptly committed its forces to the British, French, and Polish cause with a declaration of war against the Axis powers. Yet, Canadians were not united in their support of war. Quebec Premier Maurice Duplessis opposed Canadian involvement, and there was widespread opposition in Quebec to the possible imposition of conscription. A national plebiscite on conscription in 1942 found only 28% of Quebecers supportive, in contrast to English Canada, with the result that the Liberal Government never adopted full conscription before the end of the war.

Opposition to conscription did not prevent the recruitment of a substantial military force in the course of the war. By the time of the 1945 armistice, the Canadian armed forces had incorporated over one million men and women, five-sixths of them by voluntary enlistment, from a total population of less than twelve million. By comparison, the United States, which passed its first peacetime conscription law in 1940, registered thirty-one million men during the war. Including volunteers, more than fifteen million men and women served in the American armed forces before the end of the war, from a total population of more than 130 million.[3]

Canadian-American military and economic partnership during World War II contributed substantially to the growing integration of the two economies, providing a yet stronger base for a commonality of views on world affairs. Canada and the United States both strongly supported the establishment of the United Nations at the conclusion of the war. Canadians such as John Humphrey and Americans such as Eleanor Roosevelt, both involved in the establishment of the UN Human Rights Commission, were firmly committed to the protection of international human rights in the postwar era. Canadians shared with Americans the desire to establish international organizations, including the GATT and IMF, to stabilize trade and monetary relations in the postwar world.

One of the most poignant statements of the principles underlying Canadian foreign policy at the end of World War II came from Louis

St. Laurent, Secretary of State for External Affairs. Presenting the inaugural Gray Foundation Lectureship at the University of Toronto in 1947, St. Laurent stressed what he considered the essential features of Canadian foreign policy: external relations should not weaken national unity; drawing on the British and French heritage, Canadian policy should advance political liberty; Canada should demonstrate the "values of a Christian civilization" and the acceptance [by Canada] of international responsibility; and Canada should support the international rule of law, on which the "freedom of nations depends."[4]

In the context in which St. Laurent spoke, Canadian governments and peoples also generally shared the Cold War assumptions of Americans from the Harry Truman/MacKenzie King Liberal years through to the close relationship that Tory Prime Minister Brian Mulroney developed with Republican Presidents Ronald Reagan and George Bush in the 1980s and early 1990s. Although at times Canada articulated different views and pursued distinct tactics from the United States, the overall pattern of Canadian foreign policy adhered to American Cold War designs. Canada was a founding member of NATO, and Canadians fought alongside Americans and United Nations forces in Korea from 1950 through 1953. The two countries also forged strong bilateral defense links through NORAD (North American Aerospace Defense). The Diefenbaker government mobilized its military forces (although with less enthusiasm and expedition than the United States) during the Cuban Missile Crisis in October 1962, but with much confusion and debate rejected the placement of American-controlled nuclear weapons on Canadian soil.

On the other hand, Canada gained a reputation for making peace rather than war in the early Cold War, first in Cyprus, where Canada remains, in working through the United Nations to resolve the Suez Crisis in 1956, and then as part of the International Control Commission established after the Geneva accords in 1954 to assist the decolonization process in French Indo-China. Canada also retained diplomatic relations with Castro's Cuba, even after the United States and the Organization of American States severed ties and imposed an economic embargo on the rebel power; but rather than representing a break with the United States, the Canadian diplomatic presence in Havana provided a window of opportunity, and Canadian diplomats cooperated with American authorities in providing information on Cuban developments. Canadian Liberal governments in the 1960s generally supported American objectives in Vietnam, even if Prime Minister Lester Pearson raised serious questions and publicly criticized the Lyndon Johnson administration for its escalation of bombing against North Vietnam.

At least the rhetoric of a significant departure from the American link came in the late 1960s and 1970s under Liberal Pierre Elliott Trudeau. From the outset of his government, Trudeau sought a different path, ordering a comprehensive review of Canadian foreign and defense policy that flirted with the notion of Third Option diplomacy in an effort to distance Canada from the American Cold War agenda as well as to offset the high level of Canadian economic dependency on the United States. The Third Option approach was premised on the ability to make Western Europe a counterweight against American influence, but the notion foundered in part on the fact that Canada could not circumvent NATO. Canada under Trudeau did move closer to the Soviet Union and opened diplomatic relations with China; both overtures were consistent with the Nixon-Kissinger policy of detente. At the same time Europe, the Commonwealth, the Third World, and the Francophone nations gained more favour in Ottawa, even though such manoeuvring did little to alter the basic reality of Canadian economic ties to the United States.[5] The Trudeau effort both to distance Canada from the United States and to strengthen the place of French Canadians in Confederation also led logically to expanded contacts with "la francophonie." Ultimately, with stronger ties to the French world and repatriation from Britain of the Constitution, Canada would be less British; but it was not really more American. The Third Option approach thus made little significant headway in the 1970s and was, in any event, displaced by the highly pro-American Tory governments of Brian Mulroney in the 1980s. What had been policies of extreme divergence from the United States in the Trudeau years — including foreign investment review, the Third Option, and the National Energy Policy — became under the policies of the Tories ones of convergence, although leading nationalist figures such as Mel Hurtig used stronger language to describe Mulroney's pro-American posture. Prime Minister Mulroney set the tone for renewed good relations with the United States by singing Irish songs with Republican President Ronald Reagan at the Shamrock Summit in Quebec City and pursued a Reaganesque economic policy of privatization and a quest for free trade with the United States in 1988 that sent Canadian nationalists into cardiac arrest. At the time of writing, Canada was on the verge of entering into a controversial North American Free Trade Agreement with the United States and Mexico. The Conservative Government also sent Canadian forces into battle alongside the United States in the Iraq War in 1992, the first time Canadian forces had performed other than peacekeeping roles since the Korean War.

Given this long history of Canadian-American cooperation, it may seem at first glance unlikely for one to find significant differences in the foreign policies of the two countries; but those differences are there, products of varying historical legacies, of distinct political systems, of contrasting ideologies, and fundamental differences in size and power between Canada and the United States, once the latter emerged on the world stage at the end of the nineteenth century. Essentially, regardless of other sources of difference, the major factor that accounts for the distinctions between Canadian and American foreign policy is the fact that from World War I through the 1970s the United States has been a major military power and New York the financial capital of the world. Canada, in contrast, was a colony of Great Britain, with no distinct foreign policy until the twentieth century; it has been a small power, rather vaguely considered a middle power in terms of its role in the world, its military capacity, and its economic significance, even though Canada has been a member of the G-7 leading industrial nations. As a middle power, Canadian foreign policy has, almost by necessity, been reactive and internationalist in nature, although, as noted earlier, Pierre Trudeau sought to make Canada less reactive and to adopt a more clearly defined, rational policy based on national self-interest.[6]

IDEOLOGY:

Few countries in the world are as closely identified with strong ideology in foreign affairs as the United States, and its ideological traditions have deep roots in the colonial heritage, in the nature of the independence movement from Great Britain in the 1770s and in the physical isolation of the nation from Europe in the nineteenth century, until modern technology made that isolation obsolete. One of the most fundamental aspects of the American experience that has shaped its approach to the world around it has been a sense of mission and a belief in the uniqueness of the American experiment. Jonathan Winthrop, a Puritan colonist in the sixteenth century and first governor of the Massachusetts Bay colony, captured the essence of this sense of mission when he observed that the colony would serve as a beacon on a hill, providing an example of liberty to the rest of the world.

That sense of mission and a conviction of the moral rightness of America came to infuse American belief and foreign policy in the course of the nineteenth and twentieth centuries. Terms such as Manifest Destiny and mission — normally couched in terms of the destiny of the United States to spread over the North American continent — became an integral part of American vocabulary by the mid-nineteenth century. At the same time, the United States and

Americans generally came to identify with movements of liberation elsewhere in the world, as in the Latin American independence movements in the 1810s, the Greek independence movement in the 1820s, the 1848 liberal uprisings in Europe, or the Cuban quest for independence from Spain in the 1890s. In the latter third of the nineteenth century, following the Darwinian revolution and the application of Darwinian principles of evolution to the struggle for survival among peoples by Herbert Spencer and others, the American (and indeed the British) idea of mission was infused with a stronger sense of racial superiority. Thus, the "new" Manifest Destiny of the late nineteenth century contained the original notions of mission, but was honed by a belief in the superiority of white, Anglo-Saxon, and Protestant peoples. Such views were convenient, of course, as the United States joined the European nations as a colonial power at the turn of the century, acquiring control and responsibility over a small empire that stretched from the Philippines, Guam, and Hawaii in the Pacific to Cuba, Puerto Rico, and the Panama Canal Zone in the Caribbean basin.

Canadians were the products of a similar intellectual and political milieu. Victorian-era Canadians were not immune to the racial and social biases that touched late nineteenth-century American society, nor to the lure of late nineteenth-century imperialism, combining racial, economic, and religious values and perspectives. In the Canadian case this expansionist and imperialist urge was expressed largely through the British Empire and its institutions. Victorian Canadians shared with their American counterparts a belief in the desirability of spreading entrepreneurship and capitalism to the rest of the world; they also actively shared the desire to proselytize non-Christian (especially non-Protestant) peoples, with the result that Canadian as much as American missionaries found their way into Africa, Asia, and Latin America. In the same imperial spirit, the Liberal government of Wilfrid Laurier, in spite of the protests of French Canada, sent Canadian troops to fight in the Boer War.

A factor that united the Canadian and American experiences was the Canadian tendency, like the American, to consider the Canadian political, social, and economic model to be distinct from the British, purer in the absence of clear class lines, and possessing a greater degree of social, economic, and political equality. At the same time, many Canadians expressed unease at the social, economic, and political unrest they saw in their southern neighbours at the turn of the century — a failed democracy, with cities degenerating into boss rule, widespread poverty, immigrant slums, political corruption, and labour violence. Thus, the same spirit of progressive reform that swept the United States from the 1890s through World War I — urban reform, women's suffrage, temperance, electoral reform — captured the Canadian imagination; also like the United States, which strongly pursued liberal developmentalist goals overseas after the 1890s, Canadians encouraged such reforms abroad. Again, the basic difference between the two nations was neither ideology nor approach but rather their differing capacities to effect change in other countries and in the international system.

There were prominent Canadians before 1900 (and after) who shared the continentalist vision that had been articulated by some Americans in the course of the nineteenth century. Continentalists on both sides of the 49th parallel argued that there was a natural connection between the two nations that should be consummated in a more formal relationship. In the late nineteenth century, an influential Continentalist Union movement emerged in Toronto under the leadership of Goldwin Smith, an Oxford historian turned North American publicist; Erastus Wiman, a New York financier;l and Samuel J. Ritchie, an American businessman. Smith provided the intellectual rationale of the movement: Canada was an un-natural entity; the natural linkages were north-south, and Canada's destiny lay in union within a larger North American nation. Although the movement gained little popular support, it found subsequent resonance in the late 1940s with early, though aborted, discussions between Canadian and American officials over free trade, in the conclusion of a bilateral agreement in 1988, and of a North American agreement in 1992.

There have been occasional flourishes of Canadian interest in closer union with the United States over the past century and some American desire for at least closer economic union — for instance, Clarence B. Randall in the Eisenhower years. Yet, most American governments before the 1980s did not even view Canada as truly a nation of the Americas. As a colony of Great Britain in the 1820s, British North America — the embryonic Canada — was to the United States little more than a remnant of European colonialism, hardly to be distinguished at the time from Cuba, which hovered off the coast of Florida as a lingering reminder of Spain's earlier imperial glory. It was not until after World War II that Canada began to achieve the degree of autonomy in the eyes of the United States sufficient to be considered a potential "American" nation, rather than a mere British possession. From World War II through the Cold War Canada remained apart from the inter-American system, not seeking membership in the Pan American Union and its successor, the Organization of American States, until 1989. Even when Canada did finally join the OAS in 1989, a year following the completion of the Canada-United States Free Trade Agreement, Canada did not become a signatory to the Rio Treaty of Mutual Defense, a gesture of more than symbolic significance. This orientation on the part of Canada is critical to an understanding of Canadian foreign policy in the second half of the twentieth century — close to the United States, a formal ally in NATO, the major trading partner of its southern neighbour, but not without continued recognition of its deep European heritage and ties, and not without awareness of the pitfalls of being purely in the American camp.

For the United States in the nineteenth century, at the same time that American foreign policy was infused with a sense of mission, there was a competing, powerful, and contradictory tendency toward isolationism from Europe, a sentiment that made Canada, as a lingering outpost of Europe, even more alien. George Washington articulated that philosophy most effectively in his farewell address to the nation at the end of his presidency in 1796. The essential features of Washington's ideas, expressed in the midst of the controversy over the French Revolution, were: that the United States, while developing commercial relations with other nations, should have as little political connection with them as possible; that European affairs were remote from the United States and of little direct concern to the nation; that the United States should avoid formal permanent alliances; and that even in commercial policy, the United States should not seek nor grant "exclusive favors or preferences."[7]

The Monroe Doctrine of 1823, drafted in the context of the fear of a European effort to restore Spain's rebellious colonies and of Russian ambitions on the west coast of North America, rephrased Washington's philosophy. In his message to Congress, President Monroe expressly opposed any further European colonization in the "American continents." Like Washington before him, Monroe drew attention to the perceived fundamental differences of the European political systems to that of the American republics. "It is impossible," Monroe cautioned, for the European powers to "extend their political system to any portion of either continent without endangering our peace and happiness."[8]

As the nation acquired an empire of non-Anglo-Saxon and non-Protestant peoples, the United States' commitment to movements of national liberation became tempered by conflicting realities. The nationalism that continued to drive the American experiment seemed more dangerous abroad, especially following the Mexican Revolution during the 1910s and the Bolshevik Revolution in 1917, both of which presented opposing models to the American ideal of liberal developmentalism — that is economic, social, and political reform abroad under American leadership and in the American image. This American ideal included private enterprise capitalism, with a minimum of state intervention; adherence to political pluralism, with a broadly based suffrage; and the establishment of public educational systems.

During and immediately following World War I, Woodrow Wilson vigorously stressed the importance of the principle of national self-determination in American foreign policy. Franklin Roosevelt reasserted that ideal, along with other Wilsonian principles such as freedom of commerce, the rights of neutrals, the ideal of collective security, and basic civil rights, in his Four Freedoms address in the late 1930s and in the Atlantic Charter, which he and Winston Churchill concluded off the coast of Newfoundland in August 1941. In the Truman doctrine address of March 1947, President Harry Truman extended the notion of the American commitment to the liberation of oppressed peoples. Truman divided the world into two camps — the free nations and the oppressed — and committed the United States to the liberation of the latter. "I believe," he said on that occasion, "that it must be the policy of the United States to support free peoples who are resisting attempted subjugation by armed minorities or by outside pressures. I believe that we must assist free peoples to work out their own destinies in their own way ... through economic and financial aid which is essential to economic stability and orderly political processes"(*New York Times*, 13 March 1947). President Dwight D. Eisenhower applied those commitments specifically to the Middle East in the later 1950s.

Still, there were tensions in American policy between ideal and power politics. The notion of "free" peoples was a lofty ideal; but who was to determine which were the peoples struggling to be free and which were their oppressors? Thus, there emerged significant contradictions between ideal and practice, many of the contradictions the product of the East-West Cold War, which made it difficult to distinguish between subjugators and liberators, between nationalists and communists. In the 1930s, the Roosevelt administration did little to isolate the United States from association with right wing, military regimes in Latin America. In the early 1950s the Eisenhower administration actively engineered the overthrow of the elected government of Iran under Mohammed Mossadegh and reinstated the Shah. In Guatemala in 1954, in the alleged interest of anti-Communism, the CIA provided decisive aid and training to a counter-revolutionary military force to overthrow the reformist government of Jacobo Arbenz, thus facilitating not the liberation but the subjugation of the Guatemalan people for the next generation. The policies of the Ronald Reagan administration in the 1980s toward the Sandinista government in Nicaragua and the anti-government guerrilla force in El Salvador — the FMLN — paralleled those of the Eisenhower administration in Guatemala. In the interest of saving the nations from the forces of Communism and Cuban-Soviet domination in the western hemisphere, the United States funnelled billions of dollars in military aid and training — some of it contrary to Congressional legislation — to the anti-Sandinista forces in Nicaragua and to the military forces of El Salvador, while human rights, civil liberties, and notions of national self-determination played second fiddle to Cold War concerns.

In Vietnam, in the same noble, if misguided, attempt to save the Vietnamese people from Soviet-dominated communism, as well as in an effort to prevent Asia from falling into the Soviet and Chinese orbit, the United States fought its longest and most unsuccessful war, beginning with large-scale funding to the French Government in the late 1940s. By 1965, there were half a million American troops in South Vietnam fighting against what was perceived to be both internal subversion by the Viet Cong and external aggression by North Vietnam and the Soviet Union. Such intervention was consistent with President Truman's 1947 ideas but marked a sharp departure from the stress he had placed on economic and financial assistance as the means to enable peoples to resist aggression.

The Cold War thus consumed the energies of American leaders from 1945 into the Bush administration, when finally the half century of tensions came tumbling down with the collapse of the Soviet economy and the Gorbachev-led domestic and foreign policy reform initiatives, before Mikhail Gorbachev himself, caught up in a maelstrom he could no longer contain, was deposed in December 1991. Nothing so visibly symbolized the end of the Cold War as the demolition of the Berlin Wall.

With the end of the Cold War, the predictability of East-West confrontation has been displaced by the uncertainty of resurgent ethnic nationalism and religious fundamentalism as well as the continuing problems of underdevelopment, poverty, malnutrition and famine, and civil war. The end of the Cold War has made it possible for the United States to consider returning to a more isolationist stance, but it has instead chosen to move toward a more multilateral position, including peacekeeping efforts in the former Yugoslavia and Somalia, along with Canada. The more the United States reinforces the role of international agencies such as the UN and OAS at the expense of American unilateralism, the more comfortable Canada can be with its neighbour.

CONCLUSION

It should be evident that there have been basic differences in Canadian and American foreign policies during the past century. Those differences derive from contrasts in the economic and military power of the two nations, a power imbalance that has left Canada with little rational recourse except to pursue the logical foreign policy objectives of a middle power that was for its first half century a colony of the nation against which the United States had fought a war of national liberation; in its second half century Canada was caught between the world's two major superpowers. The United States may well have been driven in its international pursuits by the idealism and moralism-legalism identified by such realist critics of American foreign policy as George Kennan. The essence of Kennan's critique was that United States' foreign policy makers had historically been overly concerned with abstractions rather than *realpolitik*, with such notions as Manifest Destiny and Mission or the Open Door Policy, rather than balance of power and real national interest.[9] Canada has not been lacking in either ideology or idealism; but as a middle power it could ill afford to act without caution and did so within the protective umbrella of international organizations. A former British High Commissioner to Canada, Malcolm MacDonald, suggested that there was a "sanity, a wisdom, a true statesmanship about the Canadian outlook and policy." He also suggested that Canadians were a people with a "national sentiment pursuing national aims."[10] In the final analysis, the latter is the essence of foreign policy for all nations.

NOTES

1.   30 & 31 Vict. c. 3, Great Britain, *Statutes*, third revised edition (London, 1950), VIII, p. 22.

2.   22 & 23 Geo. 5. c.4, Statute of Westminster, *The Statutes*, third revised edition (London, 1950), XX, 496-499.

3.   U.S. Bureau of the Census, *Historical Statistics of the United States* (Washington, 1960).

4.   "The Foundation of Canadian Policy in World Affairs," The Gray Foundation Lectureship, January 13, 1947, Department of External Affairs, *Statements and Speeches* (Ottawa, 1947), pp. 1-11.

5.   The developments of the Trudeau era are brilliantly delineated in J.L. Granatstein and Robert Bothwell, *Pirouette, Pierre Trudeau and Canadian Foreign Policy* (Toronto, 1991).

6.   Michael Tucker, *Canadian Foreign Policy: Contemporary Issues and Themes* (Toronto, 1980), p. X.

7.   James D. Richardson, ed., *Messages and Papers of the Presidents* (Washington, 1896), I, 221-23.

8.   Richardson, ed., *Messages*, II, 217-219.

9.   See, for instance, Kennan's *Realities of American Foreign Policy* (New York, 1954).

10.   Cited by Louis St. Laurent, The Gray Lectureship, January 13, 1947, Department of External Affairs, *Statements and Speeches* (Ottawa, 1947), p. 11.

FURTHER READING:

Michael J. Hogan and Thomas Paterson, eds. *Explaining the History of American Foreign Relations* (1991).

Michael Hunt. *Ideology and United States Foreign Policy* (1987).

Norman Hillmer, ed. *Partners Nevertheless: Canadian-American Relations in the Twentieth Century* (1989).

J.L. Granatstein and Norman Hillmer, *For Better or For Worse: Canada and the United States to the 1990s* (1991).

Charles Doran. *Canada and the United States: Enduring Friendship, Persistent Stress* (1985).

Robert Bothwell. *Canada and the United States* (1991).

Sidney Wise and Robert Craig Brown, *Canada Views the United States: Nineteenth Century Political Attitudes* (1967).

HENRY SREBRNIK

Football, Frats, and Fun vs. Commuters, Cold, and Carping: The Social and Psychological Context of Higher Education in Canada and the United States

In 1986, I was invited to a reception at the White House in Washington at which then Secretary of Education William Bennett was a guest. We later chatted informally, and, hearing I was a Canadian, he asked my opinion of American higher education. "It seems to consist, on the undergraduate level, mainly of the three Fs," I responded, "football, frats, and fun." He was not entirely amused by my reply.

My analysis was, admittedly, largely impressionistic and anecdotal. It was based on my observations of, and, later, teaching experience at, Gettysburg College, a private, highly selective, residential undergraduate liberal arts college still loosely affiliated with the Evangelical Lutheran Church in America, and located in Gettysburg, PA, a small town of 8,000 people. The college claimed that it had a student body that was national in origin, though in reality most came from the northeastern United States; however, virtually none did come from the town itself.

The difference between such an educational establishment and a typical Canadian university became even more evident after I moved to the University of Calgary in Alberta. At this large, 24,000-student urban university offering graduate programs and professional training as well as undergraduate teaching, research took precedence over pedagogical skills and face-to-face education. Since the university was located in a major Canadian city of 750,000 people, its students were drawn largely from southern Alberta — indeed, mainly from the city itself. Most lived at home and commuted to school by car or public transit.

These are indeed very distinct types of educational environments, and each is to some extent reflective of the differing cultural and pedagogical philosophies that have emerged in Canada and the United States. What kind of impact does attendance at one type of school or the other have on the psychological and social formation of students, who are after all young adults going through a very formative period in their lives? And does this perhaps serve to explain some of the difference between the "national cultures" of the two countries?[1]

AMERICAN AND CANADIAN HIGHER EDUCATION: DIFFERENCES IN SIZE AND SCOPE

In the United States, there are some 1,800 four-year colleges and universities, divided roughly equally in numbers between public and private institutions.[2] But they differ not only in degree of quality but in kind, ranging from relatively small undergraduate liberal arts colleges through metropolitan commuter or "trolley car" schools, both public[3] and private[4], to massive universities dominating entire college towns.[5] Higher education in the United States has evolved into a highly refined institutional status hierarchy, comprised of various layers. At the top, there are a number of world-class institutions with international reputations, which draw students from across the country and around the world. Their geographic location is irrelevant and their relationship to their home state minimal — who associates Princeton University with New Jersey? Below this level are a substantial number of reputable schools, widely known and respected, certainly in their own regions; most of these are large state universities. Finally, there is a large group, numbering in the hundreds, of "invisible" schools, mainly little-known private colleges, still often church-related, with relatively small enrolments and only moderately selective to totally non-selective admissions policies.[6]

Within this framework, there are further subdivisions, involving religion, ethnicity and gender. As the frontier moved westward in the nineteenth century, hundreds of colleges were founded by various Protestant denominations, usually replicating the New England college with which they were familiar. "By 1861 denominational ambition had covered the country with colleges"; the Methodists alone opened 32 colleges (for instance, Lambuth in Jackson, TN) between 1822 and 1865.[7] Schools were established by Christian Scientists (Principia), Lutherans (St. Olaf, Gustavus Adolphus), Mormons (Brigham Young), Presbyterians (Erskine), Quakers (Earlham), Southern Baptists (Wake Forest, Furman), and many other Protestant groups. More than 260 Catholic schools were founded, mainly by various orders; the Jesuits alone created 28, including Boston College, Fordham, and Georgetown. Black (Howard, Morehouse) and Jewish (Brandeis, Yeshiva) universities were established. There are even today still 84 all-women's schools in the United States as well, ranging in quality from the prestigious "Seven Sisters," including Bryn Mawr, Mount Holyoke, and Wellesley, to such lesser lights as, for instance, Mills College in Oakland, California.

Then there are the non-denominational secular schools, both public and private. Most states have one or two major public universities — for example, in Oregon, the University of Oregon in Eugene and Oregon State University in Corvallis. States such as California, Michigan and Texas operate entire "systems," with the original campus — say, the University of Michigan in Ann Arbor or the University of Texas in Austin — now serving as the "flagship" and major research institution, and the numerous "branch plant" campuses — the University of Michigan-Dearborn or University of Texas-Pan American in Edinburg — operating as comprehensives that grant BAs and selected graduate degrees, often in education. California's system is so massive that the University of California is itself composed of nine units — the original Berkeley campus, and such major research centres as UCLA, UC San Diego, and UC Davis — along with an entire secondary California State University system comprising 19 major schools. New York State's public system incorporates more than 20 four-year colleges and universities.

The annual *U.S. News & World Report College Guide*, which ranks 1,373 American four-year institutions, notes that "Nowhere else on the globe are the young offered as wide — and bewildering — a range of academic options as in the United States."[8] American schools are too diverse to grant the nearly uniform degrees obtainable at universities in Britain or Canada and quality varies widely; Americans are willing to tolerate institutions of such low quality that hundreds of them "would not qualify in Europe as serious institutions of higher learning."[9] The system is massive; American colleges and universities enrol over 14 million students.[10]

By contrast, there are 89 degree-granting Canadian universities (14 of these affiliated with another university), from one each in Newfoundland and Prince Edward Island to 15 in Ontario.[11] Most are quite similar: except for a few primarily undergraduate-focused schools in smaller communities, universities in Canada are basically research-oriented comprehensive institutions located in big cities, and top heavy with "trolley car" commuter students. Even though the older universities were founded by various Christian denominations,[12] Canadian universities today are public institutions and they receive the vast bulk of their operating and capital funds from their provincial governments, whose grants now account for some 80% of university operating revenues. While some denominational schools continue to exist — for instance, the Anglican King's College in Halifax, or Catholic St. Thomas University in Fredericton, N.B. — they are no longer "free standing" but affiliated with degree-granting larger universities (in these two cases, Dalhousie and New Brunswick). Canada's higher education system is in effect a government monopoly. The awarding of degrees, indeed the very use of the term "university," is strictly controlled by the legislatures of the provinces, and these governments have generally been hostile to the establishment of private universities. (Canada's only private university today is Trinity Western, a small evangelical Protestant school in Langley, B.C., which gets no financial assistance from either the federal or British Columbia governments.) "The emphasis...is on universal accessibility to institutions of an approximately common standard" which may vary in regard to status and reputation but which "are not as a matter of public policy hierarchically differentiated."[13] So Canadian universities, in comparison with American ones, are characterized by much smaller differences in quality and less institutional competition and rivalry. The range of American institutions may result in both the very best and perhaps also the very worst of schools; the gap between Podunk College in some Appalachian hamlet and Harvard is infinitely wider than the distance between the very top and bottom Canadian schools, which, on an international continuum, tend to be bunched in the middle.[14] If one were to superimpose the Canadian system onto the American framework, then most of our medium to large universities would be the equivalent of decent American state universities. Top schools such as McGill or the University of Toronto, which sometimes presume to be similar to the Ivy League, are, in terms of selectivity, probably the equivalent of "Big Ten" universities such as Illinois or Minnesota. Of course there is the potential in such a system, with little "separation of education and state," for ideological hegemony. In the United States, private schools can serve as "shelters" from prevailing ideological trends, or even as places from which to marshal counterattacks. The more diverse American system, designed to satisfy many different needs and tastes, has, as former Harvard University president Derek Bok has observed, "a built-in protection against serious errors of judgment....The advantages of a competitive, decentralized system are never so evident as in periods when large social changes sweep over universities."[15]

Finally, the Canadian system is, by comparison with the American one, quite modest in size. Canada's entire post-secondary student population comprises less than 900,000 people.[16] There are almost as many faculty members in the United States as there are students in this country.

FUNDING, PHILANTHROPY, AND COSTS

With more of a tradition of private philanthropy on behalf of education south of the border, university research receives a higher percentage of funds from the private sector.

Dozens of major foundations — the Annenberg, Carnegie, Ford, Guggenheim, W.K. Kellogg, Kresge, Rockefeller, Andrew W. Mellon, and Alfred P. Sloan, to name a few — generously support research; foundations donated $8.33 billion to education in 1992.[17] The private foundations cover a wide ideological spectrum; academics can therefore apply for grants to a variety of sources and are less reliant on government agencies such as the National Endowment for the Humanities (NEH). There is consequently less ability by the state to determine their very career paths.

In Canada, there are far fewer funding agencies, and certainly nothing approximating the private sources American academics can tap. Though there are various provincial ministries that allocate research funds, the vast bulk of direct funding for research is provided by the federal government through three national granting councils, the National Sciences and Engineering Research Council (NSERC), the Medical Research Council (MRC), and the Social Sciences and Humanities Research Council (SSHRC). Humanists and social scientists, for example, are dependent largely on SSHRC, which, being in effect a quasi-monopoly, can shape the contours of a discipline by deciding who gets grants, funding for release time, and so forth. Like an established church ordaining vicars, SSHRC vets graduate students and determines which ones will become part of the professoriate. Probably the first thing that strikes a Canadian looking at the American system of higher education is the incredibly high cost, especially among quality schools in the private sector. The 1980s saw tuition, fees, room and board, and other expenses skyrocket: average tuition charges rose by 156%, while the consumer price index increased by only 64% and median family income rose 40%.[18] Annual tuition and fees alone at private, four-year colleges now average

$10,498, and total costs at many private colleges can easily exceed $20,000 a year. At Ivy League universities, the average cost now stands at $22,700, and at many schools costs continue to increase at an annual rate of 6%. In the words of one concerned student lobbyist, "Private colleges are becoming refuges for the wealthy."[19] Of course the very top ones always have been. Indeed, their elite stature reflects their connection to moneyed families: where one attends college and obtains one's credentials and "cultural capital" really does matter.[20]

Such high fees at private colleges often encourage a mentality of smug self-congratulation and too much emphasis on "rankings." Administrators, faculty, and students deal in superlatives, endlessly proclaiming how highly selective their particular institution is. Such jockeying for position has resulted in a highly refined system of stratification, with each college finding its place on a finely-calibrated hierarchical scale. Hence, most of the students on any given campus are fairly similar in terms of academic capabilities.

RECRUITMENT OF STUDENTS AND RETENTION OF ALUMNI SUPPORT

College marketing strategies, often devised by specialists, now resemble those of toothpaste and soap companies, and public relations departments have become crucial in the battle to attract attention from students and donors by enhancing the college's "name recognition." They print glossy pamphlets and fancy alumni magazines, advertise in prestigious newspapers, and try to gain the attention of the national media by publicizing the agendas of "star" academics and various events on campus. Conferences designed to teach these skills to PR directors, complete with presentations by TV news producers, magazine editors, and writers, are now commonplace. Even literary journals have become a means to market a college in an upscale fashion. That was certainly part of the reason that the Gettysburg College administration decided in 1986 to invest massive amounts of money to establish the *Gettysburg Review* — at the expense, according to some faculty, of funding for other programs.

Colleges actively court applicants: high school seniors are deluged with videos and slickly packaged promotional brochures from colleges around the country, all featuring "glossy color photos of undergraduates sitting on verdant lawns [and] students strolling and bicycling through sunshine."[21] Students are solicited at "college fairs" in major cities. About 80% of all potential freshmen visit college campuses during "get acquainted" days or weekends, during which time they are wooed by everyone from the president to the rest of the college community, including faculty and heads of student organizations.[22] There are academic presentations, informal visits to departments, information regarding expenses and financial aid, all designed to give visitors a glimpse of campus life and leave prospective students with the best impression possible of the college.

Since the physical appearance of the campus should also create a pastoral atmosphere that will appeal to parents and prospective students, the grounds should as much as possible resemble those of an idyllic colonial New England school. Even on newer campuses, the architecture is often ersatz Georgian or Colonial Revival, the landscaping manicured lawns and quads. The effect is often that of an academic "theme park."[23] Colleges and universities even sometimes tout their surrounding environment in ads, be it "a great climate with over 300 days of sunshine," "a beautiful southern campus just an hour away from South Carolina's Grand Strand Beaches," or a school "close to everything south Florida has to offer."

Also, wherever feasible, college officials promote the venerability and "traditions" of their college: the cover of a Gettysburg College publicity brochure includes the slogan "More Than 150 Years at the Forefront of Higher Education." Such hype, at this and other colleges, blends into an all-encompassing celebratory patriotism: students are inculcated with ideas of love for college and country. This is especially true at schools that can "cash in" on some historical event that took place in the vicinity. Hence, Gettysburg College, located in the town that was the site of two of the seminal events in American history — the defeat of the Confederate forces at the Battle of Gettysburg in July 1863 and Lincoln's Gettysburg Address four months later — emphasizes the hallowed story of the American republic. Even very tenuous links are milked for all they are worth: Dwight D. Eisenhower retired to a farm near the town of Gettysburg after leaving the White House in 1960, so in 1989-90, a year-long Eisenhower Centennial Celebration was held at the college; there was massive publicity, including television coverage on CNN News. By contrast, could any reader imagine the University of Calgary trying to benefit from the fact that R.B. Bennett, Prime Minister of Canada from 1930 to 1935, had lived in Calgary?

Fund-raising campaigns are now major ongoing enterprises at American schools, organized out of the "Development," "Capital Campaign," "Major Gifts," "Annual Giving," or "Institutional Advancement" offices, which are at many private schools the core of the institution, larger than most academic departments. The University of San Francisco doubled its endowment from $16 to $30 million in just 2 1/2 years after hiring professionals who computerized the development office, storing records on 70,000 people in a data base in order to match gifts sought with the resources of possible donors.[24]

A school as prestigious as Yale devotes tremendous energy to soliciting funds; as one graduate put it, "They're better than the FBI at tracking down their alumni..."[25] Alumni are therefore much more important than in Canada. Indeed, perhaps the latent function of American private schools is the production of alumni, the people who will continue to support the institution throughout their lives. As for college presidents, they are often nothing but glorified salespeople. Witness the case of Incarnate Word College, a hitherto small, struggling school in San Antonio, TX, that was "put on the map" by a new president, a "marketing genius" who decided on a million-dollar-a-year advertising blitz, including television and radio ads: in seven years, enrolment more than doubled and the college's endowment rose from $3 million to $8.7 million.[26]

It all seems to work: even in these economically uncertain times, the better liberal arts schools remain relatively affluent, cushioned by endowments and alumni contributions, whereas state institutions, more dependent on taxpayers' generosity, are suffering. Declining public support is forcing the public sector to become more aggressive: the University of Michigan, though a state school, in 1992 announced plans to raise $1 billion in private donations. Even Canadian schools are beginning to tap corporate and private pools of money: the University of Calgary recently collected more than $40 million in its first-ever national fundraiser.[27]

THE AMERICAN COLLEGE EXPERIENCE

What, though, are the genuinely positive aspects of that most American of institutions of higher learning, the small residential liberal arts college? The most significant, I would submit, involves the transformational *rite de passage* so often missing in the life of a Canadian undergraduate. An excited 17-year-old leaves home for a new environment; college is not merely an extension and continuation of high school, with the only difference often just a longer bus ride to campus! There are new friends and new perspectives. In fact, the adventure begins even before college does: an American high school senior often spends that year on a voyage of anticipation and discovery, looking over colleges far and wide. There are scores of college guidebooks, describing everything from academic programs and standards to social life on campus; they sell in the hundreds of thousands. There are even consulting services to help a prospective student, who will perhaps apply to as many as ten colleges (including the so-called "reach" and "fall-back" schools).

Indeed, a whole college culture exists in the United States, centred around residential colleges and so-called "college towns," and tied to sports, T-shirt stores, cafés, bookstores, and other services catering to students. American college students are a genuine stratum in society, not merely, as in Canada, 18- to 25-year-olds who happen to be attending university. A student who can afford it will try to live in residence at an elite university or state school even if it happens to be located in his home town (for example, a Bostonian attending Harvard, or a Seattle student enroled at the University of Washington). That is the reason such schools, even though located in large municipalities, have what amounts to a "college town" surrounding them. These are, after all, national, or at least state-wide, institutions, and not just commuter schools consisting of a jumble of office towers and modern buildings off to the side of an arterial road.

The American residential college is a "total experience." Perhaps a good analogy might be that of a soldier serving in the regular army as opposed to the reserves or national guard. In this very controlled pedagogical environment students can be shaped, moulded and motivated by professors and by other students in a way that would prove almost impossible at most Canadian universities. As a cohesive group, they will have had a genuinely shared experience for four years in a hermetically sealed, self-contained environment, unlike those random transients at a city school who continue to live to a large extent in their old environment. There are all kinds of "freshman year" activities,[28] and close supervision continues throughout the student's residency; faculty members serve as counsellors to students and as advisers to fraternities, clubs, and religious organizations. Students and faculty interact outside of the classroom; they see each other in the library and attend campus events together. The faculty in a small town or rural setting are, in a way, themselves almost in residence, even if formally off campus — they and their students form a community. The distractions of city life are absent, for both faculty and students, so there is much more interaction between them (and across departmental and disciplinary lines, at that) than at a metropolitan university. Students are even invited at regular occasions to the college president's house. They are, altogether, far less tangential to the educational enterprise than at a big research-oriented school. The college remains a fond memory long after graduation, too, and for many, "homecoming weekend" is a tradition. Alumni return to campus, often from very far away, and renew friendships; it can be a very emotional time.

Since the liberal arts college's mission is to educate the whole person, living in residence offers a community designed to broaden and enrich the educational experience of students and promote their personal growth, thus developing well-rounded individuals with social skills. The commuter, on the other hand, "not only sees less of his classmates, but more of his parents, siblings and former high school chums," and is thus not liberated from the limitations of home and neighbourhood; "even a superb academic program is unlikely to move most students very far if they return every night to home and mother."[29] Schools that aspire to greatness are almost invariably residential.

Favourable student-faculty ratios are an important selling point for liberal arts schools. At Gettysburg, the ratio was 13:1, and at more prestigious schools it can be less than 10:1 (as compared to the Canadian average of 20:1). One might perhaps call this the "boutique" treatment in education, as opposed to the "department store" feeling one gets at many large universities! There are at smaller, prestigious schools very few of those huge undergraduate classes, meeting in giant theatres, that are so common a sight in multiversities, and of course no teaching assistants. In fact, since there are no graduate students at all, professors devote their efforts to teaching undergraduates rather than supervising MA and PhD students. The teaching load is heavier than at a university — indeed, at lesser-quality colleges, eight courses a year. For students, there is less specialization than at the undergraduate level in Canada, where people often have been shunted into narrow honours programs by second year and take only one or two subjects thereafter, and more flexibility in the selection of courses. Amherst College, in Amherst, MA, with its 1,500 students and a student-faculty ratio of 9:1, eschews a core curriculum, leaving it up to students and their faculty advisers to make sure each graduate receives a well-rounded education. Small-group workshops and seminars allow students to debate issues, rather than passively acquire information. "It isn't really the mechanism that makes it work," according to history professor Hugh Hawkins, "it's much more the ethos of the place."[30] Historically, attempts have been made to limit any "professional" training at liberal arts schools. That is why the creation of departments of management, which grew rapidly in the 1980s, was such a bone of contention; they were seen as not really being a part of a liberal arts education. In Canadian terms, the whole college is in effect a faculty of arts and sciences. Indeed, some very small liberal arts colleges are almost completely interdisciplinary in their curriculum. The residential liberal arts college attempts to socialize students into near-reverence for the faculty. After all, students are paying a tremendous amount of money and have been inculcated with the virtues of their institution. By extension, therefore, the faculty must be excellent and special, and their control over classroom matters should remain virtually unchallenged. At many schools, attendance in courses is compulsory and students who miss more than a certain number of classes can be suspended by a professor, something which would be unthinkable at most Canadian institutions. Many of the evening events and lectures scheduled by various departments or programs require attendance by students; they are not just events for the professors.

Close relations and warm friendships are also the norm among the faculty, and not just within individual departments. At Gettysburg, I knew by name and sight at least 100 of the 150 or so faculty; they were a daily presence in my life. There were numerous occasions for intellectual and social commingling.[31] It was, all told, a very friendly and hospitable atmosphere. Having come from Canada, the atmosphere of the liberal arts school often reminded me of a commune or kibbutz.

Why does it appear that American students have more "fun" while in college? We know there are all kinds of sports, frills, and frivolities: many schools resemble summer camps, the students all coming to class in shorts and baseball caps as though they had just rolled out of their beds in the nearby dorms, and treating their classes almost as part of the camp curriculum. Perhaps the most important reason is the central place occupied on many campuses by the "Greek system" – the ubiquitous fraternities and sororities.[32]

Fraternities are a major presence on liberal arts campuses, despite their expense. In many American schools more than two-thirds of the men and more than half the women are members. Fraternity houses are centres of life. At many campuses, they are housed in huge Victorian mansions – "frat row" – just off campus. Those outside the fraternity system, known as "independents," often feel like second-class citizens. Though fraternities and sororities do exist at some Canadian schools, they do not have nearly the same visibility, impact or influence.

Of course there is a downside to this: alcoholism, date rape and sexual harassment, hazing and physical abuse, and various other forms of loutishness, especially at so-called "party schools." Fraternities can instill very reactionary attitudes and an almost tribal mentality: many have even into recent times tried to preserve very narrow ethnic memberships, not allowing Blacks, Jews, or other minorities to "pledge." Fraternities came to be identified with certain groups, especially "jocks," and their members would often roam through town in packs, drinking and carousing in bars, and wreaking general havoc. Indeed, by the late 1980s many faculty and administrations were debating whether to abolish the system. They wanted to eradicate what they saw as an elitist, often racist, and definitely sexist institution. At many schools, rules were established controlling fraternity activities and some particularly egregious practices, such as "hell week-end," when pledges are initiated into the fraternity, were banned. Some chapters were suspended altogether and lost their official status, although this often merely drove them "underground." But fraternities and sororities are in a sense the *reductio ad absurdum* of the snobbery and elitism that bedevils many private schools, where students are largely the self-satisfied, smug sons and daughters of the privileged, and abolishing the "Greek system" would therefore prove difficult even at those schools where it dominates the social life of a campus in totally negative ways. Former fraternity brothers are often the most "loyal" alumni, and therefore bigger donors to endowment funds than other graduates. As well, in a situation where a student has been cut adrift from family, residence, and often also ethnic and religious ties, fraternities do provide an alternative social structure and new relationships. Indeed, at most American colleges, a whole administrative machinery is devoted to "co-curricular" activities, up to and including deans or directors of Student Life, Student Activities, or Residence Life.

As already noted, many American schools are a veritable training ground for patriotism. And this is especially obvious at those major universities which emphasize team sports, especially basketball and football, organized under the umbrella of the National Collegiate Athletic Association (NCAA). If the battle of Waterloo was won on the playing fields of Eton, then probably many a wartime American victory began, so to speak, on a crisp autumn afternoon in front of some 110,000 screaming fans at, say, the University of Michigan football stadium in Ann Arbor as the Michigan football team took the field against an arch-rival such as Ohio State. The very terminology of college sports smacks of nationalism: major schools are known as football or basketball "powers," and exceptional players are given the revealing title of "All-American." In the sports sections of many newspapers, even in those big cities with professional teams, college sports receive priority in coverage. Nationally, college football is a bigger draw than is the professional National Football League, and the same holds true for college basketball over the National Basketball Association. The NCAA basketball tournament is a month-long playoffs that begins with 64 invited teams and reaches a crescendo of excitement and hoopla at the end of every March; the football season culminates with more than 20 bowl games in December and January; the Rose Bowl, Cotton Bowl, Sugar Bowl, and Orange Bowl games are New Year's Day traditions going back decades.

Clearly, American schools have become more than just institutions of higher learning; they seem to represent a whole way of life. The licensing of American university logos is now big business: college crests now grace T-shirts, pants, caps, jackets, mugs, dishes, bags, car decals, and a host of other products — including dog food and burial caskets. Various college names imply certain life-styles: "Harvard suggests technocracy and prestige; Yale, high artiness as well as blueblood elitism; Notre Dame, striving Catholicism and scrappy Irish sportiness....Schools have reputations, they've got alumni identification, they've got sports teams — hey, they've got school spirit."[33] As Ernest L. Boyer has noted, "Only in America is the decal from almost any college displayed proudly on the rear window of the family car. The message: here's a family on the move."[34] American motorists proudly plaster these insignia on their fenders and rear windows, like flags or other tribal markings.

In America, schools like Notre Dame, Texas, Duke, and Georgetown have created national constituencies for themselves, and the market for their products extends beyond the students, alumni, and their relatives; the majority of purchasers are people who simply "like" the school, for its sports teams, academic standing, or even location (this last is especially the case for sunbelt schools in tourist areas such as Hawaii, Florida, and California). Indeed, the appeal of American college products goes far beyond the borders of the United States. How many times have we seen *Canadian* or *European* university students wearing not the T-shirt of their own university, much less that of another Canadian or European university, but instead that of an American school? As the head of the University of Alabama licensing office put it, "We'll emphasize a *lifestyle*, the American college lifestyle. That's what they're hungry for."[35]

CANADIAN EDUCATION: THE BUREAUCRATIC "NON-EXPERIENCE"

How does Canada's higher education system fare in comparison with the American one just described? Certainly, on the level of cost to the student, Canadian schools are a bargain, especially when compared to top-of-the-line American institutions. Average tuition at a Canadian university is $2,250 a year; McGill's tuition and fees are still just $1,904, and British Columbia's four universities each charge about $2,000 a year. This is less than one fifth of the real annual cost of educating a student.[36] Obviously, low tuition costs make universities more affordable, hence within reach of a larger number of people. But perhaps we only value what we pay for. Unlike the sense of adventure with which many American students set out on their odyssey through college, Canadians might apply only to the one or two universities in their home city or nearby area. Even though Canadian tuition fees are incredibly low when compared to those at private American colleges (or even at state universities if the student is not a resident of that state), the parents of a Canadian might still consider it ridiculous for their child to leave home to study, since it would entail extra costs such as room and board. As the whole stratification system is less developed and schools are treated as basically interchangeable (certainly on the undergraduate level), why bother to leave home? There is no stigma attached to attending one's home institution, nor, in most cases, any particular social advantage in going off to another. Universities are treated by many students as comparable to the various outlets of a chain of fast-food restaurants — are they not all much the same? There is no great aura, no glamour or mythology built around most of our universities, and choosing a school is usually just a matter of selecting an institution in a horizontal catchment area. So most Canadian students pick the closest school to which they have been accepted.

Only a very few residential universities, such as Queen's in Kingston, Ont., and the University of Western Ontario in London, Ont., are exceptions to this rule: Queen's, founded in 1841, has been described as "Canada's most exclusive university," one "known for its strong school spirit." Most students come from somewhere other than Kingston and are thus away from home. "Queen's is one of the few places in Canada that students choose to attend, not because it's close, but because they *want* to be there." The university has always produced a high percentage of Canada's mandarins, or top civil servants. Western, established in 1878, has been called "Canada's preppiest university." A wealthy school with "snob appeal" and "school pride," its alumni, very often private-school graduates, are the most generous in the country. It, too, is largely residential and a campus where "fraternities and sororities thrive." Along with a few other long-established universities such as Dalhousie in Halifax, McGill in Montreal, and the University of Toronto, these schools retain the residue of *cachet*. Insofar as there was once a Canadian "Ivy League," this is it.[37] There are also a few primarily undergraduate-oriented schools, such as Mount Allison University in Sackville, N.B., St. Francis Xavier and Acadia universities in Antigonish and Wolfville, N.S., and Bishop's in Lennoxville, Que., that are primarily residential. St. Francis Xavier "aims for excellence as an undergraduate teaching university" and, with its beautiful Georgian buildings on a "huge and manicured campus," is among the closest approximation we have in this country to the American liberal arts college. Mount Allison, a school of 2,000 students, prides itself as a "caring" and "close-knit" community that is a "total immersion experience." Its annual tuition is $2,625, as is that of Acadia University, a "party school" where sports matter and students go to have "fun." These two schools have the highest fees in Canada (except for the small, atypical Trinity Western University, which receives no government monies). But at Mount Allison there is a 12:1 student-faculty ratio and every student gets a faculty adviser. Comparable private American schools would cost at least $15,000.[38]

Since the overly-regulated, taxpayer-supported, Canadian system supports only a limited number of colleges and universities, these are, because of budgetary constraints, increasingly unable to accommodate the numbers of qualified applicants who wish to enrol. In many provinces, thousands of students are being turned away — and have nowhere else to go. The University of Victoria in the 1992-93 academic year had to reject 1,800 students who met the entrance requirements because the university simply could not accommodate them. In Ontario, the number of high school students applying to that province's universities in 1993 was up 2% from the previous year, but available places declined by 3%. York, for instance, said it would admit 5,300 first-year students, down by 1,200 from 1992. Underfunding is the major problem facing Canadian universities today. According to a 1992 report issued by the Council of Ontario Universities, American universities receive 45% more revenue per student than comparable Ontario schools. Across Canada, operational revenue per student has declined 13% over the past 15 years.[39] Contrast this with the American system: California's public universities face the same financial crisis as ours, and budgets for the state's massive University of California and California State University systems have been slashed drastically since 1990, leading to limits on enrolment, reduced course offerings, and higher costs. At UC campuses, fees have doubled since 1990, to $4,039 a year; at Cal State, undergraduates will now pay $1,778. There is, however, an alternative — if one has the money. Enrolments at California's private colleges have increased dramatically, by almost 20% at some colleges, because these schools guarantee graduation within four years, if all course requirements are met, and point to the fact that the reduction in courses and staff at public colleges may now result in a lengthier stay for many students. In any case, there is a choice, so no one who meets the qualifications (and has the resources) will be unable to attend some post-secondary institution.[40]

Since Canadian schools are underfunded, the resulting lack of resources leads to fewer teachers, increased class sizes, and less evaluation of students' work. Students become anonymous faces within a large crowd in an amphitheatre. "Here, even the basic social graces fall by the wayside," writes University of Manitoba psychology professor David Koulack. "Talking, crackling sounds of crisp bags, and the popping of soda cans opening are all part of the classroom cacophony. It's hard to believe it is a place of learning rather than a ball game or vaudeville show."[41] Only at the graduate school level does one find the intellectual intimacy between students and faculty that at a small college can be obtained at the undergraduate level.

Since the liberal arts college, with its emphasis on teaching, hardly exists in Canada, the universities must be all things to all people, and therefore cannot be as research-oriented as a Harvard or Princeton or Stanford. In the United States, smaller colleges which emphasize teaching take up the slack, so to speak, enabling Ivy League and even top public universities to concentrate on graduate school training and research.[42] A national survey conducted for the Association of Universities and Colleges of Canada in November-December 1992 showed that, while most Canadians felt universities were "doing a good or very good job," only 7% of respondents thought research and development, rather than teaching, was a university's most important task.[43]

Since education is much more bureaucratised in Canada, professors have less control over their courses and are less free of rigid, even ridiculous, rules. Students are treated not as members of a community of scholars, but as in a contractual relationship in which fees are paid in return for services rendered. So ironically, even though Canadian institutions may have more productive scholars than many an American college, the students often relate to their professors as though the latter were civil servants merely delivering a public service — almost like the clerks at a Bureau of Motor Vehicles who hand out driver's licenses. And academics, too, often begin to treat their calling as a nine-to-five job. While at a liberal arts school, "service to the college" is a truly meaningful phrase, and faculty often feel a proprietary interest in the school, at a Canadian institution the atmosphere is often like that at an industrial enterprise: professor-workers vs. administrator-employers.[44]

There is no genuine "college life" at most Canadian schools, since the majority of students are commuters whose lives continue to revolve mainly off-campus. "Universities in Canada often resemble high schools precisely because they're full of slightly older high-school students." Hamilton's McMaster University is a typical example: most students come from 10 nearby high schools and continue to live at home with their parents. Only 5% of the 16,500 students are from outside Canada or even Ontario. In Ottawa, the Carleton University campus is "plopped on the empty plain near the airport" and 88% live off-campus. Like most Canadian institutions, neither school has fraternities or sororities. Not surprisingly, such schools are considered dull and prosaic and largely bereft of social life.[45] Though the University of Calgary is almost 30 years old, it remains a campus with no surrounding academic community or provisions for student life. The only nearby commercial establishments are a few shopping centres, so one cannot saunter off-campus, with a fellow student or professor, and relax at a nearby café or restaurant — one must frequent the facilities at the campus student union. Some of the other new universities in Canada, such as York in suburban Toronto, are aesthetic disasters; an American colleague who visited the university referred to its "brutalist" architecture. Apart from itself looking like an industrial park, York actually *is* surrounded by bleak and ugly commercial wasteland, miles from anything of interest. York is not meant to be a fun place; most students are first-generation university attenders, and congregation by ethnic group on this commuter campus is the norm. Even Simon Fraser University in Burnaby, B.C., built with such fanfare in the 1960s, today sits atop a mountain, isolated from the surrounding Vancouver region, yet with little in the way of an inner communal life. Nor is such an atmosphere confined to newer campuses: the much older University of Manitoba is also situated at the very edge of its city, Winnipeg, far from downtown and quite isolated, with no nearby student district. In Canada, students treat their institution as they might a company where they work: they arrive on campus, attend classes, and go home (or to a part-time job). It can be a grim and listless existence.

Nor do college sports do much to alleviate this ennui; in Canada, they do not usually receive much network TV coverage or front-page sports attention, nor do they attract many spectators. Such accolades are reserved for professional sports teams. In 1993, both the national (Canadian Interuniversity Athletic Union) basketball and hockey championships, held at Halifax and Toronto, respectively, drew crowds of 8,569 for the basketball final and 7,842 for the hockey final. (Both of the victorious schools were small Maritimes universities which more closely approximate the American liberal arts school.) Canadian college sports are truly amateur, and sports scholarships and commercialization in the American sense are forbidden. However, they also provide little revenue, are largely unsupported by alumni and students, and so in an era of financial stringency find themselves in danger of being axed. In the past few years, sports programs at large universities such as Alberta, Calgary, and Toronto have been threatened with closure due to lack of funding. The lack of enthusiasm and interest in college sports in Canada also results in a "brawn drain," as many Canadian students migrate south on athletic scholarships, usually to play on college hockey teams, but sometimes basketball, football, or other sports. It all becomes a vicious circle: students feel no pride or loyalty to their school, hence, unlike their American counterparts, do not become loyal alumni who later donate funds.

There is now a further trend exacerbating this problem. Due to the decline in quality at Canadian schools, all of which are public institutions that depend on shrinking tax allocations, more and more of the wealthy are sending their children to prestigious private American schools. At Upper Canada College in Toronto, Canada's most exclusive boarding school, more than one quarter of graduates now elect to attend American colleges. Other private schools also report the proportion of students heading south after graduation increasing dramatically in the past decade — primarily for the "snob appeal," but also to take advantage of the superior facilities and enviable student-faculty ratios offered by these immensely richer institutions.[46] Like former Prime Minister Brian Mulroney and Governor General Raymon Hnatyshyn (who have a daughter and son, respectively, at Harvard), many in Canada's elite thus have little personal stake in the quality of higher education in Canada. It is not their children, after all, who will suffer from the deficiencies in our higher education system. Also, those who attend American schools will very likely develop networks of friends who are predominantly American, perhaps continue on at professional schools south of the border, and become integrated into American society. They will be lost to Canada, part of a brain drain that is no less serious for its being overlooked. "A nation that sends an important segment of its young people abroad," notes University of Toronto's John Polanyi, winner of the 1986 Nobel prize in chemistry, "risks losing them forever. It has chosen provincialism as a way of life, and thereby calls into question its reason for existing."[47] America, of course, has no such problems.

CONCLUSION: A TRANSFORMATIONAL EXPERIENCE VS. LIMITED HORIZONS

There are significant psychological and cultural ramifications for students passing through such vastly different types of schools. Leaving home to study enables, even forces, people to acquire all kinds of social skills and "grow up." It probably makes the American student acquiring his bachelor's degree at 22 a much more mature person than the Canadian who has continued to live in his home city with his parents, remains in the same social and psychological orbit, and may never have left home for any extended period of time. Could this go some way towards explaining one of those truisms with which we are all familiar in this country: that Americans are less timid than Canadians, more adventurous, and ready to take risks?

The American system, with its national-level colleges and universities, also creates more national cohesion. The top schools attract students from across the nation, who form networks that transcend state or region. President Bill Clinton is a perfect example — as an undergraduate he attended a national institution, Georgetown University in Washington, rather than his own state school in Arkansas, much less some local institution within commuting distance of his house. No one took more advantage of networking possibilities than Clinton, who came from an obscure background in a small town in a peripheral and unimportant state, geographically far from the centres of power in America. The rest, as we know, is history. In Canada, on the other hand, there is much less mobility, hence less geographically-based diversity at most universities; the vast majority of students on a campus come from the same city, certainly from the same province. (Our own former prime minister, Kim Campbell, raised in Vancouver, attended home-town University of British Columbia.) This leads to provincialism: little interaction with Canadians from other regions, hence less national elite formation.

The lack of transformation at a Canadian school is especially true for ethnic and/or immigrant children. Since little attempt is made to construct a new person, and education is not seen as a way of making someone different, undergraduates are not expected to break away from the status ascribed by their community of origin. The Hartzian idea of America as a new republic, a break with the past, the embodiment of liberal enlightenment and progress, was reflected in the liberal arts notion of education as a transformational experience. Canada was founded with no such grandiose notions, nor was it intended as an experiment in nation-building or as an example for humanity; this more modest, conservative enterprise also shaped our ideas regarding higher education. In Canada, the expectation is that students will basically remain, ethnically and geographically, "who they are" and "where they come from," and become merely better-educated versions of their parents. Perhaps the word "self-esteem" has become much overused in the 1980s and 1990s, but nonetheless there are students who could really benefit from the attention provided by liberal arts professors who emphasize teaching. In Canada, a shy or timid student can easily get lost in the shuffle of huge classes and research-obsessed professors.

Author Clark Blaise, who holds dual American-Canadian citizenship and has lived and worked in both countries for extended periods of time, contrasts the Canadian awareness of human limitations to the American notion that "any true American can do whatever he wants to do."[48] American higher education plays its part in the cultural and psychological process through which many Americans transcend their specific origins and become socialized into acceptance of the hegemonic values of the larger society. Attending college is part of the process of, if not assimilation, then certainly acculturation, and those who graduate become, not just people with degrees, but also more full partners in the Lockean liberal "social contract" that makes them citizens of a political republic and an overarching civic culture of individualism. In Canada, higher education makes no such transformational claims — nor, given the nature of Canadian society, would it really be able to fulfil such promises.

NOTES

1. This article will compare the American college and university with only the English-Canadian university. To have included Quebec's post-secondary system would have required a separate piece all to itself.

2. There are another 1,300 two-year schools, as well.

3. For instance, Wayne State University in Detroit, MI; the various branches of the City University of New York; the University of Toledo in Toledo, OH.

4. The American University in Washington, DC; Northeastern University in Boston, MA; Case Western Reserve University in Cleveland, OH; Pace University in New York, NY; the University of Southern California in Los Angeles, CA; and so forth.

5. Stanford University in Palo Alto, CA; University of Colorado in Boulder, CO; University of Massachusetts in Amherst, MA; University of California in Berkeley, CA; University of Wisconsin in Madison, WI; and University of North Carolina in Chapel Hill, NC, to name a few.

6. Alexander W. Astin and Calvin B.T. Lee, *The Invisible Colleges: A Profile of Small, Private Colleges with Limited Resources* (New York: McGraw-Hill, 1972), p. 1.

7. Frederick Rudolph, *The American College and University: A History* (New York: Knopf, 1962), p. 55. This book remains the definitive work on the subject.

8. Merrill McLoughlin and Michael Ruby, eds., *America's Best Colleges* (Washington, DC: U.S. News & World Report, 1992), p. 4. The *Guide* divides American schools into 14 categories, using the guidelines established by the Carnegie Foundation for the Advancement of Teaching, based on location, size, selectivity, types of degrees offered, and dollar amount of campus research. Among the groupings are national universities (204 schools), national liberal arts colleges (140), regional colleges and universities (558), and regional liberal arts colleges (384). See p. 6. The Carnegie Foundation's own categories are doctorate-granting institutions, subdivided into two types of research universities and two types of doctorate-granting colleges and universities; two types of comprehensive colleges and universities, which typically offer some professional education and graduate education through the master's degree; two types of liberal arts colleges, which are undergraduate institutions; two-year community and junior colleges; and various specialized institutions. See *A Classification of Institutions of Higher Education 1987 Edition* (Princeton, NJ: Carnegie Foundation for the Advancement of Teaching, 1987), p. 7.

9. Derek Bok, *Higher Learning* (Cambridge, MA: Harvard University Press, 1986), p. 29.

10. *Chronicle of Higher Education* [hereafter *CHE*], March 3, 1993, p. A31.

11. There are also 201 community colleges across the country. Some of these — for instance, Cariboo and Fraser Valley colleges in British Columbia — are now permitted to grant degrees as four-year "university colleges" affiliated with universities.

12. For the development of Canadian universities, see David M. Cameron, *More Than an Academic Question: Universities, Government, and Public Policy in Canada* (Halifax: The Institute for Research on Public Policy, 1991), pp. 1-291.

13. Michael Skolnik, "Higher Education Systems in Canada," in Alexander D. Gregor and Gilles Jasmin, eds., *Higher Education in Canada* (Ottawa: Research and Information on Education Directorate, Department of the Secretary of State of Canada, 1992), p. 17.

14. Not all Canadian educators approve of this levelling process. Criticizing the Canadian system, University of Western Ontario president George Pedersen observed that "We have a tradition in this country of bringing everything down to the lowest common denominator." *Maclean's*, Nov. 9, 1992, p. 51.

15. Bok, *Higher Learning*, p. 22.

16. Norman Uhl and Anne Marie MacKinnon, "Students," in Alexander D. Gregor and Gilles Jasmin, eds., *Higher Education in Canada*, p. 48.

17. *CHE*, May 26, 1993, pp. A25-27. Annenberg alone recently announced donations of $265 million to three universities: Harvard, Pennsylvania and Southern California. *CHE*, June 23, 1993, pp. A24-25. [Readers should note that I have not converted American into Canadian currency; all figures quoted from American sources are in American dollars, which in terms of the exchange rate are worth approximately 20% more in Canadian terms.]

18. *New York Times*, March 23, 1988, p. B8; *Washington Post*, April 1, 1990, p. C2.

19. Some specific examples: Yale, where the total bill for students in 1993-94 is $25,110; Harvard, where it costs $24,880; Williams College, Williamstown, MA, $23,250; and Syracuse University, Syracuse, NY, $20,400. *CHE*, Feb. 17, 1993, p. A41; March 17, 1993, p. A37; *U.S. News & World Report*, April 12, 1993, p. 55; *Washington Post National Weekly Edition*, May 17-23, 1993, p. 19; McLoughlin and Ruby, eds., *America's Best Colleges*, p. 28.

20. See Lionel S. Lewis and Paul William Kingston, "The Best, the Brightest, and the Most Affluent: Undergraduates at Elite Institutions," *Academe* (Nov.-Dec. 1989): 28-33.

21. This is especially necessary for those colleges that do not sport "designer labels," that is, national name recognition. Jay Amberg, "Higher (-Priced) Education," *American Scholar* (Autumn 1989): 521, 525.

22. Ivy League Dartmouth College in Hanover, NH, felt its relatively remote location might hinder applicants from visiting

its breathtakingly beautiful campus and surrounding ski areas, so admissions officials instituted "Air Dartmouth," a fly-in program that provided serious applicants with round-trip airline tickets to Hanover. *Washington Post*, Oct. 7, 1988, p. B5.

23. Ernest L. Boyer, in *College: The Undergraduate Experience in America* (New York: Harper & Row, 1987), p. 17, says that the physical appearance of the campus may be the most important determinant in influencing students during campus visits.

24. Amberg, "Higher (-Priced) Education," pp. 523-524.

25. *New York Times*, March 29, 1993, p. B6.

26. *CHE*, April 7, 1993, pp. A15-17. College presidents justify their salaries by reference to their fund-raising abilities. The president of Millsaps College in Jackson, MS, noted that, since his arrival in 1978, the endowment had increased 10-fold, to more than $50 million, and that two successful capital campaigns have raised a further $47 million. So Millsaps has earned a good return on its investment in him. *CHE*, May 5, 1993, p. A16.

27. *New York Times*, March 29, 1993, p. B6; *Calgary Herald*, April 28, 1993, p. D1.

28. The "freshman year experience" has assumed such importance that the University of South Carolina, Columbia, SC, houses a Center for the Freshman Year Experience, which organizes conferences and seminars on the first-year experience.

29. Christopher Jencks and David Riesman, *The Academic Revolution* (Chicago: University of Chicago Press, 1977), pp. 182-183. Indeed, despite the lower costs of attending a local commuter school, studies show that it results in "a short-run saving and a long-run loss of opportunity." David Riesman, *On Higher Education: The Academic Enterprise in an Era of Rising Student Consumerism* (San Francisco: Jossey-Bass, 1980), p. 347.

30. *U.S. News & World Report*, Oct. 15, 1990, pp. 122-123.

31. There were monthly faculty meetings, which began with a prayer or invocation by the Lutheran chaplain and which everyone felt obliged to attend; regularly scheduled faculty get-togethers at which people presented papers on their research; informal Friday evening social gatherings for all faculty hosted by various departments; and numerous other events. The college provided a faculty dining hall where most professors ate lunch, and where anyone could sit with anyone else. This was very different from the set-up at the University of Calgary faculty club, which demanded monthly membership fees, and where in any case people sat together at their own tables in pre-arranged groups, like in a commercial restaurant, rather than at "communal tables" which any faculty member could join.

32. For the development of fraternities in the nineteenth-century American college, see Rudolph, *The American College and University*, pp. 144-150.

33. Katharine Whittemore, "Rah-Rah Revenue," *Lingua Franca* (Jan.-Feb. 1993): 53.

34. Boyer, *College*, p. 11.

35. Whittemore, "Rah-Rah Revenue,", pp. 56-57.

36. *Maclean's*, March 1, 1993, pp. 44-45; *McGill News* (Spring 1993): 14. The financial crisis facing most Canadian universities has however resulted in calls for increased levels of tuition, which are at present tightly regulated by provincial governments. University of Alberta president Paul Davenport, for one, favours scrapping tuition ceilings. *Calgary Herald*, June 26, 1993, p. B1.

37. Linda Frum, *Linda Frum's Guide to Canadian Universities* (Toronto: Key Porter, 1990), pp. 127, 199-201; *Maclean's*, Nov. 9, 1992, pp. 76, 78. However, it should be noted that even these schools charge ridiculously small tuition fees, by American elite-school standards — each costs only $1,894 a year. Dalhousie (founded 1818), McGill (1821), and Toronto (1827) are also old and respected universities, but their locations in larger cities made them more accessible to non-elite commuter students.

38. Frum, *Linda Frum's Guide to Canadian Universities*, pp. 8-9, 100, 147-149; *Maclean's*, Nov. 9, 1992, pp. 28-29, 76.

39. *Maclean's*, Nov. 9, 1992, p. 34; March 1, 1993, p. 45; *Globe and Mail (National Edition)*, June 18, 1993, pp. A1-2.

40. *CHE*, April 21, 1993, p. B3.

41. *Guardian Weekly*, Feb. 7, 1993, p. 21.

42. Boyer, in *College*, p. 121, cites a study that showed only 8% of the faculty at research universities spent 11 or more hours per week teaching undergraduates. At liberal arts colleges, the figure was 38%.

43. *University Affairs/Affaires universitaires* (April 1993): 40.

44. Former Queen's University principal J.A. Corry once likened the modern Canadian university to a "public utility." See his "Canadian Universities: From Private Domain to Public Utility," in *Farewell the Ivory Tower: Universities in Transition* (Montreal: McGill-Queen's University Press, 1970), pp. 101-112.

45. Frum, *Linda Frum's Guide to Canadian Universities*, pp. 46-47, 85-88.

46. *Maclean's*, Nov. 9, 1992, pp. 50-51. I recently noticed an item in a newspaper about a man who had been appointed dean of the Faculty of Medicine at the University of Toronto. Though he was originally a Montrealer with degrees from McGill, all three of his children were attending elite liberal arts colleges in the United States.

47. *Maclean's*, Nov. 9, 1992, p. 49. In fact, should these graduates return to Canada, we would then face the situation that obtains in many former colonial countries: the big cultural gap between those who go off to study in the metropole — "Oxbridge" or the Sorbonne — and those who attend "inferior" native universities. My own University of Calgary students were aware of this problem and made reference to it when discussing the increasing cleavage between elites and masses in Canada.

48.   Interview in the *Calgary Herald*, July 17, 1993, p. B5.

FURTHER READING:

Paul Axelrod. *Making a Middle Class: Student Life in English Canada During the Thirties*. Montreal: McGill-Queen's University Press, 1990.

Paul Axelrod and John G. Reid, eds. *Youth, University and Canadian Society: Essays in the Social History of Higher Education*. Montreal: McGill-Queen's University Press, 1989.

Jacques Barzun. *The American University: How it Runs, Where it is Going*. 2nd. ed. Chicago: University of Chicago Press, 1992.

Mary E. Clark and Sandra A. Wawrytko, eds. *Rethinking the Curriculum: Toward an Integrated, Interdisciplinary College Education*. New York: Greenwood, 1990.

Arthur Levine, ed. *Higher Learning in America, 1980-2000*. Baltimore: Johns Hopkins University Press, 1993.

Gary E. Miller. *The Meaning of General Education: The Emergence of a Curriculum Paradigm*. New York: Teachers College Press, 1988.

Francis Oakley. *Community of Learning: The American College and the Liberal Arts Tradition*. New York: Oxford University Press, 1992.

Page Smith. *Killing the Spirit: Higher Education in America*. New York: Viking, 1990.

M. Lee Upcraft and John N. Gardiner, eds. *The Freshman Year Experience: Helping Students Survive and Succeed in College*. San Francisco: Jossey-Bass, 1989.

Bruce Wilshire. *The Moral Collapse of the University: Professionalism, Purity, and Alienation*. Albany, NY: State University of New York Press, 1990.

Ian Winchester, ed. *The Independence of the University and the Funding of the State: Essays on Academic Freedom in Canada*. Toronto: OISE Press, 1984.

Terry Wotherspoon, ed. *Hitting the Books: The Politics of Educational Retrenchment*. Toronto: Garamond, 1991.

Conclusion

It was suggested at the outset that readers would be left to draw their own conclusions: it would be extremely difficult to try to summarize the profound and perplexing points made in nineteen chapters. Brief though they are, each contains a wealth of information. The sheer scope and variety of the topics also mean that overriding themes and clear generalizations are difficult to divine. Nonetheless, I think it appropriate to offer some concluding remarks about the book in general and to pose three questions.

The first of these is what is the overall tenor of *Differences That Count*; does it appear, for example, to be obviously pro or anti- American? There are undoubtedly chapters that should give American readers pause, particularly those on health care (Evans), taxation and deficits (Perry), banking and depository institutions (Binhammer and Bartholomew), gender and society (Tremblay), foreign policy (Randall) and federalism itself (Rocher). Yet in most of these areas there are also caveats: the penalty for not reforming health care "may be the same on both sides of the border — the present American system!"; Canada's annual federal budgetary deficit may be lower but its overall indebtedness (federal and provincial) is, in percentage terms, greater and the tax burden on most individuals is higher; Canadian banks and trust companies have not been immune to failures, to moral hazard questions or to the need for risk-based deposit insurance; federal-provincial relations in Canada have been and will be extremely contentious; the achievements of Canadian feminists are unique and considerable, but "the future remains uncertain."

Some conclusions should also give Canadians pause. The widespread Canadian assumption that Canadian environmental standards are superior "is clearly unjustified" (Hoberg). Similarly, American labour laws have served as a model for Canada to emulate, and higher union density in Canada may have contributed significantly to increased unemployment — and is not necessarily the result of a more finely honed social conscience or of more public support for unions (Richards). There is more serious, in-depth, journalism in the United States, notwithstanding the tabloids at every supermarket checkout; the Canadian media may exhibit commendable restraint in not delving too far into the dirty laundry in politicians' closets, or may be guilty of docility and deference and lack the resources to do a thorough job (Taras). The American judicial system, for all its flamboyant features, is more innovative; it is also far less secretive when it comes to key appointments, and the courts have better control over their own budgets (Kerans). American higher education offers — at a price — far broader choice of institutions that are both physically and pedagogically attractive and which provide a transformational and nationalizing environment (Srebrnik).

On the basis of conclusions such as those above (and many more examples are to be found) it seems safe to say that *Differences That Count* is not overtly or resolutely pro or anti either country; the authors have been willing to subject Canadian as well as American practice to critical scrutiny.

The second question I want to pose is: what, if any, lessons may be learned from these comparisons? One lesson, perhaps, is that there is little cause for smugness on either side of the border, but we probably knew this already. What is also apparent is that while comparisons are endlessly fascinating, we should not assume that either the institutions or the policies of one country can necessarily be duplicated and transferred successfully. What works in one setting and culture may have quite different and inappropriate effects in another, as several authors explicitly note. For example, in the extremely important case of aboriginal claims to self-government "the American model may be a chimera which does not deliver on its initial promises" (Brock). Such differing results are usually ascribed, not surprisingly, to the lasting effects of founding events and original national values.[1] This emphasizes the point that the perception of Canada as a conservative "counter-revolutionary alter ego of the American revolutionary tradition" is very deeply entrenched and often "frames our discussion" as to how and why we differ.[2] A historically-rooted approach is particularly useful when studying political institutions. Thus a comparison of presidential and prime ministerial powers rests largely upon the differences between the parliamentary, British-style system of responsible government and the American system of checks and balances; it largely comes down to a case of effectiveness versus openness and consultation (Smith). The discussion of Senate reform in Canada leads to the perhaps surprising conclusion that the American model "is too deeply embedded in a very different philosophy of government to provide much useful guidance" (Gibbins).

This having been said, *Differences That Count* also shows that changes in institutions or policies may have enormous but largely unpredictable effects — effects that may, or may not, always be in accord with our presumed values and formative circumstances. This is particularly true of the development of the federal systems and the role played by economic factors. It is also to be seen in the ways in which the old and the new combine to create unanticipated constitutional problems; the referendum as a political device in Canada now sits uneasily with parliamentary supremacy.

The third and last question I want to address is one that I suspect Canadian readers will inevitably ask: is there evidence of increasing convergence? To which I will resolutely answer "yes, to some extent". (I am reminded here of the contest run by *Maclean's* magazine which asked readers to complete the phrase "As Canadian as..." The winner was "As Canadian as possible under the circumstances.")

In spite of obvious historical differences, a melting pot looks a lot like a mosaic, although the state myths differ and are important (Palmer Seiler). The "Tangled Tale" of the role and place of unions in Canada may, comparatively speaking, be a case of "lagged convergence". The Canadian Charter of Rights, even though it contains some unique features, has brought Canada closer to an individualistic, rights-based legal culture and has greatly elevated the status of the Supreme Court so that it now looks far more like its American counterpart (Manfredi). Our electoral systems and their associated problems look increasingly similar; debates over "effective" representation, boundaries, campaign expenditures, and the recall of legislators, all illustrate a border that is "permeable to political ideas" (McCormick). Both federal governments are attempting to off-load their responsibilities for programs and expenditures onto states or provinces as budgets tighten and deficits grow. There are still enormous differences in the systems of post secondary education, but fiscal pressures are going to make Canadian university presidents look more like their American counterparts: concerned with alumni, fund raising, investment management, restructuring, and all the other aspects of running a bottom-line oriented big business. These pressures will force student fees upwards, creating even more incentives to send Canadian students to prestigious American schools.

Not all movement to greater convergence is on the Canadian side of the border. If the United States succeeds in its attempts to reform health care and is able to adopt a version of comprehensive insurance coverage for all citizens, one of the greatest and most politically important differences between our two countries will have been lessened. Internationally the United States is moving from unilateralism and imperialism to a more multilateral role. The president must cooperate with other national leaders; the United Nations and peacekeeping loom far larger in American foreign policy consciousness than was the case not long ago. Hitherto, these have been areas where Canada's size, history, and role within the United Nations have made it distinctive, as Stephen Randall's essay demonstrates. The powers of a president and a prime minister are very different, but in both countries public opinion polls and television news have brought about similar changes in electoral tactics, in diminished party identification, and in the need to focus on style and media manipulation.[3] Mention of television raises, inevitably, the question of Canadian culture. Here we expect to find not convergence but domination. And indeed this is the case; report after report has documented the need to maintain a Canadian cultural identity and discussed how this is to be done, but, if anything, the problems worsen (Portman).

There is one arena where differences still appear to be stark; Canada's sustained constitutional turmoil has no American equivalent. The very future of the Canadian state is being debated. Yet even here the influence of American ideas — on equality, citizenship, accountability, and rights — has grown. Canada has created an amending formula that is as Byzantine, federalized, and difficult to use as is its American counterpart. This places greater pressure on a Canadian Supreme Court that may be politically ill-suited to the task it is called on to perform (Thomas).

In 1991 the prestigious British journal *The Economist,* in a special issue on Canada, concluded by offering these pessimistic words of prophecy:

> It will continue to be prosperous, peaceful, middling. It will also continue to have a truculent French-speaking minority, and to live in the shadow of the United States, above all in its broadcasting shadow. Many Canadians will hang onto their traditions. But the two founding nations will count for less and less: Quebeckers will diminish in number, and the descendants of the British will be an ever-smaller share of the rest. Sooner or later Canadians are going to become Americans. Too bad.[4]

This is a popularized version of the late George Grant's *Lament For A Nation* thesis and is nothing new; even so, it is still sobering for Canadians to read such assessments from abroad. But *Differences That Count* shows that, despite the areas of convergence, significant patterns of difference remain. Structural arrangements and social and economic policies do matter. So does geography, as the United States struggles to control a flood of illegal immigrants along a border that is impossible to close.

Governmental action (or inaction) can confer country-specific advantages in a host of different areas such as education, labour markets, capital costs, taxation, social safety nets, fiscal policy, urban infrastructure, and crime control and prevention. Institutions are not merely artificial creations to be reshaped at will; they are inextricably tied to belief, behaviour, and vested interests. Canadian provinces are more politically powerful than are American states, and multiple loyalties are a complicating feature of Canadian political life. According to a recent wide-ranging work on public policy, there is widespread "institutionalized ambivalence" in Canada:

> ...ambivalence about the appropriate roles of the state and the market, about national and regional conceptions of political community, and about individualistic and collectivist concepts of rights and responsibilities. This ambivalence arises from tensions that are endemic to three fundamental features of the Canadian context: the relationship with the United States, the relationship between anglophones and francophones within Canada, and the regionalized nature of the Canadian economy and political community.[5]

The United States suffers from different ailments, as tourists to Florida are finding out.

Perhaps, as Richard Collins has argued, Canada's "cultural" distinctiveness is kept in place by its systems of law, public welfare, and civic order — its culture in an anthropological sense rather than an artistic one:

> Canadians' use of their leisure time to watch American television seems to have no stronger links to their political actions, their assumptions of citizenship and national self-definition than does their choice to eat in Indian, Chinese, French rather than Canadian restaurants.[6]

Reassuring words — if one believes them.

Whatever the state of our Canadian-American differences, both countries have now to deal with what is often called the "post modern" world. This is usually taken to mean a world in which the old power centres crumble, in which our collective myths and stories evaporate (or are eviscerated); in which hierarchies and authorities are challenged and suspect, and in which the old verities no longer hold sway. It may be more useful to think of the problems facing the state less as "post modern" than as, to use social theorist Anthony Giddens' term, "post traditional."[7] This places the emphasis upon the erosion of legitimacy, consent and obedience — in relationships, in families, and in political systems. It places a premium upon dialogue and not upon control and power. Populism and regionalism are reviving both in Europe and in North America at the same time that economic globalization and environmental problems are blurring boundaries.

Canada and the United States are thus challenged by unprecedented diversity, by claims to social and political recognition and redress, and by global shifts in economic power. Both remain a magnet to those seeking to escape the social and political horrors of our times. Whatever label we give this epoch, it calls for a reassessment of roles and rules, and comparing our two systems, somewhat parochial though this may be, is vital to such appraisals. Set against world events and trends, our federations may be doing rather better than we allow.

NOTES

1. To prevent duplication the introductions to several chapters were trimmed; these general cultural points recurred frequently.

2. For a recent provocative analysis of Canada's political culture see Cynthia Williams and Doug Williams, "Political Entanglements: Ideas and Identities in Canadian Political Life" in Alain-G Gagnon and James P. Bickerton (eds,), *Canadian Politics: an introduction to the discipline* (Peterborough: Broadview Press, 1990), 111.

3. See, for example, Richard Rose, *The Postmodern President: The White House Meets the World* (Chatham, New Jersey: Chatham House Publishers, 1988).

4. *The Economist,* June 29th, 1991,18.

5. Carolyn J. Tuohy, *Policy and Politics in Canada: Institutionalized Ambivalence* (Philadelphia: Temple University Press, 1993), 4.

6. Richard Collins, "Broadcasting and National Culture in Canada" *British Journal of Canadian Studies,* 4 1988,55. For an interesting and useful\distinction between a"civilization" (American) and a "culture" (Canadian) see Douglas V. Verney, Three Civilizations, Two Cultures, One State: Can-

ada's Political Traditions (Durham: Duke University Press, 1986).

7. This idea was developed in a lecture presented at the annual meeting of the *British Association for Canadian Studies* Cambridge, March 1993. Discussion of value change raises the whole complicated question of new values and value convergence.. There is evidence of both. See Neil Nevitte and Roger Gibbins, *New Elites in Old States: Ideologies in the Anglo-American Democracies* (Toronto: Oxford University Press, 1990). See also M. Basanez, R. Iglehart and N. Nevitte *North American Value Convergence: Free Trade and Integration* (Princeton University Press: Forthcoming). This work examines the important hypothesis that as "transactions" between states increase, so will value convergence, mutual trust, support for closer economic ties and support for political integration. See also Richard LaRue and Jocelyn Létourneau, "De la unitè et de l'identitè au Canada. Essai sur l'eclatement d'un état," *International Journal of Canadian Studies*, Spring-Fall 1993. They discuss the imposition and explosion of the modern state, our loss of identity and ballast, and the emergence of a new elite culture, the value of which is measured symbolically in "aero-miles." For further evidence of the rise of "new politics" in Canada and the United States see Neil Nevitte, "New Politics, The Charter and Political Participation" in Herman Bakvis (ed.), *Representation, Integration, and Political Parties in Canada* (Toronto: Dundurn Press, 1990) 355-417. This is volume 14 of the research studies undertaken for The Royal Commission on Electoral Reform and Party Financing.

Contributors

Philip F. Bartholomew is Director of the Bank Research Division at the Office of the Comptroller of the Currency. Prior to joining the OCC in May 1993, Dr. Bartholomew served as a Principal Analyst at the Congressional Budget Office. At CBO he was responsible for making budget projections of the federal deposit insurance funds as well as writing studies on depository institution issues. Prior to 1988, Dr. Bartholomew was an Assistant Professor of Economics (1981-1988) and Coordinator of Canadian Studies (1986-1988) at the University of Michigan-Dearborn. Dr. Bartholomew has a B.S. in mathematics from Villanova University, and an M.A. and Ph.D. in economics from the University of Pittsburgh. In addition to editing books on international banking and Canadian studies, he has published several articles on deposit insurance, the thrift crisis, the Canadian banking system, and the international regulation of depository institutions.

Helmut H. Binhammer is Professor of Economics and former Dean of Arts at the Royal Military College of Canada. His major publications include, *Money, Banking and the Canadian Financial Systems*, now in its sixth edition; *The Development of Financial Infrastructure in Tanzania*; *Canadian Banking and Monetary Policy* (with James Cairns and Robin Boadway); and *Deposit-Taking Institutions: Innovation and the Process of Change* (with Jane Williams). His more recent research interests have focused on deposit insurance, financial structure and regulation and international finance.

Kathy Brock is an Assistant Professor of Political Science at the University of Manitoba. She was the Research Director of the Manitoba Task Force on Meech Lake, 1989-90, has advised on the constitutionalisation of Aboriginal self-government, and has written numerous articles on the constitution and Aboriginal self-government. Currently, she is writing the study of relations between Aboriginal peoples and the Manitoba government for the Royal Commission on Aboriginal Peoples.

Robert G. Evans is Professor of Economics at the University of British Columbia, where he has held a National Health Scientist award since 1985. Since 1987 he has been a Fellow of the Canadian Institute for Advanced Research, and Director of its Program in Population Health. He is the author of *Strained Mercy: The Economics of Canadian Health Care* as well as numerous other works. He has recently served as a Commissioner of the British Columbia Royal Commission on Health Care and Costs, which reported at the end of 1991.

Roger Gibbins is currently a Professor in, and Head of, the Department of Political Science at the University of Calgary. He received his Ph.D. from Stanford in 1978 and has pursued a variety of research interests spanning western alienation, Canadian constitutional politics, political belief systems, Senate reform, American and Australian politics, and aboriginal politics. He has authored (or edited) ten books and over 50 articles and book chapters. Publications include *Regionalism: Territorial Politics in Canada and the United States*; *Conflict and Unity: An Introduction to Canadian Political Life*, and *New Elites in Old States* (with Neil Nevitte). Dr. Gibbins is currently the English Language co-editor of the *Canadian Journal of Political Science*.

George Hoberg is an Associate Professor of Political Science at the University of British Columbia. He is the author (with Kathryn Harrison) of *Risk, Science and Politics* (McGill / Queen's University Press: forthcoming), as well as a number of scholarly articles.

The Honourable Mr. Justice **Roger Philip Kerans** has been a member of the Court of Appeal of Alberta since 1980. Prior to this appointment he was a trial judge for 10 years with the District Court and the Court of Queen's Bench. Born in Lashburn, Saskatchewan, he was appointed a judge at age 36 in 1970. In 1975, he was asked to move to Calgary as Associate Chief Judge after residing for 30 years at Edmonton as a student, lawyer and judge. He has also been, since 1972, a judge of the Supreme Court of the Yukon, and is a member of the Court of Appeal for the Northwest Territories of Canada.

Christopher P. Manfredi is Associate Professor in the Department of Political Science, McGill University. His research interests centre on the politics of Charter litigation, and he has published articles on this subject in the Canadian Journal of Political Science, Canadian Public Administration, and the American Journal of Comparative Law. He is also the author of *Judicial Power and the Charter: Canada and the Paradox of Liberal Constitutionalism*, published in Canada by

McClelland and Stewart and in the United States by the University of Oklahoma Press.

Peter McCormick is Professor of Political Science at the University of Lehthbridge, where he teaches Canadian politics, constitutional law, the legal system, and political theory. He received his doctorate from the University of London (School of Economics) and is the author of numerous monographs and articles on a wide range of topics including federalism, regionalism, Senate and and parliamentary reform, voting and representation, voting behaviour, party systems, the recall of elected officials, the work of provincial Courts of Appeal, the Supreme Court of Canada, and the role of judges. He is also the author of "Politics and Public Policy in Alberta" published annually (in the *Canadian Annual Review*).

David B. Perry Senior research associate, Canadian Tax Foundation since 1968; regular contributor to Canadian Tax Journal; author and supervisor of the Foundation's annual publication, The National Finances, and the biennial Provincial and Municipal Finances; author of Financing the Canadian Federation, 1867 to 1991: Setting the Stage for Change, forthcoming; author and commentator on matters of taxation and public finance in Canadian periodicals and on radio and television.

Jamie Portman is a graduate of the University of Manitoba. He has worked for the Winnipeg Free Press, the Calgary Herald (nine years as editorial writer, theatre and music critic and entertainment editor). Since 1975 he has been national fine arts correspondent for Southam news. He is a contributor to numerous journals and reviews in Canada and the United Kingdom, and is the co-author (with the late John Pettigrew) of *Stratford: The First Thirty Years*. Awards include: a National Newspaper Award citation for criticism, three Nathan Cohen awards for criticism, and a Canadian Conference of the Arts Award for Excellence in Arts Journalism.

Stephen Randall currently holds the Imperial Oil-Lincoln McKay chair in American Studies at the University of Calgary. He has taught at the University of Toronto, Universidad Nacional Bogotá, and McGill University, where he was chair of the Department of History. He obtained his Doctorate from the University of Toronto and is the author of several books including *Hegemony and Independence* (1992) and, with John H. Thompson, *Ambivalent Neighbors: Canada and the United States* (forthcoming). He has also edited several works including *North America Without Borders* (1992). His main scholarly interest is U.S. foreign policy in Latin America. He is currently the co-editor of the *Canadian Review of American Studies* and the editor of the *International Journal* of the Canadian Institute of International Affairs.

John Richards was born in England and raised in the Prairies. He is a former NDP member of the Saskatchewan legislature. He currently lives in Vancouver and teaches economics in the Business Faculty of Simon Fraser University. He has written on a wide range of subjects from natural resource economics to labour relations, social policy and the prospect for social democratic politics and is the co-author (with Larry Pratt) of *Prairie Capitalism*.

Francois Rocher is Associate Professor of Political Science, Carleton University in Ottawa. He specializes in Canadian and Québec politics, intergovernmental relations, the constitution and political economy. He has recently edited *Bilan québécois du fédéralisme canadien* and has published many articles in academic journals and edited collections. He is currently examining the economic pressures associated with "globalization" and their impact on Canadian constitutionalism and federalism.

Tamara Palmer Seiler has published two books and a number of articles in the fields of western Canadian history, ethnic studies and Canadian literature, and is currently Director of the Canadian Studies Program at the University of Calgary. Although she was born and grew up in the United States, she has spent most of her adult life in Canada. Educated in both countries, with a specialization in Canadian and American studies, she has both an academic and personal interest in Canadian/American comparisons.

Jennifer Smith is Associate Professor of Political Science at Dalhousie University, from which she received her Ph.D. in 1981. She teaches Canadian and American government and politics, and modern liberal theory. She has served as the Commissioner of the Provincial Electoral Boundaries Commission and as Chair of the Province's Advisory Committee on the Division of Powers and Government Institutions. Recent publications include articles on representation and constitutional reform, on democratic rights and electoral reform in Canada, and on the influence of American federalism on Canadian confederation.

Henry Srebrnik is an assistant professor in the Department of Political Studies at the University of Prince Edward Island, Charlottetown,

PEI. He has taught history and political science at the University of Calgary, Alberta, and at Gettysburg College, Pennsylvania. A specialist in comparative politics and ethnic relations, he earned BA, MA and PhD degrees from McGill, Brandeis and Birmingham Universities, and he has recently completed a book on ethnic politics in east London, 1935-1945.

David Taras is Professor and Assistant Dean (Research) in the Faculty of General Studies at the University of Calgary. He is the author of *The Newsmakers: The Media's Influence on Canadian Politics* and editor of among other works *Seeing Ourselves: Media Power and Policy in Canada* (with Helen Holmes). His work spans a wide range of media, leadership, and policy related topics.

David Thomas teaches political science at Mount Royal College in Calgary. A former Dean of the College's Faculty of Business (1981-88), for the past two years he has been the chair of the Department of Economics and Political Science. In 1993 he received the College's distinguished teaching award. He teaches Canadian and comparative politics, and recent publications include articles on constitutional abeyances in Canada, the lessons of the October referendum (with Roger Gibbins) and parliamentary reform in Alberta (with Thomas Bateman).

Manon Tremblay is an assistant professor in the department of political science at the University of Ottawa. She obtained her doctorate from the University of Laval and her current research is focused on the relationship between women and political life in Australia, Canada and the United Kingdom and on representation of women in political caricatures. She has published articles in a number of scholarly journals and will shortly publish (in collaboration with Réjean Pelletier) a book on the differences between the sexes in the exercise of political power in the House of Commons and the Quebec National Assembly. She is also directing (with Marcel Pelletier) a work on the parliament of Canada.

INDEX

pollution See *environmental policy*
Polyani, John 397
populism 79, 183, 189, 204, 412
Porter, John 315, 316
poverty 9, 11-12, 13, 277-8, 312, 329, 373
Prentice Hall 352
presidents 148ff., 192, 331ff.
Prevention of Significant Deterioration Program (PSD) 105, 106
primaries 150, 151, 152
Prime Ministers 148ff., 331ff.
Prince Edward Island 56, 166, 176, 181, 382
private sector 38, 69ff., 74
Progressive Party 185
Progressive Conservative Party 152, 163, 176, 353
prohibition 208
property rights 130, 132, 133, 254, 257ff.
property taxes 49ff.
provinces 23, 30, 42-3, 49, 50, 51, 52ff., 63, 106, 107, 120, 127ff., 127ff., 140ff., 176, 181, 209, 218, 222, 224, 225, 236, 263, 280, 294
public broadcasting 334ff.
pulp and paper industry 109, 110
QPP (Quebec Pension Plan) 43-4, 51
Quayle, Dan 328
Quebec 10, 12, 43-4, 51, 52, 63, 85, 90-1, 128, 131, 139, 140, 141, 166, 169, 176, 181, 182, 196, 197, 198, 199, 201ff., 221, 222, 225, 236, 243, 262, 265, 272, 273, 274, 279, 292-3, 304, 305, 307, 338
Quebec Deposit Insurance Board 90-1
Quebec Act 305
R. v. Big M Drug Mart 238, 241
R. v. Keegstra 243ff.
racial discrimination 11-12, 130, 208, 221, 247, 311, 312
Randall, Stephen 410
Reagan administration 112
Reagan, Ronald 106, 112, 137, 138, 168, 195, 231, 257, 277, 282, 354, 366
REAL Women 295
recall of elected representatives 177, 183, 409
referenda 141, 203, 209, 409
Reform Party 200, 204
refugees 313-314
regulation 105ff., 135, 172
religion 13, 199, 241, 373, 375, 381, 383
repatriation of constitution 141, 236, 280
representation (political) 166, 170, 195, 279-80, 294
Republican Party 138, 199
reserves (banking) 88ff.
residual power 130, 132
Resolution Trust Corporation 84
Retail, Wholesale and Dept. Store Union v. Dolphin Delivery 242, 250
revolution 306, 367, 375
Reynolds v. Sims 179, 182
Riddell, Craig 68-9, 81, 82
risk-benefit analyses 112
Robb, Charles 328
Roberts, Peter 360

Robertson, Pat 327
Roe v. Wade 278
Roosevelt, F.D. 65, 153, 155, 339, 369
Rosen, Jay 339
Royal Trust Company 97
Royal Proclamation of 1763 254
RRSPs (Registered Retirement Savings Plans) 53
Russell, Peter 201
Sabato, Larry 326, 333, 340
safety 73, 106, 135
safety nets (banking) 88ff.
sales tax 49, 52, 53, 63
Saskatchewan 52, 54, 56, 66, 75, 176, 181, 186, 253, 260, 294, 314
savings and loan crisis (US) See *thrifts.*
Savings Association Insurance Fund 84
Scandinavia 72, 73
Schedule II banks 95
Schedule I banks 95
Seaboyer v. the Queen 246
securitization 88, 98
self-government, aboriginal 256ff. See also *aboriginal rights.*
Senate (US) 138, 140, 153, 155, 162ff., 173, 208, 227, 279
Senate (Canada) 162ff., 197, 408
separation of financial institutions 86
Seventeenth Amendment 167
sewage treatment 109
sexism See *women's rights.*
'sin taxes' 53
Smiley, Donald 132
Smith, Goldwin 374
'social contract' (Ontario) 76
social security (US) 44, 45, 49, 59, 136
Social Credit 81, 185, 189
South Carolina 128
sport 391ff., 396
Sports Illustrated 350
SSHRC 384ff.
St. Laurent, Louis 369-70
state constitutions 226
states 40, 42-3, 49, 50, 51, 52ff., 63, 87, 127ff., 136, 158-9, 184, 204, 209, 222, 226, 236-7, 294
Statute of Westminster 131, 367
Stevenson, Garth 142
suffrage movement 272ff.
sulphur dioxide 118, 120
Supreme Court (Canada) 134, 176, 187, 188, 197, 206, 209, 215, 223, 224, 235ff., 278, 313
Supreme Court (US) 134, 135, 155, 164, 174, 175, 194, 195, 179, 187, 198, 222, 223, 224, 235ff., 256, 261, 263, 336, 410
Sweden 73
Taney, Chief Justice Roger 134
taxation 42ff., 136, 139, 208
Taylor, Paul 332
television 334ff., 343, 345
Tenth Amendment 130, 135
'Third Option' 371
Thomas, Clarence 199, 227, 329
thrifts 83ff., 86, 93, 97
Time Magazine 349, 364